# NEW ZEALAND

# Kia Ora!

New Zealand, known to the Maoris as Aotearoa (land of the long white cloud), is a paradise of overwhelming beauty – scarcely anywhere else in the world is there such variety of scenic beauty as on these two islands in the South Pacific.

In fact the islands, formed by the friction of two continental plates, continue to develop. Earth tremors are frequent, geysers spout high into the air, hot mud bubbles in crater depressions and volcanoes sporadically spew out fire. Not far from these hot spots soar the majestic snow-capped summits of the Southern Alps. The imposing fjords and river valleys carved by glaciers are a reminder that the southern hemisphere, like the northern, has had its ice ages.

*The Maori* still preser ancient tra

Only in New Zealand are so many contrasting landscapes found within a relatively small area: expanses of evergreen primeval forest with tall ferns and giant kauri trees, areas of inhospitable wasteland, gleaming white glaciers, rugged peaks

*Colonial heritage:* a mission church in Hokianga Harbour

*Majestic Mount Taranaki:* an extint volvano

*A quiet cove* in Marlborough Sounds

and crystal rivers, white and gold sandy beaches against the turquoise sea, parkland and lush green pasture, dense forests of timber, and vineyards and orchards.

This land across the world has long been a magnet to people seeking an escape from the stress of life in the West; and also to those who seek the delights of the great outdoors – walkers, climbers, off-road enthusiasts, white-water canoeists, yachtsmen and anglers.

And as they go about the country – perhaps in the beautiful Rotorua area – visitors see something of the life of the Maoris who came to New Zealand from Polynesia many generations ago. In contrast to the peoples of the West, Maoris attach importance not to the individual but to the tribal community. Reverence for their ancestors also plays a major part in their society. Their daily life is dominated by traditions and myths, even though externally they have adapted to the way of life of the European immigrants who have settled in the country. Fascinating too are their arts and crafts, for example the superb carvings of their meeting houses.

But visitors will also enjoy meeting the friendly 'Kiwis', as the New Zealanders of European (mostly British) origin call themselves. In their attitudes and activities visitors can recognise the character of an island people whose nearest neighbours are thousands of kilometres away to the west, in Australia. Splendid isolation indeed!

# CONTENTS

*Baedeker*  SPECIALS

# Principal Sights

## ★★

### NORTH ISLAND
Auckland

Bay of Islands

Napier

Rotorua

Taupo

Tongariro National Park

Waipou Kauri Forest

Wairakei

Waitamo Caves, Te Kuiti

Wellington

Whanganui National Park

### SOUTH ISLAND
Abel Tasman National Park

Arthur's Pass

Christchurch

Dunedin

Franz Josef Glacier

Fox Glacier

Lake Manapouri

Lake Te Anau

Lake Wanaka

Marlborough Sounds Maritime Park

Milford Sound

Mount Aspiring National park

Mount Cook National Park

Queenstown

Westland National Park

### COOK ISLANDS

## ★

### NORTH ISLAND
Bay of Plenty

Coromandel Peninsula

Hamilton

Hawke's Bay

Kaitaia

Puhoi

Taranaki

Tauranga

Urewera National Park

### SOUTH ISLAND
Arrowtown

Banks Peninsula

Blenheim

Catlins

Fiordland National Park

Greymouth

Haast Pass

Hanmer Springs

Hokitika

Lake Pukaki

Lake Tekapo

Moeraki Boulders, Oamaru

Nelson

Nelson Lakes National Park

Paparoa National Park, Pancake Rocks

Stewart Island

Westport

Following the tradition established by Karl Baedeker in 1846, buildings, places of natural beauty and sights of particular interest are distinguished by one ★ or two ★★ stars. The places listed above are merely a selection of the principal sights – there are of course many other sights in New Zealand, to which attention is drawn in the guide by the Baedeker stars.

# Principal Sights
# in New Zealand

❇ major sights
❇❇ outstanding sights

*Cape Reinga
**Bay of Islands
*Ninety Mile Beach
*Kerikeri  **Waitangi
*Waimate North  **Russell
*Hokianga Harbour  Pahia
*Whangarei
**Waipoua Kauri Forest
Hauraki **
Gulf  Great Barrier Island
Puhoi
*Kaipara Harbour  *Coromandel Peninsula
*Waiwera  *Mayor Island
**Auckland  East Cape
**Waikato River  Pukekohe
*Te Aroha  **Bay of Plenty
*Hamilton  Tauranga
*Kawhia  *Urewera Nat. Park
Waitomo  Rotorua
Caves  **Wairakei  *Gisborne
*New Plymouth  Tongariro Nat. Park
Lake Waikaremoana
**Egmont Nat. Park  Wanganui River  Lake Taupo
Stratford  Napier
Hawke Bay
North Island
*Wanganui  *Cape Kidnappers
Palmerston North
**Cape Farewell  **Marlborough Sounds  *Foxton
*Kapiti Island  *Otaki
**Abel Tasman Nat. Park  Masterton  Castlepoint
Nelson  *Greytown
*Westport  Nelson Lakes Nat. Park  **Picton
Buller River  Lake Grassmere  **Wellington
**Pancake Rocks  **Hanmer Springs
Tasman Sea
*Shantytown  **Arthur's Pass Nat. Park  Kaikoura
**Franz Josef Glacier  **Mt. Cook Nat. Park
**Fox Glacier  **Westland Nat. Park  Christchurch
*Haast Pass Road  Lake Ohau  **L. Tekapo  *Banks Peninsula
L. Pukaki  Ashburton
**Mt. Aspiring Nat. Park  *Peel Forest Park
Milford Sound  *Wanaka  *Lindis Pass  Timaru
**Queenstown  *Arrowtown  *Waitaki Valley
Fiordland Nat. Park  Lake Te Anau  *Clyde  *Alexandra  Moeraki Boulders
L. Manapouri  *Lawrence  *Port Chalmers
Lake Hauroko  *Gore  **Dunedin
South Island
**Invercargill
*Nugget Point
South Pacific Ocean
*Stewart Island  *Bluff

© Baedeker

# Introduction

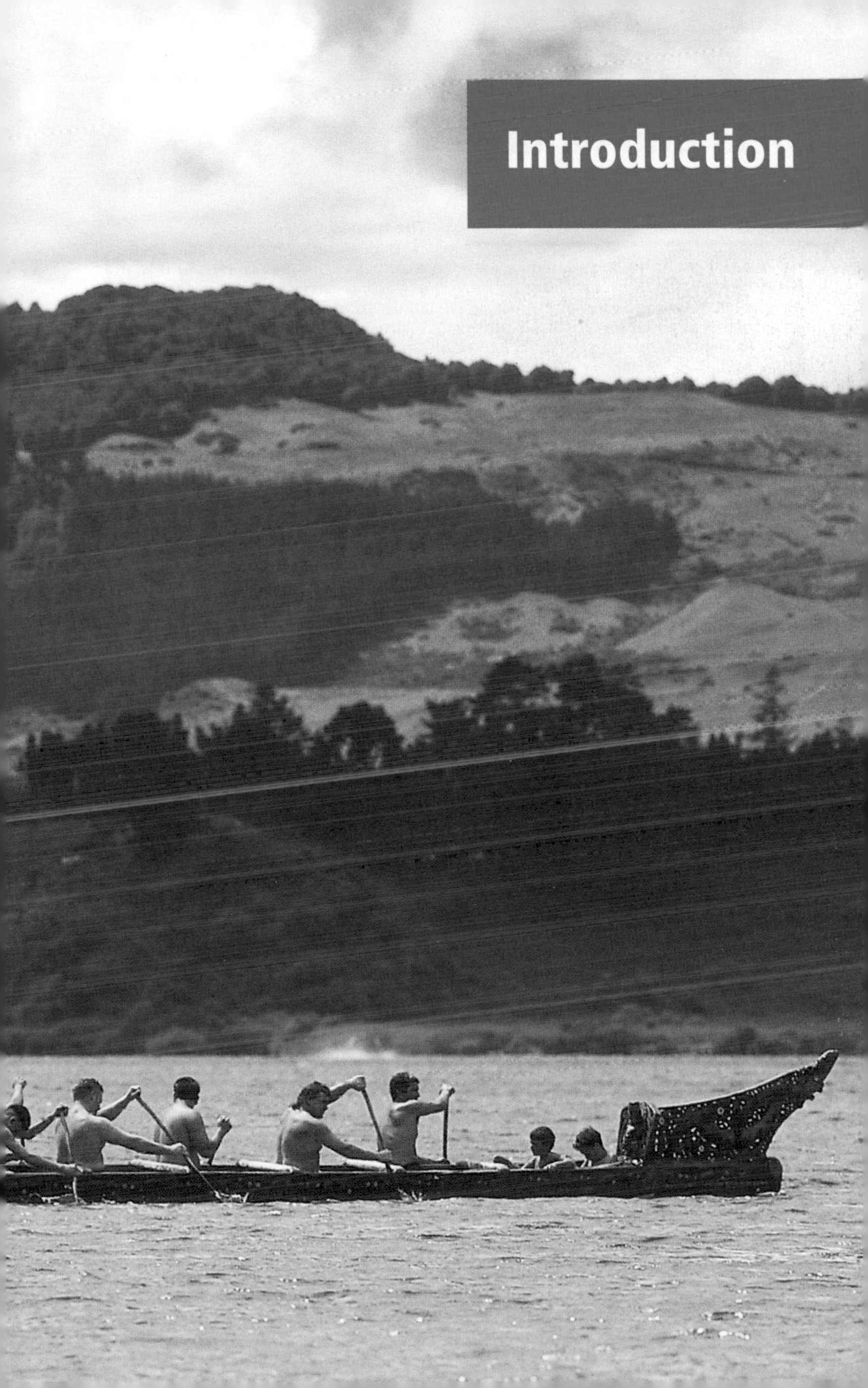

# Facts and Figures

## General

New Zealand occupies an isolated position in the South Pacific, roughly half way between the equator and the South Pole. It is about as far away from Europe as it is possible to get – a 25 hr flight – and even its nearest neighbour, Australia, is a 3 hr flight to the north-west.

With a total land mass of around 270,534 sq km (the two main islands and a number of smaller ones), New Zealand's area is rather greater than that of the United Kingdom. The North Island (114,597 sq km) and South Island (151,757 sq km) extend between 34° and 47°S, with a total distance of 1770 km between the most southerly and the most northerly points. The southernmost settlement in New Zealand is on Stewart Island. From west to east New Zealand extends between 166° and 179°E. No point on the two main islands is further than 110 km from the sea.

◄ A Maori war canoe

### The islands

New Zealand's territory includes a number of smaller islands and island groups at varying distances from the two main islands (North Island and South Island). The largest is Stewart Island to the south, with an area of some 1746 sq km. Among the furthest away are the Kermadec Islands to the north, Chatham and Bounty Islands to the east and Campbell and Auckland Islands to the south.

Other New Zealand island groups are the **Tokelau Islands** in Polynesia, the **Cook Islands** and **Niue**. The Cook Islands and Niue are associated with New Zealand as self-governing territories.

Also belonging to New Zealand is the **Ross Dependency** in Antarctica (area 4.75 million sq km), an unpopulated territory consisting of the Ross Sea, the Ross Ice Shelf and eastern and north-eastern Victoria Land.

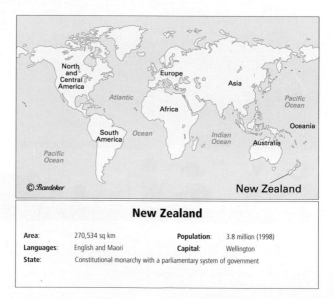

© Baedeker

**New Zealand**

## New Zealand

| | | | |
|---|---|---|---|
| **Area**: | 270,534 sq km | **Population**: | 3.8 million (1998) |
| **Languages**: | English and Maori | **Capital**: | Wellington |
| **State**: | Constitutional monarchy with a parliamentary system of government | | |

### Down under

Visitors to New Zealand soon realise that life in the southern hemisphere differs from life in Europe or North America. When it is winter in the northern hemisphere it is summer in New Zealand; when the days grow longer in Europe and the trees come into leaf it is autumn in New Zealand; and when the leaves begin to fall in the northern countries there is a feeling of spring in New Zealand. During the day the sun reaches its highest point in the north, not in the south, and accordingly the warmer slopes of a hill are on the north side, not the south.

## Topography

### Variety of landscape

Although New Zealand is not a continent but consists mainly of two large islands separated by the 30 km wide Cook Strait, it offers a remarkable variety of landscape. The two main islands have basically different structures. The North Island is a region of volcanic features and low mountain ranges, with some volcanoes reaching heights of over 2500 m. In the South Island features of volcanic origin are much less common: here the landscape is patterned by folded mountains of alpine type, much altered in the ice ages. This difference in topography is matched by differences in climate: lying closer to Antarctica, the South Island has a markedly rawer climate than the North Island.

### Coastal landscapes

Both the main islands have varied and rapidly changing coastal landscapes. The west coast of the Northland region is lined by long sandy beaches and dunes. Common to both islands are alluvial plains, deltas and at some points imposing stretches of cliffs. Notable features are the rias (river valleys inundated by the sea) in the north-east of the South Island and the fjord-like valleys carved out by glaciers in the south-west of the South Island.

### North Island (Te Ika a Maui)

Volcanic activity is very evident in the central region of the North Island. Here the landscape, shaped by volcanic action, is dominated by the **volcanoes**, still in some degree active, of Mount

Ruapehu (2797 m; the highest peak on the North Island), Mount Ngauruhoe (2290 m) and Mount Tongariro (1968 m). Lake Taupo is a huge crater lake, evidence of a gigantic volcanic explosion. Just to the north of this is the Rotorua thermal region, where the whole range of volcanic and post-volcanic phenomena can be observed. In addition to many smaller crater lakes, numerous geysers and hot mud pools there are sinter terraces and hot springs, whose characteristic odours are likely to remain in visitors' memories.

The North Island's central volcanic region is surrounded by hills rising to over 1700 m, giving the island its characteristic hilly relief. From the southern tip of the North Island to East Cape can be seen the continuation of New Zealand's youngest range of folded mountains, which begins at the southern tip of the South Island and reaches its highest points in the Southern Alps. In the west of the North Island is Taranaki (Mount Egmont, 2518 m) with its beautifully regular cone (frequently hidden in cloud).

The hilly **Coromandel Peninsula** on the north side of the North Island is of radically different structure from the other hills of the island. It is built up from volcanic material, mainly sandstone, clay and limestone.

To the north of Auckland extends the **Northland** region, with rolling hills and a subtropical climate. The highest peaks are just under 800 m. This region, favoured both climatically and scenically, offers ideal conditions for agriculture and tourism.

### South Island (Te Wahi Ponamu)

The predominant feature of the South Island is the **Southern Alps**, a range of folded mountains that in geological terms are relatively young. In the centre is New Zealand's highest peak, Mount Cook (3759 m). In its vicinity are other mountains over 3000 m – Mount Tasman, Mount Sefton and a number of other snow-capped peaks. The charm of these mountains is enhanced by numerous imposing glaciers, the most spectacular of which are the 26 km Tasman Glacier, the Hooker Glacier and the Mueller Glacier. This mountain region is now protected as the Mount Cook National Park. To the west the

## New Zealand Mountains, Lakes and Rivers

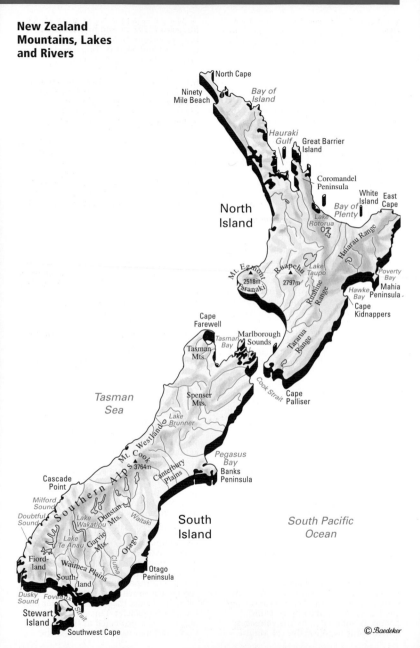

North Cape

Ninety Mile Beach

*Bay of Island*

*Hauraki Gulf*

Great Barrier Island

Coromandel Peninsula

White Island

East Cape

*Bay of Plenty*

**North Island**

*Lake Rotorua*

Huiarau Range

Mt. Egmont Taranaki 2518m

Ruapehu 2797m

*Lake Taupo*

Raukine Range

*Poverty Bay*

Mahia Peninsula

*Hawke Bay*

Cape Kidnappers

Tararua Range

Cape Farewell

*Tasman Bay*

Marlborough Sounds

Tasman Mts.

Spenser Mts.

*Cook Strait*

Cape Palliser

**Tasman Sea**

*Lake Brunner*

Westland

*Pegasus Bay*

Mt. Cook 3764m

Canterbury Plains

Banks Peninsula

Cascade Point

Southern Alps

*Milford Sound*

*Doubtful Sound*

*Lake Wakatipu*

Dunstan Mts.

Waitaki

**South Island**

**South Pacific Ocean**

Fiord-land

*Lake Te Anau*

Garvie Mts.

Otago

Clutha

Waimea Plains

South-land

Otago Peninsula

*Dusky Sound*

Foveaux Strait

Stewart Island

Southwest Cape

© *Baedeker*

Southern Alps descend to the sea by a strip of land only 50 km wide. This steep gradient over a relatively short distance has produced the long tongues of the Fox Glacier and Franz Josef Glacier, reaching down to only 300 m above sea level.

The island's **western coastal plain** is separated from the Southern Alps by the Alpine Fault.

The **eastern slopes** of the Southern Alps fall away more gradually. In this region there are numerous lakes, which give this area its particular charm.
In the northern part of the South Island there are two ranges of low mountains. To the north-west are the **Tasman Mountains**, while to the north-east is the hilly Marlborough region, the continuation of the Southern Alps (see above). The coastal region known as the **Marlborough Sounds** is an extensive system of rias (river valleys drowned by the sea).

At the other end of the South Island, to the south-west, is the beautiful **Fiordland** region, which formed in much the same way as the rias to the north. The fjords are river valleys carved out by glaciers that flowed down to the sea during the ice ages; the walls of these glaciated valleys, which are frequently U-shape. There are numerous lakes, such as Lake

Te Anau, formed by the melting of the ice masses. The mountains, of granite, gneiss and slate, are traversed by numerous valleys and reach heights of over 1700 m.

In the southern part of **Central Otago** is another mountainous region, with hills rising to 2000 m. This landscape has a continental aspect with wide river valleys and a gentler pattern of relief.

To the south and east of the South Island there is a mixture of mountains and extensive **plains**. From the Canterbury Plain in the east the **Banks Peninsula** reaches out into the sea. It is formed by an extinct volcano, whose crater lake is open to the sea and serves as a natural harbour.

## Making of New Zealand

### Continental plates
The geological history of New Zealand is largely due its situation on the boundary between two tectonic plates, the Indian-Australian plate and the Pacific plate. When the primeval super-continent of Pangaea began to split up, some 200 million years ago, there formed the two continents of Laurasia to the north (North America, Europe, Asia) and Gondwana to the south (South America,

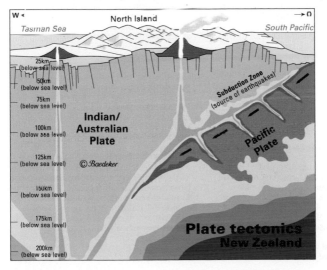

Africa, the Indian sub-continent, Antarctica, Australia). The further separation of these continents began about 150 million years ago. About that time Gondwana was divided into the present continents of South America, Africa and India; Australia, Antarctica and New Zealand still formed a single land mass. Then about 80 million years ago New Zealand was separated from Australia and Antarctica by the formation of the Tasman Sea. New Zealand was thus already isolated when Australia and Antarctica began to separate about 50 million years ago. A globe shows how the regions bordering the Pacific Ocean are caught between ranges of mountains and deep marine trenches. These are part of what is known as the unstable circum-Pacific mobile belt, the border region marked by the collision of continental and oceanic plates. Typical features of this unsettled zone are earthquakes, volcanic activity and the formation of mountain ranges and marine trenches. With its frequent earthquakes and active volcanism this belt is well known as the Ring of Fire.

### North Island

The frequent earthquakes, numerous faults, volcanic activity and young folded mountains are the consequence of forces generated by the collision of the Indian-Australian plate with the Pacific plate. The two plates move both towards one another and past one another, and as a result the Pacific plate is forced under the Indian-Australian one in the region of the North Island. This gives rise to enormous pressures and temperature differences in the earth's crust, which are vented on the surface in volcanoes, geysers, thermal springs, mud pools, fumaroles (openings through which suphurous gas is emitted) and solfataras (craters containing fumaroles).

### South Island

In the region of the South Island, on the other hand, the Pacific plate is thrust over the Indian-Australian plate, leading to the folding of the Southern Alps. The lateral displacement of the two plates along the Alpine Fault now extends for a distance of over 450 km. It is clearly visible in rocks of the same age in the north-west and south of the South Island.

### Earthquakes and volcanism

The liberation of enormous energies on the boundary between the two tectonic plates has created the landscape patterns of New Zealand. In general the formation of mountains is accompanied by volcanic activity, the extrusion of basalts and frequent violent earthquakes. Continuing volcanic activity and recurrent earthquakes are evidence that the movements under the earth's surface still go on. The movements of the two plates do not proceed steadily but give rise to tensions that are spontaneously discharged. Hence the earthquakes: at least one each year in New Zealand reaches a strength of 6 on the Richter scale. During the last 150 years severe earthquakes – for example in the Napier region in 1931 – have repeatedly resulted in heavy loss of life. New Zealand's capital, Wellington, is built on unstable ground: like San Francisco in California, it lies close to a major fault line. It was devastated by a severe earthquake in 1855. Volcanic eruptions are less of a threat, but the eruption of Mount Tarawera at the end of the 19th c. and of Mount Ruapehu in the early 1950s caused some loss of life. In the central volcanic zone round Mount Tongariro on the North Island the volcanoes are still active. Along fault lines magma comes to the surface. This can be observed from a flight over White Island in the Bay of Plenty. Above this small volcanic island, lying on the northern continuation of the fault lines in the central volcanic zone of the North Island, there are always whitish-yellow swathes of sulphurous vapour.

### Mountain formation

The most ancient rocks on the South Island, some 600 million years old, show that parts of the New Zealand land mass have been in existence since the Precambrian period (ending about 570 million years ago), when they formed part of the continent of Gondwana. During the Cambrian, Ordovician, Silurian and warly Devonian periods (570–380 million years ago) sediments were deposited in a zone of subsidence in the earth's crust near the continent of Gondwana. The subsequent process of mountain formation, which lasted until about 300 million years ago, is known as the Tahua orogenesis. A consequence of this orogenesis was the formation of a further subsidence zone known as the New Zealand geosyncline. The oldest, though untypical, rock in this

Sinter terraces at Whakarewarewa (Rotorua)

sedimentation zone is the Upper Carboniferous marble (320–290 million years ago) that outcrops at Kakahu in South Canterbury, pointing to earlier deposits of limestone. The characteristic rocks of this subsidence zone, however, are slates, sandstones, limestones and volcanic tuffs, which can be dated to the Permian period (290–245 million years ago). In the Triassic period (245–208 million years ago) greywacke (sandstone containing a high proportion of rock detritus) was formed. This constitutes the backbone of New Zealand and has been subject to folding in the region of the Southern Alps. This last phase of mountain formation took place from the end of the Jurassic period (146 million years ago) to the Middle Cretaceous (100 million years ago). In the Upper Cretaceous era (100–65 million years ago) the mountains were worn down by erosion. The present natural topography is due to a continuing process of mountain formation that began 25 million years ago and reached its climax in the late Tertiary period (10–1.64 million years ago).

All three periods of upthrust were accompanied by volcanic activity, with the deposition of lava and ash. At the same time there were repeated intrusions of plutonite (magma that had hardened under the surface) into the deeper strata. During the Tertiary period sandstone, limestone and clay strata were formed according to changing conditions.

The Pleistocene epoch that followed lasted until about 10,000 years ago. Developments on the earth's surface were shaped by the ice ages, interrupted by warmer periods.

In the most recent period of the earth's history, the Holocene, the existing land forms have undergone practically no change. Only the most recent sediments in alluvial plains and river valleys are evidence of erosional processes. Earthquakes and local displacements of soil masses, like the most recent landslide on Mount Cook (1991), can take on catastrophic dimensions.

### Ice ages (Pleistocene period)

The beginning of the first cold period, the Hautawan, with the Ross glaciation, marks the end of the Tertiary period and the beginning of the Pleistocene epoch, some 1.64 million years ago . Moraines and banded clay are evidence of the first glaciation. The first cold period was followed, about 1.5 million years ago, by the first warm period (interglacial), the Nukumaruan. The Okehuan cold period, beginning 1.2 million years ago, was less marked than the Hautawan. The following warm period, the Putikan, lasted from 700,000 to 300,000 years ago. The period from 300,000 to 10,000 years ago was marked by the frequent alternation of cold and warm periods. The earliest ice age in this period was the Porikan, which was followed by the Waiwheran warm period. This in turn was followed by the Waimaungan ice age and the Terangian warm period. The second-last ice age, the Waimean, lasted until 120,000 years ago, and the last interglacial, the Oturian, was followed 80,000 years ago by the last ice age, which ended with the beginning of the post-glacial period some 14,000 years ago. U-shape valleys, fjords, hanging valleys, terminal, lateral and ground moraines, glacier lakes and deposits of fluvial detritus are among the most obvious evidence of these periods, demonstrating the landscaping force of the ice. The still surviving glaciers – for example the Franz Josef Glacier, the Fox Glacier and the Tasman Glacier, which flow down from the mountain region round Mount Cook in the Southern Alps – are relics of the ice ages.

## Climate

New Zealand's climatic conditions relate to the different parts of the country. Thus in the west of the South Island, on the slopes of the Southern Alps, there are rainy areas with an annual precipitations well over 2500 mm. Further east, in the rain shadow of the Southern Alps, it is much drier, with annual precipitation under 700 mm. Temperatures show lesser variations, with annual averages ranging between 9°C at the south end of the South Island and 14°C to the north of Auckland; and even in the height of summer offshoots of Antarctic cold fronts can briefly bring day temperatures in the Southern Alps and Central Otago on the South Island below 10°C and the snowline down to 1000 m, while on the North Island it is high summer.

The climate of New Zealand is determined mainly by three factors: its position in the zone of westerly winds, the mountains opposed to the direction of the wind, and the country's insularity, far from any continent and surrounded by the Pacific Ocean.

### Westerlies

Lying between 35° and 47°S, New Zealand is situated in the medium latitudes of the southern hemisphere. Only the most northerly part of the North Island, the Northland region, lies in the boundary area of the subtropical and marginally tropical high-pressure zone, with a milder climate. Like the higher latitudes of the northern hemisphere (e.g. Europe), the lower latitudes of the southern hemisphere have the four seasons of spring, summer, autumn and winter. Here too the position of the sun changes over the year. But when the sun reaches its highest position in the northern hemisphere it is at its lowest in New Zealand; that is, when it is summer in Europe it is winter in New Zealand, and vice versa.

The west winds that prevail throughout the year are also characteristic of the medium latitudes and are mainly responsible for the distribution of rainfall. Again typical of the medium latitudes is the alternation of passing low-pressure areas (cyclones) and high-pressure areas (anticyclones). The former are normally coupled with cold fronts and are characterised by high rainfall and high wind speeds. In the Cook Strait between the two main islands stormy winds prevail almost all year. Thus Wellington, New Zealand's 'windy city', has wind speeds of over 50 kph on more than 170 days in the year. Stable weather conditions with light winds are usually the result of anticyclones. In the coastal regions landward and seaward winds prevent sultry weather from developing.

### Rainfall

#### Weather side

The Southern Alps on the South Island, lying almost at right angles to the prevailing westerlies, and the lower mountains of the North Island influence the frequency and intensity of rainfall in New Zealand. There are marked differences between the weather side of the hills, which is exposed to the wind,

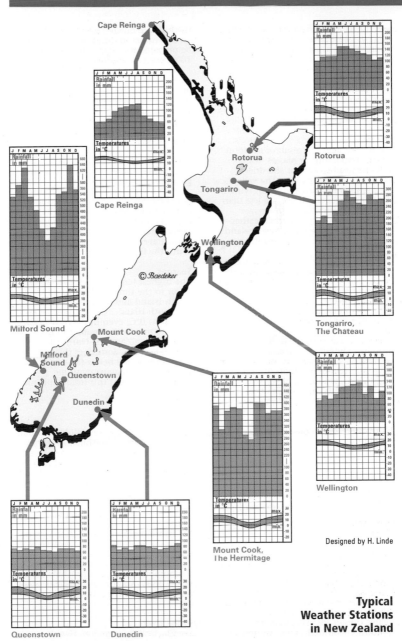

Cape Reinga

Rotorua

Tongariro

Wellington

Milford Sound

Mount Cook

Queenstown

Dunedin

Rotorua

Tongariro, The Chateau

Wellington

Mount Cook, The Hermitage

Designed by H. Linde

**Typical Weather Stations in New Zealand**

© Baedeker

and the lee side. The air masses coming from the west gain increased humidity during their passage over the Tasman Sea, but then come up against the mountains and are compelled to rise up, leading to intensive cloud formation and high rainfall. This is particularly evident on the Southern Alps, which in some areas have an annual rainfall on the weather side of over 7000 mm.

**Lee side**

On the lee side, as a result of the föhn effect (descending air masses, which become steadily warmer and drier), rainfall is markedly lower. The valleys, intramontane basins and plains lying in the wind shadow can average less than 500 mm of rainfall.

Apart from such extreme weather-side and lee-side regions, New Zealand's rainfall ranges from 1000 to 1500 mm.

**Seasons**

During the winter (June to August) the North Island comes under the influence of the westerlies and has most of its rainfall during these months. The summer months (December to February) are under the influence of subtropical and marginally tropical high-pressure areas. The consequence is stable weather with low rainfall. This stability can be disturbed by low-pressure areas of tropical origin or offshoots of tropical whirlwinds, producing heavy rain and strong winds in the north and east of the island. This occurs only during the summer months.

On the South Island, on the other hand, there are no precisely defined dry or rainy seasons: the months of maximum and minimum rainfall vary from region to region. In the south the highest rainfall is during the summer; in the east and north-east the wettest months are May and June (late autumn in the southern hemisphere); while in the west and north of the South Island the highest rainfall is in spring (September to November).

## Temperatures

**Relief and latitude**

Relief also produces considerable differences in temperature. Temperature falls, for example, by around half a degree Celsius for every 100 m of altitude; and at night temperatures in the hills are much lower than at sea level. Visitors to the Southern Alps must be prepared for temperatures below 10°C, even in summer.

Because of the moderating influence of the surrounding ocean, the differences of temperature between the north and the south of New Zealand are smaller than the distance of 1500 km might suggest. New Zealand's oceanic climate seldom has differences of temperature over the year or over the day of more than 10°C. The main exception to this is Central Otago, a region almost of continental character, where there are greater ranges of temperature.

The highest annual average temperatures, 13–14°C are found in the north of the North Island. For the extreme north of the South Island and other parts of the North Island the annual average is around 12°C. Further south the figure falls to 9°C.

**Seasons**

The highest temperatures, over 22°C, occur in the summer months on the North Island and the north and east of the South Island. Temperatures seldom fall below 0°C, even in the New Zealand winter. Only in the Southern Alps, Central Otago and the North Island's central volcanic zone does the thermometer fall below freezing point. In the coastal regions maritime influences prevent this from happening.

## Sunshine

In spite of its heavy rainfall New Zealand has long hours of sunshine, with the annual average ranging between around 2500 hrs at Nelson and Blenheim in the north of the South Island and 1500 hrs in the Southern Alps and Fiordland. For the South Island there are normally between 1600 and 2000 hrs of sunshine over the year, decreasing from north to south. In the lee of the Southern Alps the figure is around 2200, in the coastal regions of the North Island between 2000 and 2200; only in the central volcanic zone of the North Island does the number of hours of sunshine fall below 1800. An annual average of 2000 hrs of sunshine is equivalent to 5½ hrs a day.

**Ozone layer**

See Practical Information, Health

**When to go**
See Practical Information, When to Go

## Flora and Fauna

Some 80 million years of isolation from other land masses allowed the flora and fauna of New Zealand to develop independently. It is not surprising, therefore, that more than 70 per cent of the flora is found only in New Zealand. The endemic fauna is confined mainly to birds and insects, though there are also a few species of reptiles and freshwater fish native to New Zealand. For many millions of years plants and animals were isolated. The development of the flora and fauna has been affected by volcanic eruptions and a series of ice ages, but more recently by the arrival of the Europeans. In a period of 200 years – in geological terms no more than a moment in the earth's history – numerous plant and animal species have been driven out of their natural habitat or exterminated; even today many species are in danger of extinction.

## Flora

### Native flora

Originally New Zealand was covered with great expanses of **forest**. Only small areas – mainly in the high mountain regions and in the lee of the Southern Alps – were unsuitable for trees, either because they were too cold or too dry. Vegetation adapted to the temperature gradient that falls from north to south: thus the forests in different parts of the country tend to be of different species. Typical of New Zealand's primeval forests are evergreen deciduous trees and conifers, which have adapted to cold winter temperatures so that they do not, like many European species, shed their leaves.

Areas of subtropical climate in New Zealand – mainly the Coromandel Peninsula and the Northland region, but also the area round Auckland – were originally covered with forests of **kauri**, a species of spruce notable for its gigantic size.

A gigantic tree fern

In the **undergrowth** of New Zealand's forests there are ferns, mosses, lianas, climbing plants and epiphytes, giving visitors something of an impression of a primeval forest. A particularly typical representative of New Zealand's flora is the **silver fern**, which has been adopted as the country's national plant.

The commonest forest tree is the evergreen **southern beech**. On the North Island it is found associated with other species of tree, such as the tall totara, but on the South Island, for example in Fiordland and Westland, it forms large forests, with light undergrowth composed of relatively few species. In other forests the undergrowth consists of plants growing to different heights, including tree ferns, shrubs and shade-tolerant trees. At higher altitudes the beech gives place to forests of conifers.

The **rimu** is found throughout New Zealand, growing in mixed forests with other trees. Its sturdy growth makes it a popular decorative tree. It grows very slowly and some trees may be as much as 1000 years old. Its hard wood is a much used building timber.

The magnificent crimson flowers of the **Pohutukawa** appear in December – hence its popular name of the Christmas tree. It is found mainly on the beaches of the North Island.

The **rata**, a tree with beautiful deep red flowers, is most at home on the South Island. It has an unusual method of reproduction: its seeds are carried by the wind and deposited on other trees, where it forms aerial roots and gradually kills the host plant.

The yellow blossoms of the **kowhai** provides another touch of colour in New Zealand's forests.

Tall tussock or tuft **grasses** are characteristic of the plains. Expanses of dry grassland are found in the lee of the Southern Alps. Also common is toetoe grass, a species related to the pampas grass of South America.

In summer the **alpine meadows** of mountain regions are covered with a magnificent show of flowers. In addition to the daisy-like celmisias there are gentians, various species of orchid and numerous other alpine flowers, including the Mount Cook lily and the white buttercup, the largest species in its genus.

The most widely distributed New Zealand shrub is the **manuka**, which flourishes nearly everywhere and is valued as providing good protection against erosion. It is one of the first species that established themselves on land cleared of forest. Its dried leaves were once used to make a kind of tea: hence its name of the Tea Tree.

New Zealand **flax**, which has adapted to conditions in the rainy plains, was formerly of great economic importance to the Maoris. The fibres of this plant are used to make baskets, textiles and other wares.

### Foreign plants
The Maoris brought with them various useful plants from their Polynesian homeland, including the kumara or sweet potato. With the arrival of European settlers new plants were brought in on an enormous scale. More than 2000 species came to New Zealand in this way, often unintentionally. The fast-growing Californian pine is now common in New Zealand. It is grown for its timber, frequently a monoculture. The Californian giant redwood has also been successfully established in New Zealand. Other imports from different parts of the world are various species of tree (including oak), fruit trees (among them the Chinese gooseberry or kiwi fruit), garden plants, decorative flowers (especially lupins, which grow in the wild everywhere during the summer), clover and broom. Several species of eucalyptus and acacia have found their way from Australia to New Zealand. In many areas the new plants have upset the delicate ecosystem.

## Fauna

### Native fauna: birds
New Zealand's native fauna is represented in the first place by more than 250 bird species. Some are very rare, including the kiwi (☞22, Baedeker Special), a nocturnal, flightless bird. Before the arrival of humans birds had no natural enemies except other members of their own species, and as a

result a number of other flightless species were able to develop.

Other well-known New Zealand birds are the weka, the kakapo, the takahe and above all the **moa**, now extinct. There were more than two dozen species of the moa, a flightless bird similar to the ostrich. The largest of them could reach a height of 4.5 m. The early settlers in New Zealand, particularly the Maoris, hunted these birds as an addition to their diet and wiped them out before the arrival of the Europeans.

Of the four New Zealand species of **parrot** the mountain parrot known as the **kea** has the worst reputation. It is said that it attacks and kills sheep. It has become accustomed to people, and tents, sleeping bags and other human possessions are not safe from it. The kea is particularly fond of rubber items such as windscreen wipers and tyres. Untypically for a parrot, it has adapted to conditions in the mountain regions of the Southern Alps.
  Other common species of parrot in New Zealand are kakas and parakeets. Now very rare, and therefore strictly protected, is the kakapo, a flightless nocturnal parrot.

Various species of **honeyeater**, including the bellbird and the stitchbird, are relatively common in New Zealand's natural forests. They live mainly on nectar but also on fruit and insects. Perhaps the best-known New Zealand songbird is the black-plumaged tui, which also belongs to the honeyeater genus.

**Rails** are not uncommon in New Zealand. One of the largest representatives of the species is the **takahe**, a flightless bird that was believed to be extinct until a takahe colony of some size was discovered in Fiordland after the second world war.

Another flightless bird is the **weka**, which also belongs to the rail family. This inquisitive, duck-like bird is often seen on camping and picnic sites, where, like the magpie, it looks out for shiny and glistening objects.

The coasts of New Zealand are home to numerous species of **seabird**. The most striking is the **royal albatross**, which has a wingspan of up to 3.5 m. Other denizens of the coastal regions are species of gull, cormorants, petrels, terns and muttonbirds.

The **yellow-eyed penguin** is found only in New Zealand. Its habitat is the south coast of the South Island.

**Insects**
New Zealand has innumerable insect species, which are the main source of food for the country's birds. One of the most interesting insects is a tiny fly related to the gnat whose larvae are found mainly on the roofs of dark caves. They have a fascinating method of obtaining their food. They produce long sticky threads like a spider's web, and during their digestive process generate a faint light – hence the name **glow-worm**. The light attracts insects, which are caught on the sticky threads and become the fly's larder. Such glow-worms – unrelated to the European species – can be observed in the Waitoma Caves on North Island.
  Towards evening the masses of mosquitoes and sandflies that then emerge can be a nuisance.

New Zealand also has a number of species of **spider**. The most dangerous is

A giant moa

*Baedeker* SPECIAL

# 'Kiwii, kiwii' and 'Quaak, quaak'

Walking through a New Zealand forest at night, you can sometimes hear a shrill 'kiwii, kiwii' and a muffled 'quaak, quaak'. This is likely to be your only contact with New Zealand's most famous native animal, the kiwi, a shy creature that is mainly active at night.

The kiwi is a flightless bird belonging to the *Apterygidae* family. About the size of a domestic hen, it has a long, curved and pointed beak and straggly greyish-brown plumage. Its wings have receded so that it is quite unable to fly. In compensation it has an excellent sense of smell via the end of its beak.

The kiwi, of which there are three species, gets its name from the cry of the male bird. The cry of the female is more like the croak of a frog. They can live for up to 25 years. It searches for food after dark, following carefully contrived paths through New Zealand's forests, finding grubs and worms in the foliage with its beak or digging them out with its strong claws. During the rainy season and when the woodland berries are ripening the kiwi covers great distances in its nightly foraging.

It is only during the mating season that kiwis, which are normally loners, become more sociable. After mating a pair of kiwis will spend the day asleep in their hole and go out together at night in search of food. After the female produces one or two eggs, relatively large in proportion to her own size, it is the male who sits on

them. The young birds very quickly become independent, for their parents pay little attention to them, but it may be 5 or 6 years before they are sexually mature.

The Maoris regarded – and still regard – kiwis as desirable game birds. Kiwi feathers were woven into the mats of their chiefs.

The kiwis have been much decimated by hunters, particularly since the arrival of Europeans, and are now in danger of extinction. Since they cannot fly and are not particularly swift on their feet they are an easy prey, particularly for the animals brought in by the Europeans – rats, dogs, cats, martens and hedgehogs. The kiwi, as New Zealand's national animal, is now strictly protected.

the **katipo**, which is closely related to the American black widow and the Australian redback. A bite from a fully grown female is painful and can be fatal.

### Reptiles
The reptile family is represented in New Zealand by several species of gecko and small lizards. There are few snakes.

The **tuatara** is a lizard-like reptile that represents a long-past period in the earth's history: a species that in all the other parts of the world died out before the dinosaurs. It is found only in caverns on the offshore islands to the east of New Zealand.

### Fish
The waters round New Zealand are well stocked with fish and appeal particularly to deep-sea anglers. In addition to many smaller fish there are tiger and hammerhead sharks, marlin, swordfish and tuna.

### Mammals
As a result of New Zealand's early isolation it has no native land mammals apart from two species of bat. Off the Kaikoura coast in the north-east of the South Island there are schools of whales and dolphins, including sperm whales and even killer whales.

### Foreign animals
Rats and dogs came to New Zealand with the first incomers in the early historical period and great numbers of animals were brought in by European immigrants – agricultural and domestic animals such as cattle, sheep, horses, goats, pigs, turkeys and peacocks, plus game animals (including red deer) and species of freshwater fish. These were brought in to provide food for the immigrants, but other animals include opossums, martens, cats and dogs.

Red deer, opossums, rats, cats and dogs are the species that have had the most devastating effects on the delicate **ecosystem** of New Zealand. The country's flightless birds were easy prey for dogs and cats that had gone back to the wild, and the nesting places of many birds were defenceless against martens and cats. The red deer, without any real natural enemies, multiplied enormously and by biting off young shoots they hindered the natural rejuvenation of the forests. The opossum, which for many years has been increasing in numbers, has devastated great tracts of forest. The authorities concerned with the protection of nature have launched expensive campaigns for dealing with the population explosion of certain species, including the use of helicopters to hunt them down.

## State

### National emblems
The New Zealand flag has the Union flag in the upper left corner, and in the right half, on a blue ground, the constellation of the Southern Cross. The national coat of arms, adopted in 1956, also features the Southern Cross, symbolising the state, as well as a sheaf of corn, a sheep's fleece and a miner's tools, symbolising agriculture, stock farming and mining. In the centre are three sailing ships, reminders of the importance to New Zealand of maritime trade and the settling of the islands from the sea. The supporters are a white woman, representing the European immigrants, on the left, and a tattooed Maori in traditional costume and holding a spear, symbolising the original inhabitants, on the right; both figures stand on silver ferns, New Zealand's national plant. Above the shield is the British crown.

New Zealand's national animal is the kiwi: hence the name Kiwi applied to New Zealanders.

### Parliament and monarchy
New Zealand is a parliamentary democracy on the British model and a constitutional monarchy within the Commonwealth of Nations. The head of state is Queen Elizabeth II, who is represented by the Governor General. The British political tradition is reflected in the absence of a written constitution, the basis of constitutional law being provided by decisions of the British and New Zealand courts. New Zealand constitutional law, however, was collected in the Constitution Act of 1986. Politically, New Zealand is completely independent of Britain.

### Governor General
The Governor General is appointed by the Queen for a 5 year term. He opens and closes the parliamentary session, reads the 'speech from the throne'

# New Zealand

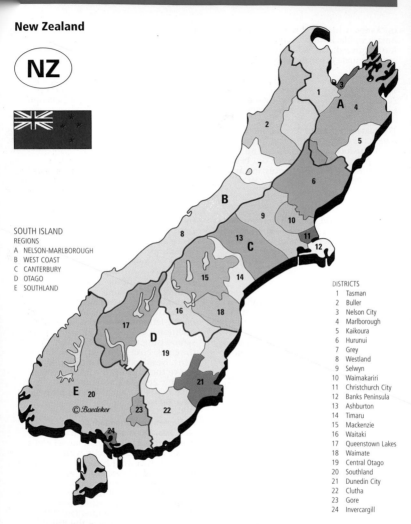

SOUTH ISLAND
REGIONS
A NELSON-MARLBOROUGH
B WEST COAST
C CANTERBURY
D OTAGO
E SOUTHLAND

DISTRICTS
1 Tasman
2 Buller
3 Nelson City
4 Marlborough
5 Kaikoura
6 Hurunui
7 Grey
8 Westland
9 Selwyn
10 Waimakariri
11 Christchurch City
12 Banks Peninsula
13 Ashburton
14 Timaru
15 Mackenzie
16 Waitaki
17 Queenstown Lakes
18 Waimate
19 Central Otago
20 Southland
21 Dunedin City
22 Clutha
23 Gore
24 Invercargill

setting out the government's plans for the session, makes various appointments and grants honours. He is head of the executive but can act only in agreement with the executive council, which consists of the cabinet and himself. He may, however, refuse his consent to laws that he believes to be contrary to the constitution. His most important function is to ensure continuity during a change of government. After a general election he is obliged to invite the leader of the victorious party to form a government.

**Parliament**

The New Zealand Parliament in Wellington has since 1952 comprised the House of Representatives. It has 120 members, who are elected for a 3 year term by universal, secret and direct suffrage. Four seats are reserved for

## NORTH ISLAND
DISTRICTS

1   Far North
2   Whangarei
3   Kaipara
4   Rodney
5   North Shore City
6   Waitakere City
7   Auckland City
8   Manukau City
9   Papakura
10  Thames Coromandel
11  Franklin
12  Hauraki
13  Waikato
14  Matamata-Piako
15  Western Bay of Plenty
16  Tauranga
17  Hamilton City
18  Waipa
19  Otorohanga
20  South Waikato
21  Rotorua
22  Kawerau
23  Whakatane
24  Opotoki
25  Gisborne
26  Waitomo
27  Taupo
28  Ruapehu
29  New Plymouth
30  Wairoa
31  Hastings
32  Stratford
33  Rangitikei
34  Wanganui
35  South Taranaki
36  Napier City
37  Central Hawkes Bay
38  Manawatu
39  Tararua
40  Palmerston North City
41  Horowhenua
42  Masterton
43  Carterton
44  South Wairarapa
45  Upper Hutt City
46  Porirua City
47  Lower Hutt City
48  Wellington City

REGIONS

A   NORTHLAND
B   AUCKLAND
C   WAIKATO
D   BAY OF PLENTY
E   GISBORNE
F   MANAWATU-WANGANUI
G   HAWKES BAY
H   TARANAKI
J   WELLINGTON

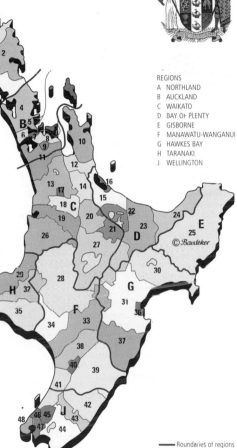

Boundaries of regions
Boundaries of districts

Maoris, who are elected in four constituencies with separate Maori electoral rolls. The electorate consists of all New Zealanders over the age of 18 and also foreigners with a long-term residence permit who have lived in the country for more than a year. Under a recently introduced system of mixed-member proportional representation electors have two votes, a constituency vote and a party vote. This is said to be fairer to the smaller parties. As in Britain, the leader of the opposition and their deputy have official salaried posts.

The government consists of the prime minister and the cabinet; all members of the cabinet must be members of Parliament. Executive powers are in the hands of the Governor General and the cabinet, who together form the executive council.

### Judicial system
The judicial system is largely based on English common law, supplemented by parliamentary legislation. The supreme court of appeal is the Privy Council in London. Since 1962 New Zealand has had an ombudsman to consider complaints of maladministration by government departments.

### Local government
Under a reorganised system of local government introduced in 1989 New Zealand is divided into 14 regions, nine on the North Island and five on the South Island, which in turn are divided into territorial authorities (towns and districts). In addition there are numerous local authorities. Education, social services and the police are the responsibility of central government .

### Parties
Under the majority voting system the political scene in New Zealand was dominated by two parties, the conservative National Party and the social-democratic Labour Party. The new voting system is likely to favour the larger minority parties, such as the Mana Motuhake, a Maori party, the Alliance Party and the New Zealand First Party.

### Trade unions
The New Zealand trade-union movement was encouraged by the state from the turn of the 19th c., so that numerous small unions were established. Until 1984 membership of a trade union was compulsory. More recently the influence of the unions has been reduced. In 1992 collective wage agreements were discontinued and replaced by individual or factory agreements.

### Foreign policy
New Zealand was a founding member of the United Nations and is also a member of the OECD and the Antarctic Treaty. Since the second world war cooperation with the United States has continued to be a central feature of New Zealand's security policy. but its increased concern with the Pacific area is shown by its participation in the Colombo Plan of 1950, under which the richer countries of Asia and the Pacific area promised development help, particularly in the technical field, to the less developed countries in the region; its membership (since 1989) of APEC, which seeks to coordinate the economic policies of the countries bordering the Pacific; and by its military alliance with Britain, Australia, Singapore and Malaysia under the Five Power Defence Agreement.

## Society

### Population
An official census has been held in New Zealand every five years since 1851. In 1998 the country had a population of 3.8 million inhabitants, about 500,000 more than it had 20 years before. During the 1970s and 1980s the rate of population growth was just under 20 per cent.

New Zealand has a land area, excluding its Antarctic territories, of around 270,534 sq km. It has thus a rather larger area than the United Kingdom (241,752 sq km) but is much more thinly populated: 13 persons per sq km, compared with 244 per sq km in the United Kingdom. This average figure, however, gives a misleading picture of the distribution of population in New Zealand. The North Island – favoured by climate, economy and communications – has an area of 114,597 sq km and a population density of just under 24 per sq km, while the rather larger South Island, with an area of 151,757 sq km, has a density of only six per sq km.

### Distribution of population
The low average population densities also obscure the fact that a large proportion of the population lives in towns with a population of over 30,000. These urban areas also show particularly high growth rates. The process of urbanisation, which has been in progress for decades, is the result mainly of economic development. Extensive rationalisation of agriculture has reduced the number of workers required, while the processing industries and the growing services sector in the towns have provided new jobs.

This development is particularly marked on the North Island. In 1996 about 30 per cent of New Zealand's population lived in Auckland, the country's largest city with more than a million inhabitants. The regions established some years ago – nine on the North Island, seven on the South Island – show very different changes in their populations between the censuses of 1986 and 1996.

The table below demonstrates clearly the movement into the large towns, on the North Island mainly to Auckland, on the South Island to the climatically favoured and scenic region around Marlborough and Nelson. The more remote parts of the country in the east and west of the North Island and the west and south of the South Island are less attractive in terms of climate and employment. This northward movement of population began in the late 1870s. The South Island, which had largely been spared by the Maori wars and had prospered thanks to the discovery of gold in Otago and on the west coast, declined in economic importance with the decline of the gold boom. In 1951 68 per cent of the population of New Zealand lived on the North Island; in 1996 the proportion had increased still further to 75 per cent.

## Immigration

The settlement of New Zealand by Europeans (mainly Britons) in the 19th c. was held up by continuing conflict with the Maoris. It was only after the end of the Maori wars and the discovery of gold that a considerable growth in the white population began. Thereafter immigration was promoted by the government and by 1880 the country had a population of 500,000. The million mark was passed in 1908, after the end of the economic depression of the late 19th c. following the collapse

of the price of agricultural produce on the world market. After the second world war the population increased rapidly as a result of immigration and the baby boom, reaching its second million in 1952 and its third 20 years later. Since the late 1970s population growth has slowed markedly. This is not solely the result of a stricter immigration policy that does not allow entry to everyone who wants to make a fresh start in New Zealand. The country's economic difficulties, particularly after the United Kingdom joined the European Community (January 1st 1973), and the necessary reorientation of the economy has led many skilled workers to leave New Zealand.

## Age pyramid

About one-sixth of the country's inhabitants were not born in New Zealand, and the large numbers of young immigrants who have come to New Zealand in recent decades have had a marked effect on the population structure. The age pyramid is more regular than in some European countries. Children and young people up to the age of 14 make up just a quarter of the population, with about two-thirds between 15 and 64 and about one-eighth 65 and over.

## Immigration

The immigration system has recently changed. The former selective procedure favouring certain trades and professions ('occupational priority') has given place

| Region | Population 1996 | % change since 1986 |
|---|---|---|
| NORTH ISLAND | | |
| Northland | 141,865 | +11.1 |
| Auckland | 1,077,205 | +22.3 |
| Waikato | 357,294 | +9.9 |
| Bay of Plenty | 230,465 | +18.4 |
| Gisborne | 46,089 | +0.3 |
| Hawke's Bay | 144,292 | +2.4 |
| Taranaki | 106,570 | −0.9 |
| Manawatu-Wanganui | 229,989 | +3.1 |
| Wellington | 416,019 | +5.2 |
| SOUTH ISLAND | | |
| Tasman | 40,036 | +16.5 |
| Nelson | 42,073 | +17.4 |
| Marlborough | 42,242 | +16.1 |
| West Coast | 35,671 | +2.2 |
| Canterbury | 478,912 | +9.7 |
| Otago | 193,132 | +5.6 |
| Southland | 100,758 | −4.5 |

## Immigration and Settlement of New Zealand after 1840

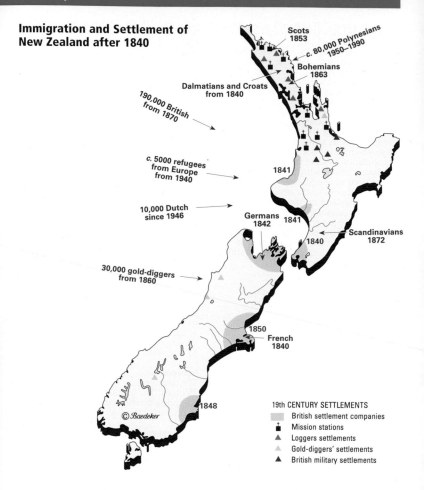

Scots
1853

c. 80,000 Polynesians
1950–1990

Bohemians
1863

Dalmatians and Croats
from 1840

190,000 British
from 1870

c. 5000 refugees
from Europe
from 1940

1841

10,000 Dutch
since 1946

Germans
1842

1841

Scandinavians
1872

1840

30,000 gold-diggers
from 1860

1850

French
1840

© Baedeker

1848

**19th CENTURY SETTLEMENTS**

British settlement companies
Mission stations
Loggers settlements
Gold-diggers' settlements
British military settlements

to a complicated points system divided into various categories, in which age, education and training, work experience, capital and readiness to invest are all taken into account as well as the question of uniting families.

**Europeans and Maoris**
About four-fifths of New Zealand's inhabitants are of European origin. They or their ancestors are mostly British. About 14 per cent of the population claims either pure or mixed Maori blood: that is, they are descendants of the indigenous inhabitants who came to New Zealand from the islands of the eastern Pacific centuries before the discovery of the country by Europeans (☞History). Some 4 per cent of the total population are so-called Pacific Island Polynesians, who came to New Zealand mainly from the tropical Cook Islands and from the islands of Niue, Samoa, Tokelau and Tonga. Most of them live in the Auckland region.

The population of European origin differs in age structure from the Maoris and Pacific islanders. Up to the age of 25 the Maoris and Polynesians feature more prominently; in the age group from 25 to 34 they are about level with the Europeans; but above 34 the proportion of Europeans increases sharply.

In 1998 7.6 per cent of the working population described themselves as unemployed. The relatively high unemployment among young people and the extremely high unemployment among Maoris and Polynesians was conspicuous.

Around the mid-19th c., after the Maoris had been decimated by tribal wars, wars with the British settlers and by European diseases, and were reduced to a rootless and aimless existence, it was believed that they faced extinction. The German traveller and scholar, Ferdinand von Hochstetter, who published a detailed description of New Zealand in 1863, expressed great concern about the decline of the Maori population (by around 20 per cent within 15 years). In the mid-19th c. there were no more than 56,000 Maoris. Von Hochstetter was convinced that by about 2000 they would have died out altogether. He also estimated that the European population of New Zealand, which was about 84,000 in 1860, would be half a million in the year 2000. In both cases he was far out. As a result of government measures to protect and integrate the Maoris, combined with the influence of leading Maori figures, the Maoris began to grow in numbers and to become conscious of their cultural independence.

### Ethnic minorities

There are small minorities of Indians and Chinese, whose ancestors came to New Zealand at the time of the gold rush. In the 19th c. numbers of Dalmatians came to Northland to dig for kauri gum; their descendants specialised in growing wine and citrus fruits. Also in the 19th c. a large group of German immigrants settled in Christchurch. Their monument to the explorer and museum founder Julius von Haast can be seen in the entrance of the Canterbury Museum. In Upper Moutere (Ranzau and Sarau) in the Nelson region, Ferdinand von Hochstetter reported encountering fair-haired German children and their parents, who described the hardships of their first years in New Zealand.

### Religion

In the last census about a quarter of the population declared themselves as of no religion; 22 per cent were Anglicans, 16 per cent Presbyterians, 15 per cent Catholics, 5 per cent Methodists and 2 per cent Baptists, while the remaining 15 per cent of the population belonged to a variety of other religious groups.

## Maoris

The Maoris, New Zealand's Polynesian inhabitants, are much smaller in number than the white New Zealanders. Only a sixth of the population describe themselves as Maoris, and the percentage of Maoris of pure blood is smaller still. In spite of their adaptation to the way of life of the European immigrants the Maoris have preserved many of their traditions.

The word *maori* means 'usual' or 'common' and was originally an adjective that the early European settlers used to distinguish the native population, who then took over the term to refer to themselves. Before, the Maoris had no general name for their race: the largest unit they recognised was the tribe.

### Social organisation

At the time of the European settlement of New Zealand there were between 100,000 and 120,000 Maoris, most of them on the North Island, which they called Aotearoa (the land of the long white cloud). Only about 5 per cent of them lived on the South Island, with its less attractive climate.

The largest social unit, the tribe (*iwi*), was divided into a number of *hapus*, clans consisting of some 500 people belonging to various related families. The *hapu* was headed by a chief known as the *ariki*, who derived his legitimacy from the *mana* (see below) of his ancestors – though he could lose his right to rule if he fell short in some way. Important decisions were taken not by the chief alone but by a meeting held on the *marae*, the central space of the village, in front of the meeting house. The head of each family had the right to speak, but the chief had the first and last word, summing up at the end of the meeting the opinions that had been expressed.

There were trading connections between the various tribes, mainly foodstuffs, but craft products and the semi-precious greenstones were also exchanged. From time to time there were armed conflicts between the tribes about rights to land or about *mana*. Usually, however, these conflicts involved only a few hundred men and casualties were few. This changed with the arrival of the first Europeans, from whom the Maoris obtained arms and ammunition that made the tribal wars fiercer and bloodier (☞History).

### Settlements

The early inhabitants of New Zealand had originally lived in unfortified settlements known as *kaingas*. It was only in the 14th c. that they began to build fortified villages (*pas*). These consisted of a group of houses set round an open space (*marae*). Here too stood the richly decorated meeting house (☞Culture), a building or underground rooms for storing food, cooking huts (since meals might not be eaten in the dwelling houses) and men's houses in which unmarried men lived and in which tools and implements were made and restored.

## Areas of Maori Settlement

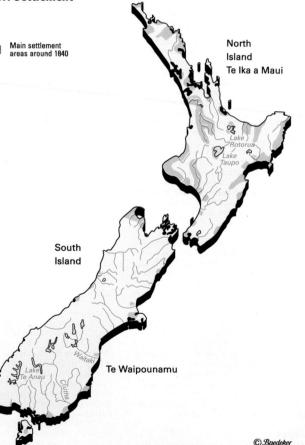

Main settlement areas around 1840

North Island
Te Ika a Maui

*Lake Rotorua*

*Lake Taupo*

South Island

*Lake Te Anau*

*Waitaki*

*Clutha*

Te Waipounamu

© *Baedeker*

## Religion

The Maori religion was animist: that is, various natural phenomena were personified and regarded as gods or spirits. The principal Maori god was Tane, who had separated his parents, the sky and the earth (☛33, Baedeker Special). He created the first woman from red earth. Tane was god of the forest, of the great trees that were of such importance for the construction of canoes and houses, and also of craftsmen, particularly boat builders and house-builders. When a tree was felled an offering had to be made to Tane to avoid incurring his divine wrath. The offerings to the gods were usually foodstuffs. Human sacrifices, common in Polynesian culture, were demanded only by the war god Tu, who was also entitled to the first enemy killed.

Communication with the gods was through a *tohunga* (the master, or the elect, a priest figure) – a title that was also given to experienced craftsmen such as woodcarvers or tattooers. The *tohunga* was required to be of high descent, with a long line of ancestors. Certain ritual functions were also performed by chiefs.

*Karakias* (sacred chants and magic formulae, whose exact performance was essential) played a part at sacrificial offerings, as prayers and invocations in various ritual acts.

## Mana

Two central elements in the life of the Maoris were *mana* and *tapu*. *Mana*, best translated as 'prestige' or 'honour', was a power and distinction that was granted to men by the gods and was transmitted to their descendants.

A man's *mana* could be increased by victories in battle, but could be lost by errors in celebrating ritual formulae or by offending against *tapu*. When enemy chiefs were defeated and enslaved they lost their *mana*.

## Tapu

To the Maoris *tapu* (taboo) is a positive force that cannot be interfered with in any way. The sacred utensils used by a *tohunga* were *tapu*, as were the persons of the priest himself and of the chief. *Tapu* could also apply at certain times to natural and environmental phenomena. There were protected times for newly

The favourite Maori colours are black, white, red and green

cultivated kumara fields, for hunting fish and birds, and for the harvest. Everyday objects, on the other hand, were *noa* (profane, ordinary); the terms could be applied, for example, to meals or even to women.

If anyone offended against a *tapu*, this inevitably brought misfortune or even death.

### Cult of ancestors
The wooden sculptures and carved figures on and in the Maoris' meeting houses and on the high prow and stern of their large war canoes represented not gods but venerable ancestors, who as the founding fathers of the tribe or family had the power to transmit their *mana* to the tribe (*iwi*) or clan (*hapu*). The fame of their great deeds was kept alive in ceremonial speeches and songs. The meeting house was the embodiment of the revered ancestors (☛Maori Culture).

### Food
The first Maoris who came to New Zealand brought various useful plants, including the kumara (a kind of sweet potato), taro and yam, which formed their staple foods. They also ate fish and birds, as well as the flesh of the rare Maori rat. The protein content of their diet was low, and this may have been one of the causes of cannibalism; but, particularly in later times, enemies killed in war were eaten in the hope of acquiring some of their qualities.

### Rights of property
The personal possessions of the Maoris included stores of food, spears and fruit trees. Enemies captured and enslaved in war belonged to the chiefs. Within the tribe the *hapus* possessed areas of land, which they distributed between individual families.

### Renaissance of Maori culture
In the 19th c. the Maoris felt themselves to be strangers in their own country, but in the course of the 20th c. they increasingly gained in self-confidence, starting to demand their rights. Since the 1970s there has been a renaissance of Maori culture. Many Maoris now regard their traditions and culture with pride. Signs of this new feeling are, for example, the establishment of new assembly areas (*maraes*), the inculcation of Maori culture in kindergartens and primary schools, and the greater use of the Maori language. Although most Maoris also have English as their mother tongue, the Maori language, which is closely related to other Polynesian tongues, is now taught in numbers of schools and educational establishments for adults, and there are also television and radio programmes in Maori.

### Maori King Movement
The traditional values of Maori culture are incarnated in Te Arikinui Dame Te Atairangikaahu, who was crowned Maori queen in 1966 and has her residence in Ngaruawahia. She is the sixth supreme chief (the first female one) of the Waikato tribes, in direct descent from Potatau, the first Maori king. The Maori King Movement from 1858 was an attempt to unite the many Maori tribes in a single unit that could counter the superiority of the Europeans settlers. The Maori queen's principal functions are representational.

### Maoris in modern society
Although the Maoris are much outnumbered by the white immigrants and there is a considerable gulf between the two cultures, the Maoris are by no means an oppressed minority in present-day New Zealand society. They are, however, markedly disadvantaged as compared with the white population. They have disproportionately large numbers of unemployed, and a high proportion of them depend on social assistance. One consequence of this is a high crime rate, the main cause of which is inadequate educational facilities. Descent and social values are still more important to many Maoris than success or possessions, and their culture has no interest in competitiveness.

Although the extended family and family relationships still play an important part in the life of the Maoris, the great majority of them now live in nuclear families. Externally their way of life is little different from that of the population of European descent.

Maori mythology and artistic skills now attract wide interest from New Zealanders as well as from visitors (☛Maori Culture).

## Economy

When the United Kingdom joined the European Community in 1973 New

# In the Beginning

The myths of the Maoris, passed from generation to generation by word of mouth, tell of the creation of the world, of the gods and of their distant ancestors in Hawaiki, and their legendary original homeland. Other myths speak of the Maoris' ancestors and their voyage in the great tribal canoes over the ocean to Aotearoa (the Maori name for New Zealand). Similar myths are found throughout Polynesia. They are related in Tahiti in very much the same terms as in New Zealand.

In the beginning, for an inconceivably long time, there was darkness. Mother Earth and Father Sky lay so closely together that their children, the gods who inhabited nature, never saw light. Discontented, they resolved to separate their parents. After unsuccessful attempts by his brothers this was at last achieved by Tane, god of the forests. He thrust himself with all his strength between his father and mother and heaved up the sky with his feet. The light of the sun and moon, the half-light of daybreak and the light of full day, now shone down on the earth; but blood from the wounds of the parents who were thus torn apart tinged the sunset and the earth with red (a sacred colour to the Maoris).

Tawhiri, the god of storms, the only member of the family who had opposed the plan to separate their parents, sent down hurricanes to the earth that was now flooded with light, devastating Tane's forests and creating such a tumult in the sea that even the sea god Tangaroa sought refuge from his raging brother in the depths of the ocean.

The love between Mother Earth and Father Sky survived their separation, and the sky poured down such floods of tears in the form of rain that they covered what had previously been dry land with water. Unable to bear the sight of their parents' grief, the gods turned their mother Earth gently round, whereupon the Sky's sorrow was relieved and his tears turned to dewdrops. The clouds that rose from the valleys into the sky were the answering sighs of Earth. When she was turned round Mother Earth had her youngest son, Ruaumoko, suckling her breast. Now covered by earth, he became the god of earthquakes and was given the fire of volcanoes to keep him warm.

The best-known mythic figure of the Maoris is the demigod Maui, a prematurely born member of the family. A sly and tricky character, he wheedled a magic jawbone out of his blind grandmother. Since the days were very short because the sun sank below the horizon immediately after rising, Maui conceived a plan to keep the sun above the horizon for longer. With his brothers he made strong ropes from flax with a noose to catch the sun; then one night they set out with the rope and came to the steep abyss where the earth ended and the sun rose in the morning from its deep cave. As the sun slowly rose the brothers captured it with the noose and Maui struck it with his magic jawbone until it became weak and covered with wounds, so that when it was released again it followed its course over the sky only very slowly and daylight over the earth lasted longer.

Zealand lost its important British market. Combined with the dependence of New Zealand's exports on world markets and the continuing rationalisation of the economy, this brought the country into deep crisis. The economy was also held back by strong state controls. In 1984 the government set about establishing a free market economy. State control of interest and exchange rates was ended, a value-added tax was introduced, state subsidies were much reduced and restrictions on imports were lifted. Many state-run enterprises were privatised, including postal services and telecommunications, the railways, banking and insurance, house-building and electricity corporations. As a result of these privatisations, cuts in social services and higher taxes inflation was reduced from over 15 per cent to 0.7 per cent (1999) and new state debt from 9 per cent to 2 per cent. Over the same period, however, unemployment increased from 3.4 per cent to over 7.6 per cent, for the privatised state enterprises cut staff and many industrial and property companies went bankrupt. In the last few years, after a long period of recession, the economy has begun to grow again, but there seems little prospect of bringing down the high unemployment rate in the immediate future. The economic reforms were accompanied by sharp changes in structure. Industry accounted for an ever greater proportion of the gross domestic product, while the proportion contributed by agriculture fell steeply.

In addition to the loss of the British market, the lack of a strong domestic market and the high transport costs resulting from the country's geographical situation created considerable problems for the country's economy. Nevertheless New Zealand has managed to develop its trade with the states bordering the Pacific (particularly Australia and Japan) and with the countries of the European Union. Since the mid-1970s it has cooperated with Australia in the New Zealand-Australia Free Trade Agreement (NAFTA) and since 1990 there has been a common free trade zone, as a result of which trade with Australia has more than doubled. New Zealand's exports to the countries of Asia, too, have tripled. Meanwhile, the proportion of exports to Europe almost halved during the 1970s and was just 20 per cent in the 1990s. New Zealand therefore welcomed the successful conclusion in December 1993 of the Uruguay round of the General Agreement on Tariffs and Trade (GATT) with its long overdue reduction of restrictions on trade.

## Agriculture

In 1997 8.7 per cent of the working population were employed in agriculture, forestry and fisheries, which contributed 9 per cent of the gross domestic product. About 80,000 farm holdings, including 7500 large farms of over 400 ha, worked a total of 17.8 million ha of land, 14 per cent of which consisted of arable. More than half of the arable land was irrigated. In recent years low world prices for agricultural produce and import barriers have badly affected New Zealand agriculture, and sharp cuts in government subsidies and the cost to farmers of interest on loans have led to loss of income, reduced investment and the abandonment of some farms.

Villages are rare in New Zealand: the typical pattern of rural settlement is one of scattered farmsteads, mostly consisting only of the farmhouse and sheds for equipment and stores. Stalls for the stock are not necessary: due to the mild climate, with only rare frosts, the animals can stay outdoors throughout the year.

### Sheep farming

The long-held belief that New Zealand has twenty times more sheep than people is no longer true. As a result of a catastrophic drought in 1988 and, more seriously still, the fall in wool prices during the 1990s, the number of sheep has fallen sharply. Between 1988 and the end of the 20th c. it fell from from 64.6 million to about 50 million. After Australia New Zealand is the world's second largest exporter of wool. In 1988 wool exports brought in almost NZ$1.8 billion; in 1997, with almost the same level of production, the figure fell to only NZ$932 million dollars.

The main sheep-farming areas are in the uplands of the North Island and the south and east of the South Island. The average flock size is about 1800, the sheep being shorn three times in a period of 2 years. The predominant breed in the moist New Zealand climate is the Romney sheep, which has

A good sheep shearer can shear up to 300 sheep a day

relatively coarse wool but yields meat of excellent quality. New Zealand produces 400,000 tonnes of lamb and 150,000 tonnes of mutton annually.

The breeds most commonly reared for their wool are Romney (ca 40 per cent), Coopworth (ca 20 per cent), Petendale (ca 10 per cent), Corriedale (ca 5 per cent) and Merino (ca 5 per cent).

### Stock farming

In the 1990s New Zealand had 8 million beef cattle and dairy cows and produced over 500,000 tonnes of beef and 13,000 tonnes of veal. The predominant breed is Aberdeen Angus, which has been reared in New Zealand since the end of the 19th c. and is prized for its robustness and the quality of its meat.

Cattle were originally reared in New Zealand alongside sheep to firm up the newly cleared pastureland and crop the remaining shrubs and bushes. They are now found all over New Zealand, frequently still along with sheep. For beef cattle steep slopes in the less good locations are preferred. In such areas the hillsides are patterned with paths

trodden out by the cattle, running along the contours. Dairy cows are found only in locations where the pasture can be intensively grazed. Dairy farming involves high investments in money and time (for milking) and requires good accessibility for refrigerated transport. New Zealand's climate, high rainfall and long hours of sunshine give its dairy farmers an advantage over their European competitors.

### Game farms

Travelling through New Zealand, visitors will be struck by the number of enclosures with herds of grazing deer. The red deer that were brought to New Zealand for sporting purposes soon became a destructive element in the forest ecosystems. Accordingly, particularly in nature reserves, the large herds of deer were hunted down, captured alive and transferred to game farms for rearing. The first licences for game farms were issued in 1970 and there are now several thousand throughout the country, rearing mainly red deer, fallow deer and wapiti. More than 5000 tonnes of meat from these farms are now exported annually.

### Goats
In recent years there has been been a substantial development of goat rearing as a result of the high demand for goat's wool (mohair, cashmere), milk and meat. Goats are also prized for their grazing habits, since they eat wild herbs and bushes that sheep and cattle disdain.

### Horse breeding
High-quality pastureland is particularly suitable for the rearing of horses and there are a number of stud farms in New Zealand, notably to the south of Auckland. Racehorses are much esteemed in New Zealand, where almost every town has a racecourse, but horses are also very profitably exported to Australia and the United States.

### Arable farming, fruit growing, horticulture
Compared with New Zealand's endless pastureland its areas of arable are very modest. But its intensively cultivated special crops (hops, fruit, particularly kiwi fruit and grapes) in relatively small,

climatically favoured areas are of great economic importance.

### Kiwi fruit
The kiwi fruit, now popular throughout the world, was developed in New Zealand in the early 20th c. from the Chinese gooseberry. It is a climbing plant that is grown on a trellis and requires protection from the wind, to which it is highly sensitive. It flourishes particularly in the Bay of Plenty (☛Sights from A to Z) on the east side of the North Island, where kiwi plantations pattern the landscape.

### Other fruit
Besides the kiwi's popularity as New Zealand's best-known fruit, apples and pears too are widely exported to Europe. The main growing areas are in the Bay of Plenty round Tauranga and Hawke's Bay, round Napier and Hastings on the east side of the North Island and the sunny country round Nelson in the north of the South Island. Apart from the export trade in New Zealand fruit, fresh fruit is used in high-tech processing factories to produce juices and preserves. This

Kiwi fruits, now exported all over the world

applies particularly to European types of berry grown in New Zealand, in particular the recent boysenberry. Stone fruits (particularly apricots) are grown in the south of the South Island (Otago region) and mainly exported to Australia. Citrus fruits have traditionally been grown in the subtropical Northland round Kerikeri.

New Zealand is now in process of conquering the Asian market (including Singapore and Japan) with new exotic fruits and crosses. The United States and Australia also offer good markets for new types of fruit such as persimmons, avocados, nashis, passion fruit and tamarillos. In 1997 New Zealand exported fruit and vegetables to the value of NZ$1.2 billion.

### Wine
Viticulture was introduced to New Zealand in 1819 at Kerikeri, the vines brought in by early European settlers. Pests and restrictive laws on alcohol at first hindered any extension of the wine-growing area, but New Zealand now has over 6000 ha of vineyards. The main wine-producing areas are round Blenheim on the South Island and on the east side of the North Island, particularly round Gisborne/Poverty Bay, Hastings/Hawke's Bay and Henderson (Northland).

### Cereals
Cereals (mainly barley and wheat) are largely grown on the great plains round Canterbury on the South Island.

## Forestry

Fully a quarter of New Zealand's area is still covered by forest. The ancient kauri forests in Northland were stripped by the early European loggers, leaving only a few surviving stands of majestic kauri trees, which are now strictly protected (☞Sights from A to Z, Waipoua Kauri Forest). The modern forestry industry now depends on non-native species of tree brought in by European settlers. Imported conifers, such as the Californian pine, which are ready for felling in 25–30 years, do very well in New Zealand. Reafforestation has proceeded without difficulty. Of the total forested area (just under 8 million ha) roughly three-quarters is worked for timber, and two-thirds of this is state

owned, with the rest in private ownership. 1.6 million ha are in forest reserves in which timber may not be worked and 0.4 million ha are in inaccessible areas where logging would be uneconomic. Half the timber felled is exported, mainly to Australia and Japan, in the form of logs, sawn timber, shavings and wood pulp for papermaking. Timber is New Zealand's third most important export, after meat and dairy products but ahead of wool.

## Fisheries

In 1978 New Zealand introduced a protected fishing and economic zone extending for over 370 km round the islands. Its coastal waters have largely been fished to exhaustion and the prospects of the fishing and fish-processing industries lie mainly in deep sea fishing. Oyster and mussel farms have been successfully developed. There are valuable catches of orange roughy, squid, snapper, tuna and crayfish. Fish exports worth around NZ$1 billion go to Japan, Australia and the United States.

## Industry

The secondary sector of the economy, which includes energy and water supply, mining and the processing and construction industries, employs 24 per cent of the working population and contributes 30 per cent of the gross domestic product. By far the major employers are the processing industries.

New Zealand's industry covers a wide spectrum, from heavy industry, mechanical engineering and civil engineering, by way of woodworking, papermaking, textiles and leather goods, to the various food industries. Altogether there are almost 20,000 firms in the processing industries, most of them small with no more than five employees. Over the last quarter of the 20th c. the number of workers employed in the processing industries has fallen by 40,000 to 260,000, mainly as a result of increasing automation.

The lifting of restrictions on imports threatens the existence of smaller firms in particular.

### Energy
The object of New Zealand's energy

Energy from the earth: the hot underground water of the Wairakei thermal field provides electric power

policy is to reduce the country's dependence on imported sources of energy, mainly oil; natural gas produced in New Zealand makes a considerable contribution to its energy needs. Liquid gas and compressed gas are widely available as fuel.

The country's hydroelectric and geothermal power potential is being exploited with the aid of elaborate and advanced technical installations (reservoirs, thermal power stations), but the changes to the unspoiled natural landscape resulting from the construction of large reservoirs and water channels have attracted opposition from environmentalists. The North Island, which consumes more electricity than the thinly populated South Island, is dependent for its energy supply on thermal and hydroelectric power stations (including a number on the Waikato River) and on geothermal stations (in the volcanic zone, between Taupo and Rotorua). The geothermal power stations work on superheated steam from boreholes in the volcanic region. There are large geothermal stations at Wairakei (1958) on the Waikato River and Ohaaki

(1987). There are no nuclear power stations in New Zealand. The use of local coal in the production of energy and the manufacture of steel is to be intensified.

In order to meet the higher energy needs of the North Island a 40 km deep-sea cable runs across the Cook Strait, so that surplus power produced by hydroelectric stations on the South Island can be conveyed to the power-hungry north.

## Mining

New Zealand was long regarded as a country lacking in minerals. Nowadays, however, it produces substantial quantities of coal, oil, natural gas, iron, gold, sand and construction aggregates. Its coal reserves are estimated at several billion tonnes, mainly on the South Island. Oil is extracted in the McKee Field off the North Island and at Ngaere/Taranaki, natural gas at Kupuni/Taranaki and in the Maui Field (50 km offshore at Taranaki); it is used for the production of energy, in the petrochemical industry and in the manufacture of synthetic fuel. Iron ore is found in the form of black iron sand in extensive areas on the west coast of both islands, with reserves amounting to several hundred million tonnes. It is processed and smelted at Glenbrook, to the south of Auckland.

### Gold

Gold played an important part in the opening up and development of New Zealand. It was found in Otago in 1861 and in Westland 3 years later, when tens of thousands of prospectors flocked to New Zealand. It comes mainly from the Coromandel Peninsula on the North Island and Otago and Westland on the South Island.

### Pounamu

*Pounamu* (the Maori name for greenstone, nephrite or jade) occurs in river beds in Westland (South Island). In the traditional Maori culture, which knew no metals, it was an important substance for exchange or for the manufacture of weapons (e.g. axe blades) and jewellery. It is now mainly used, particularly at Hokitika, in the manufacture of ornaments and jewellery decorated with Maori motifs.

### Construction industry

A very common type of dwelling in New Zealand, even in the suburbs, is the detached family house with its own garden. Most houses are timber-framed and single storey. Well over 10,000 dwellings a year are built, in addition to offices and industrial buildings.

## Commerce

### Service sector

The service sector accounts for 61 per cent of the gross domestic product and provides employment for about two-thirds of the working population. 28 per cent of workers in the service sector are employed in communal, social and private service industries, 21 per cent in commerce and the hotel industry, 10 per cent in banking, insurance and real estate and 6 per cent in transportation and communications.

### Foreign trade

In 1997–8 imports costs NZ$22.6 billion and largely comprised machinery, electrical goods and electronics, motor vehicles, oil and petrochemical products. The main suppliers were Australia, the United States, Japan, the United Kingdom, China and Germany. During the same period exports totalled NZ$21.75 billion, mainly dairy products, meat, timber and paper, fruit and vegetables, fish and seafoods, wool, aluminium and products of aluminium. The main customers for New Zealand exports were Australia, Japan, the United States, the United Kingdom, South Korea, China and Germany.

### Tourism

New Zealand is an increasingly popular holiday destination, with the total number of visitors rising from 487,000 in the tourist year 1983–4 to 1,460,000 in 1997–8, bringing an income of over NZ$3 billion. It was thought that income from tourism would rise to about NZ$8 billion by 2000 and the number employed in the tourist industry, at present 120,000, would double. However, the economic crisis in Asia during the late 1990s forestalled this outcome. The income from tourism in any case makes a significant contribution to improving New Zealand's balance of trade.

New Zealanders are increasingly concerned about this invasion by holidaymakers. Their apprehensions about damage to New Zealand's largely unspoiled natural environment are not without foundation. Recommendations are already being put forward that restrictions should be imposed on access to particularly precious nature reserves or that visitor quotas should be established. But thought is also being given to the possibility of reconciling the needs of tourism with the protection of the environment. An exemplary attempt has been made in Milford Sound since 1991, one of New Zealand's tourist highlights, to channel the stream of visitors in such a way as to safeguard the environment. Careful planning and good management are essential if chaos and devastation are to be avoided.

## Transport

### Roads

New Zealand has a total of some 93,000 km of roads, of which around 52,000 km are surfaced; 11,500 km are classified as national highways, highways and main roads. There are short stretches of motorway round the cities.

### Railways

New Zealand Rail, privatised since 1993, runs a network of 3973 km (1067 km of which are narrow gauge) linking all the country's major centres. Few routes are electrified. In their early days the railways made a major contribution to the opening up of New Zealand and to the development of its export trade. Imposing old station buildings bear witness to the former importance of New Zealand's railways. The railway system is not remarkable for its speed: express trains average about 70 kph.

### Shipping

Several large ferries or catamarans ply the Cook Strait between Wellington and Picton. Before the arrival of the Europeans New Zealand's numerous rivers provided communication with the roadless interior, and the canoes of the Maoris were soon followed by the river steamers of the Europeans, for example on the Wanganui River.

Because of its location in the Pacific, its dependence on overseas commerce and the great distances to its export markets, New Zealand depends on sea transport. The growth of container traffic gave an impetus to the development of the ports of Auckland, Wellington, Lyttleton (Christchurch) and Port Chalmers (Dunedin). There are also special installations in regional ports for the loading of cement or the shipping of petrochemical products (Port Taranaki). Coastal ships ply between the various New Zealand ports, carrying mainly cement, oil and natural gas.

In 1997 New Zealand's merchant fleet consisted of about 400 ships with a number of tankers. In 1997 the New Zealand ports handled well over 20 million tonnes of freight. There is almost no overseas passenger traffic now that passengers mainly travel by air.

### Air services

In relation to its population New Zealand has an unusually large amount of passenger air traffic. The two most important international airports are Auckland and Christchurch, which are served by international airlines. The airport at Wellington, the national capital, is the hub for domestic flights and services to and from Australia.

# History

## The coming of the Maoris

### Migration

In contrast to the settlement of Australia
by the aborigines, who moved onto the
continent 40,000 or 50,000 years ago
over the then existing land bridges from
south-east Asia, the discovery and
settlement of New Zealand are of much
more recent date. The Aborigines of
Australia and the Maoris of New Zealand,
peoples of very different racial and
geographical origins, probably never
came into contact with one another.
*Maori* means 'usual' or 'common' and
was originally a term applied by the
early European settlers to the natives of
the country, who then took it over and
applied it to themselves. The Maoris
called the white settlers *pakehas*
(strangers). They had no name for
themselves as a whole: there were only
the names of the various tribes.

New Zealand was settled by the
Maoris in the course of the Polynesian
migration that began some 4000 years
ago in the western Pacific. They travelled
by way of Samoa, Fiji, Tonga, the Society
Islands, the Marquesas and the Cook
Islands and finally reached the remote
islands of New Zealand around 2000
years ago. The Polynesian islanders were
skilled seamen. Their long voyages in
outrigger boats and catamarans were not
merely involuntary extensions of fishing
trips but planned colonisation
enterprises.

### Archaic and classic Maori periods

For the former inhabitants of tropical
islands the climate of New Zealand was
harsher than they were used to. They
lived as hunters and gatherers of berries,
fern roots and birds, as fishermen and
hunters of seals. On the South Island
they hunted the moa, a flightless bird
resembling an ostrich, which soon died
out as a result of changes in climate and
vegetation and constant hunting. The
inhabitants of Northland learned to
cultivate the kumara or sweet potato, an
import from South America, though it is
not known how or when this reached
New Zealand. The cultivation of this
vegetable and the storage of the crop
made possible the transition from the
archaic culture of nomadic hunters and
gatherers to the classic Maori culture of
sedentary tribal groups living in
unfortified or fortified villages. Modern
research and archaeology have
established that there was only one early
immigration movement, unaffected by
later arrivals. From this early nomadic
society there developed the classic Maori
culture, whose principal centre was in
the warmer Northland region. From
there tribal groups in fleets of canoes
travelled along the coast or on rivers into
the regions further south, where they
subjugated or exterminated the archaic
groups they encountered. The classic
Maori culture is believed to have
established itself throughout the main
islands of New Zealand by about AD
1500. The older culture survived only in
the Chatham Islands, far away to the
east.

### Mythology

Maori mythology presents a different
picture of the settlement of New
Zealand. It relates that around AD 925 a
seafarer named Kupe, setting out from
the legendary island of Hawaiki near
Tahiti, became the first man to discover
New Zealand, which he named Aotearoa
(the land of the long white cloud). There
he had to fight a gigantic cuttlefish, after
which he returned to Hawaiki. Some 225
years later a chief named Toi sailed from
Hawaiki to New Zealand and established
the first Maori settlement there. The full
occupation of the country is ascribed to
a large wave of immigrants from Hawaiki
at a later date. From there the islanders
set out about 1350 in seven great tribal
canoes – the origin of the various Maori
tribes.

## Discovery by Europeans

### Abel Tasman

In 1642 the Dutch seafarer Abel Tasman
(1603–59), sailing from Batavia
(Indonesia) on a mission for Antonij van
Diemen, the Dutch governor general of
Batavia, rounded Australia and
discovered what is now known as
Tasmania. On December 13th 1642 he
became the first European to sight the

coast of New Zealand, landing in the north of the South Island. The Maoris attacked the dinghy of his ships the *Zeehan* and the *Heemskerck*, killing a number of his men, and the Europeans responded with their cannon, after which Tasman left the scene of this encounter – which he named Murderers' Bay, now known as Golden Bay, at the northern tip of the South Island – without setting foot on New Zealand soil. He sailed back to Batavia, skirting the west coast of the North Island. Tasman named the new land Staten Lands after the Dutch States General, taking it to be the west coast of a large unknown southern continent. Dutch scholars later gave the newly discovered South Pacific island world the name of Nieuw Zeeland after the Dutch province of Zeeland (Zealand).

Abel Tasman and his companions later discovered Tonga and the Fiji islands.

## Captain Cook

Following the radical changes in Europe after the Thirty Years War, the Dutch provinces' conflict with Spain and the war with Britain, the Dutch withdrew from the south Pacific and the initiative passed to Britain and France. Decisive were the three voyages of Captain Cook in 1768–71, 1772–5 and 1776–9, on each of which he called in at New Zealand (☛Famous People).

The official purpose of Cook's first voyage, in the *Endeavour,* was to observe and plot the transit of Venus in 1769 from Tahiti; but he also had a secret mission to sail on from Tahiti to look for the legendary southern continent. Following Abel Tasman's record of his trip, he took a south-westerly course from Tahiti and on October 6th 1769 sighted the east coast of the North Island of New Zealand. On October 8th he landed on the island near the site of present-day Gisborne. Soon afterwards he hoisted the British flag in Mercury Bay on the Coromandel Peninsula and took possession of the land in the name of King George III. He then spent 6 months sailing round the coasts of New Zealand, establishing that there were two main islands and giving names to many bays and promontories. In 1770 he anchored in Queen Charlotte Sound. On his second voyage, with the *Resolution* and the *Adventure*, Cook returned to New Zealand, accompanied by astronomers, naturalists and artists, including the German scientists Dr Johann Reinhold Forster and his son Georg. After spending some time in Dusky Sound in the Fiordland area (South Island) he put into Ship Cove in Queen Charlotte Sound to refit.

On his first landing in New Zealand in 1769 Cook found the **Maoris** unspoiled by European contact. They were eager to

An entry in Abel Tasman's log (December 13th 1642)

Captain Cook frequently put into Ship Cove (Queen Charlotte Sound)

acquire the objects offered by the Europeans by way of gift exchange, principally iron nails, axes and tobacco. Alcohol they disliked. On Cook's second voyage (1772–5) he found the Maoris very ready to barter. They supplied his ships with fish, sweet potatoes and water in return for the desirable European goods.

### French successors to Cook

The French followed in Cook's footsteps. In 1769–70 Jean-François de Surville landed at the north end of Doubtless Bay; then in 1772 Marion du Fresne landed in the Bay of Islands on the North Island and took possession of the territory, which he called France Australe, in the name of King Louis XV. He was unaware of the earlier visits by Cook and his countryman Surville. Relations with the natives were at first friendly but soon degenerated into conflict. The Maoris killed du Fresne and two dozen of his men, whereupon the remaining members of the crew burned down three villages and shot many of the inhabitants.

### Changes in Maori life

The British government saw Australia, also discovered by Cook, as an ideal place for a penal colony, and in 1788 the First Fleet, under the command of Captain Arthur Phillip, arrived in Botany Bay with a consignment of convicts and their guards. Soon afterwards the town of Sydney and Britain's first colony in Australia, New South Wales, were founded. From there ships soon sailed to New Zealand: in 1791 the first whaler arrived, and in the following year seals were hunted for the first time in Dusky Sound. Other Europeans came to barter with the natives for flax and to plunder the forests for timber. Contact with the Europeans brought changes and problems for the Maoris. They acquired wheat and potatoes, pigs and horses, but also steel axes and above all firearms. The Maoris were particularly anxious to get guns: the tribes living in Northland near the trading post in the Bay of Islands were prepared to provide anything the Europeans wanted – even the dried heads of their enemies, elaborately decorated with tattoos – in exchange for muskets. The possession of firearms gave the Northland tribes an enormous advantage in the endemic wars with other tribes who had no direct contact with the Europeans and their weapons. Hordes of warriors equipped with firearms led by power-hungry chiefs like Te Rauparaha in 1819 were thus able to defeat, kill, eat or drive away other tribal groups without firearms on the North Island, and later also on the South Island. Particularly ruthless was Hongi Hika, who visited Britain in 1820 and was received by George IV. On his way home he stopped over in Australia and exchanged the gifts he had received in Britain for weapons, with which he began his predatory expeditions in 1821.

### Europeans and Maoris

In the early 19th c. there were still relatively few *pakehas* (strangers, i.e. Europeans), and they established close relations with the Maori tribes, to their mutual advantage. In the course of a few decades, however, the port settlement of Kororareka in the Bay of Islands developed into an infamous haunt of whalers and traders that became known to seamen as the 'hell-hole of the Pacific'. Maoris were employed by the settlers to do heavy work, and misunderstandings, maltreatment of Maoris and disregard of Maori customs and the laws of *tapu* led on occasion to serious disturbances and riots.

## Missionaries and colonisation

### First mission station

Missionary activity in New Zealand began with the establishment of a mission station in the Bay of Islands by Samuel Marsden (1765–1838) at Christmas 1814. In 1816 Thomas Kendall (☛Famous People) founded the first school for Maori children. These Anglicans were soon followed by the Methodists, who built a mission in Whangaroa Harbour in 1823, and by French Catholics. It was a long time, however, before the first conversions were achieved, since the Maoris were put off by competition and conflict between the different Christian denominations. It was only the increasing impotence of the tribal priests (*tohungas*) in the face of the diseases brought in by the Europeans and the apparent ability of the settlers to disregard the rules of *tapu* without bringing down punishment by the gods

that led to a slow increase in conversions. By the mid-19th c. most Maoris had accepted Christianity in one form or another. Cannibalism had disappeared at an early stage.

### British rule

In 1823, when the number of Europeans in the Bay of Islands had increased, the British government decreed that British subjects in New Zealand were under the jurisdiction of Sydney. But Sydney was more than 2000 km away and in Kororareka (Russell) arbitrary justice and chaos prevailed. In 1827 Hongi Hika and his warriors attacked the Whangaroa mission station and destroyed it. Finally in 1833 James Busby arrived in the Bay of Islands, where there was now a white population of over 2000, as the official representative of British interests.

### Colonisation

The increasing numbers of settlers were now demanding land to cultivate: the Maoris sold them land that did not belong to them personally but to the tribe in return for weapons and tobacco. The inevitable consequence was bloody conflict when the settlers began to cultivate the land that they had acquired in good faith. The Europeans also disregarded either unknowingly or intentionally the laws of *tapu* and took possession of Maori land illegally, provoking retaliation by the Maoris. In 1834, during the occupation of Waimate Pa (Taranaki), there were the first encounters between British troops and Maori warriors. The conflict over land escalated after the establishment of the New Zealand Land Company in 1838. Its initiator, Edward Gibbon Wakefield, had already made a name for himself by his plans for the colonisation of southern Australia. The company bought up land on a large scale, mostly from individual Maoris without the consent of the tribe as a whole. The settlers, to whom this land was sold on at high prices, were then exposed to attack by the tribe. In order to bring order into this chaos, and also to forestall possible French plans for annexation of the territory, Captain William Hobson (☛Famous People) was sent to New Zealand in July 1839 as representative of the governor of New South Wales. His mission was to protect both the Maoris and the European settlers and, in agreement with the

Maoris, to proclaim British sovereignty in New Zealand.

## Treaty of Waitangi

### February 6th 1840
On February 6th 1840 Hobson and 45 Maori chiefs from Northland assembled in Waitangi and signed the Treaty of Waitangi, a document that marks the birth of the state of New Zealand. The chiefs acknowledged the sovereignty of the British Crown and in return received confirmation of all existing rights to property, both private and collective, an assurance that Maori land could be acquired only by the Crown, and all the privileges of British citizenship.

Messengers carried the treaty to all Maori tribes, so that it finally bore more than 500 signatures. Some chiefs, however, foresaw the loss of the Maoris' political power and independence and would not sign. A large number of Maoris still reject the treaty and on the anniversary of its signing there are demonstrations at the Treaty House in Waitangi where the treaty – the 'Cheaty of Waitangi' – was signed, calling for the return of Maori rights. In 1975 the government established a special agency, the Waitangi Tribunal, to consider Maori complaints about breaches of the treaty.

### 1841: a Crown colony
In May 1840, on the basis of the treaty, Britain annexed the North Island and assumed the right to explore the South Island and thus gain possession of it too. In May 1841 New Zealand was declared a Crown Colony, with Hobson as its first governor. He moved the chief town of the colony from the still troubled Bay of Islands to Auckland (founded 1840).

## War with the Maoris

### Aftermath of the Treaty of Waitangi
With the signing of the Treaty of Waitangi it seemed, in spite of the dissent of some chiefs, that all problems between *pakehas* and Maoris had been resolved. The government established commissions to examine all disputed sales of land, and some land was returned to the tribes. In practice, however, the government sold on – at considerable profit – the land they had acquired to European settlers, who from 1840 onwards were flocking to New Zealand in thousands, usually under arrangements made by the New Zealand Land Company.

Wellington, Wanganui and New Plymouth were now founded on the North Island, while French immigrants established settlements at Nelson and

A New Zealand Expedition, by Henry Williams (published in the Quarterly Papers of the Church Missionary Society, 1835), shows a fleet of Maori war canoes on one of the North Island's many rivers

Akaroa on the Banks Peninsula, near present-day Christchurch. Although the company's utopian settlement plans often turned out to be empty words, nevertheless they brought in more than 19,000 new settlers in 57 ships between 1839 and 1843.

In 1844 the company was forced due to shortage of funds to suspend its activities. The more land was acquired by the settlers, however, the clearer it became to the Maoris that they would soon be left with nothing. The colony's electoral law also put the Maoris at a disadvantage, since only personal owners of land had the vote; and as the Maoris' land belonged to the tribe and not the individual they had no right to vote. Conflict was inevitable.

### 1843–7: Maori risings

In 1843 what came to be known as the Wairau affray took place in the Wairau Valley, to the south of Nelson. A party of European settlers from Nelson led by Captain Arthur Wakefield, defying warnings, were passing through the Wairau Valley on their way to survey a piece of land whose ownership was disputed when they encountered a force of Maori warriors of the Ngati Toa tribe. A bloody conflict developed – the only such encounter over land rights on the South Island – in which 21 settlers, including Wakefield, were killed.

There were also troubles in the north. In 1844 Chief Hone Heke several times cut down the British flagstaff in Kororareka (Russell), and in 1845 burned down the whole settlement. In the following year George Grey, who had been appointed governor in 1845, ordered British troops to bombard and capture Hone Heke's stronghold of Ruapekapeka. In 1846 there were attacks by Maori tribes in Hutt Valley, near Wellington in the south of the North Island. And in 1847 Maori attacks at Wanganui in the south-west of the North Island were repressed. Thereafter the country remained peaceful until 1860.

### Constitution Act

During this decade the beginnings of a government answerable to Parliament and a system of responsible regional administration began to emerge. The Constitution Act of 1852 reduced the powers of the governor, as the settlers wished, and established six provinces

(Auckland, New Plymouth, Wellington, Nelson, Canterbury and Otago) with their own governments.

## The Maori King Movement

The Maoris reacted to the increasing scale of European settlement by withdrawing further into the inaccessible interior of the country. In the late 1850s, in the area round the Waikato River in the centre of the North Island, a movement developed for the union of as many tribes as possible in order to counter the land hunger of the settlers. In 1857 the Maori-Kingitanga or Maori King Movement (mainly formed from the Waikato and Maniopoto tribes) chose Chief Te Wherowhero to be King Potatau I. Although he was not recognised by all the Maori tribes, his Waikato tribes put up fierce resistance to government troops for many years.

### War in Taranaki and Waikato

There were further risings in other parts of the country. In New Plymouth in 1860, on the northern slopes of Mount Taranaki, where the shortage of land was particularly acute, an under-chief sold land at Waitara against the will of the tribe. Consequently, the Maoris, led by Chief Wiremu Kingi, attacked the settlers who set about working this new land. The government sent troops to the area, and the fighting at Waitara marked the start of a series of land wars. Although an armistice was signed in Taranaki in 1861 there was recurring guerrilla activity over the next 20 years.

From Taranaki the conflict spread into the very centre of the North Island as far as the Waikato River. Government troops moved into the Waikato area and there were skirmishes at Bombay, Pukekohe and Pokeno. The supporters of the Maori King Movement were driven south. Attacks were launched from gunboats on Maori positions at Meremere and Rangiriri and the Maori king's capital at Ngaruawahia was taken. Finally, after holding out for three days at Orakau, 300 Maoris were defeated and put to flight by 2000 British troops. The troops pursued the fleeing Maoris only as far as the Punui River, to the south of Orakau. South of the river lay the King Country, as it is still called, which the government left in the hands of the surviving supporters of the Maori king – an area into which no European dared venture until the conclusion of peace. The tribal lands of the rebels were confiscated.

After the repression of the Waikato risings rebellion flared up on the east coast. In a battle for the Maori stronghold of Gate Pa at Tauranga in 1864 government troops had heavy losses. A few weeks later, however, the Maoris suffered an annihilating defeat at Pa Te Ranga and their tribal territories were taken over by the state.

### Religious resistance

In the mid-1860s the character of Maori resistance changed. It was now motivated by religion. The **Hauhau** movement (or Pai Marire) – so called after its battle cry – was a Maori revivalist movement based on the Old Testament. Like the Israelites in Egypt, the Maoris felt themselves oppressed and enslaved by the Europeans, whom they wanted to drive out of their country. The founder of the movement, Te Ua Haumene, claimed in 1862 to have had a vision at Taranaki of the Archangel Gabriel, who had enjoined him to propagate the new religion. Members of the Hauhau movement believed that their steadfast faith would protect them from enemy bullets and accordingly ran into battle with their right arm raised, screaming their war cry. By 1865 the sect had spread across the whole of the North Island from Taranaki to the east coast. The Hauhau prophet Kereopa and his followers recruited new believers among the east coast tribes that were loyal to the government and fought government troops at Ruatoria and Gisborne before finally they were defeated.

Another religious leader who came from the east coast was Te Kooti. Although he could claim a long ancestry he was not a chief and had no tattoos. He cooperated with the government in repressing the Hauhau movement, but in 1866 he fell under suspicion of collaborating with the enemy and was banished, along with 300 Hauhau supporters, without trial, to the remote Chatham Islands, where he founded the **Ringatu** sect. He saw himself as the Moses of the Maoris, with a mission to give them back their Promised Land. In 1868, after escaping from his place of exile, he and his followers killed 70 white men and Maoris loyal to the government in Poverty Bay. The troops sent after Te

Kooti never managed to catch him, and in 1872 he settled in King Country, where he lived under the protection of the Maori king Tawhiao until he was pardoned by the government in 1883.

### Civil disobedience

The land wars ended with a campaign of passive resistance centred on the village of Parihaka on Mount Taranaki, where from 1866 onwards two Maori prophets, Te Whiti and Tohu, called on their followers to resort to civil disobedience in their opposition to the settlers and the government. Te Whiti became one of the leading figures in the Maori revival.

### Defeat of the Maoris

The European settlers and the government emerged from the land wars victorious, with the much desired land at their disposal, and the Maoris had been unable to unite. They had at any rate been granted four seats in Parliament in 1867; but it was only in the 20th c. that they received partial compensation for the injustices they had suffered during the land wars. In 1881 peace was officially concluded between the Maori king and the government; the rebels were granted amnesty and were allowed to leave the King Country.

## Gold Rush on the South Island

### War and prosperity

Even as war was raging on the North Island, cattle and sheep were spreading ever further over the great expanses of potential grazing land on the South Island. In 1847 the first cargoes of butter and cheese were shipped from the South Island to Sydney. But a means of gaining wealth much more rapidly than by agriculture was provided by the discovery of gold. After small finds at Milton in 1855 and in the Buller River in 1859, the real gold rush began in 1861 when Gabriel Read, a prospector from Tasmania who had gained experience in California and Australia, discovered rich deposits of gold in what became known as Gabriel's Gully at Lawrence, south-west of Dunedin, and announced the fact in the local newspaper. By this time the goldfields of California and Victoria (Australia) were exhausted, so that prospectors flocked from there, along with many newcomers, to Central Otago and soon opened up gold workings at Clyde, Queenstown and Arrowtown. As a result Dunedin gained in wealth and importance; and in 1869 the University of Otago, New Zealand's first university, was established in the town. When too the gold in this area was exhausted, prospectors and adventurers moved to the remote west coast. Hokitika now grew in size and became an important supply port; passages through the high Southern Alps were explored and provided with roads; and in 1866 a mail coach service started between Christchurch and Hokitika.

With the end of the gold rush in the late 1860s the population moved northward – not to the newly established capital, Wellington, but to Auckland, which, encouraged by the peace with the Maoris, took over the role of the country's economic metropolis, a position held by Dunedin during the gold boom.

**Separatist movement**
The wealth brought to the South Island by gold awoke in its inhabitants a desire for political independence from the North Island, still involved in its wars with the Maoris. As a concession to this feeling the capital was transferred in 1865 from Wellington to Auckland, at the south end of the North Island. The General Assembly of the colony was firmly against separation: in 1876 the Centralists overrode the opposition of the Provincialists and secured the abolition of the provincial governments. The central government thus recovered the initiative in the development of the country.

## The Liberal period

**1891–1912**
The final decades of the 19th c. saw new developments in agriculture. The New Zealand economy gained a fresh source of revenue in the export of frozen meat: in 1882 the refrigerator ship *Dunedin* sailed from Port Chalmers (Dunedin) with the first cargo of frozen meat for Britain. But New Zealand's export trade, concerned mainly with agricultural produce, was badly hit by the collapse of prices on the world market. In addition the country was heavily in debt, having taken out large loans in London to finance the development of its infrastructure by public works in the

1870s. In the recession that set in after the loss in value of agricultural exports unemployment rose sharply. The government, which from 1891 was in the hands of the Liberal Party, developed an exemplary social policy under prime ministers Ballance and Seddon that made New Zealand a model for the rest of the world. New land laws put limits on the ownership of large estates, which were particularly common on the South Island, and made it possible for agricultural workers to have land of their own. Other social and economic measures provided for restrictions on hours of work (eight-hour day introduced in 1899), protection for children in employment, factory inspection, accident insurance, health care and state pensions – though these provisions applied only to members of trade unions.

Electoral law had already been reformed in 1889; the 'one man, one vote' system was introduced in 1890; and in 1893, after repeated petitions and demonstrations by feminists, women were given the vote.

## The Maori existence

While the population as a whole rose steadily – reaching 815,853 by the 1901 census – the number of Maoris fell alarmingly to around 40,000. Feeling like strangers in their own country, the Maoris withdrew into themselves or sought to eke out a living, in competition with white workers, on the fringes of mainstream society. The extent of the Maoris' despair was exemplified by the gift made to the government in 1887 by Chief Te Heuheu Tukino IV. Faced with the continuing occupation of land by Europeans, he handed over to the government the three volcanic peaks of Tongariro, Ngauruhoe and Ruapehu, which were sacred to the Maoris, asking that a reserve should be established for their protection. This was the origin of Tongariro National Park, New Zealand's first national park.

**Maori revivalism**
A number of Maori revivalist movements sought to counter this trend. Many had religious foundations and Messianic elements, such as Hauhau and Ringatu, Wiremu Ratana's Ratana Church and the prophets of non-violent resistance Te

Whiti and Tohu. The most influential was the charismatic Wiremu Ratana, who had gained an enormous following with his spiritual healings and also carried considerable political weight through the Ratana movement; for many years the four parliamentary seats assigned to the Maoris were held by followers of his.

### Kingitanga

A movement for Maori unification with a long tradition is Maori-Kingitanga, the Maori King Movement (see above), though this was confined to tribes in the Waikato area. The current king or queen has no constitutional, administrative or political functions: their role is social and cultural, including the preservation of Maori traditions. The present queen, like her predecessors before the land wars, has her residence in Ngaruawahia, at the confluence of the Waikato and Waipa rivers. She is informally recognised by the government.

### Kotahitanga

In the 1890s Maori-Kingitanga faced a competitor in Kotahitanga, the Maori parliament movement, which originated at Papawai, near Masterton in the south of the North Island. It demanded an independent parliament for the Maoris. Its objectives were given political expression by the Young Maori Party, founded in the early 1890s mainly by students of Te Aute College, near Hastings, among them Apirana Ngati (1874–1950), Maui Wiremu Pomare (1876–1930) and Peter Buck (Te Rangi Hiroa, ca 1877–1951). Apirana Ngati, the first Maori to take a university degree, became secretary of the Young Maori Party and for many years represented Maori interests in Parliament. Maui Pomare and the famous anthropologist Peter Buck, who ended his career as director of the Honolulu Museum, were also members of Parliament. James Carroll (1853–1926), the son of a chief's daughter and a white farmer in Wairoa, a Member of Parliament who became a minister and then prime minister, sought to promote Maoritanga, the sense of Maori cultural identity. For all these representatives of Maoritanga the only chance of Maori survival lay in assimilation. Following government measures for promoting Maori identity, the Maoris were in the process of recovering lost ground when the influenza epidemic of 1918 hit them disproportionately hard – an event interpreted by some Maoris as the vengeance of the gods they had once worshipped.

## New Zealand in the 20th century

### 1907: Dominion

New Zealand did not join with the British colonies in Australia that formed the independent Commonwealth of Australia, but remained a Crown colony until 1907, when it was given the status of Dominion. In 1911 the population passed the million mark. The Liberal era ended in 1912, when William Ferguson Massey's Reform Party, whose main support was among farmers, gained power. His victory was an expression of the farmers' fears of nationalisation of their land and the increasing strength of the workers' movement, which had demonstrated its power in the strikes of 1912 and 1913 and finally led to the foundation of the Labour Party in 1916. Caught between these two poles, the Liberal Party declined, and in the 1920s re-formed itself as the United Party.

### First world war

In the first world war New Zealand supported the British motherland, forming along with Australia the Australian and New Zealand Army Corps (ANZAC). The Anzacs fought in Egypt and at the Dardanelles against the Turks and in France and Belgium. At Gallipoli thousands of Australians and New Zealanders fell on April 25th 1915 – now commemorated annually as Anzac Day. New Zealand was represented at the Versailles peace conference and subsequently became a member of the League of Nations. In 1920 it became the mandatory power for the former German possession of Western Samoa.

The inter-war period saw a succession of economic crises and a major political change when the Labour Party came to power for the first time in 1935. It sought to overcome the depression by various job creation schemes, measures for the protection of agriculture and improvements in the state health service with the Social Security Act of 1938.

### Second world war

All this was thrown into the background by the second world war. New Zealand again sent troops, who fought in Greece and on Crete, in North Africa and later in Italy. And this time the country itself was exposed to a direct threat: after the fall of Singapore in 1942 there was the possible danger of attack by Japan. Only the intervention of American forces in the South Pacific averted this threat. American help for New Zealand also signalled a shift in the country's foreign policy towards the South Pacific area and the United States. This change was given expression in the ANZAC Pact between Australia and New Zealand in 1944 and above all in the ANZUS Pact of 1951, under which Australia, New Zealand and the United States formed a defence community.

## A sovereign New Zealand

In 1947 New Zealand achieved full independence when Parliament adopted the Statute of Westminster of 1931 and New Zealand became a member of the British Commonwealth of Nations. In the first half of the 20th c. Britain was still 'home' for most British immigrants and their descendants, and those who could afford to do so sent their children to school in Britain. Only in recent decades has Britain ceased to be regarded in this way. In the later part of the century New Zealand looked more towards its south-east Asian, Australian and Pacific neighbours, at first politically in mutual assistance pacts such as SEATO and then economically. Thus New Zealand troops took part in both the Korean and Vietnam wars. After Britain joined the European Community in 1973 New Zealand was compelled to seek new markets for its products, which were mainly agricultural. Successes in this field were the lifting of restrictions on trade with Australia in 1982 and the creation of a free trade zone that was destined to serve as a model for the south-east Asian region.

New Zealand's attitude to the United States changed in the 1980s. The anti-nuclear policy of Lange's Labour government finally brought about the termination of New Zealand's obligations to the United States under the ANZUS Pact, though the pact itself continues in force. New Zealand thus sent troops to the Gulf War. When France tested atomic weapons on the Mururoa Atoll the government remained consistent in its policy, recalling its ambassador from Paris.

## Maoritanga in the 20th century.

The Maori revivalist movement achieved some successes during the 20th c. A royal commission decided in 1918 that the confiscation of land after the land wars had been wrong; but only Crown land was returned to the tribes, land that had passed into private hands being excluded. Various compensation payments were also negotiated in the 1920s. The Waitangi Tribunal established in 1975 investigates Maori claims against the government based on the non-observance of rights and privileges guaranteed under the Treaty of Waitangi. The tribunal is also a point of contact on the position and prospects of the Maori tradition. A great step forward was the Maori Language Act of 1987, which established the equality of the Maori and English languages in the public life of New Zealand. The earlier phase of assimilation now gave place to a multicultural approach that gives stronger emphasis to the specific features of the different cultures and also does something to help with the difficult situation of the Pacific islanders in New Zealand.

A good indication of the revival of Maori culture is the large number of new assembly places (*maraes*) being laid out, even in towns, where Maoris can meet one another, guests and other New Zealanders. Further signs of the revival are the reflowering of the traditional arts of woodcarving and weaving and a great interest in Maori mythology and dances. Since the late 1960s, if not earlier, young people have also been involved in the Maori movement. There have been demonstrations against Europe-oriented teaching in schools and occupations of land and marches to Waitangi on the anniversary of the signing of the Treaty of Waitangi. The Maoris do not want to be dependent on the welfare state and seek to achieve cultural and economic emancipation. This will be difficult in view of the economy and high unemployment, the latter being relatively higher for young Maoris – a consequence of the poorer education and training of the Maoris.

In May 1995 the New Zealand prime minister, in the presence of the Maori queen Te Atairangikaahu, signed a document in which the government apologised for the expropriation of land by British troops in the 19th c. At the same time the union of Tainui Maoris was awarded US$110 million and 170 sq km of land by way of compensation. This agreement was confirmed by Queen Elizabeth II during a visit to Rotorua in November 1995.

### Political change in the new millennium

There was a change of political direction with the elections in October 1999, unseating the conservative National Party after 9 years in power. This was the consequence of the significant drop in New Zealand living standards in recent years. The Labour Party led by Helen Clark has already introduced changes to the conservative-supported free market economy.

## Natural catastrophes

### Earthquakes

As a result of New Zealand's situation on the circum-Pacific mobile belt (Ring of Fire) it suffers occasionally from severe earthquakes. In February 1931, for example, an earthquake in the town of Napier (North Island) cost 256 lives.

### Hell explodes

The volcano of Ruapehu (Maori for 'exploding hell') on the North Island becomes active from time to time. In September 1995 and June 1996 there were several violent eruptions that caused alarm and terror to the population of a wide area.

Ruapehu becomes active at irregular intervals. In 1945, for example, there were rumblings throughout the year; then on Christmas Eve in 1953 a violent eruption killed 151 people and a mighty avalanche of mud destroyed a railway bridge, and soon afterwards the Auckland–Wellington express crashed.

# Famous People

This section contains brief biographies of notable people who were born, lived or worked in New Zealand.

### Sir Peter Buck
### (ca 1877–1951) Ethnologist
Peter Buck was born Te Rangi Hiroa in Urenui, to the north of New Plymouth. After studying medicine at the University of Otago he served as a medical officer in the first world war . After the war he was able to devote himself to his real passion, ethnology, and became one of the leading experts on Polynesia. Later he became director of the Honolulu Museum in Hawaii and professor of ethnology at Yale University. One of the founders of the Young Maori Party, he represented Maori interests in Parliament for many years. He died in 1951 in Honolulu; his ashes are buried near his birthplace at Okoki Pa under a gravestone in the form of the prow of a canoe.

### James Cook
### (1728–79) English seafarer
James Cook, born in Marton, near Middlesbrough, is famed for his three circumnavigations of the globe, which yielded ground-breaking new information about the Pacific and sub-Antarctic regions. He joined the Royal Navy in 1755, sailed on a number of long voyages, was promoted to lieutenant and finally was selected by Lord Hawke to command the research ship *Endeavour*. On his first voyage (1768–71) – on which he was accompanied by the astronomer Charles Green, the scientist Joseph Banks and Daniel Solander, a Swedish botanist – he was sent to Tahiti to observe the transit of Venus; but he also had secret orders to sail beyond Tahiti to look for the legendary southern continent. After discovering the Society Islands he followed Abel Tasman's route to New Zealand and on October 8th 1769 landed near the site of present-day Gisborne in a bay that he named Poverty Bay because he found neither water or food there. His first encounter with the Maoris left several of them dead but later he was able to establish good relations with them. He circumnavigated New Zealand, thereby establishing its insular character, and discovered the strait, now named after him, between the North and South Islands. He then reconnoitred the east coast of Australia and in August 1770 passed through the southern part of the Torres Strait, thus providing definitive proof of the separation between Australia and New Guinea. On his second expedition (1772–5) Cook sailed eastwards round the globe and three times reached south of the Antarctic Circle. He reconnoitred and named the New Hebrides, Norfolk Island and New Caledonia. From New Zealand, where he put in at Ship Cove in Queen Charlotte Sound to refit, he continued eastward to Tierra del Fuego, rounded Cape Horn

James Cook

Sir George Grey

Sir Edmund Hillary

and at the beginning of 1775 discovered South Georgia and the Falkland Islands. After his return to England he was promoted to captain and became a member of the Royal Society.

The objective of his third voyage (1776–9) was to look for the north-west passage between the Atlantic and the Pacific. Again making for Queen Charlotte Sound, he discovered the Sandwich Islands (Hawaii), landed on Alaska and sailed along the Behring Strait and up the coast as far as latitude 70°44'N. During his second stay in the Sandwich Islands Cook's relations with the natives were at first friendly but later deteriorated and he was killed on February 14th 1779.

Cook gave names to many places in New Zealand, and a number of places are named after him, including Mount Cook, the highest peak in the Southern Alps, Mount Cook National Park and the Cook River to the south of the Fox Glacier in Westland.

### Sir George Grey
### (1812–98) Politician
George Edward Grey, born in Lisbon on April 14th 1812, was one of the most influential figures in New Zealand in the 19th c., holding a number of important government posts. He was governor 1845–53 and again 1861–8, and prime minister 1877–9. After being stationed in Ireland at an early stage in his career he became a political liberal and was one of the founders of the Liberal Party in New Zealand.

After three years in Australia, where he became governor of South Australia, he succeeded Sir Charles Fitzroy as governor of New Zealand in 1845, at a time when a group of Maoris had taken up arms against the government. With more troops at his disposal than his predecessors had had, he was able to crush Hone Heke and Kawiti's rising in the Bay of Islands with the help of friendly Maori tribes. In 1853 he was sent to South Africa as governor of Cape Colony, but in 1861, on the outbreak of the land wars in Taranaki, was recalled to his old post and successfully repressed the rebellion.

Grey's great merit, however, was his ability to understand and promote Maori culture. He learned the Maori language, recorded Maori myths and tribal legends, previously handed down orally, and published them in London in 1854.

Thanks to his unique knowledge of the Maoritanga and his intuitive understanding of the Maoris he was much respected by the chiefs. He died in London on September 19th 1898.

### William Hamilton
### (1899–1978) Sheep farmer and inventor
William Hamilton, a sheep farmer in Mackenzie Country, was fascinated by engines, and built racing cars in his own workshop. His particular interest, however, was in the construction of a boat suitable for the wild rivers of the South Island with their numerous rapids. In 1953 he produced the fast and manoeuvrable jet boat, with a turbine propulsion system instead of a propeller, which is now found on rivers all over the world on which traditional types of boat cannot operate. Jet-boat trips on the Shotover River, near Queenstown (☛Sights from A to Z), are now a very popular attraction.

### Sir Edmund Hillary
### (b. 1919) Mountaineer and explorer
Edmund Hillary, born in Auckland on July 20th 1919, is perhaps the most widely known New Zealander. He became world famous when, along with the Nepalese Sherpa Tenzing Norgay (1914–86), he was the first to reach the summit of Mount Everest, the world's highest mountain, on May 29th 1953, Queen Elizabeth II's coronation day – a feat for which he was knighted. In 1957, with a British expedition, he made the first journey to the South Pole by motor vehicle. In 1960–1 and 1963–4 he returned to the Himalayas on research expeditions. He now spends most of his time there, where he is active in social work with the native population. His books are very popular in New Zealand.

### William Hobson
### (1792–1842) British naval officer
Captain William Hobson was born in the Irish town of Waterford on September 25th 1792. In July 1839 he was sent out to New Zealand as lieutenant-governor on a delicate mission – to persuade the Maori chiefs to accept British sovereignty. His negotiations with them led to the signing of the Treaty of Waitangi (February 6th 1840), under which, in return for accepting British sovereignty, they were guaranteed ownership rights to their land. Although his health was poor as a result of an

Hone Heke Pokai with his wife and some of his followers

attack of yellow fever while serving in the Caribbean, Hobson then set out on a tour of the whole of New Zealand to persuade other chiefs to sign the treaty. The treaty cleared the way for New Zealand to become a Crown colony, of which Hobson was appointed the first governor. His decision to buy land on Waitemata Harbour led in 1841 to the transfer of the colony's capital from Russell to Auckland (named after the then First Lord of the Admiralty).

During his period of office Hobson was caught between a variety of interests. The New Zealand Land Company's new settlers in Wellington pressed him with their desire to get land, which the Maoris understandably were unwilling to give up, since it had been guaranteed to them by treaty. Finally some of the Maoris took up arms, and Hobson had great difficulty in dealing with the rising, since the young colony had no troops and no money. Hobson

therefore, on his own authority, issued Treasury bills. The Maori chiefs had little respect for a sick man without military support and Hobson had no success in his dealings with them. The decision had already been taken in London to recall him when he died in Auckland on September 10th 1842.

### Hone Heke Pokai
### (ca 1810–50) Maori chief

Hone Heke Pokai, a nephew of the notorious Hongi Hika (see below), came from Pakaraka, near the Bay of Islands. He was one of the signatories of the Treaty of Waitangi. Until 1841 his tribe, the Ngapuhi, had profited from the dues that all ships entering the port of Kororareka (Russell) had to pay; but this source of income was taken away when the government introduced customs duties in 1841. As a result the whalers, already hit by the falling price of whale oil, ceased to use the port. This loss of income, combined with mistrust of the government, led Hone Heke to cut down the flagstaff on the harbour, the symbol of British sovereignty, on four occasions in 1844 and 1845. On the last occasion he also attacked the settlers, who fled to Auckland. All the buildings in the settlement except the churches and the mission station were burned down. This was the beginning of Heke's War, which ended only in 1846 when he was defeated by a strong British force at Ruapekapeka. Hone Heke Pokai died in Kaikohe on August 6th 1850.

### Hongi Hika
### (ca 1772–1828) Maori chief

Hongi Hika, chief of the Ngapuhi tribe, was born in Kaikohe in about about 1772. He had good contacts with the European settlers and was regarded as a model of the educability of the Maoris. As a result he was able to travel to Britain in 1820 along with the missionary Thomas Kendall and a Waikato chief. While there he helped to compile a Maori dictionary and grammar. He was presented to George IV and was loaded with presents, which he sold in exchange for weapons on his way home. He realised that firearms were far superior to traditional Maori weapons and that with their use he would be able to make himself sole ruler over all Maoris. From his base at Kerikeri he and his heavily armed warriors carried out a series of raids, travelling in canoes, that brought devastation and death to the Waikato area, Rotorua, the Bay of Plenty, the East Cape and as far south as Wellington. He was severely wounded in battle in 1827 and died in Whangaroa on March 3rd 1828.

### Friedensreich Hundertwasser
### (b. 1928) Artist

The Viennese artist Friedensreich Hundertwasser (real name Friedrich Stowasser) was born on December 15th 1928. He first achieved fame with his paintings and drawings, which were notable for their decorative curving lines and bold use of colour. Then in the 1950s he turned to architecture, designing the famous Hundertwasser House in Vienna (1983–5).

Hundertwasser visited New Zealand for the first time in 1973 and in 1986 he became a New Zealand citizen. He settled at Kawakawa on the Bay of Islands and

practises, here and elsewhere, an environment-friendly way of life, given expression also in his 'green' guest house with its earth toilet.

Famous also is the new flag he designed for New Zealand, though it has not yet been officially recognised. It shows a green spiral on a white ground, representing an opening fern leaf, which also resembles a favourite Maori type of ornament.

### Thomas Kendall
### (1778–1832) British trader and missionary

Thomas Kendall, a native of Lincolnshire, was originally a trader but, seized with religious zeal, entered the service of the (Anglican) Church Missionary Society. In 1813 he went to Australia and in the following year, along with other missionaries, he explored the Bay of Islands in New Zealand. Later he made a second visit along with Samuel Marsden. Kendall is mainly remembered for his establishment of the first school for Maoris in 1816. He believed that to carry out successful missionary work in New Zealand it was essential to know the language, the customs and the beliefs of the Maoris. Despite his piety, Kendall had an unusual character for a missionary: he quarrelled with other missionaries, drank heavily with the whalers and traded in weapons. In 1820 he accompanied the powerful Maori chief Hongi Hika to London, where with Hongi Hika's help he compiled the first Maori grammar and a Maori dictionary. But he was probably also involved in helping Hongi Hika to obtain large quantities of firearms so that he could attack other tribes. In 1823 his way of life led to his dismissal by the Church Missionary Society. Thereafter he lived peaceably among the Maoris and then embarked on a new career as a timber merchant in New South Wales. He died in a shipwreck in August 1832.

Kendall was much criticised and disparaged, but it must be said that without his interest and activity many Maori traditions would have been lost.

### Te Kooti
### (ca 1814–1893) Maori leader

Te Kooti, or Arikirangi Te Turuki, was born in Poverty Bay in about 1814. Although not a chief, he was of noble lineage. He fought on the government side against the Hauhau movement, but was imprisoned on suspicion of collaboration with the enemy and was condemned, without trial, to be deported, along with 300 Hauhau supporters, to the Chatham Islands. It is supposed that jealousy and resentment were the causes of his arrest. While in exile he founded the Ringatu sect – known as the 'raised hand' because he made his raised arm glow in the dark by the application of phosphorus – which still has a few thousand adherents. Te Kooti saw himself as the Moses of the Maoris, whose mission it was to lead them into the Promised Land. In November 1868, after seizing a ship and escaping from the Chatham Islands, he and his followers attacked the settlement of Matawhero, near Gisborne, and killed 33 whites and 37 Maoris loyal to the government. In the fighting that followed he always contrived to escape capture, but many of his supporters were taken and executed. Te Kooti sought refuge in the inaccessible Urewera area and from there launched repeated guerrilla attacks. In 1872, after years of unsuccessful pursuit by government forces, he withdrew to King Country, where he lived under the protection of the Maori king until the official conclusion of peace. He was then pardoned and in 1891 was granted land at Ohiwa in the Bay of Plenty by the government. He died at Te Karaka on April 17th 1893.

### Count Felix von Luckner
### (1881–1966) German naval officer
Count von Luckner, famed as the 'Sea Devil', was born in Dresden on June 9th 1881. During the first world war, in 1916–17, he broke through the British blockade with his auxiliary cruiser *Seeadler* and sank or captured many Allied ships in the Pacific until his own ship was wrecked in a tidal wave. He then sailed in a lifeboat to the Cook Islands and on to the Fiji Islands, where he was taken prisoner and interned on Motuihe Island, near Auckland. His daring flight in the camp commandant's yacht during a Christmas concert caused a sensation throughout New Zealand. He then seized a coastal ship and fled to the Kermadec Islands, where he was again arrested and then held under close guard on an island in Lyttleton Harbour, near Christchurch. He was again planning escape when the war ended and he was released. When von Luckner returned to

New Zealand 20 years later he received a surprisingly friendly reception: it became known that during his exploits with the *Seeadler* he had shown great consideration for the safety of the crews of the ships he sank.

Count von Luckner, who wrote various epic accounts, died on April 13th 1966 in the Swedish town of Malmö.

### Katherine Mansfield
### (1888–1923) Writer
Katherine Mansfield (real name Kathleen Mansfield Beauchamp), born in Wellington on October 14th 1888, the daughter of a banker, is the best-known figure in New Zealand literature. As a girl she attended Queen's College in London but returned to New Zealand in 1906. In 1908 she persuaded her father to let her go back to London, where she led a liberated life in the literary and bohemian world. In 1909 she married George Bowden but left him a day after the wedding. In 1911 she entered on a liaison with the socialist literary critic John Middleton Murray, whom she finally married in 1918. In her wild life she gave little thought for her health and finally fell ill with tuberculosis. She travelled to France, Switzerland and Germany for treatment, and died while under treatment at Fontainebleau in France on January 9th 1923.

Katherine Mansfield's literary fame rests on her short stories, a genre in which she excelled. Her first published collection, *In a German Pension* (1911), was based on her experiences while taking the cure at Bad Wörishofen in Germany, but after 1915, when her much loved younger brother Leslie visited her in London and soon afterwards fell on the western front, she turned to her earlier days in New Zealand for her subjects. Among the best known of her later works are 'Prelude', 'At the Bay' and *The Garden Party*.

### Sir Apirana Turupa Ngata
### (1874–1950) Maori politician
Apirana Turupa Ngata was born about 1874 at Te Araroa on the East Cape. In 1906 he took a degree in law – the first Maori to gain a university degree. One of the founders of the Young Maori Party and its Secretary General, he became an influential Member of Parliament, active in promoting the education and training of Maoris, their ownership of land and the better use of land. In 1928 he was

Katherine Mansfield

Te Rauparaha

Edward Gibbon Wakefield

appointed the first minister for Maori affairs. His lasting achievement was the revival of Maori traditional arts and crafts, and he was responsible for the establishment of a school of arts and crafts in Rotorua.

### Wiremu (Bill) Ratana
### (1870–1939) Maori leader

The Maori revival movement of Wiremu Ratana was one of the most successful in the recent history of the Maoris. For many years Ratana lived quietly as a farmer on the family land at Wanganui, but after a vision in 1918 he believed that he had been chosen as God's mouthpiece and enjoined to gather the Maori people and lead them to God. A series of healings, whether real or imagined, brought him an immense following, and not only of Maoris. He met opposition from the Maori King Movement and from the Anglican church, from which he broke away in 1925. The Ratana Church was now established in close cooperation with the Methodists. Wiremu Ratana did not, however, confine himself to religion, but associated his movement with the political objectives of the Labour Party. For many years the four parliamentary seats reserved for Maoris were held by his supporters. His death in 1939 attracted wide sympathy and his funeral was attended by the prime minister, many members of Parliament and 3000 of his supporters. In 1991 his church still had 47,200 members.

### Te Rauparaha
### (ca 1768–1849) Maori chief

Te Rauparaha, who bore the honorific name of Great Snake, was chief of the Ngati Toa tribe. In the 1820s, from his base on Kapiti Island, off the west coast of the North Island, he started a series of campaigns of annihilation directed against other Maori tribes, particularly in the south. One of the last great chiefs before the coming of the Europeans, he was described as shrewd, valiant, cruel, wily and unpredictable. He soon came into bitter conflict with the New Zealand Land Company over their land purchases at Nelson and Wellington. In 1846 he was captured at Porirua, to the north of Wellington, and held in prison without trial for a year and a half. He died at Otaki on November 27th 1849.

### Ernest Rutherford
### (1871–1937) Physicist

Ernest Rutherford, born on August 30th 1871 at Spring Grove, near Nelson, was recognised as the leading experimental physicist of his day and the father of atomic physics. After taking his first degree in Christchurch, and then Cambridge in the United Kingdom, he did research in Montreal and later returned to Cambridge as director of the Cavendish Laboratory. His ground-breaking scientific achievements were the discovery of alpha and beta radiation in 1898, gamma radiation in 1900 and the recognition of radioactivity as the result of the disintegration of elements. He formulated the disintegration theory and the Rutherford model of the atom. In 1919 he published evidence for the first artificial transmutation of matter. He had already received a Nobel Prize in 1908, but for chemistry, not for physics. In 1931 he was created Lord Rutherford of Nelson. He died in Cambridge on October 19th 1937 and was buried in Westminster Abbey.

### George Augustus Selwyn
### (1809–78) Anglican bishop

Born in Hampstead on April 5th 1809, the scion of a well-to-do family, George Augustus Selwyn was the first Anglican bishop of New Zealand. He was educated at Eton and Cambridge, ordained as a priest in the Church of England in 1834 and appointed a missionary bishop in 1841. A year later he arrived in New Zealand to take up his duties as bishop. He had the advantage of having been a sportsman – he had rowed for Cambridge – and a good walker, for his congregation were widely scattered on the two islands of New Zealand. In his travels he covered over 11,000 km, usually in small ships or boats but often on foot. He also took an interest in politics; he was an adviser to the government and tried to act as a mediator in political conflicts. In 1867 he returned to England as bishop of Lichfield, and died there on April 11th 1878.

In New Zealand he is commemorated by the Selwyn churches, built to the design of his architect, Frederick Thatcher, in neo-Gothic style, usually of wood.

### Baron Charles de Thierry
### (1793–1864) French traveller

Charles de Thierry, who is believed to have been born in the Netherlands in April 1793, the son of French émigrés, is one of the most colourful figures in New Zealand history. After serving in a British cavalry regiment he became a student at Cambridge, where he met the missionary Thomas Kendall and the Maori chief Hongi Hika. He helped them to purchase weapons and was allegedly granted the whole Northland region by Kendall. After he had unsuccessfully tried to sell his supposed property to the Dutch government he set out for New Zealand to claim his land for himself. He travelled by way of the United States, where he stayed for 8 years. He finally arrived in Hokianga in 1837, accompanied by a group of adventurers whom he had enlisted, and proclaimed himself 'sovereign chief of New Zealand'. He was unable to make good his claim, having quarrelled both with the Maoris and with the European settlers. His

hopes that France would intervene on his behalf were frustrated when the Treaty of Waitangi was signed in 1840. In 1845 the 'monarch of Maoriland' went to Auckland where he became a music teacher, then prospected unsuccessfully for gold in California and finally set up as a businessman. He died in poverty in Auckland on July 8th 1864.

### Alexander Turnbull
### (1868–1918) Collector

Alexander Turnbull was born in Wellington in 1868 but was educated in Britain. Thereafter he lived in London and later returned to Wellington as a wholesaler. His passion was books and from the age of 17 he collected books systematically, spending lavishly. His particular interests were the Pacific area, Antarctica and New Zealand, Captain Cook and his voyages, and English literature, particularly Milton. He also collected coins and Maori works of art, which he presented in 1916 to the Dominion Museum (now the National Museum in Wellington). He bequeathed his huge collection of books – 55,000 volumes, valuable manuscripts, pictures and maps – to the state. The Alexander Turnbull Library was opened to the public in 1920 and has since then been systematically added to, making it one of the most important research libraries in New Zealand.

### Wakefield brothers
### (18th–19th century) British settlers

The Wakefield brothers all left their mark, in different ways, on the history of New Zealand.

The best known, and the one with the most lasting influence, was Edward Gibbon Wakefield (1796–1862). He drew up a plan for the settlement of the colony of South Australia, but it was only with the settlement of New Zealand that his theories and plans were put into effect. As one of the founders of the New Zealand Association, which later developed into the New Zealand Land Company, he was largely responsible for the influx of settlers into the new colony. Uncontrolled immigration led to conflicts with the Maoris, and many of the settlers were taken in by Wakefield's promises, which were not always reliable – for the company was of profit mainly to its founders. Wakefield himself remained in London, pulling the strings, and it was only at a later stage that he went out to Wellington in 1852. He died there and is buried in the Bolton Street Memorial Park.

William Wakefield (1803–48) brought the first settlers to Wellington in 1839–40. He was the driving force in the foundation of the settlement, and is justly called the 'father of Wellington'.

Arthur Wakefield (1799–1843) also worked for the New Zealand Land Company. In the course of a journey of exploration in the north of the South Island he came into conflict with Te Rauparaha and his warriors over a disputed land deal and was killed, along with a party of settlers from Nelson, in the Wairau affray. This encounter led to the Maori wars of the 1840s.

Daniel Wakefield (1798–1858) was a judge in Wellington.

Felix Wakefield (1807–75), the youngest of the brothers, became an engineer and a horticultural expert on the South Island.

### Te Whiti o Rongomai
### (ca 1830–1907) Maori leader

Te Whiti o Rongomai was the leader of a passive resistance movement aimed at preventing further losses of Maori land. He established a model village in Parihaka, at the foot of Mount Taranaki, with new methods of agriculture. The Maoris sought to prevent further acquisitions of land by settlers by setting up fences across roads, removing boundary posts and destroying crops by ploughing them in. In 1881, when Governor Gordon, who was well disposed to the Maoris, was out of the country, Te Whiti and his associate Tohu were arrested and imprisoned on the South Island, without trial, for almost two years and the village was destroyed.

Te Whiti was a gifted orator and one of the first modern Maori leaders, who gave his people courage and hope. He showed that new forms of resistance – civil disobedience, passive confrontation and solidarity – were effective, rather than resorting to arms.

# Culture

## Maori Culture (Maoritanga)

Visitors can get some impression of the ancient traditions and art forms of the Maoris in the museums of New Zealand, which almost all have examples of fine war canoes and meeting houses with carved decoration. But Maori culture does not consist solely of museum exhibits: visitors can experience the artistic skills, customs and traditions of the Maoris in special presentations of songs and dances, for the object of the Maoritanga movement initiated by a number of Maori leaders is to revive and to cherish the culture and history of the Maori people.

Maoris still make up a relatively high proportion of the population on the volcanic plateau in the centre of the North Island, round Rotorua and Taupo, and also in the Waikato area, Northland, East Cape, Taranaki and Wanganui. And in these areas too the evidence of

traditional Maori culture – the place of assembly (*marae*), with its community or meeting house – is at its most visible. The oldest meeting houses date from the 19th c., but in recent decades, with the increased self-awareness of the Maoritanga movement, many new houses in traditional style have been built all over the country. The places of assembly are still special and visitors too must respect them. As in the past, they are the scene of welcoming ceremonies and dances; here traditional speeches and songs are recited, weddings, christenings and birthdays are celebrated and solemn ceremonies of mourning (*tangi*) are held.

### Rock drawings

Rock drawings are among the oldest evidence of Maori culture and are mainly found in South Canterbury and North Otago, on the South Island. Their exact age has not been established but they

Maori woodcarvers were held in high esteem and usually belonged to the upper social stratum

The richly decorated storehouse in the Totowhio Pa

certainly go at least as far back as the period before the arrival of the Europeans. Their meaning is also unknown. Usually drawn with charcoal or ochre, they show a variety of themes, including human figures and animals.

**Woodcarving**

The woodcarvings of the Maoris rank among the finest artistic achievements of the South Seas. The preferred material was the durable yet easily worked wood of the totara tree. Most of the richly decorated meeting houses and storehouses so much admired today are no more than 150 years old, and all the carving is done with modern iron tools. Before the coming of the Europeans the only implements available to the Maoris were stone and obsidian.

Since the cult of ancestors played such an important part in Maori life, **human figures** are among the most important of the carvings. The proportions of the figures are distorted, particular emphasis being given to the head, the most *tapu* (prestigious) and therefore the most important part of the body. The feet were regarded as the least sacred parts, and accordingly are disproportionately small. The hands had usually only three fingers, like birds' claws, and the slanting eyes, inlaid with mother-of-pearl from paua shells, are also like birds' eyes. The figures are depicted in a warlike attitude, with a stone club in one hand, wide-open eyes and stuck-out tongue. The same attitudes are adopted in the haka war dance: they are deliberately provocative gestures, designed to show contempt for the enemy and ward off evil spirits.

The carvings, whether in relief or free-standing, were often painted red – a colour that had high symbolic value throughout Polynesia as the colour of the gods. The paint, which was made from red ochre and fish oil, brought out the grain of the wood and the delicacy of the carving. Unfortunately many old carvings, even those displayed in museums, have been covered with a thick coat of oil paint.

Canoes, paddles, musical instruments, everyday objects and the entrance gates of villages were all richly carved. The decoration of the bone caskets in which the skeletons of great chiefs were preserved was particularly elaborate.

**Objects made from semi-precious stones**
Maori artists also showed great artistic skill in making jewellery and weapons of greenstone. Greenstone, jade or nephrite (*pounamu*) occurred only in rivers on the west coast of the South Island and was a valuable object of exchange. Many hours of patient work were required to transform this very hard material into axes and clubs for chiefs or the amulets in human form (*hei-tiki*) that both men and women wore round the neck. After the Maoris gained access to iron tools and weapons the old greenstone axes were reworked to make *hei-tiki*, which were much sought after by the European settlers. Greenstone jewellery and ornaments with traditional motifs are still made at Hokitika and Greymouth.

The missionaries who from 1814 onwards sought to convert the Maoris disapproved of these naked figures and particularly of the sexual motifs. By the end of the 19th c., with the decline in numbers of the Maoris, the art of woodcarving had been almost entirely forgotten. With the development of Maoritanga and the help of new teachers of the art like Pine Taiapa, however, Maori woodcarving has taken on a fresh lease of life.

**Carvings as objects of trade**
A number of European collections have examples of Maori woodcarving, which became much sought after as objects of trade in the early 19th c.

**Meeting houses**
The Maori meeting house (*whare runanga*) represents an embodiment of the revered ancestors of the tribe. The roof ridge is crowned by a standing figure (*tekoteko*) of an ancestor, the mask (*koruru*) below this is his face and the bargeboards fronting the roof are his outstretched arms (*maihi*), with his fingers (*raparapa*) at the ends. The interior of the house is his thorax, the beam forming the roof ridge his spinal column, the side posts of the walls his ribs. The rich carving in the interior also has symbolic meaning, with figures of other ancestors, mythical beings, ornamentation and sometimes gods. The carvings were thus a kind of picture book that illustrated the story of the ancestors in songs and tales – for

written accounts were unknown.

The motifs, which have descriptive names, are painted mainly in red, but also in black and white.

**Tattooing**
The long-abandoned art of tattooing was not used for purely decorative purposes but to indicate status. In men the whole face, the buttocks and the upper thighs were tattooed, in women only the chin and lips. Tattooing was an extremely painful process, since it involved piercing the skin.

**Music and oratory**
Traditional Maori music and oratory was instrumental in handing on traditions, myths and history, in a society that lacked written records. The music consists almost exclusively of songs (*waiata*), with little variation in pitch but highly complex rhythms. The songs were accompanied by flutes and the performers marked the rhythm by stamping their feet and striking their thighs and breast with their fists.

Oratory and singing were an integral part of ceremonial occasions at the place of assembly (*marae*) and in the meeting house. Both were part of Maori formal rhetoric and took their themes mainly from mythology. There were a great variety of songs, but the commonest, apart from the *karakias*, the sacred songs sung only by a priest (*tohunga*) in the course of ritual acts, were mourning songs, sung at solemn funeral ceremonies, and love songs.

Modern songs are based in greater or lesser degree on the Christian choral traditions of the European immigrants; but some modern music groups are also giving fresh life to the old Maori music.

# Art

The larger New Zealand museums and art collections contain fine paintings by European masters and rare books.

**Art of the immigrants**
The first European explorers were accompanied by cartographers and draughtsmen, who made accurate records of their landing, and in the early days drawings were made of the native inhabitants, the flora and fauna and the landscape. On his travels in New Zealand in 1844 George F Angas (1822–86)

painted numerous pictures of scenery and of the Maoris. Many museums also have drawings, often charmingly naive, by early settlers. The explorer and surveyor Charles Heaphy (1820–81) drew very attractive landscapes in his travels about the country. Gottfried Lindauer (1839–1926), a Czech immigrant, painted many lifelike portraits of Maoris and scenes from their life. Charles Frederick Goldie (1870–1947), a native of Auckland, became one of the best-known and most highly paid artists in New Zealand, mainly because of his portraits of Maoris.

### 20th century

Until the 20th c. New Zealand art still followed European models, and New Zealand artists trained, worked and exhibited mainly in London. The painter Frances Hodgkins (1869–1947), who came from Dunedin, became well known and successful in Britain. Her still lifes and landscapes showed strong European influence, particularly of expressionism. After the death of her mother in 1913 she never returned to New Zealand.

Important 20th c. New Zealand artists are Rita Angus (1908–70), the landscapist Mountford T Woollaston (b. 1910), Ralph Hotere (b. 1931) and the outstanding and original Colin McCahon (1919–87), who is notable for his large oil paintings on religious, mythological and social themes. Maori themes have increasingly featured in art since the mid-20th c.

Len Lye (1901–80) became famous for his mobile sculptures, particularly in America, where he spent most of his time. He was also a painter and film director. Other notable sculptors and designers were Guy Ngan (b. 1926) and Molly McAlister (1920–79).

Many artists have settled in the sunny regions of Nelson (South Island) and Northland, particularly in the Bay of Islands. Among them is the Austrian painter Friedensreich Hundertwasser, who has spent much of his time since 1973 in the Bay of Islands.

### Decorative art

The decorative arts have a long tradition in New Zealand in the woodcarving and weaving of the Maoris. In recent decades large numbers of potters have established themselves throughout the country. Avant-garde craft shops and galleries do good business.

## Architecture

### Maori architecture

At the time of the discovery of New Zealand by Europeans the Maoris lived in huts either in an open village (*kainga*) or in a fortified settlement surrounded by a palisade (*pa*). A Maori village, Rewa's Village, has been reconstructed at Kerikeri. A striking feature of Maori houses is the rich carved decoration, including figures and masks with protruding tongues.

### 19th-century houses

The first European whalers and seal hunters relied on a tent or reed hut (*raupo*) for shelter. The better-off settlers brought prefabricated wooden houses with them. With the wider establishment of sawmills wooden houses became the normal type of dwelling, while public buildings were usually of stone. The first European houses were built when missionary activity began in the Bay of Islands, for example at the Kerikeri and Waimate North mission stations.

Settlers' houses dating from the mid-19th c., usually surrounded by verandas, have survived in Parnell (Auckland), New Plymouth and the Christchurch area. In the goldfields houses were mainly built of corrugated iron, which stood up to earthquakes better than stone buildings.

The usual dwelling of the settlers was a cottage. Examples of houses of higher pretensions can be seen in Larnach Castle (Dunedin), Holly Lea (Christchurch) and Alberton (Auckland).

### Public buildings

The preferred style for the early public buildings was neo-Gothic, whose repertoire was taken from English and Norman Gothic. Most buildings were of wood. In the time of the first Anglican bishop, George Selwyn (1809–78), and his architect Frederick Thatcher (1814–90), a number of churches were built in this style – for example, St Mary's in New Plymouth (1845–6) and All Saints in Howick (1847) – as well as secular buildings such as St John's College in Auckland (chapel 1847, College Hall 1849). Another architect who made a name for himself for imposing neo-Gothic public buildings was Benjamin W Montfort (1825–98). Montfort, who came to New Zealand as an immigrant in 1850, designed the

Canterbury Museum and Canterbury College in Christchurch and St Mary's Procathedral (1888) in Parnell (Auckland).

The other predominant style in New Zealand in the 19th c. was neoclassicism. Government House in Auckland (1856; now part of the university) was the work of William Mason. William H Clayton designed Government Building – the largest wooden building in the southern hemisphere – for the new capital, Wellington, in 1876.

William Armson (1834–83), who came to New Zealand from Melbourne in 1862, contributed to the neoclassical townscapes of Christchurch, Dunedin, Oamaru and Hokitika. RA Lawson (1833–1903) built a number of neoclassical buildings in Dunedin and Oamaru.

## 20th century

In the early 20th c. British and European architecture still provided the models for New Zealand. John Campbell chose neo-baroque for the Public Trust Building in Wellington and the Chief Post Office in Auckland. His design (1911) for Parliament House in Wellington, which

had been burned down in 1907, was carried out only in part. The building's left wing – a controversial design by the British architect Basil Spence – was built in 1964–82 and has become known as the Beehive. Other textbook examples of the neo-baroque style in New Zealand are the railway station in Dunedin (1904–7) and the town hall of Invercargill (1906).

Functionalism came to New Zealand after the first world war. The first steel-framed high-rise buildings, showing the influence of the Bauhaus, were erected in the 1920s. In 1931 Napier and Hastings were largely destroyed by a severe earthquake in Hawke's Bay and in spite of the economic depression were rebuilt in uniform art-deco style, giving Napier its distinctive townscape.

More recently two buildings in particular have given rise to controversy: the Beehive in Wellington (see above) and the Aotea Centre in Auckland, a concert hall built in 1974–89 on the model of Aalto's Finlandia Hall in Helsinki (1971). The city centres of Auckland, Wellington and Christchurch are now dominated by high-rise buildings – older facades have been

Colonial architecture: the old Chief Post Office, Christchurch

preserved on the lower storeys of modern buildings. In the new housing estates of New Zealand the single-storey detached family house predominates. Because of the danger of earthquakes they are built of wood. Many old buildings have been pulled down as being unsafe in an earthquake.

# Literature

## 19th century

In 1854 Governor George Grey published the first collection of the oral traditions of the Maoris. The earliest New Zealand writer of any note was Frederick Manning (1811–83), an adventurer, sawmill owner and timber merchant, who lived with his Maori wife on Hokianga Harbour, in western Northland, at the time of the timber boom. After 1860 he wrote two books under the pseudonym A Pakeha Maori: *Old New Zealand, a Tale of Good Old Times* and *War in the North*, the story of Hone Heke's fight against the British colonial authorities in the 1840s, seen from the viewpoint of a Maori.

### Samuel Butler

Samuel Butler (1835–1902) left Britain at the age of 25 and settled on a remote large farm on the east side of New Zealand's Southern Alps. After long journeys of exploration on the South Island he returned to Britain and devoted himself entirely to writing. His account of his experiences, drawn from his letters, *A First Year in Canterbury Settlement* (1863), and his utopian satire *Erewhon* (1872) reflect his wide travels in the inaccessible hinterland of Canterbury.

## 20th century

### Katherine Mansfield

The outstanding figure in early 20th c. New Zealand literature was Katherine Mansfield (☛Famous People). The daughter of a Wellington banker, her real name was Kathleen Mansfield Beauchamp. At the age of 19 she persuaded her father to let her go to London, where she lived in literary and bohemian circles. In 1909, for health reasons (she had tuberculosis), she

moved to Germany and lived for some months in the spa of Bad Wörishofen. This period of her life is reflected in her first book of short stories, *In a German Pension* (1911). After her much loved younger brother Leslie died on the western front she looked back to her earlier days in New Zealand for her subjects ('The Dolls' House', 'Prelude' and 'At the Bay').

### John AA Lee

The slum quarters and schools of Dunedin, then a flourishing metropolis, marked the early years of John AA Lee (1891–1982). His books, particularly his autobiographical novel *Children of the Poor*, tell of his experiences as an outsider and of the life of the poor and the social outcasts.

### Ngaio Marsh

Ngaio Marsh (1899–1982), a native of Christchurch, worked in the theatre before moving to London to start a new career as a writer of detective novels. Among her best-known works are *A Man Lay Dead*, *Vintage Murder*, *Surfeit of Lampreys*, *Died in the Wool* and *Final Curtain*. During the second world war she went back to New Zealand, where she again turned to the theatre and put on some remarkable productions of Shakespeare. In 1950 she returned to London, where, with her financial position secured by the success of her novels, she was able to devote herself to her great love, the theatre.

### Maurice FR Shadbolt

Maurice FR Shadbolt (b. 1932) belongs to the older generation of contemporary New Zealand writers. In his novel *Among the Cinders* he gives a vivid picture of the past world of gold prospectors, loggers and early settlers. He describes not only the life of the white settlers but also the very different way of life of the Maoris and the relations between the two.

### Hone Tuwhare

The life of the early settlers, seen from the Maori point of view, features in the plays of Hone Tuwhare (b. 1922).

### James Baxter

James Baxter (1926–72) is New Zealand's most celebrated lyric poet. Born in Dunedin, he was associated with the pacifist movement, under the influence of his father. He converted to

Catholicism and in 1969 founded an alternative commune for alcoholics, drug addicts and the homeless in the remote village of Hiruharama (Jerusalem) on the Whanganui River. The commune broke up after his early death.

### Allen Thomas Curnow

Allen Thomas Curnow (b. 1911) taught English literature in Auckland for many years and started writing poetry in 1940.

### Witi Itimaera
### Patricia Grace

The short stories of two Maori female writers, Patricia Grace (b. 1937) and Witi Itimaera (b. 1944), have attracted international interest. Patricia Grace's book *Potiki* pictures the Maoris' struggle against the destruction of their habitat. Further novels include *Mutuwhenua – The Moon Sleeps* (1978) and *Cousins* (1992). Witi Itimaera has written *Tangi* (1973), *Whenau* (1974), *The Matriarch* (1986) and *Bulibasha* (1994).

### Keri Hulme

Keri Hulme (b. 1947) is one of the few New Zealand female writers who are known and read in Europe. She has some Maori blood in her veins and her books are concerned with problems that have their origin in New Zealand's bicultural past. Her novel *The Bone People*, which won the prestigious Booker Prize, depicts the forlornness of the individual when deprived of their traditional bonds. Other successful books are her collection of poetry and prose, *The Silences Between*, and her collection of short stories, *The Wind Eater*.

### Janet Frame

For Janet Frame (b. 1924 in Dunedin) writing was of existential importance. She spent many years in psychiatric institutions until the discovery of her great talent as a writer led to her release. Her first volume of short stories, *The Lagoon*, was published when she was 27. The film version of her biography, *An Angel at My Table* (directed by Jane Campion), made her work known in Europe.

## Theatre

### Development

The New Zealand theatre followed British and European models longer than other cultural activities did. Only after political reorientation in the Pacific area did the country turn away from mainstream European culture. The first professional theatre company was established in the Downstage Theatre in Wellington in 1964: previously there had only been performances by visiting foreign companies and amateur groups. In the 1970s professional community theatres were established in the larger towns such as Auckland, Christchurch, Dunedin and Palmerston North.

### Bruce Mason

Fresh impetus was brought to the New Zealand theatre by Bruce Mason (1921–83). His first play, in 1953, is a critical judgment of white society, while his later plays dealt with the change in the world of the Maoris. The first of his five plays on Maori themes, *The Pohutukawa Tree* (1957), is now almost a classic. Mason's view of Maori culture as a whole is pessimistic. In 1965 he wrote *Awatea* for the Maori opera singer Inia Te Wiata, and this led to the formation in 1966 of the first Maori professional theatre company. The Maori theatre is now an established feature of the New Zealand drama scene.

### Maori theatre

A new Maori theatre movement emerged the late 1970s, differing from earlier movements in its consciousness of a political mission. Performances of song, dance and oratory, frequently with passages in the Maori language, were presented on assembly areas (*maraes*), in universities, public halls and theatres. A drama by the Maori poet and playwright Hone Tuwhare, *In the Wilderness without a Hat* (1977), was not staged until 1985. The starting point of the action is a funeral ceremony (*tangi*). In the course of an argument over the performance of the ceremony a carved ancestor figure (*tapu*) comes to life and intervenes in the discussion. The representation of a *tapu* on the stage was no doubt explanation of the 8 year delay in the production of the play.

A characteristic of Maori theatre is that the distance between spectators and actors has been abolished. The theatre thus becomes a community experience, similar to the traditional ceremonies on the *marae*.

A Maori dance group in a richly decorated meeting house

## Cinema

### Beginnings

The first films produced in New Zealand around the turn of the 19th c. were documentaries, newsreel features and silent films in which the Maoris and the unspoiled natural landscape of New Zealand served as the backdrop for banal love stories. Rudall Hayward, the well-known New Zealand director of the 1920s and 1930s, invented a special camera and a sound system that enabled him to produce talking films.

### After 1945

After the second world war all the films shown in New Zealand came from Hollywood. It was only in the 1970s that the New Zealand film industry came to life. In 1977 Roger Donaldson produced *Sleeping Dogs*, and in the same year the Film Commission was established to support the young New Zealand film industry through subsidies paid from tax revenue or the proceeds of the state lottery. While only three films were produced in New Zealand between 1940 and 1970, more than 40 were produced

between 1977 and 1985. The Film Commission proved a powerful protector of the New Zealand film industry with its small domestic market. Most of the films produced with help from the commission were concerned with the history of New Zealand, with the central event of the land wars and with the problems of a bicultural society.

Among the best-known New Zealand directors are Vincent Ward (*In Spring One Plants Alone; State of Siege*), Geoff Murphy (*Goodbye Pork Pie*), Michael Firth (*Off the Edge*) and Mereta Mita (*Patu*). Yvonne Mackay received the first prize at the 1984 Frankfurt International Film Festival for Youth for her film *The Silent One*.

The greatest success of the New Zealand cinema, which won eight prizes at the Venice Film Festival in 1990, has been *An Angel at My Table*, Jane Campion's film version of the autobiography of the writer Janet Frame (☛Literature). Jane Campion's next film, *The Piano*, won several Oscars in Hollywood in 1994. In the same year the film *Once Were Warriors*, based on a book by the Maori author Alan Duff, set new box office records. Since his roles in *The Piano* and *Jurassic Park* the New Zealand actor Sam Neill has become known to wider audiences. Actor Russell Crowe became more known in the American film *LA Confidential* and won an Oscar in the 2000 film *Gladiator*.

# Music

### Classical music
The problem of a relatively small domestic market affects the musical scene in New Zealand no less than the artistic scene. Internationally renowned artistes like the opera singers Kiri Te Kanawa and Donald McIntyre appear more frequently on European and American stages than in New Zealand; and the New Zealand Symphony Orchestra plays in many other countries as well as New Zealand.

### Pop music
Many pop music groups, too, do not stay in New Zealand, since with a small potential audience they cannot survive. New Zealand music, centred mainly in Dunedin and Auckland, is subject to constant change. Bands are ephemeral though successful groups usually start by going to Australia and then move on to London or the United States. This was the case, for example, with Split Enz, New Zealand's best-known group.

Flying Nun, New Zealand's most successful recording company, started in 1981 with groups on the South Island (Pin Group, Christchurch; The Clean, Dunedin). Their popular group The Chills set out on a foreign tour in 1985 and had some success in Britain. In the 1980s recordings by Straitjackets Fit, The Bats and Headless Chickens were issued, and their exposure and image abroad were improved by cooperation with an Australian record company.

# Quotations

**Georg Forster**
... As we approached we discovered that it was an Indian [sic], who was standing on the cliff-top, armed with a club and a battleaxe, and behind him we could see in the distance, at the entrance to the woods, two women, each holding a spear. As soon as our boat reached the foot of the cliff, we called to him in the language of Tahiti: *Tayo Harre maï*, meaning 'Friend, come here!' But he did not do so, but remained standing at his post, leaning on his club, and in this posture he made a long speech, which he uttered in some places with great emphasis and violence, at the same time swinging his club round his head. As he could not be persuaded to come nearer, Captain Cook went forward in the boat, called to him in a friendly way and threw him his own and some other people's handkerchiefs, which, however, he refused to pick up. The captain therefore took several sheets of white paper, climbed unarmed up the cliff and held the paper out to the native. The good fellow trembled visibly all over, but in the end he took the paper, though still with clear signs of fear. As he was now so near to the captain, the latter took him by the hand and embraced him, at the same time rubbing noses with the native, which is their way of greeting each other. These signs of friendship immediately dispelled his fear, for he called the two women to him, who then came up without delay, whilst from our side likewise several men went ashore to join the captain. A short conversation followed between us and the Indians, though no one really understood much of it, because neither side knew the other's language. Mr Hodges at once drew an outline of their faces, and you could see from their expressions that they understood what he was doing. For that reason they called him *tóa-tóa*, a word which must refer in some way to the visual arts.
*Journey round the World* (1778–80)

**Dr Ferdinand Ritter von Hochstetter**
The water tests neutral, has a slightly salty, but by no means unpleasant taste and possesses to a high degree the property of petrifying, or more accurately of over-sintering and incrusting. As with the Icelandic springs, the deposit is siliceous sinter or tuff, and the outflow of the foaming water has formed on the slopes of the hill a system of sinter terraces which, as white as though hewn from marble, present a sight which no description or depiction can do justice to. It is as though a waterfall tumbling down over a series of steps had been suddenly turned to stone ...

The shallow, broad river reaches far up into the Rotomahana. Here the terraces begin, with low deposits held in shallow basins. The higher up you go, the higher the terraces become, 2, 3, some even 4 or 6 foot high. They are formed from a series of semicircular steps or pools of which, however, no two are at precisely the same height. Each of these steps has a small raised edge, from which delicate stalactites hang down onto the next level below, onto a platform – sometimes narrow, sometimes broad – enclosing one or more basins shimmering with a most beautiful blue colour. These basins form natural swimming pools, which the most stylish luxury could not have made more splendid or more comfortable. You can choose a shallow or a deep pool, a large or a small one, just as you please, and at any temperature, for the pools on the higher steps, nearer the main basin, contain warmer water than those on the lower levels. Some of the basins are so large and deep that you can easily swim around in them.

As you climb up the steps, you have to wade through the lukewarm water which spreads out over the platform of the steps next to the lower basins, but which seldom comes up above your ankles ...

The pure white siliceous formations, contrasting with the blue water, the green of the surrounding vegetation and with the intense red of the bare earth walls of the water crater, the swirling clouds of spray – all this makes a picture which is unique. The collector nevertheless has ample opportunity to fill whole basketfuls with beautiful examples of the most delicate stalactites, of incrusted twigs, leaves and the like, for everything that is on the terraces soon becomes incrusted again. *Neu-Seeland* (1863)

A description of the sinter terraces of Rotomahana, later destroyed by an earthquake in 1886.

### WFA Zimmermann

The second item is a saw made from sharks' teeth, which is used to widen and extend in a regular fashion the incisions in the skin made during tattooing. You can imagine what a pleasant sensation that must be. The designs are first sketched in a black colour by a fine stick; when this colour is dry, the person who is to be tattooed lies down on the lap of the priest who is to complete the work, offering him the part of his body which is to be covered with the design. The doctor-priest then takes a well-honed chisel made of human bone, places it on a line of the design and strikes it with a little hammer until the chisel penetrates the flesh; the chisel is then moved along and the same procedure is followed, perhaps 20 times. The blood is swabbed off with a swab of moistened moss, and the artist judges whether the line is continuous and well made. If he finds that this is not so, he uses the above-mentioned saw, placing it in the wound and drawing it back and forth a number of times, until the line is perfectly correct; the work with the chisel then continues until the design is completed, which usually takes two or three hours. The black colour is now applied to the gaping, torn places, which affects the healing of the flesh whereby the designs stand proud of the more or less dark brown flesh. As the deep cuts do not heal together, the flesh grows out round them and the drawn lines form a continuous bulge, as though cut lengths of cord were lying on the skin. Every incision is raised, and as the cut is not cleanly done but torn in the cruellest of fashions, the bulge also looks unpleasant and it is hard to grasp how such a disfigurement can be considered an ornament. Tattooing of the whole body takes 10 to 12 years, and each operation on an arm, one side of a leg or half of one side of the face causes such a terrible inflammation that even the strongest man is laid low in bed for three or four weeks.
*The islands of the Indian and Pacific Oceans. The journey of a Dutch doctor and explorer* (1863)

### New Zealand national anthem

ENGLISH

God defend New Zealand

God of nations at thy feet
In the bonds of love we meet.
Hear our voices, we entreat,
God defend our free land.
Guard Pacific's triple star
From the shafts of strife and war,
Make her praises heard afar,
God defend New Zealand.

Men of evr'ry creed and race
Gather here before thy face,
Asking thee to bless this place,
God defend our free land.
From dissension, envy, hate,
And corruption guard our state,
Make our country good and great,
God defend New Zealand.

MAORI

Aotearoa

E Ihoa Atua,
O nga Iwi! Matoura,
Ata whaka rongona;
Me aroha roa.
Kia hua ko te pai;
Kia tau to atawhai;
Manaakitia mai
Aotearoa

Ona mano tangata
Kiri whero, kiri ma,
Iwi Maori Pakeha,
Repeke katoa,
Nei ka tono ko nga he
Mau e whakaahu ke,
Kia ora marire
Aotearoa.

# Sights from A to Z

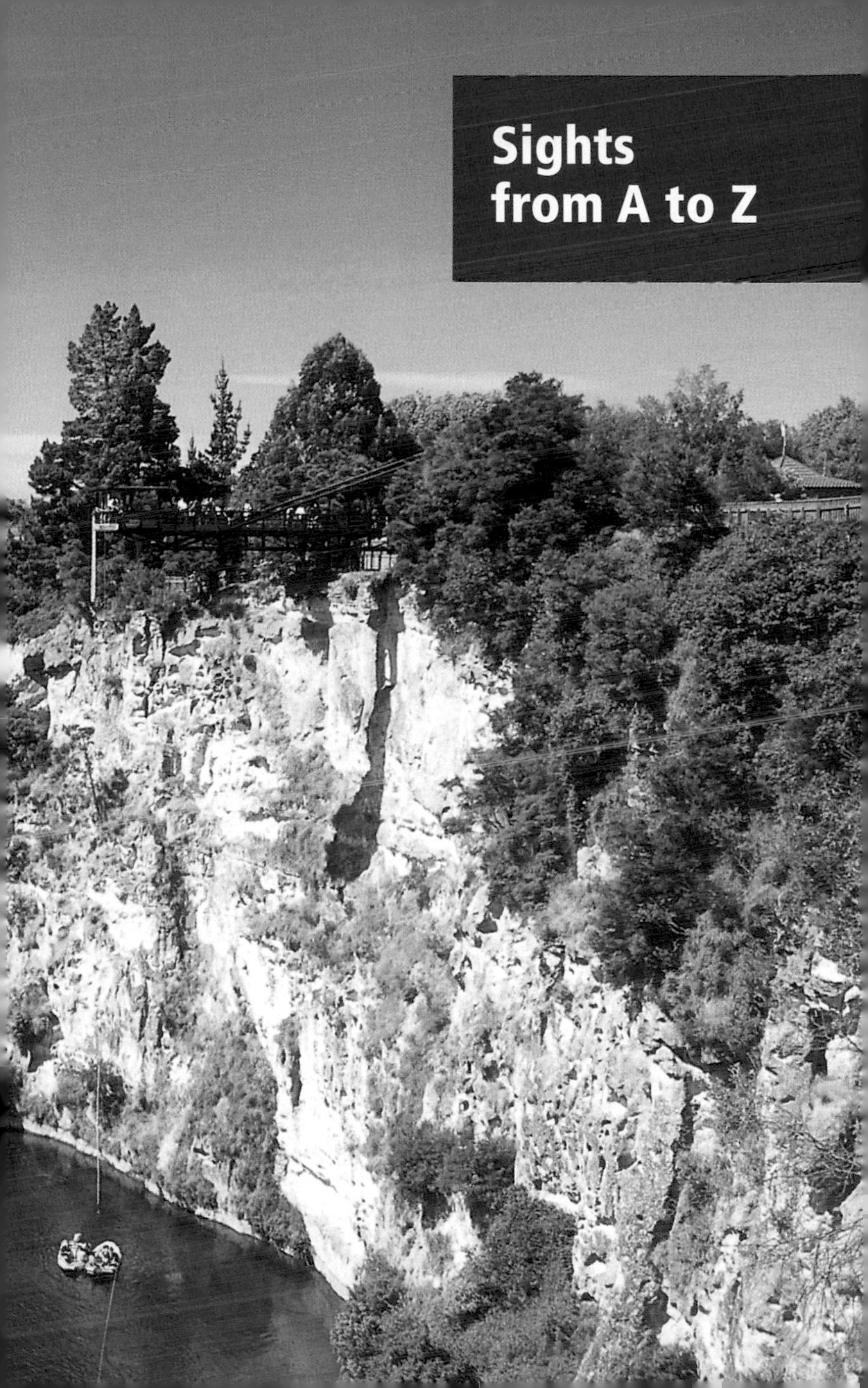

# Suggested Routes

On the North Island the attractions for many visitors are the spectacular volcanic areas, the almost tropical vegetation, the idyllic beaches and the surviving Maori culture. The appeal of the South Island lies in the snow-capped peaks and glaciers of the Southern Alps, the west-coast fjords, the wild coastline, the expanses of pastureland and the old colonial settlements and mansions.

This section presents a grand tour of New Zealand, with a number of detours and alternative routes. The routes cover all the main sights of New Zealand and provide the best views of the country's natural and man-made landscapes. Places that are the subject of a separate entry in the Sights from A to Z section of this guide are given in **bold** type and places mentioned as sub-entries in *italics*; these places can also be found via the Index at the end of the book. The map opposite gives a general view of the routes, which can be followed using the fold-out map at the end of the book.

## Grand tour (North and South Islands; ca 4600 km; 3–4 weeks)

The route starts from the multicultural city of Auckland. The tour begins with a detour to the Bay of Islands and Cape Reinga, the most northerly point on the North Island. You then return to Auckland and head south-east for the Bay of Plenty. From there the route turns south and runs inland through the volcanic heart of the North Island; the main attractions are the Rotorua area, Lake Taupo and Tongariro National Park. It continues down the North Island to its southern tip, with the national capital, Wellington – the 'windy city', but one with many attractions. From there a ferry crosses the South Island and from Picton you turn west. The route runs via Nelson and the valley of the Buller River to the wilder west coast with its numerous sights, including the Franz Josef Glacier and the Fox Glacier. The coast road ends at Haast.

◄ Bungee jumping on the Waikato River

From Haast you cut through the Southern Alps and come to the lake district on their eastern slopes. Skirting Lake Wanaka and Lake Hawea, you reach Cromwell, a road junction and the road west to Queenstown. From there the route runs south to Lumsden, from which a detour to Milford Sound and Lake Manapouri is a must. Then continue to Invercargill, at the southern tip of the island, and follow Highway 1 to the Pacific coast and along the coast to Dunedin. You then continue northward up the coast to Christchurch, Blenheim and Picton, completing the circuit of the South Island.

### Auckland–Paihia (ca 240 km)
The starting point of the tour is ★★**Auckland**, a city of international standing that is known as the 'City of Sails'. From here Highway 1 runs north along the Hauraki Gulf into the **Northland** region, passing close to the little town of ★**Puhoi**, founded by immigrants from Bohemia. The road then continues to the industrial town of ★**Whangarei** with its large oil refinery and beautiful surroundings. Beyond this is the ★★**Bay of Islands**, the starting point of modern New Zealand. Features of interest are the old Maori settlements, whaling stations and mission stations such as *Paihia*, ★*Kerikeri* and ★*Russell*. At ★*Waitangi* the important treaty of 1840 was signed between the Europeans and the Maoris.

### Paihia–Cape Reinga–Kaitaia (ca 330 km)
From Paihia the road continues north-west to end at **Kaitaia**, from which a detour can be made along ★*Ninety Mile Beach* to ★*Cape Reinga*.

### Kaitaia–Auckland (ca 330 km)
After returning from Cape Reinga to Kaitaia take Highway 1, which runs south-east and at ★**Hokianga Harbour** bears south to Taheka, where you go on Highway 12. This runs west to the point where Hokianga Harbour opens into the Tasman Sea and then continues south, running parallel to the coast and through ★★**Waipou Kauri National Forest**, one of the last remnants of primeval forest, with its giant kauri trees. Further south is beautiful *Bayly's Beach*. Here too

# Suggested Routes

Grand Tour
NORTH ISLAND
Taranak Route
East Cape Route
Napier-Taupo Route
Urewera Route
SOUTH ISLAND
South Island alternative route
Tasman-Heaphy Route
Arthur's Pass Road

North Island

South Island

Tasman Sea

South Pacific Ocean

* Cape Reinga
** Bay of Islands
* Ninety Mile Beach
* Waitangi
* Waimate North
Kerikeri
** Russell
* Hokianga Harbour
Paihia
** Waipoua Kauri Forest
* Whangarei
Hauraki **
Puhoi
Great Barrier Island
* Kaipara Harbour
* Coromandel Peninsula
* Waiwera
** Auckland
Mayor Island
Pukekohe
** Waikato River
* Te Aroha
** Bay of Plenty
East Cape
* Hamilton
* Kawhia
Tauranga
** Urewera Nat. Park
** Waitomo Caves
** Rotorua
Waikei
* Gisborne
* New Plymouth
* Tongariro Nat. Park
Lake Waikaremoana
** Egmont Nat. Park
Wanganui River
Lake Taupo
** Napier
* Stratford
Hawke Bay
** Wanganui
* Cape Kidnappers
* Cape Farewell
** Marlborough Sounds
** Palmerston North
* Foxton
** Abel Tasman Nat. Park
* Kapiti Island
* Otaki
* Masterton
Castlepoint
Nelson
** Picton
Greytown
* Westport
Nelson Lakes Nat. Park
Lake Grassmere
** Wellington
Buller River
** Pancake Rocks
** Hanmer Springs
* Shantytown
** Arthur's Pass Nat. Park
* Kaikoura
** Franz Josef Glacier
Mt. Cook Nat. Park
** Fox Glacier
** Westland Nat. Park
* Christchurch
* Haast Pass Road
L. Tekapo
* Banks Peninsula
Lake Ohau
** Milford Sound
* Mt. Aspiring Nat. Park
L. Pukaki
* Timaru
* Peel Forest Park
** Fiordland Nat. Park
* Wanaka
Lindis Pass
Waitaki Valley
** Queenstown
* Arrowtown
* Lake Te Anau
* Clyde
* Alexandra
Moeraki Boulders
L. Manapouri
* Lawrence
Port Chalmers
** Dunedin
* Lake Hauroko
* Gore
* Invercargill
* Nugget Point
* Stewart Island
* Bluff

* major sights

** outstanding sights

© Baedeker

the little settlement of *Dargaville*, just off the road, is worth a visit. Beyond this Highway 12 comes to the drowned valley system of ★**Kaipara Harbour** and soon afterwards runs into Highway 1. This goes south to Welsford, from which Highway 16 provides an alternative route westward back to ★★**Auckland**.

### Auckland–Tauranga (ca 310 km)
From Auckland you set out on a journey through the hot heart of New Zealand. Highway 1 runs south to Pokeho, where you turn east and follow Highway 2 to the ★★**Coromandel Peninsula**, which can be explored in a round trip on Highway 25. The route then continues to the ★**Bay of Plenty** and the port of ★**Tauranga**, inland from which are extensive fruit plantations (particularly kiwi fruit) and forests.

### Tauranga–Rotorua (ca 90 km)
Beyond Te Puke, Highway 33 turns off and runs south into the geothermal region of ★★★**Rotorua**, where it converges with Highway 5. Here you must allow plenty of time to see the variety of post-volcanic phenomena – geysers, pools of boiling mud, hot springs. Also in the area are a number of well-preserved Maori villages.

### Rotorua–Taupo (ca 90 km)
South of Rotorua on Highway 5 is the geothermal area of ★★**Taupo/Wairakei**, including the large lake and a geothermal power station. To the north the ★**Waikato River**, now tamed, flows through romantic, wild gorges.

### Taupo–Tongariro National Park (ca 100 km)
A few kilometres south of Taupo, Highway 1 runs past ★★**Tongariro National Park**, a UNESCO World Heritage Site. In this mountainous region, marked by continuing volcanic activity, are the two volcanoes of Ruapehu and Ngauruhoe, both regarded as sacred by the Maoris . This is now a popular climbing and skiing area.

### Tongariro NP–Wellington (ca 350 km)
From Tongariro National Park, Highway 1 continues south via Foxton (near which is beautiful Foxton Beach) and Levin to ★★**Wellington**, New Zealand's capital, with numerous attractions.

### Wellington–Picton (ferry)
From Wellington a ferry crosses the Cook Strait into the beautiful ★★**Marlborough Sounds**, at the north-eastern tip of the South Island, and puts in at **Picton**.

### Picton–Nelson (ca 420 km)
From Picton the route runs west to the pleasant port of ★**Nelson**.

### Nelson–Greymouth (ca 300 km)
From Nelson there is a rewarding detour on the **Tasman–Heaphy Route** to the ★**Abel Tasman National Park**. The main route continues on Highway 6 through the valley of the ★**Buller River**, with its old gold-mining settlements, to its mouth at ★**Westport**. Highway 6 then runs south along the rugged west coast, worn by the fierce surf of the Tasman Sea. The first highlight is ★**Paparoa National Park**, with the layered ★★*Pancake Rocks*. A few kilometres south of ★**Greymouth** is the gold-diggers' settlement of ★*Shantytown* (restored), which preserves something of the atmosphere of the 19th c. gold rush.

### Greymouth–Franz Josef (ca 190 km)
Via ★**Hokitika**, where the Maoris quarried the desirable greenstone, and Ross, where gold was found, the road comes to ★**Westland National Park**, with its two principal sights, the ★★**Fox Glacier** and the ★★**Franz Josef Glacier**. These two great rivers of ice, many kilometres long, flow down from the névé fields of the Southern Alps to the evergreen rain forests on the coast.

### Franz Josef–Wanaka (ca 280 km)
The coastal section of Highway 6 ends at Haast, where it turns south-east, follows the Haast River upstream and cuts through the Southern Alps at the ★**Haast Pass**. It then winds southward between two glacier lakes, ★**Lake Wanaka** and ★*Lake Hawea*, towards Wanaka.

### Wanaka–Queenstown (ca 70–100 km)
From Wanaka it is possible, with an all-terrain vehicle, to take the direct route to ★**Arrowtown** and ★**Queenstown** on Highway 89. With a larger car or camper van (or RV) the easiest route is on Highway 6, which takes the long way round via ★*Cromwell*.

### Queenstown–Te Anau (ca 180 km)
Among the many sights round Queenstown are ★*Shotover Canyon*, ★*Lake Wakatipu* and the ★*Remarkables*. From Queenstown follow Highway 6, which runs south to Lumsden. From

here Highway 94 branches off and runs west to the beautiful ★★**Fiordland National Park**, with ★★**Lake Manapouri** and ★**Lake Te Anau**.

### Detour to Milford Sound (ca 240 km)

From Te Anau the road continues to ★★**Milford Sound**, which is sometimes claimed to be the epitome of New Zealand. Do not miss the Glow-worm Cave on Lake Te Anau and the impressive underground power station on Lake Manapouri.

### Te Anau–Invercargill (ca 160 km)

Returning to Te Anau, we continue south to ★**Invercargill**, from which a side trip can be made to the ★*Bluff aluminium smelter* and the beautiful ★**Stewart Island**, to the south.

### Invercargill–Dunedin (ca 260 km)

From Invercargill Highway 92 runs through beautiful scenery along the south-east coast through the ★**Catlins** region, passing a number of sights (Cathedral Cave, Nugget Point). At ★**Balclutha** it runs into Highway 1, which goes north-east to ★★**Dunedin**. From here you can detour to the Otago Peninsula (colonies of seals and seabirds), with ★*Larnach Castle*.

### Dunedin–Timaru (ca 200 km)

From Dunedin Highway 1 runs north along the Pacific coast to ★**Oamaru**, passing the imposing ★*Moeraki Boulders* and the old fishing port of ★*Moeraki*. It then continues by way of *Waitaki* to ★**Timaru**, from which excursions can be made to ★*Peel Forest Park* at *Geraldine* and to the rock paintings near the hamlet of *Cave*.

### Timaru–Christchurch (ca 170 km)

The road then runs over the Canterbury Plains, with the little town of ★**Ashburton**, and finally comes to ★★**Christchurch**, capital of the South Island. From here you can visit the ★**Banks Peninsula**, with the two natural harbours of ★*Lyttelton* and ★*Akaroa*.

### Christchurch–Kaikoura (ca 300 km)

From Christchurch Highway 1 runs north-east to Culverden, from which a detour can be made to ★**Hammer Springs**. The route then continues to ★**Kaikoura**, located at the foot of the Kaikoura Range. From here a whale-watching trip is a must.

### Kaikoura–Picton (ca 200 km)

From Kaikoura the road runs north-east to ★*Lake Grassmere*, where salt is produced from the waters of the lagoon, and the famous wine-growing region round the attractive little town of ★**Blenheim**. The tour of the South Island can be concluded with a trip round the Marlborough Sounds (see above).

## Taranaki route (North Island; ca 1000 km)

This alternative to the main route on the North Island runs from Auckland to Wellington, via the Waikato River area, Hamilton and the western tip of the island, with the volcano of Taranaki.

### Route

From Auckland the road runs south, passing through the river landscape of the **Waikato River**, to ★**Hamilton**. It then comes into the **Northland** region, the highlight of which is the karstic ★★**Te Kuiti/Waitomo Caves** area, with the world-famous Glow-worm Cave. Further south-west is the port of **New Plymouth**, under the north side of the volcano of ★★**Taranaki** (Mount Taranaki or Egmont), the central feature of Mount Egmont National Park; a scenic road runs round the volcano. From **Hawera**, under the south side of Taranaki, the road runs along the coast to ★**Wanganui**, from which a rewarding excursion can be made northwards to ★★**Whanganui National Park**. The road then goes via *Foxton* and **Levin** to ★★**Wellington**.

## East Cape route (North Island; ca 1300 km)

This alternative to the main route on the east side of the North Island runs from Auckland to the Bay of Plenty, circles the East Cape and continues via Gisborne to Hawke's Bay, with the art-deco town of Napier. It then turns inland via Hastings, Dannevirke and Masterton to Wellington. On the tour there are two possible detours into the volcanic heart of the North Island, the Urewera Route and the Napier–Taupo Route.

### Route

From Auckland the route runs south-east to the ★**Bay of Plenty**, with the towns of ★**Tauranga** and ★*Whakatane* and the old

Maori settlement of *Opotiki*. If time allows, there is a rewarding excursion to two offshore islands with good bathing – ★*Mayor Island* and the volcanic ★*White Island*.

The route then continues to the ★**East Cape**, the most easterly point on the North Island, where it turns south for ★**Gisborne/Poverty Bay**. An excursion can be made from Gisborne to the *Mahia Peninsula*, to the south. In ★**Hawke's Bay** is the little town of *Wairoa*, from which the **Urewera Route** (180 km) runs north-west through the ★**Urewera National Park** to the volcanic ★★**Rotorua** area. At the south end of Hawke's Bay is the town of ★★**Napier**, from which the **Napier–Taupo Route** (150 km) runs north-west to the thermal area of ★★**Taupo/Wairakei**.

From Napier the route turns inland through a region of kiwi plantations and vineyards, via ★**Hastings** and **Dannevirke**, to **Masterton**, at the foot of the ★*Tararua Range*. Then via *Greytown*, *Upper Hutt* and *Lower Hutt* to ★★**Wellington**.

## Alternative route on South Island (ca 700 km)

This alternative route from Invercargill to Christchurch through the interior of the southern half of the South Island takes in the Otago region and the Mackenzie Country as well as the grand mountains of the Mount Cook National Park and the Canterbury region.

**Route**
From Invercargill the route runs north via *Gore* into the uplands of **Otago** and on to **Alexandra**, from which there are two possibilities: a round trip in the footsteps of the gold prospectors or a visit to the *Clutha Hydroelectric Scheme*. The route then continues north via ★*Cromwell* and over the ★*Lindis Pass* into ★**Mackenzie Country**. From ★*Twizel* an excursion to ★**Lake Pukaki** and ★★**Mount Cook National Park** is a must. From Twizel Highway 8 runs north-east past ★**Lake Takepo** and over *Burke's Pass*

to *Fairlie* and *Geraldine*. From there the route follows Highway 72 to ★**Peel Forest Park**, then to *Erewhon* and *Mesopotamia* and on to ★★**Christchurch**.

## Arthur's Pass road (South Island; ca 260 km)

This route cuts through the South Island from east to west between Christchurch and Greymouth, passing magnificent scenery. The trip can also be done by rail (TraNZAlpine Express).

**Route**
From Christchurch Highway 73 runs north-west and at Springfield reaches the eastern foothills of the Southern Alps. It then climbs steadily to the watershed at ★**Arthur's Pass**, in the centre of ★★*Arthur's Pass National Park*. Beyond the pass the road runs down into the wild ★*Otira Canyon*. It then follows the Otira River to its mouth, at the reconstructed gold-diggers' settlement of ★*Shantytown*, and finally comes to an end at ★*Greymouth*.

## Scenic Touring Routes

A number of scenic or culturally interesting routes have recently been marked as Scenic Touring Routes. The **Twin Coast Discovery Highway** at the northernmost tip of the North Island runs through spectacular kauri forests and past beautiful bathing beaches. The **Pacific Coast Highway** in the east of the North Island goes from Auckland to Napier and the Bay of Plenty and on to the Coromandel Peninsula. Also on the North Island is the **Thermal Explorer Highway**, which runs from Napier to the Taupo volcanic region and Mount Ruapehu. The **Southern Scenic Route** on the South Island starts from Dunedin in Fiordland National Park. In addition over 100 **Heritage Trails** lead to the main cultural sights in New Zealand. Details can be obtained at local tourist offices (☛Practical Information, Information).

# Sights from A to Z
# North Island

To make it easier to locate the places listed in the Sights from A to Z section of the guide, their coordinates on the fold-out map are shown at the head of each entry.

## Auckland                                    J 3

**Region: Auckland**
**Population: 910,000 (conurbation over 1 million)**

Auckland lies on a narrow isthmus, occupied by numerous volcanic cones, between Manukau Harbour and Waitemata Harbour. The 260 m high volcanic island of Rangitoto separates Waitemata Harbour from the wide expanse of the Hauraki Gulf with its scattering of islands. To the south-west are the Waitakere Ranges.

Since its foundation over 150 years ago the city has extended far to north and south. In 1891 Rudyard Kipling called Auckland 'last, loneliest, loveliest, exquisite, apart'; but today it is hard to see any boundary between the city and the surrounding country. Villages that were once a long way from the town are now suburbs and outlying districts of the city with their own shopping and administrative centres. Outside the city centre, the central business district of Auckland, the residential areas follow the usual New Zealand pattern of detached family houses with small gardens.

### Population
About a third of the population of New Zealand live on this narrow land bridge. As the principal gateway into New Zealand, it is often called the capital of Polynesia because of the high proportion of its inhabitants of Polynesian origin. This concentration of population in a relatively small area has given rise to serious problems in recent years. There are great difficulties, for example, in providing an adequate water supply.

### City of Sails
Auckland is known as the 'City of Sails' because of its inhabitants' passion for boats. On fine summer days the Hauraki Gulf is covered with sailing boats. Statistics show that one household in four owns a boat. In 1995 a New Zealand team won the **America's Cup**, so when it came to preparing for the Louis Vuitton and America's Cup in Waitemata Harbour in the year 2000 enthusiasm was high.

### History
In Maori tradition the neck of land between the Tasman Sea and the South Pacific was originally settled by descendants of the Marama-Kikihura tribe. After numerous tribal feuds over the possession of this area of fertile volcanic soil the Kiwi Tamaki tribe prevailed in the early 18th c. and established a fortified settlement (*pa*) on One Tree Hill. There were similar settlements on many of the other volcanic cones on the isthmus. But when in the course of a burial ceremony in Kaipara Harbour (north of Auckland) the chief of the tribe killed a number of other guests he himself was overthrown and killed, his stronghold was destroyed and many of his warriors were enslaved.

When the first European and American whalers landed in the Bay of Islands the Ngapuhi tribes of the Northland region, led by Hongi Hika, were quick to equip themselves with weapons and moved south on campaigns of conquest, killing and driving out the local tribes, until the Auckland area was almost completely depopulated. Diseases brought in by the settlers also took a heavy toll among the native population. In 1840, when British sovereignty was recognised in the Treaty of Waitangi, Governor Hobson, seeking a central site as the seat of administration of the colony, chose the isthmus because of its good communications and safe harbour. In what is now Albert Park, between the city centre and the university, the Albert Barracks were built to house a garrison of 1000 men. Unlike the other three large New Zealand cities (Wellington, Christchurch and Dunedin), Auckland was not founded as a planned new town, with whole

The 'City of Sails' lies on the natural harbour of Waitemata

shiploads of immigrants. It was originally occupied by government officials, traders and craftsmen, and the first Scottish immigrants arrived only in 1842. William Hobson, the first independent governor of the new colony, was a sick man, and the Colonial Office in London failed to supply him with either the troops or the financial resources he needed. He was derided by the New Zealand Land Company because he had chosen Auckland as his capital and because he did not give them all the help they wanted in purchasing land for their new settlements. He died in 1842.

The real father of Auckland was John Logan Campbell (1817–1912), one of the first European settlers in the Auckland area. Coming to New Zealand from Edinburgh at the age of 21, he and his partner William Brown established a large farm on One Tree Hill. He was involved also in setting up banks, insurance companies and shipping lines, and was a powerful impetus in the development of the town as its mayor.

To protect the town against Maori raids the government built a chain of defendable settlements in the south occupied by troops, for example at Howick, Onehunga, Panmure and Otahuhu. When the land wars broke out in Taranaki in 1860 there was some apprehension that the conflict might spread to the capital, but the fighting took place further south and Auckland was left in peace.

After the discovery of gold on the South Island Auckland became of less importance and in 1865 the capital was transferred to Wellington. The town took on a fresh lease of life, however, when gold was found on the nearby Coromandel Peninsula and agriculture flourished in the country south of Auckland. Later industrial development and the town's favourable situation for trade and communications gave its economy a further boost.

### Name

Governor Hobson, founder of the town, named it after his former commander, then governor general of India, the Earl of Auckland (1784–1849).

### Transport

Auckland's international airport is 23 km

south-west of the city centre on Manukau Harbour.

From the city there are trains to Wellington (the Overlander; 10½ hours) and Rotorua (the Geyserland; 4 hours).

The road system in and around Auckland is excellent. Roads of motorway standard run through the city in all directions.

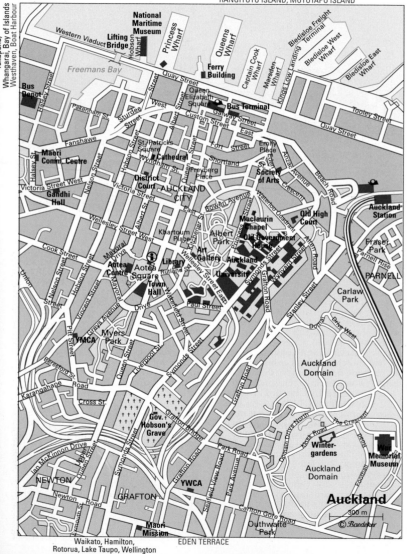

RANGITOTO ISLAND, MOTUTAPU ISLAND

Takapuna, Whangarei, Bay of Islands Westhaven, Boat Harbour

Western Viaduct
Lifting Bridge
National Maritime Museum
Princess Wharf
Queens Wharf
Captain Cook Wharf
Marsden Wharf
Kings Low Landing
Bledisloe Freight Terminal
Bledisloe West Wharf
Bledisloe East Wharf
Freemans Bay
Hobson Wharf
Quay Street
Ferry Building
Bus Depot
Halsey Street
Pakenham St.
Sturdee Street
West Street
Queen Elizabeth Square
Custom Street
Galway Street
Bus Terminal
Quay Street
Tooley Street
Fanshawe Street
Maori Comm. Centre
Nelson Street
Hobson Street
Albert Street
St. Patricks Square
Wyndham St.
Cathedral
Custom Street East
Fort Street
Shortland
Emily Place
Eden Crescent
Anzac Avenue
Beach Road
Victoria Street West
Gandhi Hall
District Court
Victoria Street
AUCKLAND CITY
Freyberg Place
Society of Arts
Albert Street East
Bowen Avenue
Waterloo Quadrant
Old High Court
Auckland Station
Cook Street
Wellesley Street West
Mayoral Drive
Khartoum Place
Albert Park
Maclaurin Chapel
Old Government House
Princes Street
Alten Road
Fraser Park
Parnell Rise
Union Street
Nelson Street
Hobson Street
Mayoral Drive
Aotea Centre
Library
Art Gallery
Wellesley Street East
Rutland St.
Auckland University
Symonds Street
Wynyard Street
Stanley Street
PARNELL
Carlaw Park
Town Hall
Vincent Street
Airedale Street
Paul Street
Grafton Road
Domain Drive West
Pitt Street
Graves Avenue
YMCA
Myers Park
Queen Street
Liverpool St.
Symonds Street
Auckland Domain
Beresford St.
Karangahape Road
Cross St.
Gov. Hobson's Grave
Grafton Bridge
Park Road
Domain Drive North
The Crescent
Knox Road
Winter-gardens
War Memorial Museum
Ian McKinnon Drive
Queen Street
Symonds Street
NEWTON
Newton Road
GRAFTON
YWCA
Seafield View Road
Park Avenue
Auckland Domain
Outhwaite Park
Carlton Gore Road
Football
Auckland
300 m
© Baedeker
Maori Mission
EDEN TERRACE

Waikato, Hamilton, Rotorua, Lake Taupo, Wellington

## Events

The Auckland Anniversary Regatta on the last weekend in January commemorates the foundation of the city. At this time of the year there are open-air concerts in Domain Park. The great Harbour Festival is held in February. At the end of March the Round the Bays Fun Run attracts tens of thousands of runners.

## Sightseeing

The attractive Waterfront Walk (7 km) runs eastward through the city from the Chief Post Office to Mission Bay. For good walkers there is the Coast to Coast Walkway (13 km), which runs from the Ferry Building at the end of Queen Street to Domain Park and on by way of Mount Eden to One Tree Hill, ending at Manukau Harbour.

A good way to see the main sights is from the Explorer Bus, which departs from the Ferry Building hourly 10am–4pm. It runs clockwise round the city, stopping at Mission Bay Beach, Kelly Tarlton's Underwater World, Rose Park Gardens (Parnell), Auckland War Memorial Museum (Domain Park; connection to Zoo), Parnell Village, Custom Street (central business district), Victoria Park Market and Hobson Wharf. Passengers can get off and on again at any of the stops.

Buses leave from The Link several times daily, stopping at Symonds Street, New Market, Parnell, Railway Station, Mid Queen Street, Casino, Victoria Park, Ponsonby Road, K' Road, Myers Park, the library and the university; trips cost NZ$1 regardless of direction or distance.

# Sights in the city centre

## Waitemata Harbour

Round the wide sweep of Waitemata Harbour extends the central business district of Auckland with its high-rise skyline. The harbour is enlivened by passenger ships and freighters and by innumerable sailing boats.

## Harbour Bridge

The harbour is spanned by a bridge more than 1 km long and some 43 m high; the steel central arch is 243 m long. The bridge was completed in 1959 and widened 10 years later. The northern districts of the city and the beautiful

bathing beaches and bays on the north side of the harbour are easily reached.

## Quay Street

Along the harbour runs busy Quay Street, on which, and on the adjoining Princess Wharf, are the popular dockside markets and the Oriental Market. The markets are held daily in summer and from Friday to Sunday in winter.

## Microworld

At Microworld (23 Quay Street) you can see the 'little things of life' – for example, the surface forms of rocks and minerals, tiny insects and other creatures – through microscopes.
Ⓖ *Daily 9am–6pm.*

## ★ New Zealand Maritime Museum

On Hobson Wharf, at the north-west end of Quay Street, is the New Zealand Maritime Museum, offering a comprehensive survey of the history of seafaring in New Zealand. The exhibits include Maori canoes and outrigger boats, whaling equipment and old instruments and implements. A section is devoted to New Zealand yachts that have distinguished themselves in

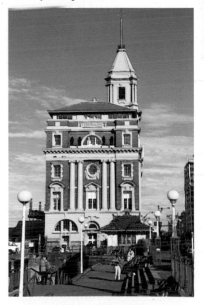

The Ferry Building

Auckland Town Hall

international regattas. The exhibition includes the yacht in which a New Zealand crew skippered by Sir Peter Blake won the America's Cup in 1995.
*Ⓘ Daily 10am–5pm, Sat. and Sun. in summer to 9pm.*

### ★Ferry Building
The imposing Ferry Building at the junction of Queen Street with Quay Street, with its fine restaurant, forms a striking landmark on the harbour front. Built in English Baroque style of brick and sandstone on a base of Coromandel granite, it was completed in 1912 to the design of Alexander Wiseman.

### Chief Post Office
Adjoining the Ferry Building is the Chief Post Office, an imposing building of 1911 designed by John Campbell.

### Downtown shopping centre
Beyond the Chief Post Office is the largest shopping mall in the city centre.

### Customs House
To the south-west of the Chief Post Office is the richly decorated French Empire-style Customs House (1889 by Thomas Mahoney). Originally occupied

by officers of the armed forces and later by the customs authorities, it now houses various cultural institutions and shops.

### ★Queen Street (Mall)
The city's busy main artery and show street is Queen Street, along which numerous high-rise office blocks occupied by banks, insurance companies and commercial firms have mushroomed. Between the Ferry Building and K' Road (see below) are department stores, shops and restaurants. There is a variety architecture in this area, with imposing colonial-period buildings rubbing shoulders with art-nouveau, art-deco and modern buildings.

### Vulcan Lane
Off Queen Street, on the left, is Vulcan Lane, a little street with many cafés that is particularly busy at lunch time and in the evening.

### St Patrick's Cathedral
To the west of lower Queen Street, at the corner of Hobson Street and Wyndham Street, is St Patrick's Cathedral (1848; RC), one of the oldest churches in New Zealand. It has a beautiful tabernacle presented by the Maoris to Bishop Pompallier, who held the first Roman Catholic service in New Zealand in 1838.

### ★Sky Tower
West of Queen Street is the 328 m Sky Tower, which is the new symbol of the city. From the viewing platform and revolving restaurant there is a magnificent panorama. Around the tower are grouped the buildings of **Sky City**, a postmodern complex with a casino, a luxury hotel and several restaurants.
*Ⓘ Daily 9am–10pm.*

### St Matthew's Church
In Wellesley Street, also to the west of Queen Street, is St Matthew's Church (1902; Anglican).

### ★Auckland Town Hall
Further south along Queen Street, at the intersection with Grey's Avenue, is Auckland Town Hall (1911 by the Clark brothers) with its imposing tower. The facade is of Oamaru marble, the base of Melbourne bluestone.

### Aotea Centre
To the right of the town hall is the Aotea Centre, New Zealand's largest concert hall. The low building was designed by the leading architect E Wainscott, apparently influenced by Aalto's Finlandia Hall in Helsinki. The construction of the building was subject to much delay and controversy, and it was only completed in 1990. In Aotea Place is a statue of the Earl of Auckland, after whom the city is named.

### Karangahape Road
On the southern fringe of the city centre Karangahape Road, familiarly known as K' Road, cuts across Queen Street. It is particularly busy on Friday evenings when the shops stay open until 10pm; a colourful touch is added by the many South Sea islanders who congregate here.

### Albert Park
East of the middle section of Queen Street is Albert Park, with its fine mature trees. This was the site of the first barracks built in Auckland.

### Auckland University
In the eastern half of the park are various institutes belonging to Auckland's renowned university. The university church, St Andrew's, was built in 1849.

### ★★Auckland City Art Gallery
The Auckland City Art Gallery, at the south-east corner of Albert Park (entrance at corner of Kitchener Street and Wellesley Street East), is a must. This impressive building, with towers and high pitched roofs in French Renaissance style, was designed by the Melbourne firm of Grainger and D'Ebro and built in 1887. It houses the famous Grey Gallery, a surprisingly rich collection of old European and contemporary New Zealand art, including works by McCahon and Wollaston. The earliest New Zealand works date from the time of Captain Cook, some of whose companions painted remarkable views of different parts of New Zealand.

There are numerous oil paintings by the Czech artist Gottfried Lindauer (1839–1926), noted for his marvellous portraits of Maoris.

The gallery also puts on spectacular exhibitions.

🅖 *Daily 10am–4.30pm; conducted tours Wed.–Sun. from 2pm.*

### Old Government House
Old Government House is a timber neoclassical building (1856 by William Mason). After the transfer of the capital of the colony to Wellington in 1865 it served as a summer residence for the governor and a guest house for important visitors. It now belongs to Auckland University.

### Old Synagogue
Opposite Old Government House is the Old Synagogue (1884 by Edward Bartley), now used for small-scale cultural events (concerts, drama).

### High Court
The High Court (1868) on Waterloo Quadrant, a richly decorated brick building complete with turrets and gargoyles, was modelled on Warwick Castle. A modern annex housing the district appeal court spoils the effect of the older building.

## West side of city centre

### Victoria Park Market
On the west side of the city centre, occupying the site of a power station (1908) fuelled with refuse, is the extensive Victoria Park Market, which sells fruit and vegetables and other goods. It also offers pleasant restaurants and pubs and a variety of entertainment. Nearby is Victoria Park, laid out in 1905.

### Ponsonby
The Ponsonby district to the west of the city centre retains, particularly in Renall Street, a number of small 19th c. houses, once occupied by workers in the nearby harbour. They are now much sought after as town houses. The Post Office (1912 by John Campbell) is a striking building in English baroque style.

## Auckland Domain

To the south-east of the city centre is the Auckland Domain, an extensive recreation area with various leisure facilities and sports grounds.

### ★★Auckland Institute and Museum (War Memorial Museum)
On the highest point in the Domain is the imposing War Memorial Museum. From the steps in front of the museum

there are magnificent views over the city centre and Waitemata Harbour.

This neoclassical building was erected in 1929 as a memorial to the New Zealand soldiers who fell in the first world war and to house the collections of the Auckland Museum, originally established in 1852. Extensions were added in the 1960s.

The War Memorial Hall commemorates the dead of all the wars in which New Zealand soldiers fought.

The museum itself contains rich collections of material on the natural and cultural history of the south Pacific and the history of the city of Auckland.

The Maori Court, a richly decorated meeting house of 1878, came from the Thames region. The magnificent Maori doorway came from Rotorua. There is also a fine storehouse with carved decoration. Of particular note is a 25 m long canoe dating from about 1836, in which Maori warriors once sailed in Manukau Harbour. There are also fine portraits of Maori chiefs by CF Goldie.

On the first floor are collections of geology, natural history, flora and fauna (particularly birds and marine mammals, including a reconstruction of a giant moa) and the seafaring history of New Zealand. Also of interest are craft products (silver, ceramics, glass), old furniture and coins.

Attached to the museum is a popular planetarium.

*Mon.–Sat. 10am–5pm (in winter to 4.15pm), Sun. 11am–5pm; performances of Maori dances daily at 11.15am, 1.30pm, preceded by guided tours of the Maori collection.*

### Winter Gardens
Close by are the Winter Gardens (glasshouses – tropical and cold), built for the Auckland Exhibition of 1913. They are now part of Auckland's Botanic Gardens.

## Parnell

### Old district
To the east of the city centre, extending to Hobson Bay, is the old district of Parnell. It retains many Victorian buildings, which in recent years have been lovingly restored. Tourists fill the nostalgic old shops (in particular craft shops) and restaurants along Parnell Road.

### ★Kinder House
At the near end of Ayr Street (No. 2; under the east side of the Auckland Domain) is the house of John Kinder, a clergyman who came to Auckland in 1855 and who also made a name for himself as a painter and photographer. The building was built for Kinder in 1856–7 by Frederick Thatcher, the architect who did much work for Bishop Selwyn. It now houses a collection of views of Auckland by Kinder.
*Daily 10.30am–4pm.*

### Ewelme Cottage
Ewelme Cottage, at 14 Ayr Street, was built in 1863–4 for the first clergyman in Howick to his own design.
*Daily 10.30am–noon, 1–4.30pm.*

### ★St Stephen's Chapel
It was in this little wooden chapel near Point Resolution, built by Frederick Thatcher in 1856–7, that the constitution of the Anglican church in New Zealand was adopted. The chapel looks out on Judges Bay. The churchyard contains the graves of many townspeople and soldiers of Auckland's early days.

### Selwyn Court
Also in the Parnell district (St Stephen's Avenue/Parnell Road) is a church-like building with a tower (1863 by Frederick Thatcher) built to house Bishop Selwyn's library. Beside this building, now used for meetings, is the bishop's residence.

### ★St Mary's Pro-Cathedral
Adjoining Selwyn Court, in Parnell Road, is St Mary's Pro-Cathedral (1888 by BW Mountfort; Anglican), in neo-Gothic style. This wooden building, one of the largest of its kind in the world, was originally on the other side of the street but was moved in 1982 to its present site beside the new Holy Trinity Cathedral.

### Rose Garden
From the Rose Garden, which is a sea of blossom from November to March, there is a fine view of Auckland Harbour.

## Outer districts

### Mount Eden
This 196 m high volcanic cone (called after the Earl of Auckland's family name) on the south side of the city, from which

**Auckland Museum**

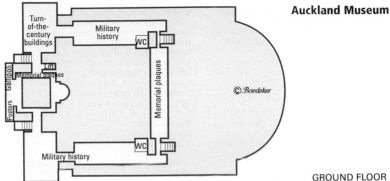

GROUND FLOOR

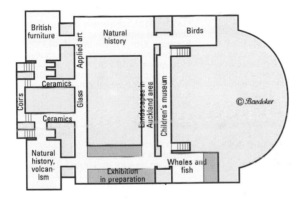

FIRST FLOOR

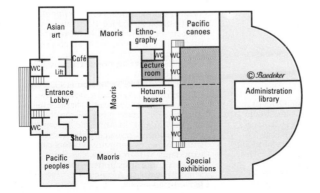

SECOND FLOOR

there are fine views of the surrounding area, was the most southerly point of the site acquired from the Maoris in 1840 for the building of the new capital. There are slight traces of the Maori fortifications, which may date from the 16th c. Nearby is Eden Garden, with fine mature trees.

### Highwic House
Near Mount Eden, in the Epsom district (Gillies Avenue), is Highwic House, rebuilt in 1862 in a 'carpenter's Gothic' style and later enlarged. It belonged to a landowner named Alfred Buckland and remained in his family until 1978. It is now a museum.
ⓖ *Daily 10.30am–noon, 1–4.30pm.*

### ★ One Tree Hill
Further south is another volcanic cone, One Tree Hill (183 m), one of the city's finest viewpoints. At the top are the ramparts of a Maori *pa* (17th–18th c.) that once occupied the site and could accommodate up to 4000 people. On the highest point of the hill there once stood a sacred totara tree, which was ruthlessly felled by the first European settlers.

John Logan Campbell, the true founder of Auckland (☛History; above), established a large farm on One Tree Hill in the late 1830s. On the occasion of a royal visit in 1901 he presented much of his land to the nation as **Cornwall Park**.

### Acacia Cottage
In Cornwall Park is Auckland's oldest surviving building, Acacia Cottage, which was built by John Campbell in 1841. When he died at a great age in 1912 he was buried on the summit of One Tree Hill. Beside his grave is an obelisk recording his respect for the Maoris and their achievements.

### Auckland Observatory
Also on One Tree Hill is Auckland Observatory.
ⓖ *Guided tours by appointment.*

### Ellerslie Racecourse
Ellerslie Racecourse lies in 12 ha of parkland under the west side of One Tree Hill. It is the venue for New Zealand's major horse races and there is also a small museum on the history of racing.

### Alberton House
Alberton House (100 Mount Albert Road), a two-storey mansion on the slopes of Mount Albert, in the south-west of the city, was built in 1862; a ballroom and other apartments were added in 1870 by Allan Kerr Taylor, a landowner who had become rich during the gold boom. Attractive features are the corner turrets and the verandas running round three sides of the building. It is set in beautiful gardens.
ⓖ *Daily 10.30am–noon, 1–4.30pm.*

### Mount Albert
On Mount Albert itself there are slight remains of Maori fortifications.

### ★★ Museum of Transport and Technology (MOTAT)
This museum, in the Western Springs district (Great North Road), is devoted to the history of technology and transport in New Zealand. Its prize exhibits relate to the aviation pioneer Richard Pearse (1877–1953), who made his first flights about the same time as the Wright brothers. Other items include old coaches, railway rolling stock, trams and vintage cars, collections of material on printing, photography and calculating machines. Between the museum and the nearby zoo runs an old-time tram.
ⓖ *Daily 9am–5pm.*

### Auckland Zoo
Also in Western Springs is Auckland Zoo, set in spacious grounds. A popular attraction is the Nocturnal House, where kiwis can be seen grubbing for worms – one of the few places in New Zealand where these shy creatures can be seen.

### ★★ Kelly Tarlton's Underwater World
East of Hobson Bay, in the Orakei district (Tamaki Drive, Orakei Wharf) is Kelly Tarlton's Underwater World, a popular tourist attraction since 1985. Visitors walk in long acrylic tunnels through huge tanks in which they can observe large numbers of fish of all sizes, including sharks and rays. There is a display devoted to the underwater explorations of Kelly Tarlton (1935–85), in the course of which he studied the marine fauna of the south Pacific and investigated wrecks lying off the coasts of New Zealand. In Antarctic Encounter, a reconstructed research station with a small colony of penguins, visitors can experience within a Snow Cat the difficult conditions under which scientists work in Antarctica.
ⓖ *Daily 9am–9pm.*

**Howick**
23 km east of Auckland, beautifully located on the Hauraki Gulf, is Howick (pop. 15,000), an outlying suburb of the city. It was founded in 1847 as part of the chain of defendable settlements established by Governor Grey to protect the new town of Auckland on the south.

**★Howick Colonial Village**
The defended settlement, with its well-preserved houses, is protected as a national monument and is now an open-air museum. Of particular note is All Saints Church (1847), which, like almost all the churches built in Bishop Selwyn's time, was designed by Frederick Thatcher. The nave was widened in 1862. The old churchyard has graves of early settlers. Other buildings of interest are the Courthouse (1848) and Bell House (1852), now occupied by a restaurant.
🕐 *Daily 10am–4pm.*

**Otara**
20 km south-east of the city centre is the Otara district, with a Polynesian market where visitors can feel something of the atmosphere of the South Seas. On the main square and in the community house there are colourful displays, particularly on Saturday mornings, of foodstuffs, clothing and arts and crafts.

**★Devonport**
North-east of the city centre, beyond Waitemata Harbour, is the exclusive residential suburb of Devonport with its elegant villas and carefully tended gardens. This is very much a holiday place, with an active beach life, a yacht marina and expensive boutiques. Devonport also affords the finest view of the Auckland skyline.

**Naval Museum**
The Naval Museum in Devonport on the north side of Waitemata Harbour (Spring Street) illustrates the history of the Royal New Zealand Navy. The collection includes uniforms, medals, ships' bells, ships in bottles and much else.
🕐 *Daily 10am–4.30pm.*

**Pavilions of New Zealand**
The Pavilions of New Zealand, which attracted great interest at the International Exhibition in Brisbane in 1988, have been re-erected in Montgomery Road, near the airport.

They now house exhibitions on the mythology, history and environment of New Zealand.

## Beaches

Due to its situation between two ramified natural **harbours** Auckland has many beautiful beaches. Particularly popular are the beaches on the north side of Waitemata Harbour between Cheltenham and Long Bay. The best beaches are at Takapuna and Milford.

**West coast**
There are some very beautiful beaches on the west coast, but with their sheer rocks, heavy surf from the stormy Tasman Sea and treacherous undertow they are dangerous for bathers. The following beaches are recommended for good swimmers: the beach at Piha (40 km west), Karekare Beach, White's Beach, Bethell's Beach and the beach at Whatipu, at the entrance to Manukau Harbour.

**Hauraki Gulf**
There are a number of good bathing beaches in Hauraki Gulf. Among the most popular are the beaches on the Whangaparaoa Peninsula (40 km on Highway 1) and at Orewa and Waiwera.

## Excursions

**★Tamaki Drive**
Tamaki Drive, starting from the Ferry Building, runs for 10 km past beautiful stretches of Waitemata Harbour to Judges Bay, below Parnell Park. It then cuts across Hobson Bay to Ohaku Bay, where many leisure craft and yachts are moored. In Orakei a *marae* constructed jointly by Maoris and whites and a meeting house can be visited.

On Bastion Point, further east, there are remains of defensive structures. Some years ago there was a major conflict over land rights between the Maoris and the government when land claimed by the Maoris was to be sold for building luxury houses. Finally in 1988 the government decided to give the land back and pay compensation.

On the point is the grave of Michael Joseph Savage (1872–1940), a very popular Labour prime minister. A commemorative column stands out

The Hauraki Gulf with its many islands is within easy reach of Auckland

against the triple volcanic peak on Rangitoto Island lying offshore from the point.

Then comes Mission Bay, with its beautiful and bathing beach. The mission station founded by Bishop Selwyn is now a restaurant. An exclusive residential district has grown up round the bay.

Tamaki Drive ends at Achilles Point, at the east end of Heliers Bay, where a tablet commemorates the cruiser *Achilles*, which in 1939, along with two other warships, sank the German battleship *Graf Spee*.

### ★Auckland Wine Trail

The Auckland Wine Trail takes in some of the best-known wineries in New Zealand at Henderson (ca 20 km west) and Kumeu (ca 25 km north-west), where visitors are shown round the establishment and can taste the wines. The winegrowers are mainly Dalmatians whose ancestors came to New Zealand to prospect for kauri gum.

### Waitakere Ranges

The green hills of the Waitakere Ranges, south-west of Auckland, are a popular recreation area. A particular attraction is the Auckland Centennial Park (64 sq km), to the south of the area. An information bureau 5 km west of Titirangi provides details about the flora of the region, particularly the last stands of kauri trees in this area.

### West coast

There are some very attractive spots on the rugged west coast, its rocks lashed by the surf of the Tasman Sea, including the beaches at Piha (40 km west of Auckland). Piha and Karekare are also good starting points for walks in the Waitakere Ranges, with their masses of green ferns. Further north is beautiful Muriwai Beach, where colonies of gannets from the offshore islands have established themselves.

## Hauraki Gulf

The Hauraki Gulf, enclosed by Northland, the city of Auckland and the long northward-reaching Coromandel Peninsula, is scattered with numerous islands and islets. The gulf is a favourite sailing area and also offers good fishing.

### Hauraki Gulf Maritime Park
Much of the gulf and some of the islands are included in Hauraki Gulf Maritime Park, which is home to numerous endegared species of birds, insects and marine creatures. A special permit is usually necessary to visit the islands, and then only on a day trip.

### ★★Hauraki Gulf islands
There are boat trips to some of the islands in the gulf, particularly Rangitoto, Waikehe and Pakatoa.

### Rangitoto
This volcanic island was likely still active at the time of the Polynesian settlement of New Zealand, for there are no remains of any fortified Maori settlements. This beautiful island with its rolling hills, lying directly off Waitemata Harbour, was purchased by the government in 1857 and ever since has been a popular excursion. From the highest point on the island (260 m) there are marvellous panoramas. Rangitoto is now a nature reserve and part of Hauraki Gulf Maritime Park. There is a ferry service from Auckland.

### Waiheke
Waiheke, a popular holiday island, is densely populated, with over 5000 inhabitants, many of who commute daily to work in Auckland. In the north of the island there are a number of beautiful beaches (Oneroa, Palm Beach, Onetangi).

### Pakatoa
East of Waiheke is the small island of Pakatoa, also popular for holidays.

### Motuihe
Motuihe (area 180 ha), lying within easy reach of Auckland, attracts many people from the city on day trips. During the first world war there was a camp for internees and prisoners of war on the island. One of the prisoners was Count Felix von Luckner (☛Famous People), who made a daring escape from the camp during a Christmas party, seized the camp commandant's yacht and, sailing under the German flag, got as far as the Kermadec Islands before being recaptured.

### Kawau
Further north is Kawau. This island, on which copper was once mined, was purchased in 1862 for £3700 by Governor Grey, who converted the mine manager's house into a mansion for himself, surrounding it with a kind of Garden of Eden containing exotic plants and animals. The house, restored and furnished in period style, can be visited. There are boat services to Sandspit and Snells Beach.

### Great Barrier Island
Great Barrier Island (area 28,000 ha; pop. 600) was so named by Captain Cook because it barred the entrance to the gulf. Once inhabited by loggers felling kauri trees, gold prospectors and copper miners, the island is now largely pasture for sheep and dairy cattle. At the end of the 19th c. letters were conveyed from the island to the mainland by carrier pigeon.

### Little Barrier Island
Now a strictly controlled nature reserve, Little Barrier Island is a refuge for rare species of birds and plants.
You can only visit the island with special permission from the Department of Conservation.

### Goat Island
This tiny islet (9 ha) lies just north of Cape Rodney. On the island is the Marine Biology Research Institute of Auckland University.

### Tiritiri Matangi
The little island of Tiritiri Matangi (207 ha) lies off Whangaparaoa and has a lighthouse. Formerly grazing land, it is now a nature reserve, to which natural forest is gradually returning. There is a good sandy beach, but apart from this the coast is extremely steep. The island can be visited only during the day.

### Motukorea (Brown Island)
This island, an eroded cone of volcanic lava and scoria, lies immediately off the mouth of the Tamaki River next to Auckland. John Logan Campbell and William Brown established their first farm here before moving to One Tree Hill in Auckland. The island is part of the Hauraki Gulf Maritime Park and can be visited only during the day. A landing should be attempted only at high tide, since at other times there may be dangerous shallows.

## Waiwera

Just under 50 km north of Auckland on Highway 1 is the pretty little beach settlement of Waiwera. Its hot medicinal springs were already famed in the 19th c.; many people came here to take the cure and spa establishments and hotels were built to cater for them.
ⓖ *Spa daily 9am–10pm.*

### Wenderholm Reserve

To the north of Waiwera is the Wenderholm Reserve, a small nature reserve with attractive picnic areas and fine views of the Hauraki Gulf.

## ★★Bay of Islands                    H/J 2

### Region: Northland

The Bay of Islands, so **named** by Captain Cook who visited the bay in 1769, lies near the north end of the North Island. It is sprinkled with more than 150 small islands, mostly green and wooded. It is a drowned river system, the result of the rise in sea level after the last ice age. Its particular charm lies in the scatter of

islands and subtropical climate. It is a popular resort for sailing enthusiasts and anglers. The Austrian artist Friedensreich Hundertwasser settled here and planted thousands of trees on his property, a former farm at Kawakawa.

### ★★Bay of Islands Maritime and Historic Park

The Bay of Islands Maritime and Historic Park extends from Whangaruru in the south to Whangaroa in the north. In addition to the islands it includes protected nature reserves and places of historical interest on the coast and in its hinterland.

The park can be explored on a network of trails or by boat and there are accommodation huts and campsites. The park offices, with an information centre, are in Russell. There is also a park rangers' station in Kerikeri.

### History

Maori tradition relates that the legendary Polynesian seafarer Kupe visited the bay in the 10th c. Much later Captain Cook rounded Cape Brett, which projects far into the Pacific, to enter the bay. The French seafarer Marion du Fresne, following in Cook's footsteps, set up

The Bay of Islands – a paradise for sailing enthusiasts

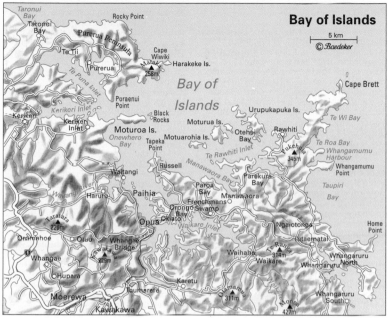

**Bay of Islands**

camp on Moturua Island in 1772 and claimed the territory, which he called France Australe, for the French Crown. After staying for some weeks and establishing friendly relations with the Maoris, du Fresne's two ships were about to continue their voyage when they were attacked by the islanders and du Fresne and some of his men were killed. The reasons for the natives' change of mood are not known: it may be that the Frenchmen unintentionally broke some *tapu*. The surviving French sailors, in retaliation, burned a number of villages and killed many Maoris before departing.

Missionary activity in the bay began in the early 19th c. under the leadership of Samuel Marsden, an Anglican clergyman. Marsden had got to know two chiefs from this area in New South Wales, and they promised him their protection. He landed in the bay in 1814 and preached his first sermon that Christmas. A year later the first mission station was built, soon to be followed by others. At about the same time European settlement began in the bay. The sheltered harbour of Kororareka attracted whalers, loggers and flax traders and by 1820 a disreputable little port town had

developed, which after the signing of the Treaty of Waitangi became the first capital of the British colony of New Zealand.

When war broke out in the north with the destruction of Kororareka (Russell) by the Maori chief Hone Heke in 1845 the capital was transferred further south to Auckland. The Bay of Islands now attracts crowds of visitors. It has a number of buildings and other relics of the early days of the colony, for example at Waitangi, Kerikeri, Paihia, Waimate North and Russell.

**Sailing and angling**

The Bay of Islands was celebrated as an anglers' paradise by the American writer Zane Grey (1875–1939), an ardent big game angler, and it remains a favourite resort of both anglers and sailing enthusiasts.

**Cream trip**

A pleasant way of exploring the islands of the bay is to take the half-day 'cream trip' cruise. The term goes back to the days when milk from the various islands was collected by boats that also delivered the mail.

## Paihia

In the south-west of the Bay of Islands is the little town of Paihia (pop. 3000), which developed out of a mission station founded in 1823 and is now the chief town in the bay. Among the missionaries active in this area were Henry Williams and William Colenso, who were present at the signing of the Treaty of Waitangi. Features of interest in the town are St Paul's Church (1926) and the Museum of Shipwrecks (on board the barque *Tui*), with treasures recovered from local shipwrecks.

### Boat trips

From Paihia visitors can take a variety of boat trips, for example the 'cream trip' mentioned above and the Cape Brett trip to Piercy Island and Cape Brett, at the southern entrance to the bay.

### Subsea Adventure

In Otehei Bay (in the outer reaches of the Bay of Islands) you can explore the colourful underwater world of the Bay of Islands in a tourist submarine.

### Cape Reinga

There are bus trips from Paihia to Cape Reinga, the most northerly point in New Zealand, with a detour to Ninety Mile Beach.

### Steam train

An old-style steam train runs between Opua and Kawakawa, to the south of Paihia.

### Haruru Falls

3 km west of Paihia are the Haruru Falls, which are particularly impressive after heavy rain.

## Waitangi

### History

2 km north of Paihia, reached over a bridge, is Waitangi, situated in an inlet off the Bay of Islands. Here on February 6th 1840 the famous treaty was signed between British officials and local Maori chiefs, which provided the basis for the formal establishment of the British colony of New Zealand. After the War of American Independence Britain was not particularly anxious to establish a new colony in New Zealand, but the government could not prevent the haphazard foundation of settlements by whalers, sealers, traders, speculators, released and escaped convicts and adventurers. Moreover Edward Gibbon Wakefield had formed a company to promote the colonisation of New Zealand, the New Zealand Land Company, which in spite of the discouraging attitude of the government was determined to press on with large-scale settlement. In addition, missionaries, who were now active in New Zealand, had appealed to the government for support in order to prevent the exploitation of the Maoris by the settlers. And finally there was some concern that the French might seek to annex New Zealand. Accordingly, in 1832 the government sent out James Busby (1801–71) to the Bay of Islands as British Resident, without giving him adequate powers or financial resources. Then in 1840 Captain William Hobson (1793–1842), a man in poor health, was sent to New Zealand as representative of the governor of New South Wales. He was given no troops and no money, but was expected to negotiate with the Maori chiefs for the recognition of British sovereignty over their country.

Hobson arrived in New Zealand at the end of January 1840. On February 5th the local chiefs met in front of Busby's house and spent the whole day discussing the terms of the draft treaty that had been prepared by Hobson with the help of Busby and the missionaries. On the following day the treaty was read a second time, discussed and finally signed by the 45 chiefs present. Copies of the treaty were then taken round the whole country by government officials and missionaries and presented to the chiefs who had not been present at the meeting. Much eloquence was applied to persuading them to sign, and advantage was often taken of their ignorance. Even so, some chiefs refused to sign the treaty.

The problem with the treaty and its complex language was that despite the explanations offered by the Europeans the chiefs were unable to understand it, for the idea of sovereignty meant nothing to them. The Maoris recognised no authority higher than the tribe.

On October 2nd 1840 the declaration of British sovereignty was published in London and acquired the force of law. The original copies of the treaty are preserved in the National Archives in Wellington.

The signing of the treaty is commemorated annually on February 6th with ceremonies in Waitangi. In recent years there have been repeated demonstrations by Maoris protesting against the treaty.

**Treaty House**
The Treaty House was built in 1833 by the Sydney architect John Verge as the private residence of James Busby, the British government's representative in the colony. The side wings were added later. In 1932 it was acquired by the then Governor General and presented to the people of New Zealand. It is now open as a historic monument.

**★★ Maori meeting house**
Nearby is a large Maori meeting house erected in 1940 on the centenary of the Treaty of Waitangi. The carving was the work of the famous Maori woodcarver Pine Taiapa. It incorporates all the different regional styles and bears witness to the Maoris' new-found national self-awareness. There is also a large canoe decorated with carving, made from the trunks of three kauri trees.

The Waitangi visitor centre can supply further information.
ⓖ *Daily 9am–5pm.*

## Kerikeri

In a beautiful setting at the head of the narrow Kerikeri inlet, which reaches far inland from the Bay of Islands, is the little town of Kerikeri (pop. 3000), a favourite residence of artists and well-to-do retired people. Citrus fruits and various tropical fruits are grown on the fertile soil in the surrounding area.

**History**
The second mission station in New Zealand was established here in 1819 by John Butler, who some 20 years later moved to the new settlement of Wellington (see entry) to continue his missionary activities.

**★ Kemp House**
Kemp House, also known as the Kerikeri Mission Building, dates from 1822. John Butler, for whom it was built, lived in it only for a year before being moved to other work. After some rapid changes of

Woodcarvings in the Maori meeting house at Waitangi

missionaries the house was occupied by James Kemp in 1832 and remained in his family until 1974. The ground floor is in the style of the 1840s, the upper floor in Victorian style.

*Summer daily 10.30am–12.30pm, 1.30–4.30pm; Jun.–Aug. Sat.–Wed.*

### Stone Store

Adjacent to Kemp House is the oldest stone building in New Zealand, which also belonged to the Kemp family. This two-storey building was erected in the 1830s to replace a wooden storehouse that was burned down. At one time it housed Bishop Selwyn's library, which the bishop felt was safer in a stone building. During the war with Hone Heke it became an ammunition store. It is now occupied by a shop and a small museum of local history, with material on the early days of the mission station.

*Summer daily 10.30am–12.30pm, 1.30–4.30pm; Jun.–Aug. Sat.–Wed.*

### ★Rewa's Village

On the opposite side of the inlet is a reconstruction of a *kainga*, an unfortified Maori village, as it may have looked before the coming of the Europeans. It gives a good impression of the way of life of the Maoris before the 18th c. The village is notably lacking in carved decoration: perhaps it was believed that the much esteemed works of art with which meeting houses and storehouses were decorated would be safer in a *pa* (fortified settlement). Rewa, after whom the village is named, was the second-most powerful man in the tribe after its chief, Hongi Hika.

### Kororipo Pa

On the terraced hill above the inlet is the fortified Maori village of Kororipo Pa; it is reached by a waymarked footpath from the Stone Store. This was the base from which Hongi Hika set out on his raids, thrusting as far afield as Wellington and the East Cape (see entries). In 1814 he met the missionary Samuel Marsden in Sydney and helped him to establish mission stations at Rangihoua in 1814 and later at Kerikeri.

### Rainbow Falls

About 3 km beyond Kerikeri are the spectacular and enchanting Rainbow Falls.

## Russell

Some 70 km north-west of Whangarei, idyllically situated on a sheltered site on the Bay of Islands, is the old whaling station of Russell (pop. 1100). The best way to reach it is by ferry from Opua or Paihia; by car it can be reached on a roundabout route via Whakapara.

### History

The settlement, originally called Kororareka, was of importance in the early 19th c. as a whaling station and trading post, where honest traders as well as more doubtful characters did business with the Maoris. There were numerous drinking houses and brothels that gave the place a bad name; but this was also the starting point of missionary activity in New Zealand. In 1840 the treaty recognising British sovereignty was signed at Waitangi, on the opposite side of the inlet, and Governor Hobson acquired land in nearby Okiato on which to establish the seat of government. But Russell did not remain long the capital, which was soon transferred to Auckland.

The name of the place was changed from Kororareka to Russell in honour of Lord John Russell, then British colonial secretary and later prime minister. In 1841 the government buildings in Russell were destroyed by fire. The change of name probably also reflected the inhabitants' desire to throw off the bad reputation of Kororareka. With the transfer of the seat of government to Auckland the Bay of Islands area declined in population and in importance. Customs duties introduced by the government led foreign shipping to avoid the port, and Hone Heke (☛Famous People), chief of the Ngapuhi tribe, lost his income from mooring fees. He had signed the Treaty of Waitangi, but he now felt himself cheated by the Europeans, and launched a fight for liberation from British rule. In 1844–5 he four times cut down the flagstaff bearing the British flag, and on the last occasion also, with his warriors, burned down the whole town except the churches and the mission station. The white population fled to Auckland by sea and the war in the north began. After suffering two shameful defeats British forces defeated Hone Heke's men at Ruapekapeka in 1846. Thereafter Russell remained a quiet and remote little town, which still preserves much of its 19th c. character.

Russell's Christ Church is the oldest church in New Zealand

### ★Christ Church

Christ Church (1836) is New Zealand's oldest surviving church. Unlike other churches in the Bay of Islands, it was built as a place of worship for the settlers rather than as a mission church. It was renovated in 1871.

Round the church are many gravestones of whalers, seamen, Maoris and early settlers.

### Pompallier House

Pompallier House (1841–2) was not, as might be supposed, the residence of Bishop Pompallier, who founded the first Roman Catholic mission station here in 1838, but housed the mission's printing press. The house was originally less elegant; it was only after the mission moved to Auckland that the new owners substantially altered it and added the veranda and chimney. Now protected as a national monument, it is furnished in period style and still contains the old printing press.
ⓖ Daily 10am–12.30pm, 1.30–4.30pm.

### The Bungalow

At the end of the beach, adjoining Pompallier House, is the house known simply as The Bungalow. It was built in 1853 for a British businessman, James R Clendon, who was also the American honorary consul. His daughter ran a school here.

### Captain Cook Memorial Museum

This museum in York Street commemorates the great explorer. Notable among the exhibits is a model of his ship, the *Endeavour*.
ⓖ Daily 10am–4pm.

### ★Harbour front

On the charming old harbour front there are many relics of the settlement's early days. Among them are the police station in the old customs house, the Duke of Marlborough tavern (which claims to have the oldest liquor licence in New Zealand) and an old cannon. Yachts and catamarans of all sizes are moored on the front, a place of great activity during the holiday season and in the evenings when the deep-sea anglers come in with their catches.

From the landing stage there are pleasant cruises in the Bay of Islands (the 'cream trip', the Cape Brett trip). Visitors can also take a bus trip to Cape Reinga or cross on the ferry (15 min.) to Paihia.

### Flagstaff Hill
There are wide views from Flagstaff Hill, on which Hone Heke several times cut down the flagstaff bearing the British flag (monument).

## Kawakawa

16 km south of the Bay of Islands on Highway 1 is Kawakawa (pop. 2000), now the administrative centre of the Bay of Islands district. It was originally a flax-processing centre, and later coal was mined here. Today Kawakawa is noted in particular as the elected home of Friedensreich Hundertwasser (☛Famous People). The artist donated to the township a toilet shack constructed in his particular style with no corners or straight edges and which is now a tourist attraction.

### Steam railway
Another attraction is the old steam railway that runs beside the main road and links Kawakawa with the old coal port of Opua.

### ★ Waiomio Caves
4 km south of Kawakawa, on a side road off Highway 1, are the Waiomio Caves. This ramified cave system attracts many visitors with its bizarre karstic features, stalactitic formations and the spectacular Glow-worm Cave. It is owned by descendants of Chief Kawiti, who fought alongside Hone Heke at Ruapekapeka.
🅖 Conducted tours daily.

### ★ Ruapekapeka Pa
The Maori stronghold of Ruapekapeka Pa is of great interest but is not easy of access. To reach it, turn off Highway 1 16 km south of Kawakawa. This was the scene of the last battle between Hone Heke and British troops. The pa, commanded by Hone Heke and his ally Kawiti in 1846, could not hold out against the sustained fire of the British forces, and after the storming of the fort, which was watched by Governor Grey himself, Grey declared peace and allowed the Ngapuhi to return to their tribal territory. The rebels' land was not confiscated, as it was later in the land wars on the Taranaki Peninsula, in the

Bay of Plenty and at Waikato. The remains of ramparts, underground positions and tunnels can still be identified, as well as the British gun positions. (The Maori defences provided a model for the trench systems of the first world war.)

From the elevated battle site there are fine panoramas of the mountains of Northland.

### Waimate North
20 km west of Paihia (see above) Samuel Marsden established the first Anglican settlement in the interior of the island in 1830. He laid out a farm on a British model so that the natives should not only be converted but should be introduced to useful work. The farm was a great success, and Charles Darwin, emerging from a long journey through primeval forest in 1835, was astonished to find himself in what seemed to him an English village. For a time Bishop Selwyn made the farm his residence and installed a theological seminary here.

### ★ Mission House
A relic of the early settlement is the mission house, built in 1832 and thus the second-oldest surviving European building in New Zealand. A good example of the early colonial architecture, it is furnished in period style.
🅖 Summer daily.

### St John's Church
Beside the mission house is St John's Church (1871), the third church on the site. The churchyard contains 19th c. gravestones.

## Bay of Plenty                K–M 4
### Region: Bay of Plenty

The Bay of Plenty lies between the Coromandel Peninsula in the west and the East Cape. The main towns are Tauranga (see entry), Whakatane and Opotiki.

### Kiwi Coast
The gently curving and shallow bay is also known as the Kiwi Coast. Over the last 30 years numerous kiwi plantations, sheltered by the windbreaks that are a feature of the landscape, have been laid out here, benefitting from the long hours of sunshine and fertile volcanic soil.

**Name**

The bay was given its name by Captain Cook (☛Famous People), who was able to take in large stores of water and victuals here, after leaving a previous port of call in Poverty Bay (near Gisborne) almost empty-handed. Cook also gave names to the offshore islands, such as White Island (after the plumes of steam from its volcano) and Mayor Island (which he named at the same time as the Alderman Islands off the Coromandel coast).

**History**

The Maori tribes in the Bay of Plenty suffered badly from the raids of the Ngapuhi warriors from Northland, now armed with guns, and these tribal wars hindered missionary activity and settlement.

Following the end of the land wars in the Waikato area there was heavy fighting around Tauranga. Many British soldiers were killed during an attack on Gate Pa in 1864, and widespread terror was caused by the Hauhau movement and later by Te Kooti's guerrilla war. After the land wars ex-soldiers were settled in the Bay of Plenty (e.g. at Tauranga, Whakatane and Opotiki) on land confiscated from the Maoris.

**Economy**

At first the settlers lived from pastoral farming, but in the 20th c. fruits gradually became the main source of income. Citrus fruits brought profits, but in the 1960s the now fashionable kiwi fruit began to be grown and it is now an export crop producing record yields.

In the hinterland of the Bay of Plenty and on the volcanic plateau pines are mainly grown. The Californian pine flourishes here and has the merit of growing very quickly. The little town of Tauranga has now developed into an important timber-exporting port.

**Tourist attractions**

The beaches of the Bay of Plenty are popular with bathers and surfers. There is also good fishing.

# Whakatane

**Region: Bay of Plenty**
**Population: 17,000**

The town of Whakatane, situated in the centre of the Bay of Plenty, at the mouth of the Whakatane River, is the supply centre for an area that depends on agriculture and forestry for a living. In its hinterland there are large kiwi plantations, and pastoral farming (dairy cattle, sheep, red deer) is also important. Further inland large areas have been planted with pines, and on the outskirts of the town there are large timber-processing plants (including papermaking factories). In summer Whakatane, with its beautiful beach, is a popular holiday resort.

**History**

Long before the arrival of Europeans this area was densely populated by Maori tribes. Toi, the legendary seafarer from Hawaiki, is said to have landed here and established a *pa* (fortified settlement) at the tip of the Whakatane Heads. An early white settlement was attacked in 1865, whereupon the governor imposed martial law and confiscated large areas of tribal land on the east side of the Bay of Plenty. In 1869 Te Kooti attacked the little military settlement and burned it down, but thereafter he was driven back into the Urewera hills. He was pardoned in 1883 and granted land at Wainui (east of Whakatane) on which he lived for the rest of his life. In 1987 a severe earthquake caused heavy damage in the area.

**Pohaturoa Rock**

On this steep-sided sacred rock in the centre of the town is a *tapu* cave in which the Maoris used to hold their ceremonies. Since 1927 it has been a memorial to the dead of the first world war. Beside the rock is a model of an ancestral canoe, the *Mataatua*.

From the almost vertical summit of the rock there is a fine view of the town – in good weather it is possible to see the plumes of steam on White Island.

**Whakatane Museum**

This little museum in Boon Street has a fine collection of Maori arts and crafts. ◉ *Daily 1.30–4pm.*

**Whakatane Heads**

Some 2 km from the town centre, Maori tradition has it that the ancestral canoe landed here.

**Whakatane Board Mills**

3 km west of the town on the road to Tauranga (see entry) are the Whakatane

Board Mills, where timber from the Matahina pine forest, 48 km away, is processed (wood pulp).
Ⓖ *Conducted tours by appointment Mon.–Fri. 10.30am.*

### Ohope Beach
Ohope Beach, 6 km east of Whakatane, is highly favoured by surfers and surf anglers. The narrow Ohiwa Peninsula separates this beach from a more sheltered one inside the natural harbour.

### Awakeri Hot Springs
12 km south-west, on the road to Rotorua, is the little thermal resort of Awakeri Hot Springs.

## Kawerau

**Region: Bay of Plenty**
**Population: 8000**

Some 30 km south-west from Whakatane, roughly halfway between Rotorua (see entry) and the Bay of Plenty, is Kawerau, a planned new town established in 1953 at the foot of Mount Edgecumbe. It lies near the large Kaingaroa State Forest with its extensive plantings of pines.

### Tasman Pulp and Paper Mill
The town is dependent on the Tasman Pulp and Paper Mill, which produces mainly newsprint and cellulose for export. Substantial quantities of sawn timber are also produced and sold mainly to Australia. A decisive factor in siting the mill here was the existence nearby of a geothermal field, and natural hot steam is used to produce power. The mill processes an annual 2 million cu. m of timber from the huge pine forests in the surrounding area.
Ⓖ *Conducted tours daily 1.30pm, starting from the main entrance.*

### ★Mount Edgecumbe
The extinct volcano (805 m) is an easy climb. It is possible to bathe in the crater lake on the summit, from which there are breathtaking views. The hill is sacred to the Ngatiawa tribe as a place of burial and there have long been protests against afforestation on the hill and demands for its return to the Maoris.

### Tarawera Falls
22km south-west of Kawerau the Tarawera River, after flowing for some distance though a system of karstic caves, plunges over a 60 m high rock face. A path runs through the forest to the falls.

## Opotiki

Opotiki (pop. 4000), near the east end of the Bay of Plenty, was formerly one of the largest Maori settlements in the bay. On the outskirts of the town is the little St Stephen's Church, built in 1864 on the initiative of Carl Volkner (1819–65), a German Lutheran missionary. Volkner, who had worked in Opotiki since 1859, was brutally murdered in the church by supporters of the Hauhau movement in 1865 on returning from a visit to Auckland; the Maoris suspected that he was a government spy and had betrayed them. Because of its nearness to the impenetrable Urewera Ranges Opotiki was frequently attacked by Hauhau groups or Chief Te Kooti's guerrillas.

## ★White Island

White Island rises out of the Bay of Plenty to a height of 300 m, some 50 km north of Whakatane. It is a highly active **volcano**, the continuation of a chain of volcanoes on the North Island that runs north from Ruapehu in the Tongariro National Park (see entry). In an eruption in 1914 the eastern flank of the hill was literally blown away and the crater lake was drained. The volcano still shows considerable thermal activity: long white plumes of steam rising into the sky (hence the name given to the island by Captain Cook), hissing fumaroles, boiling and bubbling pools of mud, emissions of foul-smelling sulphurous vapours. White Island can be reached by boat from Whakatane (see above) and Tauranga (see entry) or on scenic flights by helicopter or light aircraft. **Note**: special permission is needed to land on White Island.

## ★Coromandel Peninsula          K 3/4

**Region: Waikato**

The Coromandel Peninsula, a tongue of land marked by volcanic activity, extends northward between the Hauraki

## *Baedeker* SPECIAL

# Rough Outside, Succulent Within

It is barely 20 years since a certain New Zealand product conquered European and American markets: the kiwi fruit. This large gooseberry-like fruit is esteemed not only for its high content of vitamins C and E but also for its juicy sweet-sour flesh and good keeping quality. It originates from China and was long known as the Chinese gooseberry. The plant, which grows to a height of several metres, flourishes particularly on warm sites. It has relatively large hairy leaves and dioecious white flowers (i.e. with male and female reproductive organs in separate flowers). The fruit, oval in shape and some 8 cm long, with a thin brown hairy skin, is borne only on the female plants; the juicy greenish flesh contains small black seeds. The fruit reaches its full aroma 9 months after flowering. It is harvested in New Zealand in May and June.

After picking the fruit must be stored or processed within 2 days. With suitable refrigeration it can stay fresh for several months. The New Zealand fruit grower Hayward Wright has succeeded in producing a particularly large and succulent variety. The plants are cultivated on trellises, in the proportion of one male to seven female plants. An average plant 8 m high can yield up to a thousand fruits.

The kiwi fruit grown in New Zealand has proved an ideal export product. They can easily be preserved, refrigerated or used in the manufacture of fruit juice, wine, liqueurs, jelly and preserves.

Exports flourished due to large-scale production in plantations and New Zealand technical knowledge of refrigeration. Even by the 1950s the kiwi fruit had been sold all over the world. Every kiwi fruit exported bears a small sticker with the legend 'The world's finest kiwi fruit'. This label was one element in a brilliant marketing strategy. Gooseberries were not particularly popular, and anything Chinese was suspect in the political atmosphere of the time – hence the Chinese gooseberry became the kiwi fruit, using the name of New Zealand's national bird .

Gulf and the Firth of Thames in the west and the Bay of Plenty (see entry) in the east. The landscape of the peninsula is a contrast of wild and rugged mountains, mostly forest covered, sheer cliffs and beautiful sandy beaches. Surfers, divers and deep-sea anglers prefer the rocky indented east coast; the sheltered west coast, particularly on the Firth of Thames, is a favourite of sailing enthusiasts. In recent years the peninsula, with its largely unspoiled natural landscape, has attracted many artists and large numbers of tourists. Beautiful semi-precious stones can be found in its rivers and streams and on its beaches. Visitors should beware of dangerous abandoned mine shafts.

### Name
The peninsula takes its name from a British ship, HMS *Coromandel*, that visited the harbour in 1820 to load kauri timber for the Royal Navy. The name was originally given to the port but was later applied to the whole peninsula.

### History
Like Northland (see entry), the Coromandel Peninsula was once covered with kauri trees yielding valuable resin, but by the early 19th c. it was ravaged by loggers. They were followed by resin collectors, who dug over the soil, and then by gold miners, who soon exhausted the peninsula's easily accessible seams of gold.

### Coromandel Range
The backbone of the peninsula is the Coromandel Range, which extends to the northern tip of the peninsula at Port Jackson.

### Touring the peninsula
Visitors can explore the varied landscapes of the peninsula on a round trip on Highway 25. A good starting-point is the little town of Thames.

## Thames

**Region: Waikato**
**Population: 6500**

Thames, the largest place on the Coromandel Peninsula, lies on the west side at the point where the Waihou River flows into the Firth of Thames. It is

Steep cliffs along the Coromandel Peninsula

made up of the two earlier settlements of Shortland (the port) and Grahamtown (the old gold-miners' settlement). Captain Cook anchored in the Firth of Thames in November 1769 and surveyed the area at the mouth of the Waihou River. The local Maoris were friendly.

After the discovery in 1852 of seams of gold-bearing quartz in the Coromandel Range the population of the peninsula increased enormously in the 1870s, for a time passing the 20,000 mark. At that time the town is said to have had more than 80 hotels. The gold rush reached its peak in 1873, but even before the first world war the gold was almost worked out, and the population left Thames altogether or turned to agriculture.

### Thames Mineralogical Museum
There is an interesting mineralogical museum housed in the former School of Mines. In addition to an extensive collection of minerals it contains models of mines, stamper batteries (for crushing the rock) and miners' equipment.
🕐 *Mon.–Sat. 2–4pm.*

### Other sights
The Thames Museum recalls the days of the early settlers.

The Queen of Beauty pump, behind the power station, once pumped water out of the mine shafts at depths of up to 300 m.

The cemetery to the south of the town occupies the site of the Maori fortified settlement of Totara Pa, which was destroyed by Hongi Hika.

On a prominent site to the north of the town is a memorial to the dead of the first world war.

### Miranda
The thermal resort of Miranda is 30 km from Thames, on the opposite side of the Firth of Thames.

### Kauaeranga Valley
To the east of Thames is the Kauaeranga Valley, where in the past large numbers of kauri trees were felled and much resin collected.

### Kopu
South of Thames is the little town of Kopu, from which there is a rewarding excursion (33 km) to Hikuai; the road, winding through wild and rugged scenery, was opened only in 1967.

### ★Coromandel Forest Park
North-east and south-east of Thames extends the beautiful Coromandel Forest Park, which can be explored on a number of trails. It has a total area of 63,400 ha, of which over 8000 ha consist of young planted kauris. Large areas of this rugged highland region are covered with natural rain forest. Information about the forest and its trails can be obtained from the park offices (13 km east of Thames on the road to Kauaeranga).

## Coromandel

**Region: Waikato**
**Population: 1500**

On the north-west coast of the peninsula is the port of Coromandel, around which gold was worked in the 1860s. There is an interesting museum in the former School of Mines (open by appointment). Other features are the old Court House (1860) and an old stamper battery for crushing the gold-bearing ore.

### Excursions
From Coromandel Highway 25 runs by way of the old gold-mining town of Kuaotunu to Whitianga (48 km; see below). The narrow and in part unmade road climbs gradually to 347 m, with fine views of the natural harbours of Coromandel and Whangapoua and of Mercury Bay.

There is a shorter route to Whitianga (33 km) on a narrow winding road that runs past the Waiau Falls and through old stands of kauris. On the way it is worth climbing Castle Rock (525 m) for the sake of the wide views from the summit.

The road from Tapu to Coroglen, further south (29 km), follows a winding course through the Tapu and Waiwawa valleys, with the double peak of the Camel's Back (819 m) as backdrop. 3 km before Coroglen there is an unusual, almost square, kauri tree.

The coast road north of Coromandel is narrow and in poor condition, making the trip to Cape Colville, at the northern tip of the peninsula, slow and difficult.

### Colville
26 km north of Coromandel, the little township of Colville, an old loggers' camp, is the last place for taking in

Cathedral Cave, near Hahei on the Coromandel coast

supplies for the journey to the northern part of the peninsula (Port Jackson, Port Charles, Kennedy Bay).

### Mount Moehau

At the north end of the peninsula is Mount Moehau (892 m), regarded by the Maoris as a sacred mountain. The commander of the Arawa tribal canoe is believed to be buried on the summit. It is a steep and difficult ascent – but worthwhile for the view (in fine weather).

## Whitianga

**Region: Waikato**
**Population: 3000**

### ★ Mercury Bay

Some 70 km north of Thames, beautifully situated in Mercury Bay, is the popular holiday resort of Whitianga. The bay is full of fishing boats and pleasure craft belonging to big-game anglers and divers. Kupe, the legendary Polynesian seafarer, is said to have fished here. It was here too that Captain Cook (☞Famous People) hoisted the British flag in 1769 and took possession of New Zealand in the name of George III; the scientists travelling with him observed the transit of Mercury, thereby giving the bay its name.

Vast quantities of kauri timber and thousands of tonnes of resin from the Coromandel Peninsula were shipped from Whitianga.

### Whitianga Rock

On Whitianga Rock there was a fortified Maori settlement (*pa*) that impressed Cook with its defensive strength. It has now largely been demolished.

### Shakespeare Cliffs

At Shakespeare Cliffs (easily reached from Ferry Landing) is a monument to Captain Cook, who lay at anchor here in his ship, the *Endeavour*.

### Buffalo Beach

Near Whitianga is Buffalo Beach, named after a ship that ran aground here in 1840.

### Hahei

A few kilometres east of Whitianga is Hahei, with a beautiful beach, at the end

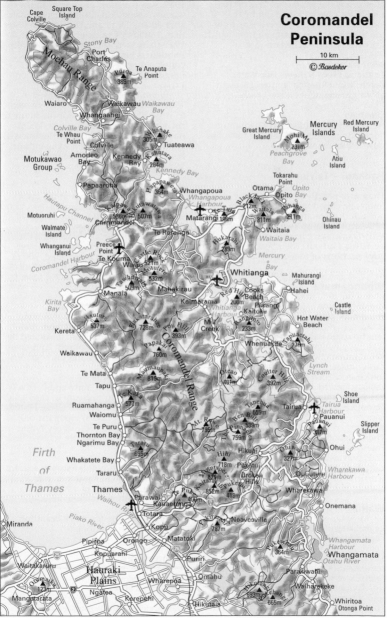

# Coromandel Peninsula

10 km

© Baedeker

of which is the ★Cathedral Cave (☞106), a wide sea cave hollowed out by the force of the waves. There is a lane from the town centre to a car park from which the cave can be reached on foot.

### ★Hot Water Beach
To the south of Hahei is Hot Water Beach, where thermal springs gush out of the ground right on the beach.

### Kuaotunu
North-east of Whitianga is Kuaotunu, once a flourishing gold-mining town but now almost deserted.

## Pauanui – Tairua

These two prettily situated holiday resorts lie close together on the east coast of the Coromandel Peninsula, between Whitianga (see above) and Whangamata (see below), separated only by Tairua Harbour. Their beaches attract large numbers of tourists.

## Whangamata

**Region: Waikato**
**Population: 4000**

On the south-east coast of the peninsula is the popular holiday resort of Whangamata, which grew out of an earlier loggers' and gold-miners' settlement. There is a sheltered beach in the bay, and there are other good beaches further north at Onemana and Opoutere and to the south at Whiritoa.

### Walks
There is good walking in the Taitua State Forest to the north and in the Wentworth and Parakowhai valleys in the interior of the peninsula. Here and there are the remains of gold workings.

## Waihi

**Region: Bay of Plenty**
**Population: 4500**

The once flourishing gold-miners' settlement of Waihi lies in the southern foothills of the Coromandel Range, near the Bay of Plenty (see entry). Gold was found here in 1878, and the gold mine on Martha Hill, which was worked until

1952, was the most productive in the the whole of New Zealand. Its deepest shaft goes down 550 m and there are no fewer than 160 km of galleries and tunnels. In 1912 there were serious clashes between the miners and the mine owners, one consequence of which was the foundation of the New Zealand Labour Party.

When the Martha Mine closed in 1952, because it was no longer economic to work, there were fears for the future of the town. Since then, however, Waihi has developed into the main commercial centre of a wide area and some industry has been established in the town. In 1988 gold mining was resumed.

### ★Martha Hill Gold Mine
There are many buildings in the town dating from early gold-mining days, and on Martha Hill are the ruins of the old pumping house. The new Waihi Gold Mining Company is now working the gold by opencast methods over a large area. A huge hole in the ground, 200 m deep, is to become the central feature of a new recreation area (conducted tours by appointment).

### Waihi Arts Centre and Museum
The Waihi Arts Centre and Museum recalls the days of the gold rush. All aspects of gold mining are illustrated by a model of the mine, miners' equipment both old and modern and photographs.

### ★Karangahake Gorge
This gorge between Waihi and Paeroa is a kind of open-air museum of early gold mining. The Karangahake Gorge Historic Walkway (ca 1½ hours) along the old railway line passes some of the huge machines in which the ore was crushed.

### Steam railway
During the main holiday season a steam train runs through the gorge from Waihi to Paeroa, a distance of 13 km.

### ★Waihi Beach
11 km east of the town is a beautiful sandy beach 10 km long.

## Dannevirke                    L 7

**Region: Hawke's Bay**
**Population: 6000**

Dannevirke, a town founded by

Scandinavian immigrants in 1872, lies on the eastern slopes of the Ruahine Range, 60 km north-east of Palmerston North and 100 km south-west of Hastings (see entries).

### History
The Scandinavian settlers were brought in to clear the primeval Totara forest, in an area between Masterton and Takapau known as the Seventy Mile Bush, and to build a road through the area. After clearing the land they lived mainly by pastoral farming, but many left when the government decided to charge for the passage to New Zealand, which had previously been free.

The construction of sawmills and the coming of the railway in 1884 gave a boost to the economy of the town, and with the arrival of many British settlers it gradually lost its Nordic character.

### Domain Park
The Domain Park is an attractive open space with its mature trees, enclosures for game and aviaries.

## Surroundings

### Norsewood
20 km north of Dannevirke is the village of Norsewood (pop. 330), which also originated as a Scandinavian loggers' settlement. In 1888 it was destroyed by fire. There is a pioneer museum in Upper Norsewood. Later the Norsewear textile factory was established here.

### Seven Star Abbey
West of Norsewood is Seven Star Abbey, a Cistercian monastery.

### Waihi Falls
These romantic falls lie in primeval forest 40 km south-east of Dannevirke on the road to Waipatiki and Horoeka.

## East Cape                    M/N 4/5

### Regions: Bay of Plenty, Gisborne

### Suggested tour
From Opotiki, on the Bay of Plenty, a road runs north-east along the coast to Hicks Bay and then turns south, bypassing the East Cape, and follows the east (Pacific) coast to Gisborne, on Poverty Bay. The distance between the

two places on the coast road is 340 km. The scenic inland road from Opotiki to Gisborne, running through the Waioeka Gorge and the Waipaoa Valley (Highway 2), is only 150 km. Both routes can be combined for a round trip. The country is at its most beautiful around Christmas, in the southern summer, when the pohutukawa trees are covered in crimson blossom.

### History
Somewhere in the East Cape area, on October 9th 1769, Cook and his crew became the first Europeans to land on New Zealand. Two days before the cabin boy, Nick Young, had sighted, to the south of present-day Gisborne, a promontory that has since been known as Young Nick's Head. The first landing in Poverty Bay, however, was a disappointment. Cook sailed on, and after calling at a number of other points on the east coast finally came to the Bay of Plenty, where he found in abundance all he needed for his ship and his crew.

### Topography
Due to the remoteness of the East Cape from the main centres on the North Island (Auckland and Wellington; see entries), and the barriers to communication formed by the wild Raukumara Range and the impenetrable primeval forests of the Urewera Range, this area long remained isolated. European settlement in the area proceeded very slowly. In spite of a massive drift to the towns the proportion of Maoris in the population is still exceptionally high, and around a quarter of the land belongs to them. Much of the land is leased to white farmers. In the early days many European farmers allowed their land to run wild when their lease expired, and in the hilly interior there was severe damage from erosion after the forests were cleared.

### Maori woodcarving
Magnificent examples of Maori woodcarving have been discovered in the East Cape area, such as the meeting houses, storehouses and war canoes kept in ethnographic museums in Wellington and Auckland. Marvellously carved meeting houses have been preserved in situ at Hicks Bay, Te Kaha, Tikitiki and Gisborne.

### Omaio Beach

56 km north-east of Opotiki is the seaside resort of Omaio Beach, which has an excellent tourist facilities.

### Te Kaha

70 km north-east of Opotiki, in a beautiful little bay, is Te Kaha. This was once the scene of many inter-tribal feuds, and a fortified Maori village stood here. From the 1830s to the 1930s many whalers came from the Bay of Islands (see entry) to the East Cape to hunt the passing whales. At Tukaki there is a richly decorated meeting house erected in 1950. Earlier Maori artefacts from Te Kaha are now in the War Memorial Museum in Auckland (see entry).

### Waihau Bay

Almost 100 km north-east of Opotiki is Waihau Bay, with a small township and a guest house established in 1914. From here there are fine views of the coast towards Cape Runaway.

### Cape Runaway

This cape marks the eastern extremity of the Bay of Plenty (see entry). Captain Cook gave it its modern name while sailing from Poverty Bay to the Bay of Plenty: a single cannon shot fired into the air dispersed the Maori war canoes that were approaching his ship.

### Whangaparaoa

120 km north-east of Opotiki is Whangaparaoa (Bay of Whales), once a favoured whalers' base.

### Hicks Bay

150 km north-east of Opotiki and 190 km north of Gisborne, Hicks Bay is named after one of Cook's officers. It has popular beaches, particularly the one in Horseshoe Bay. Other features are a meeting house at Tuwhakairiora (1872) and a glow-worm cave near the local motel.

### East Cape

The East Cape, the most easterly point in New Zealand, can be reached only on a side road from Te Araroa. On the cape is a lighthouse (140 m high) from which there is a breathtaking panorama. Round the cape are numerous wrecks.

### Te Araroa

At Te Araroa is one of the tallest and

The East Cape, once remote and inaccessible, is now an attractive holiday area

oldest pohutukawa trees in New Zealand. In 1820 there were savage raids in this area by Ngapuhi tribesmen from Northland armed with guns, in the course of which several thousand members of the Ngati Porou tribe are said to have been killed or enslaved.

**Warning**: the beach here is dangerous for swimmers because of the heavy surf.

### Tikitiki

A few kilometres south of Te Araroa, beyond the Raukumara Range, is the little town of Tikitiki, with one of the finest Maori churches, St Mary's. It was built in 1924 as a memorial to the Maori soldiers who fell in the first world war.

### Ruatoria

A short distance further south is Ruatoria (pop. ca 800), the chief place of the Ngati Porou, the principal Maori tribe on the east coast. This was the birthplace in 1874 of the Maori politician Apirana Ngata. Features include the Mangahanea Marae estate, with a meeting house (1896), The Bungalow (residence of Apirana Ngata) and the Porourangi meeting house (1888; rebuilt 1934).

**Note**: all meeting houses in this area are privately owned and can be entered only with special permission.

### Mount Hikurangi

West of Ruatoria is Mount Hikurangi (1754 m), the highest peak in the Raukumara Range. A long-drawn-out dispute over the ownership of this mountain was settled only in 1991, when it was assigned to the Maoris.

### Waipiro Bay

On the coast below Mount Hikurangi is Waipiro Bay, which at the beginning of the 20th c. was one of the largest settlements on the east coast. Its remote location, however, has been the cause of its decline.

### Te Puia

A few kilometres further south is Te Puia, a little town famed for its medicinal hot springs. From nearby Mount Molly there are magnificent views.

### Tokomaru Bay

Further south, in Tokomaru Bay, the ruins of a frozen-meat plant and port installations are witness to better times. There is a meeting house (1934) with fine carving.

### Anaura Bay

After his disappointment in Poverty Bay Captain Cook landed on the beautiful sandy beach of Anaura Bay, where the natives were friendly. The strong surf, however, prevented him from taking in supplies of water. He was told that he could get water in Tolaga Bay, a quieter bay to the south.

There are fine views from the Anaura Bay Walkway (4 km long) at the north end of the bay.

### Tolaga Bay

With its beautiful beach, Tolaga Bay attracts many bathers and anglers. A trail runs to Cook's Cove (private; open Oct.–Jul.), where Cook drew water from a spring that has since dried up.

### Waihau Beach

40 km north of Gisborne is the very beautiful Waihau Beach.

### Whangara

The little Maori settlement of Whangara lies on the coast 30 km north of Gisborne. On the gable of the carved meeting house is a figure of a man riding on a whale; according to a tribal legend the tribe's ancestor arrived here on a whale's back.

### Raukumara Forest Park

This hilly and densely wooded nature reserve covers an area of 115,000 ha between the East Cape and the Bay of Plenty (see entry). It has few facilities for visitors. The highest peaks are Hikurangi (1754 m) and Raukumara (1413 m). The Motu River flows through the park. The best way to reach it is on the old road to Motu, 35 km east of Opotiki.
Information is available from the Forest Service offices in Gisborne, Opotiki and Ruatoria.

### ★Route via East Cape

The road from Gisborne to Opotiki by way of the East Cape runs through varied scenery of great beauty that makes the longer journey (twice the length of the direct route on Highway 2) well worthwhile. But the shorter route too has great scenery, running through the Waioeka Gorge, winding river valleys and an almost unpopulated region of forest-covered hills. Halfway along this route, at Matawai, the old coach road via Motu (only in good weather; hard going) can be followed. An attractive trail, the

Otoko Walkway, runs along the Waihuka River between Te Karaka and Rakauroa, following an abandoned railway line through the dense forest.

**Gisborne**
See entry

**Opotiki**
See Bay of Plenty

## Gisborne                                    M/N 5

**Region: Gisborne**
**Population: 32,000**

The town of Gisborne lies in **Poverty Bay** (so named by Captain Cook in 1769), on the southern edge of the East Cape (see entry). Cook landed on Kaiti Beach, where the Turanganui River flows into the sea, but was prevented by the aggressive attitude of the local Maoris from taking in food and water. The country round Poverty Bay is now a fertile fruit-growing area.

### Sunrise at the world's end
Situated off the main communication routes and far from the important New Zealand markets, Gisborne was long regarded as the 'end of the world'. Even today, with improved communications, the population continues to decline. Nevertheless each year from Christmas to New Year Gisborne is extremely busy because the New Year's sun first touches land here. For the turn of the millennium all hotel accommodation in Gisborne and the vicinity was booked out months in advance.

### History
The advance of the Hauhau movement into this region by way of Opotiki in 1865 ended a period of peaceful and successful development for Gisborne. Although the Maori tribes on the East Cape were in general well disposed to the government – particularly the Ngati Porou, who had suffered severely during the inter-tribal wars – many Maoris supported the recent Hauhau movement. There was heavy fighting between government troops and rebels at Ruatoria, to the north, and north-west of Gisborne. Te Kooti, who had previously supported the government, was arrested on suspicion of treason and deported without trial, along with other Hauhau

supporters, to the Chatham Islands. Escaping from there, he returned and wrought a ruthless revenge. In an attack on Matawhero, to the west of Gisborne, 70 Europeans and Maoris loyal to the government were killed. There was further fighting with government troops, but Te Kooti eluded capture and in 1872 sought refuge in Te Kuiti (King Country), where he lived until he was officially pardoned in 1883.

### Name
The settlement's original Maori name was Turanga, but in 1870 this was changed to Gisborne (after a colonial official of that name) in order to avoid confusion with Tauranga on the Bay of Plenty.

## Sights

### Kaiti Hill (Titirangi)
From Kaiti Hill (Titirangi), at the foot of which Cook landed in 1769, there are magnificent views of the town and the surroundings. To the south there is a prospect over Poverty Bay as far as Young Nick's Head. On the summit of the hill is an observatory.

### Poko-O-Rawiri
At the foot of Kaiti Hill is the Poko-O-Rawiri meeting house (1925), one of the largest and most recent of its kind, though it departs from the old tradition. The carving is by the Rotorua school (☛Rotorua). Above the building is a small Maori church.

### Museums
**Gisborne Museum and Arts Centre** (Stout Street) illustrates the history of east-coast culture and displays works by contemporary New Zealand artists.
🅐 *Daily 2–4.30pm.*

The **Maritime Museum**, on the banks of the river, displays a variety of material, including relics of the *Star of Canada*, which ran aground on Kaiti Beach.

## Surroundings

### Matawhero
The church at Matawhero, 7 km west of Gisborne, is the oldest church in the region. Constructed of kauri wood, it was built in 1862 as a storehouse for Captain

The everpresent sheep in the hinterland of Gisborne

Read, one of the early settlers, and 10 years later was converted into an Anglican church, bought by the Presbyterians in 1872. It was the only building spared by Te Kooti when he ravaged the area in 1868.

### Manutuke

14 km south-west of Gisborne is Manutuke, with two beautifully carved 19th c. meeting houses. The bargeboards on the roof of the Te Mana-ki-Turanga house (1883) show the god Tane separating the sky from the earth and Maui drawing his great fish out of the sea. The Te Hau-ki-Turanga house (1842) that formerly stood nearby is now in the National Museum in Wellington. The other one still in Manutuke, Te Poho Rukupo, was built in 1887 in honour of the Maori chief Rupuko, who was famed as a woodcarver.

### Poverty Bay vineyards

Poverty Bay is the most famous Chardonnay winegrowing region in New Zealand. Around Manutuke are the Milton Vineyards whose wines are among the best in the country.

### Rongopai

At Rongopai, 20 km north-west of Gisborne, is a meeting house built in great haste (1888) when a visit from the Maori leader Te Kooti, who had been pardoned by the government, was expected – though he did not in fact turn up. The paintings in the interior, with their range of colours, show a radical break with Maori tradition and strong European influences. When the house was built older Maoris are said to have been appalled by the work of their younger artists.

### ★ Eastwoodhill Arboretum

The arboretum, 50 km west of Gisborne, is best reached via the Ruakaka Road. Its delightful landscaped gardens contain about 2500 species of tree indigenous to the northern hemisphere.

### Rere Falls

The wild Rere Falls are 15 km further west along a picturesque lake area.

### Beaches

North of Gisborne, along the road to the East Cape (see entry), are a series of beautiful beaches: Wainui Beach (5 km),

Makorori (14 km), Whangara (28 km), Waihau (45 km) and Tolaga Bay (55 km).

**Morere**
At Morere, 60 km south of Gisborne on Highway 2, are hot springs. The area lies within a nature reserve.

**Mahia Peninsula**
The Mahia Peninsula, a hilly promontory projecting south into the sea, separates Hawke's Bay, to the south, from Poverty Bay. Here, some 80 km south of Gisborne, are a number of beautiful beaches and peaceful holiday places.

## Hamilton                                    K 4

**Region: Waikato**
**Population: 150,000**

Hamilton, New Zealand's fourth-largest city, lies in the fertile plain of the Waikato River. The country's only inland city, it has developed spectacularly since 1950. It has a university and several agricultural and food-science research institutes, including the Meat Industry Research Institute of New Zealand.

**History**
The military settlement of Hamilton was established in 1864, after the end of the land war in the Waikato area, on the site of an abandoned Maori village. Instead of being paid the soldiers were given land to cultivate. The town is named after Captain John Hamilton, who was killed in the Battle of Gate Pa, near Tauranga on the Bay of Plenty (see entry).

Before the 18th c. the Maoris had, with much labour, laid out fields of kumara in the fertile but frequently flooded plain. When the missionaries arrived they adopted European farming methods and by the mid-18th c. there were great fields of wheat in this area, mainly supplying the needs of Auckland. Before the construction of roads the Waikato and Waipa rivers were the main routes in the interior of the country.

In the late 1850s the Waikato tribes sought to unite the Maoris, fragmented and often involved in inter-tribal feuds, against the superior power of the Europeans. They also felt themselves to be exploited when the the grain market collapsed.

The land war broke out in Taranaki in 1860, but when the fighting ended there the government was ready for action in the Waikato area. Governor Grey had built a military road from Auckland to Waikato – the Great South Road – and fortifications were built south of Auckland to defend the town. General Cameron sent gunboats up the Waikato River and with their help the Maori strongpoints, including Meremere, Rangiriri and Ngaruawahia, capital of the Maori king, were quickly taken. There was also fighting at Te Awamutu and Kihikihi. The Punui River to the south of Awamutu was now the frontier with the King Country, where the fleeing Maori king had taken refuge. Maori land up to the river was confiscated and allotted to British soldiers for cultivation. But they had difficulty in draining the swampy terrain and the land was bought up by firms in Auckland with the capital necessary to reclaim the land. In 1878 the railway came to Hamilton.

## Sights

**Waikato Museum of Art and History**
The museum (Victoria Street and Grantham Street) has a large collection of Maori material, particularly on the Tainui tribe. Its prize exhibit is a carved war canoe of 1845. Also of interest are examples of modern woodcarving and weaving from Ngaruawahia.
ⓘ *Daily 10am–4.30pm; admission free on Mon.*

**Historic buildings**
The Bank of New Zealand (1878) at the corner of Hood Street and Victoria Street is due to be converted into a cultural centre. Hockin House (1893), in Selwyn Street, is the headquarters of the Waikato Historical Society. Lake House (1873), in Lake Crescent, is a masterpiece of Victorian architecture.

**Waikato River**
The Hamilton Gardens on the banks of the Waikato River are particularly beautiful when the roses are in bloom. An excursion steamer, the *Waipa Delta*, plies along the river.

**Victoria Street, Main Street**
In Victoria Street, which runs parallel to the river, and Main Street there are a number of commercial art galleries.

**Theatres**

Hamilton has two theatres: the Founders' Memorial Theatre (London Street and Tristram Street), which tends towards the traditional, and the avant-garde Left Bank Theatre (Marlborough Place).

## Surroundings

**Temple View**

7 km south-west of Hamilton is Temple View, the headquarters of New Zealand's Mormons.

**Raglan**

50 km west of Hamilton, on the Tasman Sea, is Raglan, a pleasant seaside resort with a beach of black sand. It is named after Lord Raglan, commander of British forces in the Crimean War. The first white mission station in the Waikato region was established here in the 1830s.

**★Bridal Veil Falls**

It is worth making a detour south from Raglan to the magical Bridal Veil Falls, which really do wave in the wind like a white veil. When the sun is shining from the right direction they also glisten with all the colours of the rainbow.

**★Ngaruawahia**

20 km north-west of Hamilton is Ngaruawahia, once capital of a Maori kingdom of the Waikato tribes, where Chief Te Wherowhero was elected king as Potatau I in 1858. The present queen (since 1966) is the sixth (and first female) ruler of the Waikato tribes. A new king or queen is elected in a solemn ceremonial at the end of the *tangi* mourning ceremonies for the dead ruler, in the presence of the body on its bier.

During the land wars, which rapidly spread from Taranaki to the Waikato area, it became evident that the situation of the royal residence at the two rivers was a source of danger rather than security. After British gunboats on the Waikato had taken the Maori strongholds at Meremere and Rangiriri in 1863, Ngaruawahia was abandoned without a fight. After the battle of Orakau the king sought refuge with the tribes in King Country.

Maori land was then surveyed by the government and sold. Even after peace was concluded in 1881 it was many years before a new residence of the Maori

kings was established here. Finally in 1920 land on the river was bought back from settlers and the stronghold of Turangawaewae Pa was built. A major part in the rebuilding of the royal residence was played by the Maori princess Te Puea Hernagi (1884–1952). The first building erected was the Arehurewa shrine for relics, followed in 1923 by the Kiwikiwi meeting house. The first post of the Mahinarangi meeting house was driven into the ground by the famous Maori politician Apirana Ngati. Turongo was built in 1933, a residence for King Koroki designed by Princess Te Puea (a richly carved six-sided tower-like structure). The Kimiora Cultural Complex (1974) contains a large mural. The queen's palace is not open to the public; it can be entered only on special occasions.

Since 1896 a canoe **regatta** has been held annually in March at the Point, the confluence of the Waikato and the Waipa. Its high point is a parade of large war canoes. A monument at the Point commemorates King Potatau I. Here also is a turret gun from a British gunboat, a relic of the land war of 1863.

**Taupiri Mountain**

7 km north of Ngaruawahia, on the banks of the Waikato, is Taupiri Mountain (288 m). The hill, which to the Maoris is sacred, was returned to them by the government only in 1975. On the slopes of the hill, which has been fortified since early times, is the *tapu* burial place of the Maori kings.

**Huntly**

On the lower course of the Waikato River, 33 km north of Hamilton, is the town of Huntly (pop. 7000). Here the river cuts through two huge **coalfields** that were opened in the 1840s. The coal deposits were systematically surveyed by the geologist Ferdinand von Hochstetter in 1859. After a number of serious accidents in the underground workings opencast mining started in 1940. There are now, however, two new underground mines.

Ⓖ *Conducted tours by appointments; apply to the Coal Corporation office in Huntly.*

Huntly's coal-fired **power station** was completed in 1981. Its twin cooling towers, 150 m high, are prominent features of the landscape.

## Rangiriri

17 km north of Huntly is Rangiriri, which in 1863, during the land wars, was the scene of a bloody encounter between British troops and Maoris. It was only after two unsuccessful assaults on the Maori stronghold here that it finally fell to the British. The main fortifications stand on the west side of Highway 1.

## Te Aroha

53 km north-east of Hamilton on Highway 26 is the long-established spa resort of Te Aroha (Waikato region; pop. 3500), situated at the foot of the hill of the same name on the fringes of the Kaimai Range. It still preserves its turn-of-the 19th c. Victorian bathhouses and spa establishments. There are three different mineral springs, whose water is used both for drinking and bathing. The old bathhouse No. 1 has been replaced by a modern establishment. From Mount Te Aroha (952 m; trails, shuttle bus) there are beautiful views. Within easy reach of Te Aroha are the Kaimai Range (trails) and the imposing Wairere Falls (150 m high).

## Matamata

60 km east of Hamilton, on Highway 27, is the little town of Matamata (Waikato region; pop. 6000), the commercial centre of an agricultural region (sheep, dairy farming, horse breeding). The town owes its origin to a 19th c. British immigrant named Firth who leased more than 22,000 ha of land from the local Maori chief, Wiremu Tamihana. He drained the swamps, built a road to the military settlement of Cambridge and made the Waihou River navigable for cargo vessels. By the end of the century, however, his little empire had collapsed. He built the three-storey Firth Tower (1881; 3 km east of Matamata) as a refuge against Maori raids. Beside the tower are his house and a number of other old buildings.

## Kaimai Range

North-east of Matamata is the Kaimai Range, through which there are a number of trails. One particularly attractive trip is to the imposing Wairere Falls, 150 m high. The trail takes off from the Matamata–Okauia–Gordon road.

◀ The enchanting Bridal Veil Falls near Raglan

## Cambridge

A half-hour drive south-east from Hamilton is the English-looking town of Cambridge (pop. 11,000), on the Waikato River, in the commercial centre of an agricultural area (cattle, sheep, horses; dairy farming). Cambridge was originally a military settlement established during the land wars in the Waikato region, on the site of a fortified Maori village. British gunboats could sail up the Waikato River as far as this point. It is disputed whether the town was called Cambridge because the Waikato was thought to resemble the English river Cam or as a compliment to the then commander-in-chief of the British army, the Duke of Cambridge. Historic buildings include St Andrew's Church (1881; Anglican), the Primary School (1879) and the old Court House with its handsome facade, now housing the Municipal Museum.

## Lake Karapiro

South-east of Cambridge is Lake Karapiro, a 24 km long reservoir supplying the Karapiro hydroelectric station (viewing is possible). It is the lowest of a chain of power stations on the Waikato that were brought into operation in 1948.

## Te Awamutu

30 km south of Hamilton (Highway 3), on the Waipa River, is the old Maori settlement of Te Awamutu (Waikato region; pop. 8500). The name means 'end of the river' (that is, the highest point at which it was navigable by canoes). A mission station was established here in 1839. Te Awamutu is now the commercial centre of a dairy farming area. The last battles of the land war in the Waikato region were fought hereabouts in the late summer of 1864. The decisive battle was fought at Orakau, only 8 km from Te Awamutu, on March 31st 1864. The heroic resistance of Rewi Maniapoto provided material for the early New Zealand film *Rewi's Last Stand*.

After the end of the land war in the Waikato region British soldiers were settled on land confiscated from the Maoris. The Puniu River marked the boundary between the confiscated land and the King Country, which no settler dared enter until a peace treaty was signed with King Tawhiao in 1881. The railway reached Te Awamutu in 1880.

St John's Anglican Church (1854) has

fine stained glass and interesting gravestones. Beside it, in sharp contrast, is a modern church built in 1965.

In the Civic Centre (Roche Street) is the Te Awamutu and District Museum, which is mainly devoted to the Maoris and the land wars.

ⓖ *Tue.–Sat. 10am–4pm, Sun. 2–4pm.*

The Waipa Kokiri Arts Centre was established to preserve and maintain the craft skills of the Maoris.

ⓖ *Mon.–Thu. 9am–4pm, Fri. 2–4pm.*

### Pirongia Forest Park

Pirongia Forest Park (15 km west of Te Awamutu), centred on an extinct volcano (959 m), can be explored on a network of trails with mountain huts and fine views.

## Hastings                          L 6

**Region: Hawke's Bay**
**Population: 58,000**

The town of Hastings lies 20 km south of Napier (see entry) in the fertile Heretaunga plain with its numerous fruit plantations, vineyards and parks. The town's economy centres on food industries (canning, fruit processing, brewing, meat-freezing plants).

### History

In 1864 a group of 12 settlers, known as the 'twelve apostles', bought land in the Heretaunga plain. One of them, Francis Hicks, founded the settlement in 1873. It was originally to be called Hicksville, but this was replaced by its present name, in honour of Warren Hastings, first governor general of the East India Company. Like its neighbour, Napier, Hastings was hit by a severe earthquake in 1931, in which several dozen people were killed and many buildings were totally destroyed. The rebuilding of the town was largely in art-deco style.

## Sights

### Hastings Exhibition Centre

The Hastings Exhibition Centre (Civic Centre, Eastbourne Street) has a large collection of Maori works of art, and also houses the Ebbett Collection, an art collection assembled by an early 20th c. mayor of the town.

ⓖ *Daily 10am–4pm.*

**Leopard Brewery**
ⓖ *Conducted tours by appointment.*

## Surroundings

### Havelock North

5 km south-east of Hastings is the exclusive residential suburb of Havelock North (pop. 9000), named after Major-General Sir Henry Havelock, who distinguished himself in the Indian Mutiny.

### Te Mata

From the hill of Te Mata (400 m) there is a marvellous view of Hawke's Bay. The hill can be climbed on a narrow road or an attractive footpath.

### ★Te Mata Estate

On the slopes of the hill is the Te Mata Estate, the oldest winery in New Zealand. This relatively small estate produces an excellent wine, Sauvignon Blanc Castle Hill.

### Lourdes Chapel

On the road to Te Mata is the modern Lourdes Chapel (1960), dedicated to the Virgin Mary. Its architect, John Scott, was clearly influenced by Le Corbusier. The timber interior is reminiscent of churches built for Bishop Selwyn, such as All Saints in Howick and Old St Paul's in Wellington.

### Wineries

Particular attractions in the climatically favoured region round Hastings and Napier (see entry) are the many wineries, some of them long established.

### ★Hawke's Bay Wine Trail

Some wineries can be visited in the course of a walk on the Hawke's Bay Wine Trail. Information, including brief guides with maps, is available from tourist offices in Hastings and Napier. Notable wineries include Greenmeadows Mount St Mary's Mission, Vidal's Vineyard (Hastings), Te Mata Estate (Havelock North), Corban's Winery (Napier), Esk Valley Estate (north of Napier) and Brookfields Vineyards (Meeanee, between Napier and Hastings).

### Waimarama

30 km south-east of Hastings by way of Havelock North is Waimarama, with a beautiful sandy beach. From here there

are fine views of the high cliffs of Bare Island.

### Ocean Beach
Ocean Beach, also reached by way of Havelock North, is another excellent beach.

### Pakipaki
In the Maori village of Pakipaki, 6 km south of Hastings on Highway 2, is the Houngara meeting house (1916), with fine carving.

### Te Aute College
30 km south of Hastings is Te Aute College, a school founded in 1854, mainly for Maori pupils. The school is famed for having taught three future Maori leaders, Maui Pomare, Apirana Ngata and Peter Buck, and is seen by many as the cradle of the influential Young Maori Party. The school has a fine assembly hall, with magnificent carving by Pine Taiapa in the 1930s.

### Waipawa
### Waipukurau
43 km and 50 km south-west of Hastings are the two little townships of Waipawa (pop. 1700) and Waipukurau (pop. 3700), founded in the 1860s by the owners of large sheep farms.

44 km south of Waipukurau and 5 km before Porangahau, on a hill just off the road, is a village with the longest place name in the world – 36 letters in the official spelling and no fewer than 62 in the colloquial version. The place name is a story in itself. 'the place where Tamatea, the man with the big knees, who fell down hills, climbed up again and ate them, became known as the land-eater and played a song to his loved one on the flute' (the loved one was his twin brother, who was killed in battle).

## Hawera                                    J 6

### Region: Taranaki
### Population: 11,000

Under the south side of Mount Taranaki, at the north-west end of Taranaki Bay, is the agricultural market town of Hawera; the Maori name means 'burnt earth'. Threatened by the Hauhau movement after the land wars in the Taranaki region, the settlers withdrew southward to Patea. In 1870 a military post was

established at Hawera, and round this a settlement grew. Angered by the government's tolerance in its dealings with the Maori leader Te Whiti and the passive resistance and civil disobedience of his tribe, the local settlers drove out the Maoris in 1879 and proclaimed the Republic of Hawera; the separatist movement was quickly put down by the government.

## Sights

### Turuturu-mokai Pa
Of the fortified Maori settlement of Turuturu-mokai Pa, built long before the arrival of the Europeans, there remain parts of the ramparts and storage pits.

There also survive five outer strongpoints (2.5 km north of Hawera; signposted). In the late 1860s British troops constructed a defensive position outside the *pa*, which was attacked and overrun in 1868 by Hauhau warriors and a white defector.

### Water tower
From the water tower (50 m high) at the corner of High Street and Albion Street there are magnificent views.

### Elvis Presley Memorial Room
The Elvis Presley Memorial Room (51 Argyle Street) has a collection of records and souvenirs of the famous rock 'n' roll star assembled by a local Elvis fan.

### Tawhiti Museum
The Tawhiti Museum, housed in a former dairy, has a rich collection of material on the eventful history of the region.

## Surroundings

### Bush railway
3 km north-east of Hawera an old railway once used for transporting logs has been reopened as a tourist attraction.

### Ohawe Beach
7 km west of Hawera, at the mouth of the Waigongoro River, is Ohawe Beach, where the first moa bones were found, from which the skeleton of this long-extinct giant flightless bird has been reconstructed. It is believed that there were several species of moa still living in the Taranaki area in the 14th c.

### Te Ngutu-o-te-manu battlefield

23 km north-west of Hawera by way of Okaiawa is the battlefield of Te Ngutu-o-te-manu (1868), in which government troops suffered heavy losses in an effort to avenge the taking of their position at Turuturu-mokai Pa.

### Patea

28 km south-east of Hawera is the military settlement of Patea (pop. 2000), established in the 1860s, which played an important part in the land wars. It is now a dairy- and sheep-farming region. In good weather there is a fine view from here of Mount Taranaki (Egmont).

Here too is a 17 m long concrete model of the Aotea tribal canoe, made in 1933 to commemorate the ancestors of the Maori tribe who once lived in this area.

The South Taranaki Museum (Egmont Street) has a collection of Maori artefacts and mementos of the early European settlement.

◉ *Daily 10am–4pm.*

### Lake Rotorangi

Inland, in a densely forested area, is Lake Rotorangi, a 46 km long reservoir on the Patea River, created in 1984 to supply water to a large hydroelectric power station. The lake attracts large numbers of anglers and sailing enthusiasts. It can be reached from Hawera, or via Eltham and Patea.

## Hawke's Bay                    L/M 6

### Region: Hawke's Bay

This crescent bay lies on the east side of the North Island, near Hastings (see entry). It was given its name (after Admiral Lord Hawke) by Captain Cook in 1769. It is bounded on the north-east by the Mahia Peninsula and on the south-west by Cape Kidnappers.

### Climate

Hawke's Bay has a Mediterranean climate, with little rain and long hours of sunshine, conditions ideal for fruit growing and horticulture, including vines and various vegetables. In spite of this the population has been steadily declining in recent years.

### Cape Kidnappers

Cape Kidnappers, 21 km east of Hastings (see entry) at the south end of Hawke's Bay, near Clifton, is noted particularly as a nesting place for ★gannets. The birds arrive in the sanctuary here at the end of July. Their eggs are laid between October and November, and the young birds hatch 6 weeks later. The gannets begin to leave their nesting place in February, and by April almost all of them have gone.

The gannet colony can be reached from Clifton (5 km walk) only at low tide along the sandy beach to an observation platform. There are conducted tours from Te Awanga and trips in all-terrain vehicles to near the site.

### History

In Maori mythology the cape was Maui's magic fish hook, with which he had hauled the whole of the North Island, like a giant fish, out of the sea. It was given its present name by Captain Cook, who after his first disappointing landing in Poverty Bay had turned back, sailed south and anchored off the cape. On the following morning, when Cook was bargaining with the Maoris who had come out to his ship in canoes, some of them seized a young Tahitian named Taiata, the servant of Cook's interpreter, and carried him off. The young man managed to escape and swim back to the ship: whereupon Cook named the rocky promontory Cape Kidnappers. It was another 50 years before Europeans settled here. The first were whalers, who set up whaling stations at Mahia, Wairoa and elsewhere. Around 1840 there were still only a few settlers living in Hawke's Bay; then during the 1840s the missionary William Colenso established a mission station at Clive. He brought the natives the Bible in the Maori language, but he also showed them how to grow grain and fruit. A notable feature of the European settlement of Hawke's Bay and its hinterland is that it was carried out not by poor immigrants but by entrepreneurs with capital, who bought huge areas of land from the Maoris and established large sheep farms. They did not work the farms themselves but appointed efficient managers to do it for them.

The hinterland of Hawke's Bay is hilly and sometimes mountainous. The only flat area is the Heretaunga plain near Hastings, which was drained, divided up into smaller holdings and sold.

Cape Kidnappers, on Hawke's Bay, is one of the few places where gannets can be seen close up

In February 1931 the Hawke's Bay area was hit by a severe earthquake that caused heavy damage, particularly in Napier and Hastings (see entries), and killed more than 200 people. One consequence of the earthquake was a rise in the level of the seabed, which created over 3000 ha of new land in this area.

### Wairoa
The little town of Wairoa (pop. 5000), situated on Hawke's Bay between Napier and Gisborne (see entry), is the commercial centre of a large pastoral farming region and a good base from which to explore Urewera National Park, with Lake Waikaremoana. The first Europeans to come here in the 1820s were flax dealers, later followed by whalers and missionaries. In 1865 there was fighting between the settlers and supporters of the Hauhau movement, who were finally compelled to withdraw to the roadless fastness of the Urewera Range.

The most striking feature on Marine Parade is a lighthouse of kauri wood that from 1877 to 1958 stood on Portland Island, off the southern tip of the Mahia Peninsula. The Wairoa Museum has mementos of the early settlement and a good collection of Maori material. From the bridge there is a view upstream of the Takitimu meeting house, with carving by Pine Taiapa.

### Other sights
See Hastings, Gisborne, Napier

## Hokianga Harbour     H 2

### Region: Northland

Hokianga Harbour, a long, ramified inlet on the west side of the northern tip of the North Island, is a drowned valley system with different landscapes on each side. On the bare north side are tall sand dunes; on the green south side are the little holiday resorts of Omapere and Opononi, both of which have beautiful beaches. Many ships have come to grief on the shallows and sandbanks.

### History
Maori legend relates that Kupe, the legendary Polynesian seafarer and discoverer of New Zealand, set out from here on his voyage home to Hawaiki.

Much later, probably at about the same time as in the Bay of Islands (see entry), European, Australian and American whalers, timber and flax dealers began to put in here. It is believed that the first immigrants settled here in 1827 but for fear of the Maoris moved on to Australia. Until the early 20th c. kauri timber and resin formed the bulk of the trade in Hokianga Harbour, which became an important port of call for ships from all over the world. The population was larger than it is today; the loggers, gum diggers and sawmill workers gradually gave way to farmers, who pastured their cattle and sheep on the land that had been cleared of trees. Remnants of the original kauri forests have been preserved both north and south of Hokianga Harbour, in the Omahuta Forest Sanctuary (north) and Waipoua and Trounson forests (south).

Baron de Thierry (1793–1864), a French aristocrat living in exile in England, had made the acquaintance of the Maori chiefs Hongi Hika and Waikato in Cambridge during their visit to Britain. He obtained from them, in some dubious way, ownership rights over large territories in Northland. In 1837 he turned up in Hokianga with a group of followers, claiming to be 'sovereign chief of New Zealand', to carry out his plan for a settlement at Rangiahua. But his plan was impracticable and he was unable to establish his claims; his followers abandoned him, and he lived out his life in poverty in Auckland.

## Sights on Hokianga Harbour

### Horeke

Horeke is a picturesque little port town to the north of Taheke, with its houses built on piles. A shipyard was established here around 1827–8, but by 1830 its Australian owners had run out of money.

### Mangungu Mission House

A Wesleyan mission station was established to the west of Horeke around 1838. The Wesleyans had started their missionary work 10 years before with the support of Chief Eruera Patuone, who is believed to have had some contact, as a small boy, with members of Captain Cook's crew. One of the missionaries, John Hobbs, had good relations with the natives and spoke Maori, and later he was able to act as Governor Hobson's translator during the negotiation of the Treaty of Waitangi. When the population of the area moved south the mission station was transferred to Auckland (1855). The old mission church has gone but the churchyard with its gravestones remains. The Mission House, furnished in period style, is run by the Historic Places Trust.

◎ *Summer daily noon–4pm; other times by appointment.*

### Kohukohu

Kohukohu, on the north side of Hokianga Harbour, was once an important loggers' settlement. The first Roman Catholic mass in New Zealand was celebrated here by Bishop Pompallier in 1838 – an event commemorated by a memorial on Totara Point. Kohukohu is now favoured by artists and people who desire a life away from the city.

There is a ferry from Kohukohu to the neighbouring settlement of Rawene, to the south.

### Omapere

From Omapere travellers coming from the south on Highway 12 have a magnificent view of the spacious natural harbour. There is a pleasant walk along the beach, going west, to the harbour entrance. At high tide spray shoots high into the air from a blowhole.

### Onoke

In the little township of Onoke, situated at the point where the Whirinaki River flows into Hokianga Harbour, is a house that belonged to Frederick Maning (ca 1860), the trader and writer who became widely known under the pseudonym A Pakeha-Maori.

### Opononi

The holiday resort of Opononi, near the Hokianga Heads, has a beautiful beach. A well-known Opononi character was a dolphin called Opo who was particularly friendly with children playing on the beach and is now commemorated in a sculpture by Russell Clark. 2 km further east, at Pakanae, is a monument to the legendary Polynesian seafarer Kupe. There are fascinating cruises from Opononi on a historic steamer round the many arms and inlets of Hokianga Harbour.

### Rawene

The old loggers' settlement of Rawene

(pop. 350) is prettily situated on a promontory. Some of its houses are still built on piles in the water. This is another little place that has been given a fresh lease of life by artists and escapees from modern life. Notable buildings are the Old Hotel, the former hospital beside the landing stage and above all Clendon House, built in the 1860s for the successful British businessman James R Clendon. Clendon had first brought a consignment of convicts to Australia and then became a dealer in kauri wood. In the Bay of Islands he established contacts with American whalers and finally was appointed the United States honorary consul in New Zealand. His personal contacts gave him great influence. He built himself a number of houses, three of which have survived – in Russell, in Manawaora (east of Russell) and in Rawene. His house in Okiato (south of Russell), which served as New Zealand's first Government House, was burned down in 1842. Clendon House, furnished in period style, stands on the Esplanade in Rawene and is open to the public as a museum.
◙ *Daily 10am–4pm.*

## Kaikohe                                    H 2

**Region: Northland**
**Population: 4000**

Centrally situated in Northland, an hour drive east of Hokianga Harbour (see entry), is the little town of Kaikohe. The warlike Ngapuhi tribe had many fortified settlements in this area. After earlier inter-tribal wars the War of the North was fought out here between Hone Heke and government troops. Two months after Hone Heke's attack on Kororareka (Russell) in May 1845 he fought a battle with British troops at Lake Omapere (which is only 2 m deep and is fed by hot springs near its south-west corner). The British forces suffered heavy losses, but even more Maoris were killed in the successful defence of their *pa*, 9 km north-east of Kaikohe. A few weeks later, in battle at Ohaeawai (north-east of Kaikohe), British troops again suffered heavy losses. The battlefield is now marked by a simple little Maori church (1871) dedicated to St Michael, within the ramparts of the *pa*. Six months later Hone Heke was decisively defeated in the battle of Ruapekapeka.

**Hone Heke Monument**
Prominently situated on a hill near Kaikohe is a monument (1911) to the widely respected politician Hone Heke (1869–1909), who died young. He was a grand-nephew of the notorious and warlike Maori chief of the same name.

**Pioneer Village**
In Kaikohe's Pioneer Village visitors can see the old courthouse from Waimate North (1862), a tiny jail, a smithy and other 19th c. buildings. There is also an old railway built for the transport of timber.
◙ *Sat., Sun.*

**Ngawha hot springs**
7 km east of Kaikohe, reached on a road that branches off Highway 12, are the hot springs of Ngawha. The water, containing mercury and soda, are used in the treatment of skin conditions and rheumatism.

## Kaipara Harbour                            J 3

**Regions: Auckland and Northland**

It is an hour drive north-west from Auckland (see entry) to the southern shore of Kaipara Harbour, a vast natural harbour. The numerous indentations and inlets are part of a system of drowned river valleys. Kaipara Harbour has a total shoreline of over 3000 km. Only a few places offer a general view of its area: there are good views from Highway 1 at Bryderwyn and from the road (not asphalted all the way) between Wellsford and Helensville.

**History**
In the 19th c. Kaipara Harbour was an important route for the transport of kauri logs and resin from the great forests of Northland. Nowadays it is much quieter. Most of the peaceful little townships and villages – Helensville, Port Albert, Whakapirau, Pahi, Tinopai, Pouto – can be reached only on secondary and minor roads.

**Matakohe**
The most notable feature of Matakohe, situated on Highway 12 at the north end of Kaipara Harbour, is the Coates Memorial Church, built in honour of Prime Minister Joseph Gordon Coates (1878–1943), who is depicted as a knight

in armour in a round stained-glass window.

Adjoining the church is the famous ★Otamatea Kauri and Pioneer Museum, which has vivid displays illustrating the early days of the settlers and the history of kauri felling and resin gathering.
◎ Daily 9am–5pm.

## Kaitaia                                    H 2

### Region: Northland
### Population: 5200

Near the northern tip of the North Island is Kaitaia, a commercial centre for the surrounding area. It is a good base for excursions northward via Waipapakauri and along Ninety Mile Beach to Cape Reinga (see below) or westward to the Maori settlement of Ahipara, at the south end of Ninety Mile Beach. The road to Cape Reinga is good all the way, but most car-rental firms prohibit driving along the beach itself.

### Population
The population of Kaitaia includes a strikingly high proportion of Maoris, as well as many descendants of 19th c. immigrants from Dalmatia (at that time part of the Austro-Hungarian empire) who made a living as gum diggers.

### Aupouri Forest
In Aupouri Forest, to the north of Kaitaia, efforts are being made to halt the drifting sand and consolidate the dunes by planting pines along the beach.

### Surf-fishing competition
The Ninety Mile Beach Surfcasting Contest, held annually in January, attracts thousands of angling enthusiasts.

### History
Kaitaia was founded in 1834 as a mission station and grew rapidly when kauri prospectors arrived in Northland. After the first world war tourism began under the slogan of the 'winterless North'.

### Far North Regional Museum
The Far North Regional Museum (South Road) has displays on kauri resin. It also has an anchor that the French navigator JM de Surville lost during a storm in Doubtless Bay in 1769.
◎ Daily.

### Kaitaia Track
This trail (just under 10 km long), 3 km south of Kaitaia, runs through magnificent scenery.

### Mangamuka Gorge Track
This 11 km trail, 26 km south-west of Kaitaia, runs from the Takahue Valley to the wild Mangamuka Gorge.

### ★Omahuta Forest Sanctuary
40 km south-east of Kaitaia is the Omahuta Forest Sanctuary, with magnificent kauri trees. The original forest vegetation has largely been preserved and there are also many species of birds.

A road turns off Highway 1 to the south of Mangamuka Bridge and runs for 13 km to a parking area from which a footpath goes off into the forest.

## ★Doubtless Bay

Doubtless Bay, 35 km north-east of Kaitaia, extends from Cape Karikari in the north-west to Berghan Point in the north-east, and is easily accessible on Highway 10. Its main attraction is its beautiful beaches. Offshore there are good fishing for deep-sea anglers. Matai Bay and Cape Karikari are popular with scuba divers.

### History
According to Maori mythology Kupe, the legendary seafarer from Hawaiki, made his first landing in New Zealand here, at Taipa. The name Doubtless Bay was given by Captain Cook, who, sailing along this coast in 1769, decided that 'doubtless' it was a bay and not an island.

Soon after Cook passed this way the French navigator JM de Surville, heading for Peru, arrived in the bay and landed at Whatuwhiwhi. The natives were at first friendly but turned hostile when a dispute arose over a ship's boat that had been carried away in a storm. De Surville burned down the Maoris' huts and took their chief on board as a prisoner. The chief died soon afterwards of scurvy and de Surville himself died in an accident in a boat in heavy surf.

De Surville lost three anchors in a storm off Doubtless Bay. They were recovered in 1974 and 1982, and one of them is shown in Kaitaia Museum.

### Cooper's Beach

The little township of Cooper's Beach, between two Maori fortified settlements, has a beautiful beach.

### Mangonui

Mangonui, once a centre of the kauri trade, with sawmills and port installations for handling timber, lies in a beautiful setting. It has a number of buildings from earlier days.

At the landing stage is the Sealab, with an aquarium (
⊚ *Daily 9.30am–4pm.*

## ★Ninety Mile Beach

This seemingly endless and empty sandy beach on the west coast of New Zealand's northernmost tip does not quite live up to its name: it is in fact only 103 km long. The gleaming white sand tempts motorists to drive along the beach itself, but this can be dangerous. It should be attempted only by drivers with local knowledge and a suitable all-terrain vehicle; visitors should note that all New Zealand car-rental firms ban driving on beaches.

In January 1932 an Australian, Norman Smith, set a world speed record of 264 kph on a 16 km stretch of beach at Hukatere.

### Surf-angling competitions

Surfcasting competitions are held annually in January at Ahipara.

### Shifting sands

The shifting dunes at Aupouri, which formerly tended to move inland, have been stabilised by sowing grass and lupin seeds and planting conifers.

## Cape Reinga

Cape Reinga – the Maori name means underworld – is the most north-westerly point on the North Island. It is reached from Kaitaia on a road that runs along the narrow tongue of land fringed by Ninety Mile Beach, passing through Aupouri Forest (planted to consolidate the dunes) and an extensive area dug over by kauri gum diggers in earlier days. At some points it is like driving over a desert.

The lighthouse at Cape Reinga

### History
In 1769 Captain Cook almost met the French navigator JM de Surville in this area. During a violent storm their ships were only a short distance apart but they sailed past without seeing one another.

### ★ Lighthouse
From the lighthouse on Cape Reinga there are tremendous views – westward along the coast to Cape Maria van Diemen (so named by Tasman), eastward as far as the North Cape. If visibility is good the Three Kings Islands – so called by Tasman because he sailed past them on Epiphany in 1643 – can be seen in the distance.

The lighthouse, 165 m above sea level, was built in 1941. Below it an ancient pohutukawa tree hangs over the sheer cliff. To the Maoris it is sacred, for from here, they believe, souls plunge at sunset into the sea and down into the underworld to return to Hawaiki.

### ★ Cape Reinga Walkway
From Cape Reinga there are rewarding trails eastward to Spirits Bay (ca 10 hours) and southward by way of Cape Maria van Diemen to Ninety Mile Beach and then inland to Te Paki (ca 7 hours).

There is no overnight accommodation at Cape Reinga. Information about walks and accommodation in the area can be obtained from the information centre in Kaitaia.

### Houhora Heads
Roughly halfway between Kaitaia and Cape Reinga, in a beautiful inlet, are the Houhora Heads, with a campsite and picnic area.

### Mount Carmel
Opposite the Houhora Heads is Mount Carmel (245 m), so named by Captain Cook.

### Subritzky House
Subritzky House was built by a 19th c. Polish immigrant and has been lovingly maintained by his descendants.

### Wagener Museum
Near Subritzky House is the Wagener Museum, with a varied collection that includes Maori art, whaling equipment, firearms, everyday objects of the 19th c. and kauri resin.
◉ *Daily 9am–5pm.*

## Kawhia Harbour     J/K 4/5

**Region: Waikato**

Some 100 km south-west of Hamilton (see entry), on the west coast, is the natural harbour of Kawhia. The area was formerly of great importance to the Maoris as the resting place of the Tainui ancestral canoe.

The Maori tribes that lived here, under their chief Te Rauparaha, were driven out of Kawhia in 1821 by other Waikato tribes and moved south to Kapiti Island, where they in their turn killed or drove out the local tribes.

### Kawhia
Now a small settlement of 300 people, in the 19th c. Kawhia was an important trading centre (timber, flax, grain) that shipped cargoes to Sydney and even as far afield as California. After the land wars and the peace of 1881 it declined into insignificance.

### Te Puia hot springs
On Te Puia beach, 4 km west of Kawhia, hot springs gush out of the sand at low tide, so that visitors can have their own thermal bath.

### Taharoa
South of the entrance to Kawhia Harbour, reached on a side road, is the Maori settlement of Taharoa, round which are considerable deposits of dark ferruginous sand. It is processed in modern plants and exported, mainly to Japan.

## King Country

Inland from the North Taranaki Bight (west coast), between Mokau and Kawhia, extends the rugged and infertile area known as the King Country. It is a region of karstic limestone, with deep gorges, intricate karstic cave systems and bizarre rock formations.

### History
The first Europeans landed in this area in the early 19th c. on the wild west coast at Mokau and Kawhia. They traded with the Maoris, exchanging guns for flax and dried tattooed heads, which were much sought after in Europe. Missionaries taught the natives European farming methods, and soon wheat was being

exported from Kawhia.

Between Mokau and Kawhia lived the warlike Te Maniapoto tribes, who believed that their ancestors had arrived here in the Tainui ancestral canoe. They were keen partisans of the Maori King Movement and supported the rebels in Taranaki and Waikato against the government.

After the defeat of the rebels at Orakau the Maori king, whose residence had been at Ngaruawahia on the Waikato River, sought refuge in this area. The Ngati-Maniapoto tribes held on to their land, and settlers did not dare to venture into the King Country.

In 1881 the mighty Maori chief Rewi Maniapoto made peace with the government. He sold and leased land to the whites, against the will of the Maoris, and permitted the construction of a railway through the King Country.

Until the mid-20th c. alcohol was prohibited in the King Country. As a result smuggling and illicit distilling flourished.

## Levin                                    K 7

**Region: Manawatu-Wanganui**
**Population: 19,000**

Levin, the commercial centre of a farming region in the western foreland of the Tararua Range, lies 93 km north-east of Wellington (see entry), to which it supplies vegetables, milk and meat.

The town was founded in 1889 as a camp for railway workers and was named after a director of the railway company.

## Surroundings

### Lake Horowhenua
To the west of Levin is Lake Horowhenua, a popular recreation area. The Maoris constructed artificial islands in the lake on which they built fortified villages (pas).

The area round Lake Papaitonga, to the south, was the scene of bloody battles between supporters of the Maori leader Te Rauparaha and the local tribes.

### Waitarere Beach
8 km north-west of Levin is Waitarere Beach. Offshore can be seen the wreck of HMS *Hyderabad*, which ran aground here in 1878.

### Hokio Beach
There are beautiful stretches of beach at Hokio, to the south, and at the mouth of the Manawatu River, to the north. Efforts are being made to consolidate the dunes by planting trees, in order to prevent the sand from being blown on to the fertile fields inland.

### Foxton
20 km north of Levin is Foxton (pop. 2700), a much older European settlement. Founded in 1855, it later was given its present name in honour of Sir William Fox, several times prime minister of New Zealand. Most of the trade in the trading post at the mouth of the river was in flax and timber. When the railway was built a long way from Foxton, however, the town's development came to a standstill.

There are a number of historic buildings in Foxton's main street. The old courthouse is now a museum of local history, and the old tram station, once served by horse-drawn trams, still survives.
ⓖ *Museum Sun.*

### Foxton Beach
Foxton Beach is a pretty little settlement with many holiday and retirement homes.

### Flood control
Measures are in place for controlling flooding on the Manawatu River between Foxton and Shannon.

## Masterton                                K 7

**Region: Wellington**
**Population: 20,000**

100 km north-east of Wellington (see entry), on the fairly steep eastern slopes of the Tararua Range, is the town of Masterton, an important communications hub and supply centre. It is named after Joseph Masters (1802–74), leader of the Small Farm Association, which opposed the settlement plans of Edward Wakefield and the New Zealand Land Company and demanded that poor immigrants should also be able to acquire and work small areas of land. Masters won the support of Governor Grey, whose name is commemorated in the little township of Greytown, 23 km further south. In

1853 the association bought land from the Maoris, divided it up and sold it on to small farmers.

### Aerial top-dressing
Great improvements in agricultural yields were achieved, particularly in hilly country, by the use from 1947 onwards of aerial top-dressing, a method of distributing fertilisers, seed and pesticides from the air.

### Wairarapa Arts Centre
The Wairarapa Arts Centre, which incorporates a Methodist church of 1878 (Bruce Street), has a collection of local and regional art.

## Surroundings

### Mount Bruce Wildlife Centre
30 km north on Highway 2 is the Mount Bruce Wildlife Centre, run by the Department of Conservation. It is famed for its bird breeding station, which is particularly concerned with the survival of the endangered takahe.
🔘 *Daily 10am–4pm.*

### ★ Tararua Range
West of Masterton are the rugged hills of the densely wooded Tararua Range, which lies between the Wairarapa area and the west coast. There are a number of peaks, such as the Mitre (1571 m).

### Tararua Forest Park
Some 100,000 ha of the range constitute Tararua Forest Park, within which are a number of walking trails, with overnight accommodation in mountain huts.

### Mount Holdsworth Reserve
22 km west of Masterton, on the eastern fringes of Tararua Forest Park, is Mount Holdsworth (1474 m), the central feature of an important nature reserve.

### ★ Honeycomb Rock Walkway
50 km south of Masterton, at Falt Point, is an 8 km trail along the Pacific coast, passing curious honeycombed rocks.

### Castlepoint
### Riversdale
Castlepoint (70 km north-east) and Riversdale (ca 60 km east) are the only bathing resorts on the long stretch of inaccessible cliff coast in the south-east of the North Island.

## Featherston

**Region: Wellington**
**Population: 2600**

The township of Featherston lies 40 km south-west of Masterton at the foot of the Rimutaka Ranges. This area was first surveyed about 1840 for the New Zealand Land Company, and the town was named after a senior government official who decided that a settlement should be established here.

### History
The settlement was originally a mail-coach station. Later, when a railway was built through the Rimutaka Ranges, large numbers of railway workers settled here.

During the second world war there was a camp for Japanese prisoners of war in Featherston. In 1955 the 8.79 km Rimutaka railway tunnel was driven through the hills.

### Rimutaka Forest Park
A 16 km stretch of railway line, on a fairly steep gradient, was abandoned after the opening of the new tunnel. It is now the **Rimutaka Incline Walkway**, one of the principal trails in Rimutaka Forest Park.

### Fell Engine Museum
The Fell Engine Museum displays a steam engine specially built in 1878 for this steep stretch of railway line.

### Lake Wairarapa
Nearby is the shallow Lake Wairarapa, formerly home to large numbers of ducks and eels, which provided additions to the Maori diet.

The lake was sold to the New Zealand government in 1896. Recently it has been incorporated in a large scheme for the prevention of flooding.

### Palliser Bay
There is an attractive excursion to the wild coast of Palliser Bay and **Cape Palliser** on a road that runs south on the east side of Lake Wairarapa. This was the scene of a tragic incident in 1942, when a revolt by Japanese prisoners of war was crushed and 48 of them were shot.

# Greytown

**Region: Wellington**
**Population: 1800**

20 km south-west of Masterton is Greytown, once the centre of the fertile Wairarapa area (fruit growing, vegetables). The township was founded by small farmers in 1854 and named after Governor George Grey, who had supported the Small Farm Association in its efforts to help workers on the land own their own holdings.

The dense primeval forest was cleared for cultivation, but because of the unpredictable nature of the Waiohine River the railway was built at some distance from Greytown and the town's development was brought to a halt.

### Papawai Marae
3 km away is Papawai Marae, the main stronghold in the 1890s of the Kotahitanga movement that fought vehemently for self-government for the Maoris. Discussions were held here between the government and representatives of the Maoris. Subsequently the movement was absorbed into the Young Maori Party. The carvings round the *marae* face inwards, not outwards as was usual. A small Maori house that belonged to the *tohunga* (priest) still stands.

### Waiohine Gorge
20 km north-west of Greytown, on the edge of Tararua Forest Park, is the wild Waiohine Gorge. For the more adventurous there are trails from here up to Mount Omega (1182 m) and Mount Holdsworth (1474 m).

# Napier                                      L 6

**Region: Hawke's Bay**
**Population: 53,000**

This important port in Hawke's Bay (see entry) is named after the colonial administrator General Sir Charles Napier. The town was largely destroyed by a devastating earthquake in 1931. In spite of the prevailing economic depression the town was rapidly rebuilt, and its previous neoclassical buildings gave way to art deco designs and the American Spanish mission style. The new buildings were claimed to be earthquake proof.

Skilled publicity, emphasising the town's climate, its unique assemblage of art-deco and mission-style architecture and the varied scenic attractions of its hinterland, has made Napier a popular tourist centre.

### History
When the first settlers arrived in Hawke's Bay, many years after Captain Cook, the local Maoris had been decimated by rival tribes armed with guns or driven north on to the Mahia Peninsula. The whalers, traders and missionaries who came here found only small numbers of Maoris in the area.

In 1844 a clergyman was sent to Hawke's Bay to establish a mission station near Clive, and about the same time the hinterland was developed for pastoral farming. The new settlers came into conflict with the government in distant Wellington (see entry), which was drawing revenues from the sale of land but was doing little for the opening up and development of the Hawke's Bay area. Accordingly in 1858 the area was declared an independent province with Napier as its chief town.

During the land wars the east coast round Napier was largely spared by the fighting. In 1866 there was a Hauhau campaign against Napier, but the rebels were beaten back at Omarunui and Eskdale by the settlers themselves.

### Earthquake, 1931
On the morning of February 3rd 1931 there was a severe earthquake in the region, shocks from which were felt as far away as Europe. Buildings in Napier and the neighbouring town of Hastings (see entry) was destroyed and 256 people lost their lives. The seabed in the Ahuriri Lagoon was thrust upwards and the town thus acquired more than 33 sq km of extra land. This is now covered by pasture, various industrial installations, an airport and the districts of Marewa, Onekawa, Pirimai and Maraenui.

## Sights

### ★ Marine Parade
Marine Parade, the town's finest promenade, runs along the seafront. It is lined with Norfolk pines and is most attractive in the morning sun. It has all the attractions and entertainments of a popular tourist resort.

The busy Marine Parade is just off the town centre. The **visitor centre** provides information about Napier and the surrounding area. Well-tended gardens, including the impressive **Sunken Gardens**, mini-golf and a roller-blading rink provide entertainment for young and old. In the Mediterranean-style **colonnade** with a roofed concert platform is the ship's bell of HMS *Veronica*, which was the first source of help after the 1931 earthquake.

### ★Marineland of New Zealand

A major attraction is Marineland of New Zealand, with its displays by performing dolphins, seals and otters, as well as its penguins and gannets.
ⓖ *Daily 10am–4.30pm; dolphin shows twice daily.*

### Lilliput Railway

The Lilliput Railway is particularly popular with children.

### Stables Museum and Waxworks

The Stables Museum has films and displays about the 1931 earthquake as well as a popular waxworks show.
Further south are the Mardi Gras

Area, used for a variety of events, the Can Am Cars and a small lake (boats for hire).

### Hawke's Bay Aquarium

A little further along is Hawke's Bay Aquarium, with a three-storey Oceanarium in which visitors can see at close quarters a great variety of creatures of the Pacific – the sharks' feeding time is a great draw.
ⓖ *Daily 9am–5pm, evenings in summer.*

### ★Hawke's Bay Art Gallery and Museum

The Hawke's Art Gallery Bay and Museum has a rich collection reflecting the culture and art on the east side of the North Island. Much space is also devoted to contemporary art. Particularly interesting is the audio-visual material on the earthquake and the subsequent rebuilding of the town, with many photographs and eyewitness accounts.
ⓖ *Daily 10am–5pm.*

### ★Statue of Pania

In the gardens opposite the museum is a statue of Pania of the Reef, a mermaid-like figure who features in a Maori legend. Pania loved a man and lived with him on land, in spite of her family's

Pania of the Reef, a figure of Maori legend, on Napier's Marine Parade

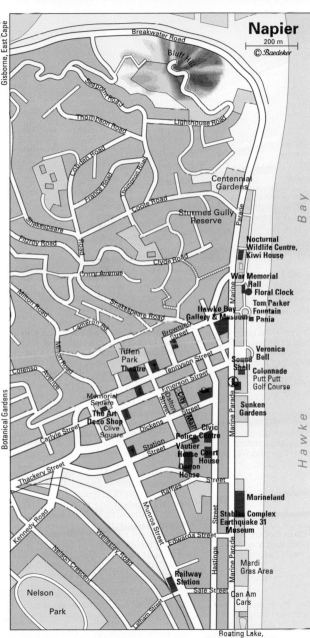

Napier

200 m

© Baedeker

Art-deco architecture in Napier

appeals to her to return to the reef. One day when she swam out to visit them she was drawn down into the sea and was unable to return to her lover.

Beside the statue is the **Tom Parker Fountain**.

#### War Memorial Hall
Close by, to the north, is the War Memorial Hall, commemorating those who fell in various military conflicts, particularly the first and second world wars. In front of the hall is the photogenic **floral clock**.

#### ★Nocturnal Wildlife Centre
Further north still is the Nocturnal Wildlife Centre, with a variety of New Zealand animals that are active at night. In the **Kiwi House** visitors can see New Zealand's national bird, which is an endangered species (☞22, Baedeker Special).
◉ Daily 11am–3pm.

#### Cathedral
From the Hawke's Bay Museum the broad Tennyson Street runs into the town centre, passing the Cathedral of St John the Evangelist, whose roof fell in during a service on the day of the earthquake. It contains a small chapel dedicated to Bishop Bennett, the first Maori bishop, and the Maori politician Apirana Ngata.

#### ★★Art Deco Walk
After the earthquake in 1931 the town was rapidly rebuilt, largely in the art-deco and Spanish-mission styles then in fashion in the United States. The result was a unique assemblage of buildings in these styles (now protected as national monuments), comparable only with the Art Deco District of Miami. The Napier architect Louis Hay, who played a major part in the rebuilding of the town, was strongly influenced by the American architects Henry H Richardson, Frank Lloyd Wright and Louis Sullivan. Among the first buildings erected after the earthquake were the Masonic Hall (1932 by WJ Prouse of Wellington) and the Criterion Hotel (by EA Williams).

The high point of the calendar is the **Art Deco Weekend** held annually on the third weekend of February. Accommodation should be booked early.

A brochure gives detailed descriptions of Napier's finest art-deco buildings in a walk round the town. Information is also available from:

THE ART DECO SHOP
Desco Centre, 163 Tennyson Street
☎ *(06) 8350022, fax (06) 8351912, email artdeco@hb.co.nz, www.artdeconapier.com*
◎ *Mon.–Fri. 9am–5pm, Sat., Sun. 10am–5pm. Guided art-deco walks Oct.–Jun. daily 10am, 2pm; Jul.–Sep. Wed., Sat., Sun. 2pm (start from the shop).*

### Botanical Gardens
West of the town centre, on the slopes of Hospital Hill, are the Botanical Gardens. Close by is Napier's cemetery, with a number of historic gravestones.

### ★Bluff Hill
To the north of the town centre is Bluff Hill, on which are the Centennial Gardens and Bluff Hill Domain. From Bluff Hill Lookout (reached by way of Lighthouse Road) there are magnificent views; in good weather the prospect extends as far as the Mahia Peninsula to the north-east and Cape Kidnappers to the south-east.

## Surroundings

### Eskdale Park
20 km north-west of Napier, on the road to Taupo (Highway 5; see entry), is Eskdale Park, a popular destination for excursions. It lies in a beautiful valley with long-established woodland and vineyards. There was fighting here in 1866 between settlers and Hauhau rebels.

### Tutira
40 km north of Napier on Highway 2, situated on a lake (bird sanctuary), is the old sheep station of Tutira that was immortalised by the farmer and writer Herbert Guthrie-Smith (1861–1940) in his books. There is an attractive circuit of the area on the Tutira Walkway (9 km; steep in places).

### Hastings
See entry

### Hawke's Bay
See entry

## New Plymouth                                            J 6

**Region: Taranaki**
**Population: 50,000**

Under the north side of the Taranaki or Mount Egmont volcano (☞Taranaki, Egmont National Park) is the port of New Plymouth, an industrial town and commercial centre of a farming region. The harbour, formed in 1881 by the construction of breakwaters, handled dairy produce (particularly cheese) and now also ships raw materials for the petrochemical industry. The proximity of rich offshore deposits of fossil fuels (at Kapuni, Maui and elsewhere) has brought a number of industrial firms to New Plymouth, creating employment.

### History
New Plymouth, so called after its English namesake, was founded in 1841; the first settlers came from Devon and Cornwall. They are said to have found only small numbers of Maoris in this area – though the presence of many fortified settlements (*pas*) and kumara fields suggests the contrary. Probably the local Taranaki tribes, who had only clubs for combat, were so harried in the early decades of the 19th c. by the Waikato tribes, who were already equipped with firearms, that they moved south, where they sought to join up with Chief Te Rauparaha in order to get guns and reoccupy their tribal territory.

Strife blew up between the returning Maori tribes and the settlers (*pakehas*), and in 1860 the conflict escalated into fierce country-wide fighting, sparked off by a fraudulent land deal at Waitara, 16 km east of New Plymouth.

## Sights

### Pukara Park
Pukara Park (Liardet Street) is laid out in Victorian style, with a fountain that is illuminated after dark and a waterfall.

### Brookland Park
Adjoining Pukara Park is Brookland Park, another attractive open space.

### The Gables
Nearby is The Gables, a wooden house built in 1848. It was originally a hospital but later was used as military quarters and an old people's home. It was moved

to its present site in the early 20th c. It is now used for art exhibitions and cultural events.

### Taranaki Museum
The Taranaki Museum (Ariki Street) has a large collection of Maori objects from the region, including a stone used as an anchor, a stone axe from an ancestral canoe, a chief's cloak, old sculpture and woodcarving. There is also material on the early days of the settlers.
◉ *Tue.–Sun. 10am–5pm.*

### Richmond Cottage
Beside the museum is Richmond Cottage, built on another site in 1853 as a schoolhouse and moved to its present position in 1962. It is furnished in period style and illustrates life in a well-to-do 19th c. household.

### Marsland Hill
Marsland Hill (wide views) can be climbed either from Robe Street or from St Mary's Church. The summit, which was gradually levelled over the centuries, was once occupied by a Maori *pa*. During the land wars British troops were stationed on the hill.

Lava cones, Pungarehu

### St Mary's Church
On Marsland Hill, in the centre of the town, is one of the oldest stone churches in New Zealand (built for Bishop Selwyn in 1842), with a fine interior. During the land wars it served as a military post and ammunition depot. In the churchyard are the graves of early settlers.

### Govett-Brewster Art Gallery
This gallery in Queen Street presents contemporary New Zealand art. The collection includes works by Len Lye (sculpture, pictures).
◉ *Daily 1–5pm.*

### Power station
New Plymouth's power station (1977; Breakwater Road) was originally coal fired, but was converted to gas after the discovery of natural gas nearby. Its 200 m chimney is a landmark visible from far and wide.
◉ *Conducted tours by appointment.*

## Surroundings

### Hurworth
A few kilometres south of New Plymouth

is the old immigrant settlement of
Hurworth, which still preserves a small
homestead built in 1855 by Harry
Atkinson (1831–92), an opponent of
Governor Grey who played a prominent
part in the Taranaki land war and later
became a highly respected politician
(three times premier of New Zealand).

### Pukeiti Rhododendron Trust
In the nearby expanse of rain forest
between mounts Patuha (683 m) and
Pouakai (1400 m) is the Pukeiti
Rhododendron Trust, a large nature
reserve that is brilliant with blossom in
spring.

### Pungarehu
At Pungarehu, 40 km south-west of New
Plymouth, a road goes off to **Cape
Egmont**, with a lighthouse built in 1881.
On the cape are numerous striking
conical lava formations.

### Waitara
17 km north-east of New Plymouth is
Waitara (pop. 6000), where the land wars
broke out in 1860. It has petrochemical
and food industries (frozen meat).

### Urenui
15 km further east is Urenui, birthplace
of the famous Maori scholar and
politician Peter Buck, who is buried
under a stone canoe prow near the old
Maori fortified settlement of Okoki Pa.

### King Country
From New Plymouth a road runs north-
east through the gently rolling grassland
of Taranaki to the mountain terrain of
the King Country.

### Taranaki
See entry

## Northland                         H/J 2

Northland is a hilly and sometimes
mountainous region at the northernmost
tip of the North Island. It lies outside the
tectonically active part of New Zealand:
there have been no active volcanoes in
Northland for a very long time and the
region is not troubled by earth tremors
of any significance.

The present coastline, much indented
and eroded by the sea, was formed by a
rise in sea level after the last ice age,
when many valleys were subsequently
drowned. Thus on the west coast there is
a series of long, ramified inlets. By
contrast, on the east coast there are wide
and deep harbour basins and numerous
offshore islands.

The mild climate with its rainy
winters and dry summers provided ideal
conditions for the growing of sweet
potatoes (kumara) and their winter
storage. It also favoured the growth of
giant kauri trees (☞164, Baedeker
Special). When these died and rotted
away they left deposits of kauri resin
(gum), a substance resembling amber in
appearance, under the ground. Along the
coasts and in the tidal reaches of inlets
mangroves grow, and pohutukawa
bushes cling to even the steepest rocks.

### History
Archaeological research indicates that
the Polynesians who settled in New
Zealand first established themselves in
Northland, which in the Maori classic
period was densely populated –
demonstrated by the fortified settlements
on many hills and mountains. Then,
when population pressure became too
great, some tribal groups moved south
into cooler parts of the country.

There is evidence in this region of
settlement in both prehistoric and
historic times. Just as the ancestors of the
Maoris had come from afar and made
their home here, so in the early 19th c.
European whalers, timber dealers and
missionaries came to Northland. Among
these settlers, too, were many former or
escaped convicts from Australia. Manners
in these immigrant communities were
rough and ready: Darwin, who arrived in
the Bay of Islands (see entry) in the *Beagle*
in 1853, was appalled by the 'scum of
society' whom he found there. Moreover
the missionaries who were active in
Northland from 1814 onwards were
unable to prevent the warlike local tribes
from obtaining guns and ammunition
and then attacking the tribes further
south who lacked modern weapons.

The Treaty of Waitangi, under which
the Maori chiefs recognised British
sovereignty in return for a guarantee of
their rights, marked the birth of the state
of New Zealand. But with the transfer of
the seat of government south to
Auckland the importance and the
economy of the north declined. In
recent years, however, tourism – basing
its appeal on the relics of New Zealand's

Idyll in Northland: a pile dwelling on one of the North Island's natural harbours

early history and the slogan of the 'winterless north' – has given the region a new lease of life.

### Sights
See Bay of Islands, Hokianga Harbour, Kaitaia, Waipoua Kauri Forest, Whangarei

## Palmerston North     K 7

**Region: Manawatu-Wanganui**
**Population: 71,000**

Palmerston North – named after the 19th c. British statesman Lord Palmerston – lies some 150 km north-east of Wellington (see see entry), on the Manawatu River. The 'North' distinguishes it from another Palmerston near Christchurch (see entry) on the South Island.

Originally a loggers' settlement, the town is now an important traffic hub and the commercial centre of a region of pastoral farming, with large creameries and frozen-meat plants.

### Agricultural research
Palmerston North is important also as the seat of Massey University, a national centre of veterinary medicine, nutritional science and biotechnology, and other leading agricultural research and experimental institutions. Among them are the Grassland Research Centre, the New Zealand Dairy Research Institute, the Palmerston North Seed Testing Station and the Awahuri Artificial Breeding Centre.

### History
The site of Palmerston North was originally covered with almost impenetrable forests, and the town was founded relatively late, in 1866. At first its only link with the outside world was the Manawatu River, on which timber felled by the loggers was transported to the coastal port of Foxton. After the railway from Wellington reached the town. in 1886 it developed rapidly. Ever larger areas of forest were cleared to make way for pastoral farming, and creameries, slaughterhouses and meat factories were established.

An agricultural college in the town became in 1928 the Massey University of Manawatu. It is named after a local farmer, William Ferguson Massey (1856–1925), who became leader of the Reform Party and from 1912 to 1925 was prime minister of New Zealand. The new university grew rapidly, and was later joined by other agricultural research institutions.

## Sights

### The Square
The hub of the town's life is the Square, originally a large open space of almost 7 ha, which in earlier days was traversed by the railway but is now a park, with fountains, and the site of the modern Civic Centre.

### Square Edge
The site of the former municipal offices is now occupied by a craft centre (showroom, sales).

### Manawatu Museum
The Manawatu Museum in Church Street is devoted to the history of the region. The collection includes Maori artefacts and mementos of the early settlers.
🄶 *Tue.–Sun. 2–4pm.*

### Manawatu Art Gallery
The Manawatu Art Gallery in Main Street West displays mainly contemporary New Zealand art.
🄶 *Tue.–Sun.*

### Rugby Museum
The Rugby Museum in Cuba Street is devoted to New Zealand's national sport.
🄶 *Daily 1.30–4pm.*

### Monro Hill
From Monro Hill, named after a British immigrant who settled here in 1870 and founded the country's first rugby club, there is a view of the spacious campus of **Massey University** (see above).

### ANZAC Park Viewpoint
From this viewpoint at the end of Cliff Road, on the southern outskirts of the town, there is a fine panorama of the town. In good visibility the volcanoes Taranaki and Ruapehu can be seen in the distance.

## Surroundings

### Feilding
20 km north-west of Palmerston North is Feilding (pop. 13,500), founded in the 1870s as a 'special settlement' on land acquired by the Emigrants' and Colonists' Aid Corporation and divided into smallholdings for immigrants without the money to buy land. The site was found by William Feilding, after who the town is named. The first 250 settlers came here in 1874, cleared the forest and established farms and in due course a meat factory was built. In addition to stock farming (sheep, cattle) fruit and vegetables are now also grown. In spite of its nearness to Palmerston North Feilding has preserved its own character. There are a number of late 19th c. buildings.

### ★Ruahine Forest Park
North-east of Palmerston North is Ruahine Forest Park (936 sq km), a nature reserve famed for its wildness. The park has many species of flora and fauna that are rare elsewhere in New Zealand. At the end of the few roads running into the forest there are mountain huts and rest areas, from which trails leading into the wilderness. The best route to the park from Palmerston North is via Ashhurst and the Pohangina Valley. Information is available from the Department of Conservation offices in Palmerston North and Wanganui (see entry).

### ★Manawatu Gorge
16 km east of Palmerston North on the road to Woodville is the entrance to this wild gorge, carved out by the Manawatu River between the Ruahine Range to the north and the Tararua Range to the south. It is a favourite location for jet-boat enthusiasts and experienced white-water canoeists.

## Puhoi                                          J 3

### Region: Auckland
### Population: ca 200

An hour drive north of Auckland (see entry), off Highway 1 to the west, is the little township of Puhoi, founded in the 1860s by immigrants from Bohemia.

### History

Martin Kippner, a sea captain from Bohemia who had visited New Zealand, gave such a good account of the country that a party of villagers from Staab, 100 km south-west of Prague, were encouraged to make the long and trying voyage. They settled in a forested area north-west of the Hauraki Gulf, where they were allotted plots of land and set about clearing the forest for agriculture. In those days the Puhoi River was their only link with the outside world.

### ★Church

Puhoi is a popular destination for excursions from Auckland. At the entrance to the village is the only **wayside cross** in New Zealand. The Church of St Peter and St Paul (1881) has an altarpiece (1885) reminiscent of others in the Bohemia. In the nearby churchyard are the graves of Bohemian settlers.

### Puhoi Hotel (Puhoi Tavern)

The Puhoi Hotel – previously called the German Hotel – has held a liquor licence since 1879. Photographs on the walls of the bar recall earlier days.

## Rotorua                                L 5

**Region: Bay of Plenty**

### Information

The Tourism Rotorua office in Fenton Street provides, in addition to information about the Rotorua area, sightseeing flights, jet-boat trips and excursions to the numerous volcanic, post-volcanic and geothermal features in and around Rotorua.

### Importance of region

The country round lakes Rotorua and Tarawera, south of the Bay of Plenty (see entry), with its variety of volcanic phenomena, is the longest-established and most visited tourist area in New Zealand. All over this landscape are jets of hot steam issuing from clefts in the ground, geysers shooting water high into the air, bubbling pools of mud and glinting deposits of minerals all the colours of the rainbow on the hot subsoil, and everywhere there is a smell of sulphur, of greater or lesser intensity. The settlers who came here in the 19th c. were filled with a mixture of curiosity, fear and wonder. The local Maoris had come to terms with their environment: they bathed in the thermal water and used it for heating and cooking. Later they acted as guides for white visitors. The tourist high spots in the 19th c. were the gleaming pink and white sinter terraces at Lake Rotomahana, which were regarded as one of the natural wonders of the world.

### Maori mythology

The legends of the local Arawa tribes have their own explanation for the origins of volcanic activity and associated phenomena. Immediately after the ancestral canoe landed, it is said, a *tohunga* (priest) climbed, with a companion, to the snow-covered summit of Mount Tongariro, where they were in danger of freezing to death. The priest then begged the gods in Hawaiki to send fire to warm them: the fire duly arrived, travelling under the sea and came to the surface first at White Island and then at various points round Rotorua and Taupo, finally emerging from the summit of Mount Tongariro. The priest was saved, but his companion had already perished from the cold.

Lake Rotorua with the island of Mokoia in its centre feature in another Arawa legend, the romantic love story of Hinemoa and Chief Tutanekai. She was a girl living on the shores of the lake, for whom her parents had chosen a suitable husband; the young chief, Tutanekai, lived on the island. He so delighted the girl with his flute playing that she swam over to the island, supported on empty calabashes, to see him – for to prevent her going her parents had hidden all the canoes.

## Rotorua town

### Spa

During the land wars the Arawa tribes on the volcanic plateau were loyal allies of the government. They even prevented Maori groups from the Bay of Plenty from travelling through their territory to help the Waikato tribes. In recognition of this Prince Alfred, Duke of Edinburgh, Queen Victoria's son, gave them a bust of his mother in 1870, which still stands on the *marae* (assembly place) in Ohinemutu, the old Maori settlement on the south bank of Lake Rotorua. The duke was welcomed by the Maoris with a greeting ceremony and traditional dances. He also drank the local water, known for its medicinal properties. Thereafter Rotorua developed into a fashionable resort, very much in the style of the European spas of the period.

### Eruption of Mount Tarawera

The sudden eruption of Mount Tarawera on June 10th 1886 occurred without warning – though an aged *tohunga* living in the area had predicted a great misfortune. Also a party of British visitors accompanied by Maoris had recently reported strange happenings on Lake Tarawera, where they claimed to have seen a ghostly canoe. The northern summit of Mount Tarawera burst open, a 19 km long crack appeared in the

ground and lava and ash buried the village of Te Wairoa and other Maori settlements. More than 150 people were killed and even the marvellous sinter terraces disappeared. The eruption, however, also created new attractions, especially in the Waimangu Valley, and the excavation of the buried village of Te Wairoa drew numbers of curious tourists.

### Heyday of the spa

The eruption did little harm to the prospects of Rotorua as a health resort – quite the contrary. The construction of a luxurious bathhouse in Government Gardens, on the shores of the lake, was now planned. The first government medical officer, Dr AS Wohlmann, had visited a number of fashionable

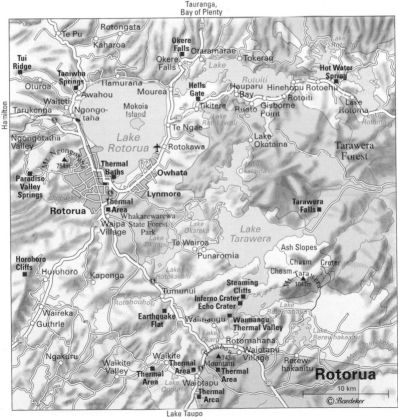

European spas and was particularly impressed by the half-timbered bathhouse of Bad Nauheim in Germany. Half-timbered construction was aslo redolent of English vernacular architecture and was cheaper than a stone building, which was more liable to damage in an earthquake. The new half-timbered spa establishment was completed in 1908. It had a veranda in front in which visitors could walk about and drink the water.

### Tourism

Due to the crowds of visitors coming to take the cure or merely to see the sights, Rotorua has now grown into a town of 54,000 inhabitants, with numerous hotels, motels, motor camps and other accommodations. There are pubs and restaurants of all types and various souvenir shops. For visitors approaching Rotorua from the south on Highway 5 it is like entering some kind of theme park.

As a result of the many private boreholes that have been drilled to supply water for baths and for heating, geothermal activity has declined sharply in some places. There are now restrictions on the use of thermal water.

### ★Government Gardens

The magnificent Government Gardens, which include a park and sports grounds, lie directly on the shores of the lake. They are trim and well cared for, the flowers providing a riot of colour. Visitors can simply stroll in the park or play golf or games if they prefer.

### ★Tudor Towers

The most eye-catching feature in Government Gardens is Tudor Towers, the old half-timbered bathhouse of Rotorua. Since the opening of a new spa establishment in the 1960s the former bathhouse now contains the Rotorua Museum (history and natural history of the Rotorua area) and the City Art Gallery (including Maori art).
*Mon.–Fri. 10am–4pm, Sat., Sun. 1–4.30pm.*

### Arawa Memorial

The memorial set up in 1927 to commemorate those who fell in the first world war depicts the varied links between Maoris and whites (the Arawa ancestral canoe, the signing of the Treaty of Waitangi, British kings and queens, a missionary preaching).

Tudor Towers, Rotorua

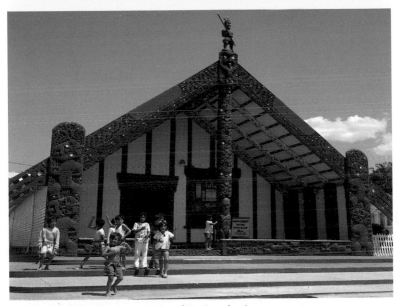

The Ohinemutu meeting house, a masterpiece of Maori woodcarving

### ★Polynesian Pools

Behind Tudor Towers is the modern spa establishment, providing for a variety of sports. Its particular attraction is the three Polynesian Pools, which are supplied with water by three different springs. The whole area is pervaded with the scent of orchids.

### ★Mount Ngongotaha

North-west of the town is Mount Ngongotaha (757 m). From its viewing platform there are marvellous views of the town and the lake. The easiest way up is in the Skyline Gondola (lower station in Fairy Spring Road).

### Mokola Island

From Rotorua there are boat trips to Mokoia Island, in the middle of the lake.

## Ohinemutu

### Bust of Queen Victoria

Adjoining Government Gardens is the Maori village of Ohinemutu, once the most important Maori settlement in the Rotorua area. On the *marae* (assembly place), beside the meeting house and the church, is the bust of Queen Victoria presented by the Prince Alfred in 1870, protected by a marvellous carved canopy. Everywhere in the area, between the houses and in the tiny gardens, clouds of steam issue from the ground.

### ★St Faith's Church

The interior of St Faith's Church (1910; Anglican) is notable for the fine Maori carving and woven fabrics. One of the stained-glass windows shows Christ in the dress of a Maori chief walking on the water of Lake Rotorua.

### ★Churchyard

In the churchyard beside the church the dead are buried in whitewashed stone or concrete coffins resting on the hot ground. Among those buried here are the American missionary SM Spencer (1810–98) and Captain Gilbert Mair (1843–1923), who was a great friend of the Arawa and the only white man to be granted the full status of a chief. He had defended Ohinemutu against Hauhau raids and attacks by Te Kooti.

### ★Maori meeting house

Opposite the church is a magnificent

Maori meeting house. The interior is richly decorated with old Maori carving; the exterior was renovated in 1941.

## Whakarewarewa

### ★Geothermal fields
The geothermal phenomena of the Rotorua area can be most easily observed in the Maori village of Whakarewarewa, 3 km south of Rotorua. There are numerous springs and three impressive geysers within a small area.

### ★Maori cultural centre
Whakarewarewa has a Maori cultural centre, with a carved gateway, palisades, a meeting house and a war canoe. There are also performances of Maori music and dances. Within the complex is a Maori arts and crafts centre, with a carving school and a showroom for the sale of craft products.
🕓 *Daily 8.30am–5.30pm.*

### Whakarewarewa Forest Park
Whakarewarewa Forest Park (38 sq km) extends south-east of the geothermal field of Whakarewarewa . There are trails to the Blue Lake and the Green Lake.

## Waimangu Valley

### ★★Volcanic landscape
The Waimangu Valley was completely reshaped by the eruption of Mount Tarawera in 1886. Old photographs show the splendour of the sinter terraces described by Ferdinand von Hochstetter, which no longer exist. The Maori villages of Te Wairoa, Te Arihi and Moura disappeared under masses of lava and ash, and roads and bridges were destroyed.

There are organised excursions to the volcanic features in the Waimangu Valley. The tour includes a walk along the shores of Lake Rotomahana, passing the Waimangu Geyser, now inactive, which in the past shot water up to a height of 400 m. Other features are the Waimangu Cauldron, a 4 ha lake of steaming hot water, the Cathedral Rocks and the Warbrick Terrace. Below Mount Tarawera (1111 m), at present quiescent, is **Lake Tarawera**, on the shores of which (particularly round Tarawera Landing) there are Maori rock drawings. Finally a boat takes visitors across the lake to the buried village of Te Wairoa, now partly excavated. At least half a day must be allowed for the tour.

### Te Wairoa
This buried Maori village lies on the south-western shore of Lake Tarawera. 14 km south-east of Rotorua the road (signposted) runs past Tikitapu (the Blue Lake) and Rotokakahi (the Green Lake) and comes to Te Wairoa. Here a small exhibition of old photographs and objects found under the lava gives some impression of what the village was like before its destruction. Among the houses that have been excavated is the one occupied by the *tohunga* who predicted a great calamity. There are also remains of a mill and a tourist hotel, as well as an ancient stone Maori storehouse with archaic figures.

## Waiotapu

30 km south of Rotorua on the road to Taupo (Highway 5) is the village of Waiotapu, famed for the spectacular post-volcanic features in the area.

### ★Lady Knox Geyser
Waiotapu's top attraction is the Lady Knox Geyser, which spouts with almost unvarying punctuality at 10.15am and sends a jet of water high into the air.

This punctuality is achieved, however, with a little help. Soap powder must be thrown into the water: the sodium carbonate therein decreases the surface viscosity and sets the geyser off. This was discovered by convicts who used soap to do their washing in pools of thermal water.

### Artist's Palette
The silicate terraces known as the Artist's Palette shimmer in all the colours of the rainbow, as the pink-and-white sinter terraces destroyed by the eruption of Mount Tarawera must have done.

### ★Champagne Pool
The effervescent thermal waters of the Champagne Pool, highly charged with minerals, have earned it its name. Like other pools in the area, it sparkles in many colours, predominantly yellow, green and blue.

The Lady Knox Geyser, which 'performs' at ➤ 10.15 every morning

## Tikitere

### Hell's Gate
In the north of the Rotorua area is Tikitere, known as Hell's Gate because of its evil-smelling springs of sulphurous water and vigorously bubbling pools of mud. The geothermal field here covers some 10 ha, with seething mud springs, a charming warm waterfall (Kakahi Falls), pools of sulphurous water and clouds of steam hovering over vegetation resembling a primeval forest. A small exhibition illustrates the character of the area.

## Surroundings

### Rainbow Springs
5 km north of Rotorua, at Rainbow Springs, are a number of attractive trails running under tall tree ferns. The pools and streams in this area teem with rainbow trout. At **Rainbow Farm** visitors can learn about sheep and cattle farming in New Zealand, with demonstrations of milking and sheep shearing.

### Ngongotaha
7 km north of Rotorua, on the western shore of the lake, is Ngongotaha, with the **Agrodome**, which puts on shows (three times daily) of many different breeds of sheep. Expert sheep shearers and self-appointed sheepdog trainers demonstrate their skills.

### Lake Rotoiti
North-west of Lake Rotorua, some 20 km from the town of Rotorua, is Lake Rotoiti, near which are a number of carved Maori meeting houses. Here too, on a north-western arm of the lake, are the Okere Falls.

### Hongi's Track
Through the forested area that extends eastward from Lake Rotoiti to Lake Rotoehu runs Hongi's Track, on which Hongi Hika and his warriors carried their canoes overland from one lake to the other during his expedition of conquest in 1823. On the track is a tree sacred to the Maoris, said to have been planted 400 years ago by Hinehopu, a chief's wife.

### Other sights
Other places of interest within easy reach of Rotorua are Paradise Valley Springs (11 km north-west on Highway 5), Taniwha Springs (14 km) and Hamurana Springs (17 km), at the north end of Lake Rotorua.

The lakes in the surrounding area are popular in summer for picnickers, trout anglers and swimmers.

## Taranaki                                     H/J 5/6

### History and economy
This region on the west side of the North Island takes its name from Taranaki (Mount Egmont, 2518 m), a volcanic cone that rears up in isolation to the south of New Plymouth. It draws the rain clouds over the Tasman Sea like a magnet, so that it has numerous streams flowing down its slopes. To the Maoris the summit of the mountain was sacred and they never climbed higher than the snowline. The summit area was declared a nature reserve in the 19th c., when the felling of trees and the use of the land for agriculture was prohibited within a six-mile radius of the summit. Lower down, however, large expanses of primeval forest were cleared and there is now lush pastureland grazed by dairy cows. The earlier sawmills have given way to large creameries. Served by a good network of roads, the Taranaki region is one of the most densely populated parts of New Zealand, though in recent years there has been no growth in population.

The commercial centre of the region is New Plymouth (see entry), on the coast to the north of Mount Taranaki. In the 19th c. there were fierce disputes in this area between the settlers and the Maoris over the seizure of land by the whites, leading in the 1860s to the Taranaki land wars.

Oil was discovered near New Plymouth in the 19th c., but this was of little economic importance compared with the discovery, more recently, of fields of natural gas off the coast of Taranaki at Maui and at Kapuni, to the south of Mount Taranaki.

## Egmont National Park

### ★★Taranaki (Mount Egmont)
Egmont National Park (335 sq km) is centred on the almost symmetrical volcano of Taranaki, whose highest peak rises up to 2518 m. With its harmonious conical form, Taranaki has often been

compared with Japan's Fujiyama. The Maori name Taranaki has prevailed over the name Mount Egmont (after the Earl of Egmont, First Lord of the Admiralty) given to the mountain by Captain Cook, though that name is borne by the national park. Within the park, which takes in the main summit (2518 m) and the subsidiary summits to the north, Pouakai (1400 m) and Patuha (684 m), the original vegetation of primeval forest and scrub has been preserved. In summer hosts of walkers and climbers make for the summits (the climb, there and back, can be done in a day from one of the mountain houses in the area), while in winter the slopes of the mountain attract large numbers of skiers.

On Mount Taranaki you should keep an eye on the weather. In these mountain regions it is very changeable: good weather can suddenly change to mist or rain and become colder. The best time to climb the mountain is in the summer month of January.

### Maori mythology

Maori tradition has it that Tahurangi, the Maoris' great ancestor, was the first man to climb the volcano,

The volcanic cone of Mount Taranaki

demonstrating in this way that he had taken possession of the whole area for the Taranaki tribes. Long ago, according to the legend, the personified Taranaki volcano lived in the centre of the North Island along with the other volcanoes, where he paid court to the beautiful wife of Tongariro, who was away from home at the time. When Tongariro returned and found the faithless pair there was a fierce fight between the two mountain giants and Taranaki was driven away to the furthest point in the west of the island, deepening the bed of the Whanganui River in his flight.

### First ascent by Europeans

The first known ascent of Taranaki by Europeans was in 1839, when Ernst Dieffenbach, who was surveying the area for the New Zealand Land Company, and James Heberley, a whaler, made the climb with Maori guides. The Maoris refused, however, to go beyond the snowline, since to them the summit was *tapu* (sacred). The Maoris climbed high peaks only to bury dead chiefs and *tohungas* (priests) in secret caves. In 1885 Frances Fantham became the first woman to reach the summit, giving her

name to Fantham's Peak, a subsidiary crater to the south.

## Taranaki returned to the Maoris

In 1978 the government, in a symbolic gesture, gave the summit of the mountain back to the Maori tribes of the Taranaki region, so that it might be included, with their agreement, in the newly established national park.

## Mountain houses

There are a number of mountain houses, at altitudes of around 900 m, that provide overnight accommodation; the sites can be reached by car. The climb to the summit from a mountain house takes about 10 hours there and back. The **Manganui skiing area** is most easily reached from the Stratford mountain house.

## Curtis Falls
## Dawson Falls

Waymarked trails lead to two impressive waterfalls, the Curtis Falls and the Dawson Falls. At the Dawson Falls accommodation is available in Dawson Lodge. From here there are trails to Lake Dive and the Stratford mountain house.

## North Egmont

25 km south of New Plymouth (see entry) is North Egmont (alt. 936 m), with a visitor centre for the national park. Attractive trails lead to the Holly Hut and Bell's Falls.

## Kori Pa

South of the little town of Oakura, a short distance inland, is Kori Pa, a fortified Maori settlement. Standing high above the river, it seems almost impregnable. However, it was abandoned in 1820 when the local Taranaki tribes fled before the Waikato tribes, who were armed with guns.

## Puniho

At Puniho, 30 km south-west of New Plymouth (see entry), is a rock that, according to the Maori legend, was brought here by the volcano Taranaki in his flight from the central plateau. To the Maoris the rock was sacred, and on certain ceremonies was draped in a chief's cloak. To touch the rock could be fatal: it is said that 70 enemy warriors who had carried it off all died that day, whereupon the rock returned by itself to its original position. The stone's magical

powers declined at the coming of the European settlers, and it can now be touched without evil consequences.

## Parihaka

3 km higher up (starting from Pungarehu) is the village of Parihaka, established by the Maori leaders Te Whiti and Tohu. In 1866 the villagers began a campaign of passive resistance and civil disobedience against the government; in 1881 the two leaders were arrested and kept in prison, without trial, for almost 2 years, and their village was destroyed. The conflict between the Maoris and the whites was not settled until 1926, when the government agreed to pay compensation. The village is now a centre of the Maori revival. Here too is Te Whiti's grave. Visitors to the village should respect the feelings of the Maoris.

## Oaonui

50 km south-west of New Plymouth (see entry) is Oaonui, the supply base for the two offshore production platforms in the Maui natural gas field. The visitor centre provides information about the extraction of natural gas from the continental shelf.

## Manaia

90 km south of New Plymouth is Manaia (pop. 1000), the commercial centre of a farming district. It has a large memorial to those who fell in the land wars. On the golf course are two blockhouses built in 1880 to provide protection against attacks by Te Whiti.

12 km north-east of Manaia is the site of a battle between Maori warriors and British troops in 1868. The Maori leader Titiokowaru enticed the British force into an ambush and annihilated it.

## Kapuni

North of Manaia, at Kapuni, are fields of natural gas that are now being worked. This industrial activity is evident in the flares burning off gas, pipelines and a fertiliser factory.

## Stratford

The little market town of Stratford (pop. 6000), on the south-eastern slopes of Taranaki, was founded in 1877 on an old Maori road. In its early days its economy centred on the processing of timber felled during the clearing of the forests. Stratford is now a popular starting point for walks and climbs on Taranaki (approach route via Pembroke to the Stratford mountain house). Stratford's power station (completed 1976) is fuelled by natural gas from the nearby Kapuni field.

### ★Heritage Trail
From Stratford the Heritage Trail runs 155 km north-east to Taumarunui. This winding route takes in some impressive natural features, such as the Mount Dampier Falls and the Tangarakau Gorge.

### Pukerangiora Pa
8 km north-east of Inglewood, in a densely forested area, is the fortified Maori village of Pukerangiora Pa.

### Waitara
16 km north-east of New Plymouth is Waitara (pop. 6000), where the land wars began in 1860. The main cause of the wars was the land hunger of the settlers, who, squeezed between the volcano and the sea, looked to the Maoris' farming land. The local tribe, the Te Ati Awa, had fled south in the 1820s before the better-equipped Waikato tribes. They gave up land in the Wellington area to the settlers so that they could return to their tribal territory around 1848. But the settlers wanted this land too. Thereupon the Maoris united in opposition to a renegade Maori leader who had gone over to the settlers' side. Government troops then intervened in order to secure the land for the whites.

### Manukorihi Pa
The fortified Maori village of Manukorihi Pa has a meeting house with magnificent carving. It was built in 1936 in honour of the influential Maori politician Maui Wiremu Pomare.

## Taupo                                    K/L 5

### Region: Waikato

### ★Lake Taupo
Lake Taupo, New Zealand's largest inland stretch of water (area over 600 sq km), is a remote and peaceful location in the heart of the North Island. After some 300,000 years of relative calm there was a series of violent eruptions in this area in the 2nd c. AD, when immense amounts of volcanic ash and pumice were spewed out and spread over a huge area. Later the empty crater collapsed, forming a caldera, and the accumulated mass of detritus prevented the water collected in the crater from draining away. Thus Lake Taupo was born.

When this last great eruption in the Lake Taupo area occurred New Zealand was probably not yet occupied by people, but its effects were felt across the world, as records from China and the Roman Empire attest. In New Zealand itself the massive beds of pumice and ash are impressive evidence of this great natural catastrophe.

The visitor centre of Tongariro National Park (in the village of Whakapapa, to the south of Lake Taupo) illustrates, by a comparison with the devastating eruptions of Mount St Helens in the United States and Krakatoa in Indonesia, the stupendous power of the explosion that gave birth to Lake Taupo.

### Rivers
Numerous rivers flow into Lake Taupo from the south, east and west. The largest is the Tongariro, which enters the lake in a delta at Turangi (see below), at the south end. The Waikato, a river with an abundant flow of water, leaves the lake at Taupo.

### Settlement
The abundance of fish and birds attracted Maoris to settle on the shores of the lake at a relatively early stage. But they were greatly in fear of the lake because of the monsters (taniwha) that were believed to inhabit its waters.

The first missionaries arrived in 1839, but settlers at first showed little interest in the area because they judged the land to be infertile. In 1841 Ernst Dieffenbach, who was surveying the area for the New Zealand Land Company, was struck with the magnificence of the landscape.

In 1869 a well-armed police force was stationed on the lake to take action against Te Kooti's guerrillas. It was then that the healing properties of the thermal waters in the area were recognised and the first bathhouses built. But many years passed, however, before any decent roads were constructed.

### Circuit of the lake
A circuit of the lake involves a drive of some 150 km. On the east and south sides the road runs almost continuously close to the shore, with magnificent

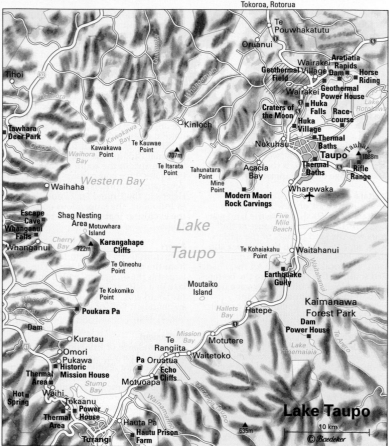

Tokoroa, Rotorua

Te Pouwhakatutu

Oruanui

Wairakei
Geothermal
Field
Aratiatia
Rapids
Horse
Riding
Wairakei
Village
Dam

Wairakei
Geothermal
Power House

Tihoi

Craters of
the Moon
Huka
Falls
Race-
course
Huka
Village

Kinloch

Nukuhau
Thermal
Baths

Tawhara
Deer Park

Taupo

Kawakawa
Point
Te Kauwae
Point
707m
Thermal
Baths
Rifle
Range
1888m

Waihora
Bay
Te Itarata
Point
Tahunatara
Point
Acacia
Bay

Western Bay

Wharewaka

Waihaha
Mine
Point
Modern Maori
Rock Carvings

Escape
Cave
Shag Nesting
Area
Motuwhara
Island

Lake

Five
Mile
Beach

Whanganui
Falls

Karangahape
Cliffs

Taupo

Whanganui
Cherry
Bay
722m
Te Oineohu
Point
Te Kohaiakahu
Point
Waitahanui

Te Kokomiko
Point
Moutaiko
Island

Earthquake
Gully

Poukara Pa
Hallets
Bay
Hatepe

Kaimanawa
Forest Park
Dam
Power House

Dam

Kuratau
Te
Rangiita
Mission
Bay
Motutere
Waitetoko
Lake
Rotoaira

Omori
Pukawa
Historic
Mission House
Pa Oruatua
Echo
Cliffs

Thermal
Area
Motuoapa
Stump
Bay

Hot
Spring
Waihi

Tekaanu
Power
House
Wairarino
635m
Lake Taupo

Thermal
Area
Hauta Pa
Hautu Prison
Farm
10 km

Turangi
© Baedeker

Tongariro National Park

views, passing a series of holiday
settlements. Beyond Waihi, because of
the hills, it runs at some distance from
the lake.

### Boat trips

There is a variety of boat trips available
on the lake. Sailing boats, steamers and
motorboats take visitors to see the rock
carvings by young Maori artists and the
cliffs at Karangahape, which can be
reached only by boat.

### ★Trout fishing

The best fishing grounds on the shores
of the lake are at the mouth of the
Waitahanui River (15 km south of Taupo
on Highway 1) and at Hatepe (10 km
further south, also on Highway 1), where
anglers sometimes stand in long rows,
almost shoulder to shoulder. Fishing is
permitted throughout the year.

## Taupo town

Taupo (pop. 19,000), at the north-east
corner of the lake, is still a relatively
young town, having grown to its present
size only since the 1950s. Its growth was

stimulated by the construction of new roads, the development of the volcanic plateau by reafforestation with pines, the harnessing of geothermal energy and above all by tourism. The lake, in which Californian rainbow trout have flourished since the late 19th c., has become a popular holiday destination. It also makes a pleasant stopover on the journey from Wellington to Auckland (see entries). Numerous hotels, motels, holiday houses and motor camps cater for visitors; many of them have their own swimming pools of thermal water.

## Sights

From the shore of the lake, where the rather characterless modern town centre lies, there are superb views. There is a fine Maori gate with delicate carved decoration. In the evening the outlines of a huge artificial trout are picked out by innumerable lights. The early days of the settlement established by the police force are recalled by a protective wall and the courthouse of 1881.

### ★Thermal baths

The luxurious Brett Thermal Pools are in the style of Japanese bathhouses. The AC Baths in Spa Road were originally established for the use of the police force, the AC (Armed Constabulary). There are also thermal baths at Tokaanu on the south side of the lake, near a small geothermal field.
◎ *Daily 8am–9 or 9.30pm.*

### ★Taupo Walkway

This walk, starting from County Avenue in Taupo, follows the Waikato River to the Huka Falls (4 km) and on to the Aratiatia Rapids (11 km). Skirting the forest, it affords a succession of beautiful views.

### Taupo Lookout

From the end of the Huka Falls Loop Road it is a short distance to the Taupo Lookout, at the local radio station. In good weather there are fine views over the town and the lake to the distant mountains.

### Waikato River Lookout

This viewpoint overlooking the Waikato River is most easily reached from Spa Road; it also known as Hell's Gate, because it overlooks steaming rocks.

## Wairakei

### ★Geothermal field

One particular attraction in the Lake Taupo area is the large geothermal field at Wairakei, which lies just under 10 km north of the town of Taupo. It is conveniently laid out for visitors travelling by car: the circuit of Wairakei Park (40 km) includes so many things to see that a full day should be allowed for the trip.

From Highway 1, going north, the Huka Falls Loop Road goes off on the right just beyond Taupo. At the Huka Falls the mighty Waikato River thunders down over an 11 m high rock face. Huka Valley, a reconstructed pioneer settlement, offers a presentation of living history.
◎ *Daily 10am–5pm.*

At Honey Hive New Zealand, visitors are given an introduction to New Zealand's highly developed beekeeping industry, and can sample the honey.

### ★★Geothermal Power Project

The geothermal power station with its visitor centre is a must for every visitor to New Zealand. An excellent audio-visual show introduces visitors, with the aid of pictures and models, to the construction and operation of the Wairakei power station and the whole chain of power stations on the Waikato River.
◎ *Daily 9am–noon, 1–4pm.*

### ★★Taupo Observatory

The new Taupo Observatory of the New Zealand Institute of Geological and Nuclear Sciences is well worth a visit for the sake of its displays, models and film shows illustrating the volcanic history New Zealand. It provides an excellent introduction to geothermal phenomena and the study of volcanic activity
◎ *Daily 10am–4pm.*

### Lookout

Visitors can continue through the organised chaos of steaming and hissing pipes and pipelines to the Lookout, from which there is a general view of the area.

### ★Wairakei Thermal Valley

The densely wooded Wairakei Thermal Valley has a variety of post-volcanic phenomena, including a small geyser (which gives rise to a hot waterfall), bubbling mud pools and multicoloured mineral deposits.

Lake Taupo, a huge crater lake formed after violent volcanic activity in the 2nd c. AD

### Aratiatia Dam

5 km north of Wairakei is the Aratiatia Dam with its associated power station, the first of a series of hydroelectric stations on the Waikato River. As a result of the diversion of water to the power station the Aratiatia Rapids are now dry; but following demonstrations against the construction of the power station water is allowed to flow in the old river bed daily 10–11.30am and 2.30–4pm.

### Wairakei golf course

Wairakei has a golf course on which, for a reasonable fee, golfers can play a round in this strange steaming and bubbling landscape.

### ★Craters of the Moon

2 km south of Wairakei are the Craters of the Moon, which steam, hiss and bubble and sometimes smell of rotten eggs. For their own safety visitors must keep to the paths.

## Orakei Korako (Hidden Valley)

### ★Geothermal field

The Hidden Valley, 30 km from Taupo, is reached from a side road linking Highways 1 and 5. To reach the thermal field it is necessary to take a boat across the Waikato River. Part of the area was flooded by the damming of the river in 1961, but this does not interfere with the walkway round the geysers, sinter terraces, mud pools and hot springs. The finest feature is the Great Golden Fleece, a range of sinter terraces 38 m long and over 4 m high.

*Boat trips daily 8.30am–5pm.*

### Turangi

At the south end of Lake Taupo is Turangi (pop. 4500), once a quiet little holiday resort, which has developed rapidly since construction began on the Tongariro hydroelectric scheme in 1964. Farmers and forestry workers have settled here as well as construction workers and technicians. Turangi has also become a centre of the timber industry. Above all, however, the town has gained from tourism: it is a good base not only for exploring the surrounding area but also for excursions to Tongariro National Park (see entry).

On the way from Turangi to Tokaanu the pipelines of the Tongariro hydroelectric scheme can be seen on the hillside above the road. Under the scheme the Whanganui, the Tongariro and other rivers are linked by channels and underground tunnels. Before the water flows into Lake Taupo it drives the turbines of another power station. Since the water level of Lake Taupo can thus be controlled, the output of the eight hydroelectric stations on the Waikato River can be optimised. During the construction of this complex system, care was taken to ensure that the flow of water in the Tongariro River was maintained in order to avoid endangering its stocks of trout.

### Tongariro National Trout Centre

4 km south of Turangi is the Tongariro National Trout Centre, a state-run hatchery where rainbow trout are bred. In addition to meeting domestic needs the centre also exports roe to other countries.

🄖 *Conducted tours daily 9am–4pm.*

### Mount Pihanga

Over Turangi looms Mount Pihanga (1325 m), which in Maori mythology, as the only 'female' volcano, is courted by the 'male' volcanoes in the surrounding area. From the Pihanga Saddle Road Viewpoint there is a marvellous view of Lake Taupo. Near here is the idyllic Lake Rotopounamu.

### Tokaanu

The little township of Tokaanu, 5 km west of Turangi, is known for its thermal springs (spa establishment open daily). St Paul's Church (Anglican) has an appealing Maori-style interior.

### Waihi

8 km west of Turangi is the village of Waihi, in an idyllic but also dangerous location. It has twice suffered severe damage from landslides. In 1846 Chief Tuwharetoa Te Heuheu Tukino and many members of his tribe were killed when a landslide dammed the stream and an avalanche of mud engulfed the village.

The village has a very handsome Roman Catholic church, St Werenfried's (1889), with a beautiful Maori-style interior and fine stained glass depicting the Virgin and Christ in Maori dress. The meeting house (1959) contains older carved decoration. Notable also is the tomb of Chief Te Heuheu Tukino.

Near the village are the 90 m high Waihi Falls.

### Kaimanawa Forest Park

South-east of Turangi is Kaimanawa Forest Park (760 sq km), with magnificent southern beeches. It lies immediately east of Tongariro National Park, separated from it by Highway 1 (Desert Road).

## Tauranga　　　　　　　　　　L 4

**Region: Bay of Plenty**
**Population: 71,000**

On the west side of the Bay of Plenty (see entry) is the town of Tauranga. Its Maori name means 'calm water' or 'sheltered anchorage' – referring to the natural harbour enclosed by the long, narrow island of Matakana. The fertile soil and temperate climate provide ideal conditions for the growing of kiwi fruit, plantations of which, with their tall hedges as windbreaks, pattern the landscape.

The settlement of Tauranga was established in the 19th c. on confiscated Maori land as a military base and became a market centre for the surrounding area. More recently the beautiful beaches near the town have made it a popular holiday resort and a favourite place for retirement.

After the infertile pumice soils in the hinterland of the volcanic plateau had been turned into good pasture with the aid of cobalt fertilisers and, after 30 years, the huge coniferous forests were ready for felling the population of the Tauranga area increased sharply. In more recent times Tauranga has lost none of its attraction. Communications have been much improved, for example by the construction of a railway tunnel through the Kaimai Range, providing direct connections with Hamilton and Auckland (see entries), and a new harbour bridge. The harbour, at the foot of Mount Maunganui, is now New Zealand's leading port for exports.

### History

Sailing this way in 1769, Captain Cook was struck by the number of fortified Maori settlements (*pas*) in the Tauranga area. He concluded that the inhabitants must have many enemies and were exposed to frequent attack. The first missionaries, in 1828, were horrified by the brutality with which villages were attacked and their inhabitants slaughtered, and their early missionary efforts were frustrated by the inter-tribal wars. They finally achieved some success in 1838 when a missionary bought land from the Maoris and built a mission station. In 1864 the government sent troops to the little settlement to prevent reinforcements reaching the Maori forces in the Waikato land war. Two defensive positions were also established. The Maoris retaliated by building a strongly fortified *pa* (Gate Pa) opposite the entrance to the missionary settlement. British troops surrounded it and there was bitter fighting. The Maoris escaped but were defeated a few weeks later at Te Ranga, and thereafter much of their tribal territory was confiscated. As late as 1928 a government commission approved the confiscation as an appropriate punishment for rebellion. The Maoris had to wait until 1981 before a law was passed giving them compensation for the confiscated land.

## Sights

### ★The Elms (Tauranga Mission House)

The missionary Alfred N Brown (1803–84) built a mission station known as The Elms in 1838 on a site he had bought from the Maoris. The house, with a small chapel and a small library in the garden, has survived almost unchanged. The garden front is particularly beautiful. The old trees, two Norfolk pines and an English oak, have grown to enormous size. Now a national monument, the house is furnished in period style.
🕓 *Conducted tours daily 2pm.*

### Monmouth Redoubt

The Monmouth Redoubt (1864), with well-preserved ramparts and a number of old cannon, can be reached from the north end of the Strand. It is named after the Monmouth Light Infantry, who were stationed here. Beside the entrance is a carved Maori war canoe set up here in 1970.

### Otemate Pa

The site of the old fortified Maori settlement of Otemataha Pa is now occupied by a cemetery containing the

The deep-water harbour, Mount Maunganui

graves of many who fell in the fighting at Gate Pa and Te Ranga. It is reached by way of the railway bridge at the end of Cliff Street.

### ★Tauranga Historic Village

The colonial period is brought to life in this open-air museum on Avenue West, with examples of old workshops, 19th c. shops and simple quarters for troops. The place is particularly lively at weekends, when traditional craft markets are held. In keeping with the period, there is also a steam train.

### Mount Maunganui

Only a few kilometres from Tauranga, easily reached over the harbour bridge, is the independent town of Mount Maunganui (pop. 12,000), situated on the other side of the natural harbour, which at this point is equipped with modern transport facilities.

In summer the town, lying at the foot of the steep hill (232 m) from which it takes its name, is a popular holiday resort. There are a number of footpaths running up the hill, which was once crowned by a fortified Maori settlement.

### Beaches

Mount Maunganui has marvellous beaches (Ocean Beach, Papamoa Beach).

### Hot water pools

A number of natural hot water pools are evidence of volcanic activity in this region (☞Rotorua).

### Mayor Island

In the north-west of the Bay of Plenty, some 35 km north of Tauranga, is Mayor Island, formed from an extinct volcano 387 m high, with two craters containing lakes. There are remains of a fortified settlement on the hill.

Mayor Island is a favourite of deep-sea anglers. Every year in late summer and autumn (December to May) there are great angling competitions in the waters round the island.

There are boat trips to Mayor Island from Tauranga and Whangamata.

## Te Kuiti                              K 5

**Region: Waikato**
**Population: 5000**

The little town of Te Kuiti lies 80 km

south of Hamilton (see entry) at an important road intersection. From here it is only a short distance to the famous Waitomo Caves, and then on to the Taranaki coast. Originally a railway workers' camp, Te Kuiti is now the commercial centre of the King Country, a region in which the main occupations are farming, mining (limestone and coal) and timber working.

### History

After the Battle of Orakau the supporters of the Maori king fled to this area, where for 17 years he was safe from pursuit – for no settler dared venture into the King Country. In 1872 the Maori leader Te Kooti also sought refuge in the King Country after his rebellion in the east was crushed. A camp was established here in 1887 to house workers employed on the construction of the railway from Wellington to Auckland.

### Maori meeting house

The pride of Te Kuiti is a magnificent Maori meeting house, built in 1878 for Te Kooti. After he was pardoned by the government in 1883 he presented the house to the tribe that had taken him in during his exile.

### Otorohanga

Otorohanga (pop. 2500), 20 km north of Te Kuiti, has a bird park with a kiwi house, in which the birds can be observed in night-time conditions, and aviaries housing other native species.
ⓖ *Bird park daily 10am–5pm.*

### Pureora Forest Park

Pureora Forest Park (830 sq km), 60 km south-east of Te Kuiti, is famed for the many different bird species found here. There are a number of trails through the park. The soil was formed from pumice ejected during the eruption of Mount Taupo in the 2nd c. AD.

## Waitomo Caves

### ★Karstic cave system

20 km north-west of Te Kuiti are the Waitomo Caves, an ramified karstic cave system famed for its bizarre stalactitic and sinter formations. The caves attract large numbers of visitors, particularly in the summer holiday season.

## ★★Glow-worm Cave

The principal attraction is the Glow-worm Cave, through which an underground stream flows. The cave was first explored in 1887. Glow-worms, which live only in conditions of fairly high humidity, produce long sticky threads like a spider's web, to which other small insects are attracted by the faint light generated by the glow-worms during the digestive process. Visitors are taken through the dark cave in boats and can observe the glow-worms hanging from the ceiling of the cave, twinkling like the stars.

🎧 *Conducted tours summer daily 9am–5.30pm, winter to 4.30pm.*

## Aranui Cave

2 km from the Glow-worm Cave is the Aranui Cave, which is dry and therefore has no glow-worms. It was discovered by a Maori in 1911. Its attractions are the varied stalactitic and sinter formations.

🎧 *Conducted tours daily from 2.30pm.*

## Ruakuri Cave

This 'Dogs' Cave', near the Aranui Cave, is the largest of the Waitomo caves. Like the Glow-worm Cave, it has a stream flowing through it, and consequently also has glow worms. Adventurous visitors can join an abseiling and black-water rafting tour or the Lost World tour.

## Waitomo Caves Museum

In addition to exhibits on caves and caving, the museum presents audio-visual shows on the Waitomo cave system and on glow-worms.

## ★Ohaki Village and Weaving Centre

The road to the caves runs past the reconstruction of a Maori village as it may have looked before the arrival of the Europeans. Visitors can watch Maori craftsmen at work and also buy souvenirs.

## ★Waitomo Walkway

This enjoyable trail, which starts from the car park in front of the Glow-worm Cave, runs through the forest, passing limestone formations in the steep gorge of the Waitomo River, to the Ruakiri Natural Bridge, an arch left by the collapse of a cave. The complete circuit takes about 4 hours.

## ★★Tongariro National Park  K 6

**Region: Manawatu-Wanganui**
**Area: 750 sq km**

Tongariro National Park, established in 1887 and a UNESCO World Heritage Sites since 1991, lies in the heart of the North Island, just to the south of Lake Taupo (see entry). It is about 350 km south of Auckland and about the same distance north of Wellington (see entries).

### Getting there

From Lake Taupo Highway 47 runs via Turangi to the national park; then continue on Highways 4 and 49 to Ohakune and Waiouru, returning to Turangi on Highway 1, the notorious Desert Road. This circuit (without detours) is about 180 km.

There are regular bus services from Turangi to the national park, Ohakune and Waiouru, and railway stations at Waiouru, Ohakune and the national park itself.

### Information

Tongariro National Park headquarters and visitor centre at Whakapapa provides general information, maps and descriptions of the various paths and trails.

🎧 *Daily 8am–5pm.*

There are interesting **exhibitions** on the national park and its flora and fauna.

🎧 *Audio-visual presentations daily 11am, 2pm, 4pm.*

There are also tourist offices in Turangi (☛Lake Taupo) and on the Mountain Road, Ohakune in the south.

🎧 *Mon.–Fri. 8am–4pm.*

### Seasons

The national park is open throughout the year. The skiing season on Mount Ruapehu usually lasts from June to October.

Since the weather in the national park is very changeable, warm clothing and protection against rain should be taken on a walk of any length. Stout footwear is necessary, particularly above the snowline. Good maps are essential, since the routes are not always waymarked. You should take sufficient food with you; water from streams in the park should be boiled because of the danger of parasites.

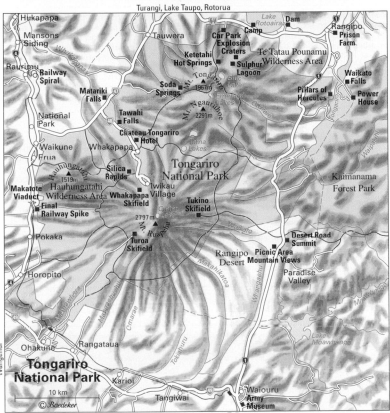

Turangi, Lake Taupo, Rotorua

Underground channels

## Accommodation

Throughout the national park there are only nine huts equipped with mattresses. The ski huts at Iwikau and Tukino can be used only by members of ski clubs. In addition to the luxury hotel Château Tongariro there are other hotels and more modest accommodations at Whakapapa, the national park railway station, Turangi, Ohakune and Waiouru.

## Topography

The central features of the national park are the three volcanoes of Tongariro (1968 m), Ngauruhoe (2291 m) and Ruapehu (2797 m). They are part of a chain of volcanoes that extends north by way of the volcanic White Island to the Kermadec and Tonga islands. These volcanoes, relatively young in geological terms, have repeatedly erupted in recent centuries, as attested by Maori legends and observations made since the European settlement, but have rarely caused catastrophic damage. The most serious recent incident was at Christmas in 1953, when the crater lake on **Mount Ruapehu** overflowed and a great volume of water and mud poured down, destroying the railway bridge at Tangiwai, derailing the Wellington–Auckland express and killing 151 people. The last time the snow-capped Ruapehu showed any volcanic activity was in September 1995, when it spewed out huge mass of rock and lava and great rivers of mud flowed down its slopes.

**Mount Tongariro**, the most northerly of the three volcanoes, is also the lowest. Its summit is broken down into a number of craters. On the slopes of the hill, at Ketetahi, there is an active geothermal field, with hot springs, fumaroles and seething mud pools.

**Mount Ngauruhoe** is still active and there are frequently plumes of smoke and steam over its summit. A series of minor eruptions since 1954 have changed the form of the mountain, particularly on the west side.

The three volcanoes are constantly monitored so that in the event of an eruption the local population can be warned in time. But the locals and foreign visitors are not unduly concerned about the dangers of an eruption: there are numerous popular skiing areas on Mount Ruapehu, and the many enjoyable trails in Tongariro National Park are well used.

The national park offers a great variety of scenery. The initial impression is of bare lava slopes and expanses of brown tussock grass; but on the rainier west side of the hills the landscape ranges from rain forest by way of montane forest and subalpine scrub to the alpine zone. Round the snow-covered craters are bizarre lunar landscapes with greenish-blue crater lakes and steaming crevices in the ground. Finally the dry east side of the mountains, towards the Rangipo Desert (Highway 1, the Desert Road), is barren and inhospitable.

**Mythology**

The Maoris revered and feared the smoking mountain peaks, which to them were *tapu*, and accordingly the volcanoes were the subject of many legends. The subterranean fires were said to have been kindled when the children of the gods forcibly separated their parents, Mother Earth and Father Sky. They resolved to turn Mother Earth round in order to put a stop to her flood of tears and her complaints. But the youngest of her children, Ruaumoko, still an infant at her breast, was turned along with his mother and came to lie under her. He was then given the underground fires to keep him warm, and became the god of volcanoes and earthquakes, who can blow away people like flies.

Mount Ngauruhoe, an active volcano in Tongariro National Park

Small mountain lakes below Mount Ngauruhoe

According to another tribal legend all the mountains on the North Island were once gathered together in the centre of the island. All were male except one, Pihanga (south of Turangi). The other mountains paid court to her, but she favoured Tongariro, who defeated all the others and drove them away. Taranaki travelled west and stopped on the Tasman Sea, having carved out the bed of the Whanganui River in his passage; Putanaki (Mount Edgecumbe) reached the Bay of Plenty and stopped at Kawerau; but Tauhara, a slow mover, got only as far as Lake Taupo.

In the tradition of the tribes of Taupo and Rotorua their ancestor Ngatoro, commander of the Arawea tribal canoe, landed in the Bay of Plenty and moved inland to take possession of the land. He decided to climb Mount Tongariro along with a slave girl, and asked his followers to fast until he returned. His people disobeyed his command, whereupon the gods were angered and sent a snowstorm that almost killed Ngatoro and his companion. In this extremity he called on the gods in his distant homeland of Hawaiki to send him fire. The fire duly came, creating on its way the geothermal fields of Rotorua and Taupo and then burst out of the volcanoes to warm Ngatoro. He threw the body of the dead slave girl, Auruhoe, into the crater of Ngauruhoe, which since then has borne her name.

### National park

The Maoris living on the south side of Lake Taupo long revered the volcanic peaks and buried their dead chiefs and *tohungas* (priests) in caves on the slopes of the mountain. In 1887 Chief Horonuku Te Heuheu Tukino, fearing that settlers would occupy this sacred site, made over the summit area, within a radius of a mile, to the state on condition that a protected area would be established to safeguard the summit as a holy place. To the original area the government added further land to bring the national park to its present size. Tongariro National Park was the first in New Zealand and the second in the world (after the Yellowstone National Park in the United States).

### Bruce Road

After the completion, in 1908, of the railway between Auckland and

Wellington (see entries), which skirts the south and west sides of the national park, the numbers of visitors increased. In 1919 the government decided to establish a skiing area on the western slopes of Mount Ruapehu, and an access road (Bruce Road) was laid up to the village of **Iwikau** (alt. 1622 m). In 1929 the luxury hotel Château Tongariro was built half way up, 9 km from the turn-off of Bruce Road from Highway 47 (Turangi to Tongariro National Park).

### Whakapapa
The holiday village of Whakapapa was established nearby, with a range of accommodations and the national park's visitor centre.

### Turoa
The Turoa skiing area, on the south-western slopes of Mount Ruapehu can be reached from Ohakune on the Ohakune Mountain Road.

### Te Porere Pa
The road to this fortified Maori village on the western edge of the national park is signposted on Highway 47 (Turangi). Here in 1869 Te Kooti was defeated in the last great battle of the land wars. The defences have been partly demolished.

### Poutu Redoubt
To the west of Rangipo, on Lake Rotoaira, is the Poutu Redoubt, the base for the British attack on Te Kooti's stronghold of Te Porere Pa.

### ★Raurimu Spiral
The Raurimu Spiral is a remarkable feat of railway engineering that achieves a sharp descent of 200 m in one complete circle, three horseshoe curves and two tunnels.

### Makatote Viaduct
The Makatote Viaduct crosses a valley between Pokaka and Erua. Constructed in 1908, it was last viaduct on the main line between Auckland and Wellington. Highway 4 runs under the viaduct.

## Walks in Tongariro National Park

The national park provides the finest walking country on the North Island. It offers scope both for short walks and for more strenuous hikes taking several days.

The 'sleeping' volcano, Mount Ruapehu

### Round Whakapapa
The best-known trails taking off from the visitor centre in Whakapapa village are the Alpine Garden Track (1.5 km), the Taranaki Falls Track (6.5 km circuit), the Whakapapanui Track (3 km), the Silica Rapids Track (7 km) and the Waihohonu Track (an all-day walk from Highway 1 to Château Tongariro or vice versa).

### Tongariro Crossing
This walk across the country round Mount Tongariro takes a whole day (about 9 hours actual walking).

### Round the Mountains Track
This walk (4/5 days), starting from the end of the Ohakune Mountain Road in the south, goes via Whakapapa, circling Ngauruhoe and Tongariro to join the Desert Road.

### Ohakune
The little town of Ohakune (pop. 1500) lies on the south-western edge of Tongariro National Park (Highway 49). The clearance of forest in this area made it possible to grow vegetables, and rich yields are obtained on the volcanic soil. The coming of the railway promoted the development of the town, which is now a popular all-year holiday resort, a good base from which to visit the national park and Mount Ruapehu.

The beautiful ★Ohakune Mountain Road winds its way up through the forests of the national park to the Mangawhero Falls and the Turoa skiing area on the western slopes of ★Mount Ruapehu. This involves climbing from 600 m to 1600 m.; at this height snow is present from June to October.

Walks From the park ranger station at the near end of the Ohakune Mountain Road there is a 3 km circuit through the Mangawhero Forest.
It is a 2-hour walk to the imposing Waitonga Falls, one of the highest (63 m) in Tongariro National Park.

### Raetihi
11 km west of Ohakune is Raetihi (pop. 1300), on Highway 4, which once marked the boundary between the Wanganui region and the King Country. In 1918 a devastating forest fire in this area destroyed nine sawmills and 150 houses. The local timber industry took a long time to recover from this severe setback. Prominent features of the town are the twin towers of a church belonging to the Ratana sect.

### Whanganui River Road
For a rewarding trip from Raetihi, take the Whanganui River Road, which runs west from Raetihi to Pipiriki and then follows a winding and fairly strenuous route through the wild and romantic valley of the Whanganui River.

### Railway bridge
20 km north of Ohakune an imposing railway bridge 79 m high (1907) spans a valley, crossing Highway 4.

### Waiouru
A few kilometres south of Tongariro National Park, on Highway 1, is Waiouru (pop. 3000). In these inhospitable uplands (alt. ca 800 m) covered with tussock grass is the largest military camp in New Zealand, with an extensive training area. The little town has the highest railway station on the North Island. In good weather there is a fine view of the volcanic mountains in the Tongariro area.

Waiouru also has a **military museum**, the Queen Elizabeth II Army Memorial Museum (uniforms and equipment of the New Zealand army; dioramas of world-famous battlefields). Ⓘ *Daily 9am–4.30pm.*

### Rangipo Desert
To the north of Waiouru is the Rangipo Desert – not a real desert, but a barren region of poor soil and dry winds.

## ★Urewera National Park    L/M 5

**Regions: Bay of Plenty, Hawke's Bay, Gisborne**
**Area: 2110 sq km**

### Information
The Urewera National Park headquarters and visitor centre at Aniwaniwa and ranger stations at Taneatua and Murupara give advice about walks in the national park, much of which is difficult of access, and information about the location of mountain huts. Walkers undertaking long hikes and requiring accommodation in the huts must inform the park authorities.

### Getting there
The principal means of access to the National Park is Highway 38, which cuts through it from north-west (Rotorua) to south-east (Wairoa, Hawke's Bay). The best approach from the north is from Whakatane (☛Bay of Plenty) along the Whakatane River.

Highway 38, the only route through the park from Rotorua via Murupapa and through the Urewera Ranges to Wairoa, was completed only in 1930. 220 km long, it is poorly asphalted, if at all, and is very hilly, with numerous bends.

### Accommodation
There is only limited accommodation at Aniwaniwa and Waikaremoana, on the east side of Lake Waikaremoana.

### Topography
The first section of the park was established in 1954 and there have been further extensions since then. It is now New Zealand's third-largest national park. It lies in the Urewera Ranges, the densely wooded hills that are still regarded as the most remote and inhospitable part of the North Island. The endless dark forests, never cleared by settlers, prevent the soil from being washed away by erosion and reduce the rate at which water drains away.

### History
The Tuhoe tribe that occupied the Urewera area was isolated and had little contact with other tribes even in pre-European times. According to their tradition their ancestor was born of a marriage between a maiden of the mist and a mountain, and accordingly they were known as the 'children of the mist'. Mist often shrouds the mountains in this rugged region, which is too cool for growing kumara (sweet potatoes). Until recently the Tuhoe tribe lived mainly on roots, berries, birds and fish.

Since the tribe had no interesting objects for barter and trade the European immigrants had no interest in the area, and even the missionaries soon gave up.

Te Kooti, who had supported the government against the Hauhau rebels until his arrest and deportation in 1866, found refuge and supporters in the Urewera Ranges. From here, in a skilfully planned campaign of guerrilla warfare, he could launch lightning attacks on military bases and settlements and swiftly withdraw. The Ringatu sect founded by Te Kooti also had many adherents here.

The other leading figure in the area was Rua Kenana (1869–1937), founder of a religious sect similar to the Mormons. He saw himself as Jesus's younger brother and a prophet. His Te Wairau Tapu sect was associated with a move for the revival of Maori self-awareness and their traditional way of life. The members of the sect, who from 1905 met in a large circular temple at Maungapohatu and revered their leader as Te Kooti's heir, achieved a new – though still modest – prosperity through common ownership of property and modern working methods.

But Rua Kenana, who was against military service, came into conflict with the New Zealand government. The police, seeking to arrest him in 1916, became involved in a gun fight with his supporters – an event often called the last battle in the struggle between the Maoris and the *pakehas* (whites).

## Sights

### Aniwaniwa
Te Kooti and Rua Kenana are still revered in the Urewera region. They are depicted together in a mural by Colin McCahon in the national park's visitor centre at Aniwaniwa.

### ★Hinerau's Track
The visitor centre is the starting point of Hinerau's Track, a beautiful trail through the park's striking landscape, with the chance of seeing many rare birds.

Other attractive walks lead to the Bridal Veil and Aniwaniwa Falls and to the little Lake Waikareiti, higher up in the hills.

### ★Lake Waikaremoana
In the centre of the national park is Lake Waikaremoana (alt. 614 m), which is 55 km long and over 250 m deep. It is believed to have formed some 2000 years ago when a landslide dammed the Waikaretaheke River. There is a hydroelectric station at the south end of the lake where the river flows out. This quiet lake attracts tourists who prefer a peaceful holiday. A walk round the lake takes between 3 and 5 days; overnight accommodation is available in mountain huts. Fishing is permitted at certain points.

Unspoiled natural beauty in Urewera National Park

### Ruatahuna

The scattered Maori settlement of Ruatahuna, on the western slopes of the Huiarau Range and the upper course of the Whakatane River, can be reached by way of Highway 38. From here it is worth making a detour (4 km) to Mataatua to see (after politely asking permission) a very fine Maori meeting house with impressive carving.

### Maungapohatu

The lonely settlement of Maungapohatu, where the self-styled prophet Rua Kenana gathered his flock, lies 20 km north of Ruatahuna, below Mount Maungapohatu (1366 m), which is almost always shrouded in clouds and mist. It was formerly a sacred burial place for tribal chiefs. Nothing remains of Rua Kenana's circular temple that stood above the present meeting house.

## Waikato River       K/L 4/5

**Region: Waikato**

The Waikato, New Zealand's longest river (425 km), rises as the Tongariro River on the snow-capped Mount Ruapehu (2787 m) volcano in Tongariro National Park (see entry), flows through Lake Taupo and emerges from it as the Waikato River at Taupo (see entry). The Maori name Waikato-taniwha-rau means 'the flowing water of the hundred water monsters'. Before the river was tamed by dams, power stations and flood barriers in the 20th c., it fully justified its name with its waterfalls, whirlpools, rapids, marshy areas and floods.

At Mercer, north of Huntly, the Waikato abruptly turns west and flows into the Tasman Sea in a wide estuary, over black ferruginous sand. Until the last great eruption of Mount Taupo in the 2nd c. AD the Waikato flowed not westward, as it does now, but east into the Firth of Thames.

### History

Ferdinand von Hochstetter, surveying the coalfields round Huntly for the New Zealand government, compared the Waikato with the Rhine and the Danube and called it the Mississippi of the Maoris. The local Tainui tribes were warlike and self-assured. The Waikato region was densely populated and bloody inter-tribal feuds were endemic; every insult and every attack called for *utu* (revenge and retaliation) in order to preserve the *mana* on which the tribe's reputation and authority depended. In the early 19th c. there was a major conflict between rival tribes in the area north of Te Awamutu, which was settled by a traditional hand-to-hand battle. From 1820 onwards many of the local Maoris were killed and even more were enslaved in attacks by Ngapuhi tribes from the north, now armed with European weapons. After this visitation the Waikato tribes were keen to trade with the Europeans, exchanging mainly flax for firearms. Missionaries too were successful in their evangelising work. The Maoris were quick to learn the modern farming methods taught by the missionaries, growing wheat on the fertile soils of the region and soon exporting it to Auckland and even to Australia.

The fertile land also attracted the increasingly numerous settlers, hungry for land. In order to present a united front against the whites the Waikato tribes joined in a tribal union and in 1858 elected an old chief, Te Wherowhero, as king. After his death in 1860 his belligerent son at once joined in the fight over land round Waitara in Taranaki. The British authorities built a military road to Mercer, on the Waikato, and British gunboats were able to sail up the river to the Maori positions. The Maoris defended their fortified positions with all the means at their disposal. The final battle in the Waikato war was fought at Orakau, and after his defeat the Maori king fled with his surviving followers into the King Country. The old tribal territory on the Waikato was confiscated; the land was cleared of trees, drained and converted into grazing and arable land by British soldiers, and Hamilton became – and remains – the commercial centre of the Waikato region.

### Hydroelectric development

The enormous potential of the Waikato as a source of electric power was soon realised and a series of dams and hydroelectric stations were built. The Tongariro Hydroelectric Power Scheme was carried out in the area south of Lake Taupo. A chain of eight hydroelectric stations was built on the river after its emergence from the lake (in order downstream): at Aratiatia (1964), Ohakuri (1961; area of reservoir 13 sq km), Atiamuri (1958), Wakamura (1956), Maraetai (1952, extented 1970), Waipapa (1961), Arapuni (1929) and Karapiro (1947). Karapiro is 188 km downstream from Lake Taupo.

These eight hydroelectric stations are supplemented, north of Taupo, by the geothermal power station at Wairakei and two coal-fired power stations at Huntly and Mercer, which use the water of the Waikato not for the production of energy but for cooling.

## Waipoua Kauri Forest          H 2

### Region: Northland

Waipoua Kauri Forest lies on the south side of Hokianga Harbour (see entry), 65 km north-west of Dargaville. This primeval forest, covering 90 sq km, has the largest surviving stands of kauri trees in New Zealand.

### Getting there

From Dargaville take Highway 12, which runs north-west to Hokianga Harbour. The 20 km stretch through primeval forest is now asphalted throughout.

### ★★Giant trees

Waymarked trails lead from Highway 12 to two imposing kauri giants: Tane Mahuta (god of the forest) and Te Matua Ngahere (father of the forest). Tane Mahuta is the largest known kauri, standing 51.5 m high, with a trunk measuring over 4 m in diameter; it is estimated to be 1200 years old. Te Matua Ngahere is only 30 m high but has a still thicker trunk than Tane Mahuta; it is about 2000 years old.

### History

New Zealand's kauri forests were bought up from the 1870s onwards to make room for new settlements. Legislation for the protection of nature was introduced only in 1952. When the European settlement began there were vast expanses of kauri forest extending from Northland to south of Auckland, as well as on the Coromandel Peninsula. The straight trunks of the kauris, with no side branches, were much sought after for use as ships' masts, and in the early days of

Tane Mahuta, the tallest known kauri ➤

settlement they were New Zealand's principal export. After the loggers came the gum diggers, who dug deep down into the ground in search of lumps of resin from long dead kauri trees. The resin was used in the manufacture of paints and lacquers.

### Trounson Kauri Park
South-east of the Waipoua Kauri Forest is the Trounson Kauri Park (500 ha) established by James Trounson in 1919. Its stands of kauris are younger but equally dense. As in the Waipoua forest, there are trails, picnic areas and campsites.

**Note** An excellent introduction to the history of kauri felling and gum digging is provided by the Kauri and Pioneer Museum in Matakohe, 50 km south of Dargaville (☛Whangarei).

## Wanganui                                    K 6

**Region: Manawatu-Wanganui**
**Population: 42,000**

The town of Wanganui lies in the estuary of the Whanganui River, on the south-west coast of the North Island.

### History
Before the arrival of the Europeans the river was an important transport route for the Maoris' canoes. There were frequent conflicts between the various tribes, as the numerous fortified villages along the river show. There was particularly fierce fighting between the local Maoris and the warriors of Te Rauparaha, who had been driven out of his home area at Kawhia on the west coast and now launched plundering expeditions from his base on Kapiti Island, much further south.

In 1840 the New Zealand Land Company, directed by William Wakefield, 'bought' (as they saw it) 160 sq km of land from the Maoris in exchange for pipes, mirrors and cloth. The Maoris, however, took a different view of the exchange: they regarded these things as gifts, which they reciprocated with gifts of sweet potatoes, sucking pigs and so on. In the same year the New Zealand Land Company began settling immigrants on the land. They were in a difficult situation, for they had far more new arrivals than they could provide for in Wellington, where there too their purchases of land had gone wrong.

The fertile plains at the mouth of the Whanganui were easy to clear and cultivate, and the wide river, navigable without difficulty in its lower reaches, was a convenient transport route that obviated the expense of building roads. Inevitably there were conflicts with the local Maoris. In 1847 British troops were sent in to support the settlers. In the following year a treaty was signed that gave the Maoris £1000 in return for 320 sq km of land. For the moment this resolved the dispute. The local Maori tribes did not take part in the land wars that had now broken out, and the settlement of Wanganui developed unhindered.

## Sights

### Queen's Park
The Queen's Park, laid out on the site of fortifications built by the early settlers, is now in effect the cultural centre of the town; within it, side by side, are the Wanganui Museum, the Serjeant Gallery and the War Memorial Hall.

### Cook's Gardens
The best view of Queen's Park is from the neighbouring Cook's Gardens that lie rather higher up, on the site of an old military fortification. The gardens are a pleasant open space with various sports grounds. In 1962 the middle-distance runner Peter Snell achieved his first world record here.

Further up the hill are a 19th c. wooden fire-watching tower and an observatory.

### ★Wanganui Museum
The Wanganui Museum has an excellent collection of Maori arts and crafts, including greenstone jewellery and weapons, as well as a 23 m long war canoe of 1810, once rowed by 70 men, and a series of portraits of Maori chiefs by the German painter Gottfried Lindauer. There are also mementos of the days of the first settlers and the conflicts with the Maoris.
◉ *Mon.–Fri. 10am–4pm, Sat., Sun. 1–4.30pm.*

### ★Serjeant Gallery
The Serjeant Gallery (named after a well-

to-do local family) occupies a large and imposing building. The collection consists mainly of works by British and New Zealand artists of the 19th and early 20th c., including CF Goldie and the local artist Frances Hodgkins.
ⓐ *Daily afternoons.*

### Moutoa Gardens
The Moutoa Gardens are a small park of historical interest on the Whanganui River, on the spot where land deals were negotiated in earlier days. It was originally intended to be the site of the town's marketplace. There are a number of monuments commemorating historical events, including the Battle of Moutoa (1864), in which the local Maoris defeated a party of Hauhau warriors intent on destroying the town. There are also a memorial in honour of Maoris who died in the first world war and a monument to the Putiki chief Te Rangihiwinui Kepa, who fought on the government side in the land war and became known as Major Kemp.

### Durie Hill
From Durie Hill, on which there are an outlook tower and a war memorial, there are fine views of the town, the coast and, in the distance, mounts Ruapehu and Taranaki.

### Putiki Church
This Maori church (1937) has magnificent carving by the great Maori woodcarver Pine Taiapa.

### Putiki Pa
Putiki Pa, a Maori stronghold on the banks of the river, held out against hostile attacks until 1829 when Te Rauparaha and his warriors overpowered and massacred the defenders. In 1891 the river overflowed its banks and washed away the meeting house and many Maori canoes. A new meeting house and a storehouse were then built.

### Beaches
The best beaches in the vicinity of Wanganui are west of the town at Castlecliff, on the Whanganui estuary and at Mowhanau and Ototaka.

## Surroundings

### Ratana
23 km south-east of Wanganui is the Maori village of Ratana (pop. 500), which gave its name to a religious movement. This had great influence on the revival of Maori consciousness and still has many adherents throughout the country. The handsome twin-towered church was built in 1927. Beside the church is a small museum devoted to Wiremu Ratana (1870–1939), founder of the Ratana sect, who had a great reputation as a healer. In the large meeting house are models of the seven Maori ancestral canoes, Abel Tasman's *Heemskerck* and Cook's *Endeavour*. Ratana's birthday is celebrated annually on January 25th as a popular festival.

### Waverley
50 km north-west of Wanganui is Waverley (pop. 1600), near which are ancient rock drawings (difficult of access).

### Whanganui
See entry

## ★★Wellington J 8

**Region: Wellington**
**Population: 326,000**

### Getting there
**Air travel** There are services from all the major New Zealand airports, particularly from Auckland and Christchurch, to Wellington International Airport (8.5 km south-east; shuttle bus to Cathedral Square).

**Rail** Wellington is the southern terminus of the main line from Auckland and there are connections with New Plymouth and Gisborne. Waterloo station is in Bunny Street.

**Ferry** There are up to four crossings daily from Picton, on the South Island (3½ hours) and two crossings daily from Lyttleton/Christchurch (10 hours). Ferry terminal: Aotea Quay.

**Road** From Auckland on Highways 1, 3 and 4 via Wanganui (655 km), or on Highway 1 via Lake Taupo (670 km; a better road).

### Capital city
Wellington, New Zealand's capital city, lies at the south-western tip of the North Island in a supremely beautiful situation, surrounded by water and steep hills,

*Baedeker* SPECIAL

# The Kauri and the Kahikatea

The giant **kauri** tree is found only on the North Island of New Zealand, north of latitude 39°S. Remnants of the much larger forests of pre-European New Zealand are found in the Auckland area, on the Coromandel Peninsula and in Northland between Hokianga Harbour and Dargaville.

Until well into the 20th c. timber from the kauri, a tree resembling a spruce, and the resin that it yielded were New Zealand's principal exports. Its easily worked wood was prized by shipbuilders and furniture makers alike, while its resin (gum) was used in the production of paints and lacquers.

Great numbers of European immigrants found employment felling the giant trees and digging deep into the ground in search of fossil kauri resin, a substance resembling amber.

As a result the kauri – one of the world's tallest trees – has been almost exterminated. Of the great expanses of forest once covering well over 10,000 sq km there survive only remnants, barely amounting to 150 ha.

Strict protective measures have been introduced and costly reafforestation programmes launched to save this tree that is so typical of New Zealand's northern regions.

The kauri, a member of the araucaria family with oval leaves about 7 cm long and a 1 cm wide, can reach a height of over 50 m. The trunk, straight and without branches, can be up to 6 m thick, and bears a magnificent crown.

Kauris are relatively slow growers. The bark of a young tree (50–70 years old) is quite smooth; that of an older tree tends to be scaly. Fully grown kauris are often several hundred years old. Individual trees (e.g. Waipoua Kauri Forest; ☞160) are anything up to 2000 years old.

The wood of the kauri, which is rich in resin and highly aromatic, was used by the Maoris until the 19th c. to build their long war canoes. Resin was also used – as it was by the Indians of Mesoamerica in pre-Columbian times – in religious ceremonies (e.g. in the preparation of incense). Soot from burnt kauri resin was incorporated in the process of tattooing.

The giant kauri trees were felled by the Maoris, with the simplest stone tools, only after solemn ceremonies had been performed. There was no overfelling later practised by European settlers.

The **kahikatea**, known to the British settlers as white pine, is a member of the evergreen *Podocarpaceae* family. It grows even higher than the kauri (up to 60 m) but has a relatively slender trunk. It is found mainly in humid areas on both the North Island and the South Island. The species has existed since the Mesozoic era.

with its picturesque natural harbour, Port Nicholson. Another characteristic of the city is the strong and sometimes stormy westerly that blows in almost constantly from the Cook Strait, giving Wellington its name of the 'windy city'. One disadvantage of the magnificent situation, however, is a shortage of level ground, so that the city has been compelled to spread into widely scattered areas of land between the hills and inlets of the sea, which are linked by a network of winding roads, sometimes running high above sea level. Some land was gained by earth movements during a severe earthquake in 1855, when the harbour area rose about 1.5 m, and more recently land reclamation schemes have created more room in the city centre and for the airport; but it has still been necessary to resort to high-rise building in the central area to meet the city's needs. Wellington has the most modern skyline in New Zealand but at the cost of losing much of its Victorian architectural heritage. Many old shops and offices were demolished on the grounds that they were not earthquake-proof, to be replaced by steel-frame tower blocks that

have turned many streets in the city centre into channels for the wind. The residential areas have now moved far out into suburbs and satellite towns – north-east to Hutt Valley (Petone, Lower Hutt, Upper Hutt), north to the Kapiti Coast (Porirua, Paekakariki, Paraparaumu). Access to the city centre is provided by urban motorways and suburban rail lines, tunnelling through the hills and destroying more of the city's older buildings.

Wellington is the seat of New Zealand's Parliament and government, and thanks to its situation on the north side of the Cook Strait is an important traffic hub for communications with the South Island. As a metropolis, however, Wellington has now been overtaken by Auckland (see entry) – a reversal of past history, when Wellington fought for years to supersede Auckland as capital.

### Culture

Wellington is the home of the New Zealand Symphony Orchestra and the New Zealand Ballet Company. The International Festival of the Arts, with some 300 events and exhibitions, is held in March in alternate (even-numbered)

The best view of Wellington is from Mount Victoria

years. An event that attracts larger attendances, however, is the rowing race in January by the city's lifeguards across the Cook Strait from the South Island. Other events in Wellington's year are the state opening of Parliament and Tulip Sunday at the beginning of October, when the Botanic Gardens are a glorious show of colour.

### Sightseeing

On offer are bus trips to the harbour, along the coast and into the hills surrounding the city, usually combined with an ascent by cable car or a cruise round the harbour. Information is available from from the visitor information centre (☛Practical Information, Information).

A good option for doing your own sightseeing is a Daytripper ticket (NZ$5) for the city's Stagecoach buses.

### Shopping

At weekends Wakefield Market, at the corner of Jervois Quay and Taranaki Street, offers a wide range of fabrics, arts and crafts and above all fashion jewellery. There are a variety of shopping centres, large department stores and elegant boutiques on Lambton Quay.

## History

### Maori mythology

According to Maori mythology Kupe, the legendary seafarer and discoverer of New Zealand, sailed into the bay and camped on the Miramar Peninsula. The first permanent settler, however, is said to have been Tara, son of Whatonga, who like Kupe had come from Hawaiki and had set out from Hawke's Bay to look for land for settlement. From him the harbour got its Maori name of Te Whanganui-a-Tara (great harbour of Tara). His descendants formed the Ngai-Tara tribe, which built fortified hilltop settlements round the harbour.

### Captain Cook

On his first voyage, in 1770, Cook saw the entrance to the harbour, but it was only on his second voyage that he noticed the arms of the sea running far inland, forming a good natural harbour. Wind and tides, however, carried the *Resolution* out to sea. Georg Forster, in his record of the voyage, described high, barren, blackish hills and the inquisitive

Maoris who came out in canoes to look at the *Resolution*.

### First settlers

Half a century after Cook Te Rauparaha and his warriors from Kapiti Island fell upon the tribes of the south. Those who survived the slaughter fled into the hills and the dense forests, and their place was taken by the Te Ati Awa tribe, who had themselves been driven out of their tribal territory in Taranaki. When the first European settlers arrived about 1840 the local Maoris, in terror of the other tribes to the north and north-east, saw the white men as a lesser evil and hoped for their protection. The first white visitors – flax traders, whalers, seal hunters – only stayed briefly in the area, and when the sailing ship *Tory* put into the bay in 1839, carrying agents of the New Zealand Land Company sent from London to assess the scope for settlement, they found hardly any Europeans there. The expedition was led by William Wakefield, brother of the founder of the company, Edward Gibbon Wakefield. No sooner had the ship anchored than Wakefield went ashore and bought from the Maoris who happened to be there, in return for 100 guns, blankets and the usual trinkets, vast stretches of land that did not belong to them – for he either did not know or chose to ignore the fact that the Maoris had no concept of private property. The *Tory* was soon followed by other vessels bringing the first settlers, and by the end of 1840 they numbered more than 2500. The first arrivals settled at Petone, in Hutt Bay, calling their settlement Britannia. But they had great difficulty in making anything of the marshy land and dense scrub, and they also had to contend with flooding and a minor earthquake (which they at first took for an attack by the Maoris). Accordingly they soon moved further south-west to the site of present-day Thorndon, where, on what is now Lambton Quay, they erected a prefabricated building that they had brought from Britain. Originally designed as a school, it also served for many years as a courthouse, a ballroom and even the seat of the provincial government. Round this building grew up the New Zealand Land Company's first and most successful settlement, named after the Duke of Wellington, who had been a great supporter of Wakefield's plans.

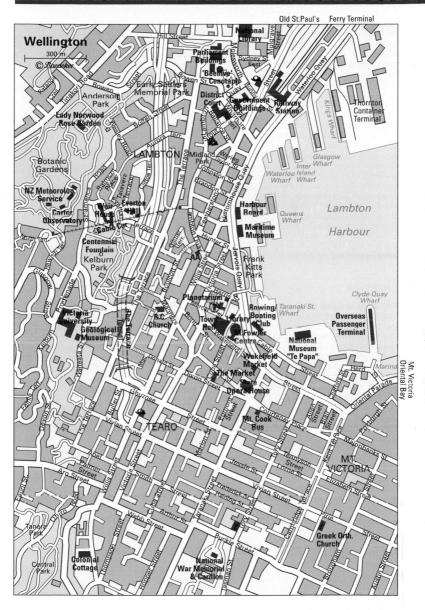

Wellington

300 m

© Baedeker

Old St.Paul's    Ferry Terminal

National Library
Parliament Buildings
'Beehive'
St. Cenotaph
District Court
Government Buildings
Railway Station
Thornton Container Terminal
Early Settlers Memorial Park
Anderson Park
Lady Norwood Rose Garden
LAMBTON
Midland Park
Glasgow Wharf
Inter Island Wharf
Waterloo Wharf
Botanic Gardens
NZ Meteorology Service
Carter Observatory
Weir House
Everton Hall
Cable Car
Harbour Board
Maritime Museum
Queens Wharf
Lambton Harbour
Centennial Fountain
Kelburn Park
AA
Frank Kitts Park
Planetarium
Clyde Quay Wharf
Victoria University
R.C. Church
Geological Museum
Town Hall
Library
Rowing/Boating Club
Taranaki St. Wharf
Overseas Passenger Terminal
M. Fowler Centre
National Museum "Te Papa"
Wakefield Market
The Market
State Opera House
Marina
TE ARO
Mt. Cook Bus
Courtenay Place
MT. VICTORIA
Majoribanks St.
Tanera Park
Colonial Cottage
Central Park
National War Memorial & Carillon
Greek Orth. Church

Mt. Victoria
Oriental Bay

## Wellington as capital

In 1865, after many years of complaints by New Zealanders in the south about the remoteness and inaccessibility of Auckland as capital, the decision was taken to transfer the capital to Wellington, situated conveniently close to the South Island. During the move the steamer *White Swan*, carrying officials and official documents, sank off the east coast. Its passengers were rescued but most of the documents were lost. Wellington now succeeded Russell/Okiato and Auckland as New Zealand's third capital and soon enjoyed a boom, due to the transfer to the new capital of diplomatic missions, banks, businesses and shipping agencies and to the foundation of Victoria University. Residential districts and industrial installations extended over the whole of Hutt Valley as far as the Rimutaka Ranges and the city also expanded over the hills to the west coast.

## Thorndon

### Parliamentary and government quarter

The most imposing building in the parliamentary and government quarter is the ★Old Government Building (1876) at the north end of Lambton Quay. Like the other buildings in this area, it stands on the old seabed that was thrust upwards in the 1855 earthquake and proved a welcome addition to the narrow strip of level ground fronting the harbour. Although this massive four-storey building in Italian Renaissance style looks as if it were built in stone, it is in fact wholly of wood – the second-largest wooden building in the world. The architect, WH Clayton, son-in-law of the then prime minister Sir Julius Vogel, used kauri, rimu and matai wood, which turned out to be so expensive that the government dispensed with an official opening ceremony. The building originally had 22 chimneys but these were removed as an earthquake risk. In front of the building is a statue of the Labour leader and prime minister (1940–9) Peter Fraser.

**Parliament buildings** North of the Old Government Building is an even more remarkable building, the modern circular structure popularly known as the Beehive, which houses ministerial and government offices and the Cabinet Room. Built in 1964–81 to the design of the British architect Sir Basil Spence, it is still the subject of controversy. Next to it is Parliament House (1922), built of granite and Takaka marble from the South Island. The chamber in which Parliament sits is modelled on the House of Commons chamber at Westminster. There are conducted tours of the building on weekdays. The chamber of the upper house, which was abolished in 1952, is now used only for the state opening of Parliament.

Here too is the General Assembly Library Building, a two-storey neo-Gothic building (1897). In the gardens are statues of Richard John Seddon, prime minister of New Zealand 1893–1906, and John Ballance, leader of the Liberal Party and Seddon's predecessor as prime minister.

★**National Library** Further north again, past other government buildings, is the National Library (Molesworth Street; opened 1987.) The nucleus of the national collection was formed by the Alexander Turnbull Library, previously kept in Turnbull's old house in Bowen Street, near the Beehive. The library now has over 250,000 volumes, including a very valuable and almost complete collection of accounts of travel and discovery in the south Pacific. In the fine Reading Room is a mural by the Maori artist Cliff Whiting depicting the separation of Mother Earth and Father Sky.

### Mulgrave Street

To the east of the National Library is Mulgrave Street, running north–south. At its south end, on the corner of Sydney Street, is the **Thistle Inn**, Wellington's oldest hotel. Originally built in the 1840s, it was rebuilt after a fire in 1866.

To the north are the **National Archives**, which have a display of important documents bearing on the history of New Zealand. They include letters written by Captain Cook, the petition that led to women getting the vote and the Treaty of Waitangi itself. The National Portrait Gallery is housed in the same building.

Beyond this is ★**Old St Paul's Church** (1866; Anglican), perhaps the finest of the churches built for Bishop Selwyn by Frederick Thatcher. Externally a plain white wooden building in neo-Gothic (Early English) style, it has a charming interior in which the beauty of the wood is enhanced by the use of light. Originally Thorndon's parish church, it became Wellington's cathedral until it was superseded in 1972 by the present cathedral opposite the National Library.

### Katherine Mansfield's birthplace
From the north end of Mulgrave Street Murphy Street continues north-west, passing the Katherine Mansfield Memorial Park (presented to the city by her father), crosses the urban motorway and runs into Tinakori Road, at the far end of which (No. 25) is the plain wooden house, very much in the style of old Thorndon, in which Katherine Mansfield (☛Famous People) was born in 1888. The house, which was built by her father in the year that she was born, has been restored to its original condition and is now a museum.
🕲 *Tue.–Sun. 10am–4pm.*

## Lambton Quay to Cuba Street

### Lambton Quay
Lambton Quay, which runs south from near the railway station, and its continuation Willis Street form Wellington's busy main artery and commercial street. The name Quay is a reminder that the shoreline originally ran here: all the land to the east of this street was thrust up from the seabed in the 1885 earthquake.

There are no spectacular sights along this street and few old buildings apart from the District Courts (1879) and the Public Trust Building (1908). There is, however, another old building in Boulcott Street, which opens off Willis Street. At No. 63 is **Antrim House**, a handsome mansion of kauri wood (1904), now hemmed in by high-rise buildings. It was built by Thomas Turnbull for the shoe manufacturer Robert Hannah.
🕲 *Mon.–Fri. noon–3pm.*

Otherwise glass-and-steel buildings predominate in this area – with the Bank of New Zealand, at the south end of Lambton Quay, towering above them all

The Beehive, Wellington

– behind which are luxury shops, department stores and shopping malls.

### Civic Centre
Nearer the harbour (see below) is the Civic Centre, with the old town hall, the elegant Wellington City Library (designed by Ian Athfield) and the Michael Fowler Conference Centre. Diagonally opposite the Conference Centre is the Capital Discovery Place (also by Ian Athfield), a hands-on museum for children in which science and technology are presented in a vivid and accessible way
ⓒ *Wed.–Sun. 10am–5pm.*

The **City Art Gallery**, housed in the former public library, has a large collection of modern art and presents exhibitions and film shows.
ⓒ *Daily 11am–5pm, Thu. to 8pm.*

### Cuba Street
Adjoining the Michael Fowler Centre is the Cuba Street pedestrian precinct, where the pace of life is quieter than in hectic and expensive Willis Street and Lambton Quay. Visitors may feel tempted to relax in one of the many restaurants.

## ★Waterfront

### Wellington's shop window
The waterfront of Wellington is very attractive. Queen's Wharf and Frank Kitts Park are surrounded by fine buildings, including the Civic Centre (see above), the modern City of Sea Bridge and the recent National Museum (1998). From Frank Kitts Park there is a good view of the nearby harbour. Features include a mast from the ferry *Wahine* that went down with 51 passengers in a storm in the harbour in 1968, and a bronze representation of the two ships in which Abel Tasman discovered New Zealand in 1642.

### Maritime Museum
The Wellington Harbour Board Maritime Museum is primarily devoted to the history of the port. It contains many models of ships and one of the harbour.
ⓒ *Mon.–Fri. 9.30am–4.30pm, Sat., Sun. 1–4.30pm.*

### Queen's Wharf Retail and Event Centre
The lively area around the museum

includes the Queen's Wharf Retail and Event Centre with various boutiques, bars and restaurants.

### ★★Museum of New Zealand Te Papa Tongarewa
The city's latest attraction is the new Te Papa (Maori expression for 'our country') National Museum opened on the south side of the harbour in 1998 and showing multimedia and interactive displays of the country's history. Mountains to Sea explains how New Zealand was created; Awesome Forces features a multimedia presentation on earthquakes; On the Sheep's Back highlights the economic significance of sheep farming; The Time Warp gives a thrilling high-tech trip through time and space. The heart of the museum is formed by Te Marae, a modern Maori shrine, the Maori meeting place Te Wharenui and a giant canoe used as a Maori warship. The new museum complex also includes collections from the **National Art Gallery** and 19th c. and 20th c. works by artists from New Zealand, Australia and Europe. It also has some works by Rembrandt.
ⓒ *Daily 10am–6pm, Thu. to 9pm.*

## Other Sights

### ★Botanic Gardens
The Botanic Gardens (26 ha) lie in the centre of the city on the Kelburn Hills. The ★**cable car** that runs up to the gardens is an experience in itself. This 610 m long funicular railway, opened in 1902, climbs from Lambton Quay, opposite Grey Street, to a height of 122 m. The old wooden cars were replaced in 1979 by modern ones made in Switzerland. From the hilltop there is a magnificent view of Wellington.

The Botanic Gardens were opened in 1869. At the entrance are the Carter Observatory belonging to the Meteorological Institute and a number of other university scientific institutes. The high points of the gardens are the Lady Norwood Rose Garden, with over 500 varieties of roses, the begonia house, the herb garden, the Maori herb beds and a garden designed to raise concern for the environment. The walk through the gardens ends at the north exit in Glenmore Street, which has retained its Victorian wrought-iron gates and porter's lodge.

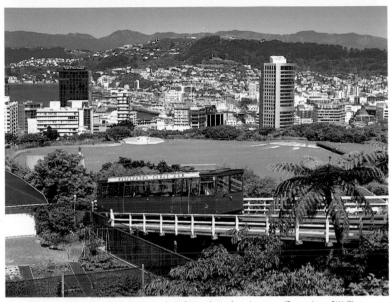

The cable car running up to the Botanic Gardens, from where there is a magnificent view of Wellington

**Bolton Street Memorial Park**
From here it is a short distance to the Bolton Street Early Settlers Memorial Park, with the Sexton's Cottage and the graves of noted citizens and politicians, including Edward Gibbon Wakefield (☞Famous People) and Richard Seddon.

**Victoria University**
To the south of the upper station of the cable car is the campus of the Victoria University. In the Hunter Building is a geological museum. More interesting perhaps for most visitors is the Roman Catholic cemetery in Mount Street, with the oldest graves in Wellington (1840).

**★★Mount Victoria**
Mount Victoria (196 m), immediately east of the city centre, is the best-known and also the windiest of Wellington's viewpoints. A narrow winding road, signposted 'Lookout', runs up from Oriental Bay to the Byrd Memorial below the viewing platform. From the terrace on the summit there is a magnificent panorama of the broad city, the harbour, Cook Strait, Hutt Valley and Kelburn Park with the university buildings. The Byrd Memorial

commemorates the American aviator Richard Byrd, who in 1929 made the first flight over the South Pole from his base in New Zealand.

## Surroundings

**★★City Marine Drive**
The 40 km City Marine Drive – suitable for bicycles as well as cars – runs round the Miramar Peninsula to the east of the city, keeping close to the coast almost all the way and passing a number of bathing beaches.

The circuit begins in **Oriental Bay**, where whales were once beached and cut up, now a select residential suburb with charming wooden houses reaching up from the shore to Mount Victoria. On the hill to the right is a large building (1905) once occupied by St Gerard's monastery and to the left is the Freyberg Swimming Pool. The latter is named after Lord Freyberg, born in London but brought up in New Zealand, much decorated in the first world war, commander-in-chief of New Zealand forces in Europe and North Africa in the second world war and the seventh Governor General of New Zealand. From here the road continues round Point Jermingham into Evans Bay, from which there is a view of the Miramar Peninsula.

Continuing past the airport, built on a reclaimed sandbank that links the Miramar Peninsula with the mainland, you come to the west coast of the peninsula, on whose northern tip, Point Halswell, is the ★★**Massey Memorial**, built on the site of a fortified Maori settlement (*pa*). It commemorates William Ferguson Massey, prime minister of New Zealand 1912–25. The exertion of the ascent is rewarded by a tremendous **view** of Wellington and Port Nicholson.

Then on to Mahanga Bay and **Point**

**Gordon**, a fort built in the 1880s when, after the opening of the port of Vladivostok, there was concern in New Zealand about the possibility of an attack by Russia.

The route continues to Scorching Bay and **Worser Bay**, both of which have beautiful bathing beaches. The harbour pilots' office was once in Worser Bay. Then on, southward, to Breaker Bay and along the south end of the airport into **Lyall Bay**, from which there is a view of the mountains of the South Island; the beach is popular with bathers and surfers.

The coast road continues past a series of rocky promontories to Houghton Bay, Island Bay (good surfing beach) and Owhiro Bay, where the road comes to an end.

**Wellington Surroundings**

5 km

© Baedeker

From here it is a 2-hour ★**walk** west to the **Red Rocks**, a volcanic formation between the footpath and the sea. At Sinclair Head, 3 km further west, a colony of seals can be observed in winter.

The return route from Owhiro Bay runs inland on Happy Valley Road, Brooklyn Road and Nairn Street (at No. 68 a cottage of 1858, now a museum) and so back to Willis Street.

### Eastbourne

Eastern Bay Drive runs along the east side of the harbour, passes through Petone and comes to Eastbourne, which also has beautiful bathing beaches. From here there is a pleasant walk on a waymarked trail through woodlands down to beautiful **Butterfly Creek**, where there is an attractive pool for bathers.

Another trail (16 km there and back) runs from Eastbourne to **Pencarrow Head**, on the east side of the entrance to the harbour, where New Zealand's first lighthouse was built (1859). From here there is a fine view of Port Nicholson.

All botanists will enjoy a visit to the **Otari Museum of Native Plants**, which is not a museum but rather a beautiful garden, with specimens of all the plants that grow in New Zealand and the Chatham Islands. The museum is reached by way of Wilton Road (signposted to Karori), west of the city centre.
🔘 *Daily 9am–5pm.*

### ★Kapiti Coast

Along the Kapiti Coast, from Paekakariki by way of Raumati to Waikanae, there are a series of beautiful bathing beaches. There are also three good museums.

### Tramway Museum

The Tramway Museum in Elizabeth Park, Paekakariki (45 km north of the city centre on Highway 1), is a popular attraction at weekends. Here tramcars that once ran along Lambton Quay carry passengers on nostalgic trips to the Memorial Gates at McKay's Crossing. The gates commemorate the 2nd US Marine Division that was stationed here during the second world war.

### Engine Shed

The Engine Shed in Paekakariki has a fine collection of working steam engines.
🔘 *Sun. 9am–5pm.*

### Southward Car Museum

Near the Tramway Museum is the Southward Car Museum, with a large collection of veteran and vintage cars, including a Cadillac that belonged to Marlene Dietrich, another that belonged to Al Capone and the first two cars – made by Mercedes-Benz – to run on New Zealand's then dusty tracks in 1898. The museum is some 50 km north of the city centre, 3 km south of Waikanae.
🔘 *Daily 9am–5pm.*

### ★★Ferry to the South Island

A trip by ferry to the South Island is an unforgettable experience. The crossing takes 3½ hours. From the harbour the ferry cuts across the Cook Strait and then sails for an hour or more through the magnificent scenery of the Marlborough Sounds to the little port of Picton.

### Lower Hutt

15 km north-east of Wellington is the outer suburb of Lower Hutt (pop. 95,000), which was named after a director of the New Zealand Land Company. It lies on the lower course of the Hutt River, which is flanked by steep hills. Near here is Petone, where the first settlers arrived in 1840; frequent flooding by the Hutt River soon led them to move their settlement further south. After reaching agreement with the local Maoris on the sale of the necessary land they cleared the forest and laid out gardens. But as the expanding city of Wellington gradually extended to the lower course of the Hutt River the settlement of Lower Hutt became a residential suburb, and some of the market gardens gave way to factories. There are now also a number of research institutes and television studios.

The **Dowse Art Museum** (Laings Road) has an excellent collection of New Zealand art and crafts. Notable items are a carved Maori storehouse and a collection of glass.
🔘 *Mon.–Fri. 10am–4pm, Sun., pub. hols. 11am–5pm.*

**Christ Church**, in Eastern Hutt Road, is the oldest church in the Wellington area. Built of wood in 1854, it was restored after a fire in 1989.

### Petone

The **Settlers Museum** in the suburb of Petone (on the Esplanade) has an collection of material on the European settlement of the area, as well as extensive archives that are of particular interest to genealogists.

◉ *Tue.–Sun. afternoons.*

**Markets** The Settlers Market in Jackson Street and the Station Village Market at the corner of Hutt Road and Railway Avenue attract large numbers of visitors on Thursdays and Sundays.

### Wainuiomata Valley
The road continues south-east through the Wainuiomata Valley and in 20 km reaches the sea. The rocks exposed here show clearly the various upthrusts caused by earthquakes. The most recent spectacular upthrust of the seabed resulted from the 1855 earthquake, The uppermost raised beach was thrust upwards some 6500 years ago.

### Rimutaka Forest Park
10 km south of Wainuiomata, in Catchpool Valley, a road goes off to Rimutaka Forest Park (campsites, picnic areas). There are a number of trails in the park, including the Five Mile Track to the Orongorongo River (4 hours), the Middle Ridge Track (2 hours) and the Butcher Track (tough rock climbing; 1 hour), from which there are beautiful views of Wellington's harbour.

### Otaki
75 km north of Wellington, on the South Taranaki Bight, is Otaki (pop. 6500). The Otaki area once had a relatively large Maori population and was controlled in the early 19th c. by Te Rauparaha from his base on nearby Kapiti Island. It is now the commercial centre of a fertile vegetable-growing area. The first Maori university, the University of Rauwaka, was founded in Otaki as the logical development of earlier Maori pre-school and school education projects.

The British missionary Octavius Hadfield (1814–1904), later bishop of Wellington, worked in Otaki from 1839 and taught the Maoris to cultivate the excellent local soil. He strove to maintain good relations between the settlers and the Maoris and was able to restrain Te Rauparaha from attacking Wellington. His uninhibited expression of his views on the Taranaki land war, however, made him unpopular with the government.

Otaki's main sight was the Rangiatea

Maori church, which unfortunately was destroyed by fire several years ago. Only a sign remains to commemorate New Zealand's finest Maori church.

Nearby is the grave of Te Rauparaha; legend has it that his body was transported to Kapiti Island.

1 km further on is a Roman Catholic mission station established in 1844. The church was built in 1857.

### Upper Hutt
30 km north-east of Wellington, in the valley of the Hutt River, is the satellite town of Upper Hutt (pop. 38,000). The population includes many commuters who travel into Wellington to work, but the town also has a number of factories and other institutions, such as the New Zealand Central Institute of Technology.

### Tararua Forest Park
Upper Hutt is a good base for walks in the wild and densely wooded Tararua Range. A particularly attractive route is the Puffer Track.

## Kapiti Island

### Region: Wellington

This long narrow island (17.6 sq km) lies off the west coast at Waikanae, 70 km north of Wellington. It is now a nature reserve but can be visited only with the permission of the Department of Conservation. There is no overnight accommodation on the island. The east side, facing the mainland, has gentle wooded slopes, but the west coast has cliffs or falls sharply to the Tasman Sea.

### History
In the early 19th c. Chief Te Rauparaha, whose tribe had been driven out of their territory round Kawhia by other Maori tribes, established himself on the island. Through trade with the settlers he acquired so many guns that, like Hongi Hika, he was able to mount plundering raids as far south as Christchurch on the South Island. Finally he was arrested and sent to prison for 2 years. Although he never became a Christian he supported the missionaries in the building of the Rangiata church at Otaki.

# ★Whanganui National Park   J/K 6

**Region: Manawatu-Wanganui**
**Area: 740 sq km**

### National park
Whanganui National Park, which extends on both banks of the Whanganui River from its mouth at Wanganui (see entry) to Taumarunui, was established in 1987. It is planned to develop Pipiriki as the headquarters of the park.

## ★★Whanganui River

The Whanganui River (290 km) rises on the western slopes of Mount Tongariro, flows through Taumarunui and then through almost impenetrable forest country, via Pipiriki and Wanganui, into the Tasman Sea. The country through which it flows is for the most part hilly and densely wooded. Below Pipiriki the river is tame enough but higher up there are rapids, waterfalls and narrow gorges. The Whanganui River Road is narrow but runs through a riverine landscape of great beauty.

### Maori mythology
Maori tradition is unanimous that the bed of the Whanganui was carved out by Taranaki (Mount Egmont) volcano when he fled west from the central plateau after being vanquished by Tongariro in the contest for the fair Pihanga. The legendary Polynesian discoverer Kupe is said to have sailed up the river, at least in its lower reaches, in his canoe.

### History
Before the 19th c. the river was an important canoe route linking the interior of the North Island with the west coast, with numerous branch routes along its tributaries. The European settlers and travellers also used the river, which was navigable as far up as Taumarunui, on their way to Rotorua. Excursions on the river, usually lasting 3 days, with accommodation in an elegant hotel in Pipiriki (now burned down), remained popular well into the 20th c.

A chain of Anglican mission stations was established along the river from 1843 onwards, and a French nun, Marie Aubert, founded a Catholic mission in 1883 under the name Jerusalem.

At the turn of the 19th c. the river valley began to be turned into farming land. On the lower course of the river, round Wanganui, and on its upper course, round Taumarunui, the transformation went well, but on the river's middle course, above Pipiriki, there were serious difficulties. Settlers, mainly old soldiers, and even Maoris who moved into this area had to contend with luxuriant vegetation, poor soils and rapid erosion, and nothing could persuade them to stay – not even the bridge built over the river at Mangapurua in 1936, which soon became known as the 'bridge to nowhere'.

### ★Boat trips
Although passenger and freight traffic on the Whanganui River was discontinued in 1958 as uneconomic, cruises on the river are now again available to meet the increasing demands of the tourist trade. There is, for example, a 5 day cruise from Taumarunui to Wanganui (October to March). From Wanganui, Pipiriki and Taumarunui there are jet-boat trips, and in summer visitors can paddle down the river in a canoe from Taumarunui to Wanganui (see entry) at its mouth, a distance of 232 km.

Information about boat trips on the Whanganui can be obtained from the visitor information centre in Wanganui (corner of Guyton Street and Hill Street).

### ★Walks
The most beautiful stretches of the river can be reached only on foot. There are a number of trails that take walkers to particularly attractive spots on the river (e.g. the Matamateaonga Track).

## Whanganui River Road

The Whanganui River Road, completed in 1934, follows the river upstream from Wanganui to Pipiriki, with many bends. There are also some roads in the Taumarunui area.

There are a number of places of interest on the Whanganui River Road:

### Upokongaro
11 km north of Wanganui is Upokongaro, with St Mary's Church (1877; Anglican) and the remains of a Maori *pa*.

Luxuriant vegetation along the Whanganui River

### Atene (Athens)

Atene (35 km) has a small meeting house (1886). There is a rewarding hike on the Atene Skyline Walk (6–8 hours).

### Koriniti

The Maori settlement of Koriniti (48 km), once a place of considerable size, has two carved meeting houses – although most of the Maoris have now left the area. The road beyond Koriniti is unasphalted and in poor condition.

### Operiki Pa

North of Koriniti is Operiki Pa (49 km), a well-planned fortified Maori settlement with high ramparts.

### Kawana

The grain mill at Kawana (56 km) was built in 1854 and was in operation until 1913. It has now been restored as a monument of industrial heritage.

### Ranana

The former Catholic mission station of Ranana (61 km) lies just downstream from Moutoa Island, once the site of a large Maori *pa*. In 1864 the local Maoris repelled an attack by Hauhau warriors.

### Hiruharama (Jerusalem)

The village of Hiruharama (67 km) is idyllically situated on a bend of the river. The French nun Marie Aubert established a Catholic mission here in 1883.

The village gained a certain notoriety as the home of a commune in which the writer James K Baxter (1926–72) spent his last years.

### Pipiriki

Pipiriki (79 km) has only an attractive campsite for accommodation. During the land wars it was a major centre of the Hauhau movement. It is planned to establish the headquarters of Whanganui National Park here.

## Whangarei                                   J 2

**Region: Northland**
**Population: 44,000**

Whangarei, the largest and most important town north of Auckland (see entry), lies on an indented natural harbour that runs far inland on the east coast of Northland. The town developed late but rapidly. The nearby deep-water harbour on Marsden Point can take large tankers and a large oil refinery was built there. The oil-fired power station that it supplied was closed down in 1992. There are also modern factories producing cement, fertilisers and glass.

### Topography
An imposing backdrop to this modern port and industrial town is provided by the five peaks of Mount Mania (404 m).

### History
Although European immigrants established a settlement here in 1839, constant disputes with the local Maoris hampered its development, and in 1845, during the war with Hone Heke, most of the settlers fled to Auckland.

The development of Northland was held back by its poor infrastructure, and an all-weather road from Auckland was built only in the mid-1930s. The breakthrough came in the 1960s when an oil refinery and an oil-fired power station were built, and these were gradually followed by other industries.

## Sights

### Clapham Clock Museum
The Clapham Clock Museum in Water Street (Rose Garden) has a collection of some 800 clocks, the earliest dating from the 17th c.
🅖 *Daily 10am–4pm.*

### Mount Parahaki
On Mount Parahaki (242 m) is a large war memorial. From the top of the hill there are fine views of the town and harbour. The hill can be climbed either on foot (from Mair Park; about 1 hour) or by car (on Memorial Drive).

## Surroundings

### Reed Memorial Kauri Park
This park, 2 km from Whangarei on the Ngunguru road, is notable for its giant kauri trees and a beautiful waterfall.

### Whangarei Falls
6 km from Whangarei on the Ngunguru road are the 24 m high Whangarei Falls.

### ★Northland Regional Museum
This open-air museum lies 8 km west of Whangarei on Highway 14 (the

Dargaville road), in the grounds of the Clarke Homestead (established 1885). The nucleus of the museum is the former doctor's house, to which a number of other houses, a schoolhouse and a chapel were later added.

### Poor Knights Islands
24 km east of Tutukaka are the Poor Knights Islands, a favourite area for divers. There are cruises and fishing trips to the islands from Whangarei.

### Other excursions
Other places of interest round Whangarei are Tutukaka, Ngunguru, Matapouri, Wolley Bay, Sandy Bay and Hikurangi (round trip ca 80 km), Parua Bay and the beautiful beaches of Pataua (round trip ca 90 km).

### Marsden Point
A prominent landmark in the Whangarei area is the striped tower (120 m high) of the former power station on Marsden Point (see above), 30 km south-east of Whangarei. The adjoining oil refinery was built so that New Zealand could import cheap crude oil rather than expensive end products. Nowadays, however, more than 40 per cent of the refinery's raw material comes from the oil and natural gas fields in the Taranaki region. The deep-water harbour on Marsden Point can accept tankers.

In Marsden Point visitor centre an audio-visual show illustrates the development of this industrial area and the technology of the refinery.
🅖 *Daily 10am–5pm.*

## Dargaville

### Region: Northland
### Population: 5000

The little town of Dargaville, founded in 1872 by an Irish immigrant, lies 60 km south-west of Whangarei (see entry). Immigrants from Dalmatia settled in the town, originally as gum diggers (prospectors for kauri resin), but later they and their descendants took up winegrowing. Dargaville rapidly developed into an important centre of the trade in kauri timber and resin. Ships sailed into Kaipara Harbour and then up the broad Wairoa River to Dargaville. Dargaville is now a popular base for excursions to Trounson Kauri Park (35 km north) and Waipoua Kauri Forest (52 km north; see entry).

### ★Northern Wairoa Museum

This museum is in Harding Park, on a hill above the town from which there is a fine view of the Wairoa River. The museum displays a variety of objects from before the European settlement and the early days of the settlers, including kauri wood and resin.

An item of particular interest is an ancient war canoe, built using only stone tools. The canoe was buried on North Head (70 km south of Dargaville) in 1809 after inter-tribal fighting and was rediscovered only 20 years ago.

A recent addition to the museum's collection is the masts of the Greenpeace ship *Rainbow Warrior*, which was sunk by French agents in Auckland Harbour in 1985.

### Bayly's Beach

13 km west of Dargaville is Bayly's Beach, a wild stretch of coast with numerous shifting dunes.

### Waipu

40 km south-east of Whangarei, picturesquely situated at the outflow of the Waipu River into Bream Bay, is Waipu (region Northland; pop. 1700), founded in the 1850s by Scottish immigrants who had previously tried their luck in Nova Scotia and at Adelaide (South Australia).

In the centre of the town is a monument commemorating the founders of the town in the form of a tall column bearing the Scottish lion rampant. The Waipu House of Memories displays mementoes of pioneering days, family trees and the collected sermons of the Reverend Norman McLeod, the minister who brought the original settlers here.

### Bream Bay

In Bream Bay are a number of beautiful beaches, including Waipu Cove and Lang's Beach (10 km south).

## ★Whangaroa Harbour                    H 1/2

### Region: Northland

### Topography

Whangaroa Harbour is a picturesque inlet, a natural harbour that is part of a drowned valley system, near the northern tip of the North Island. This wild and sparsely populated area is reached on Highway 10 and a side road that branches off it. It is an hour drive north from the Bay of Islands (Pahia).

### Massacre on the Boyd

In 1809 a ship from Sydney, the *Boyd*, sailed into Whangaroa Harbour to load kauri wood. Among the ship's crew were a number of Maoris, including a young chief, who was apparently killed by white seamen on the trip over the Tasman Sea. In revenge for this crime all the white men who went ashore were massacred, and later in the night the Maoris boarded the ship in search of plunder and set fire to the powder barrel. The ship was burned out and only four men survived.

Thereafter settlers avoided the inlets in Northland, and even the missionaries restrained their zeal.

The wreck of the *Boyd* still lies on the seabed off Red Island and is regularly visited by excursion boats (daily in summer from Whangaroa and Totara North) and by divers.

### Return of the white settlers

Settlers did not return to the area until the 1840s. In the 1870s a shipyard was established at Totara North that in the course of time built several dozen ships.

### ★Beaches

In a number of small inlets – Matauri Bay, Tauranga Bay, Wainui Bay – there are idyllic bathing beaches, reached on a road that runs along the coast (magnificent views).

### Rainbow Warrior

The wreck of the Greenpeace ship *Rainbow Warrior*, blown up by French agents in Auckland harbour in 1985, was sunk off Matauri Bay and now attracts numbers of divers.

**SOUTH ISLAND**
The majestic Mount
Cook, the highest peak
in New Zealand's
Southern Alps –
magnificent walking
country in summer and
a popular skiing area
in winter

# Sights from A to Z
# South Island

To make it easier to locate the places listed in the Sights from A to Z section of the guide, their coordinates on the fold-out map are shown at the head of each entry.

## ★★Abel Tasman National Park                                    G/H 7/8

**Region: Nelson**
**Area: 225.5 sq km**

The Abel Tasman National Park lies at the northern tip of the South Island, on the promontory between Tasman Bay and Golden Bay.

### Information
The Department of Conservation maintains visitor centres at Motueka and Takaka and ranger stations at the Totaranui and Marahau campsites; at any

of these you can obtain information and maps, and also permission to spend the night in the park (in a hut or your own tent).

### Season
The Abel Tasman National Park – one of the most visited of New Zealand's National Parks – is open throughout the year. The main season is in December and January, and to be sure of a place on a campsite or a bed in a hut at that time you must book months in advance.

### History
This national park, the smallest in the country, was established in 1942 on the 300th anniversary of Abel Tasman's discovery of New Zealand in 1642. Tasman anchored near the Tata Islands in what is now known as Golden Bay, but when the local Maoris attacked his ship's boat and killed some of his men he

Beautiful beaches on the north coast of the South Island, discovered by Abel Tasman in 1642

decided not to go ashore, and thereafter called the bay Murderers' Bay.

### Topography

The French seafarer and explorer Dumont d'Urville, who surveyed the north coast of the South Island in 1826–7, was overwhelmed by the beauty of the scenery. Nowadays tourists, walkers, water-sports enthusiasts and scuba divers are drawn to the national park by its beautiful coves and inlets, bizarrely shaped limestone cliffs, tiny islets and beaches of golden sand, some of which can be reached only by boat or on foot. Since the establishment of the national park the vegetation has recovered from the effects of earlier over-felling.

### Caves

In the south-west of the National Park there are a number of cave systems, some of them still not completely explored. The best known cave is Harwood's Hole, which is 300 m deep.

**Warning** The caves in this area can sometimes be dangerous because of the brittle nature of the rock.

## Walks

### Wainui Falls Walk

The Wainui Falls Walk (ca 2 hours there and back) runs from the Takaka–Totaranui road to the Wainui Falls (21 m high).

### Lookout Rock

The Lookout Rock, from which there are fine views of Golden Bay, is also reached from the Takaka–Totaranui road (ca 1½ hours there and back).

### Gibbs Hill

Further north is Gibbs Hill (400 m), from which there are even better panoramas. A half day should be allowed for this walk, which starts from the same road.

### Pukatea Walk

This is a half-hour walk from Totaranui along the north side of the bay.

### Skinner Point
### Goat Bay
### Waiharakeke Bay

South of Totaranui along the beach are Skinner Point (ca 40 minutes there and

back), Goat Bay (ca 1½ hours) and Waiharakeke Bay (ca 3½ hours).

### Anapai Bay
### Mutton Cove
### Separation Point

North of Totaranui are Anapai Bay (ca 1½ hours there and back), Mutton Cove (3 hours) and Separation Point (ca 5 hours), the most northerly point on the promontory.

### Cleopatra Pool
### Falls River Valley
### Cascade Falls

From Torrent Bay there are popular trails to the Cleopatra Pool (ca 1½ hours there and back), Falls River Valley (ca 1½ hours) and Cascade Falls (ca 2 hours).

### North of Marahau

There are pleasant walks to a number of beautiful coves and inlets to the north of Marahau.

### ★★Coastal Track

The Coastal Track is a 3 day walk along magnificent scenery. It begins at Marahau, on the boundary of the national park, and runs north along the coast to Separation Point, at the northern tip of the promontory, and then turns west to reach Wainui Inlet, at the north-west corner of the park. There is accommodation on some of the inlets (advance booking essential). Since some rivers and lagoons can be crossed only at low tide, you should plan your walk according to the tides. The most difficult crossing is likely to be the estuary of the little Awaroa River.

### Organised trips

Abel Tasman Enterprises, in Old Cederman House (19th c.), 4 km north of Motueka, runs guided walks and boat trips in the national park.

**Note** The walking trails in the interior of the peninsula are for experienced cross-country walkers only.

## Surroundings

### Takaka

On the north-western edge of the national park is the little township of Takaka (Nelson-Marlborough region; pop. 1300), which was founded in 1842. It lies at the foot of Marble Mountain,

A swaying footbridge leads to a hidden bathing cove

which provided the marble used in the Parliament Building in Wellington (see entry) and the cathedral in Nelson (see entry). Features of interest are the little Takaka Museum and the Golden Bay Work Centre and Artisan Shop.

### Golden Bay
There are a series of beautiful beaches in Golden Bay (Pohara, Tata, Paton's Rock, Tukurua).

### Pupu Springs
5 km away are the Pupu (Waikoropupu) Springs, which have an abundant flow of water – most of it from the Takaka River, which in a dry summer can disappear completely underground. Gold diggers were active in this area in the 19th c.

### Collingwood
30 km north-west of Takaka, at the mouth of the Aorere River, which here flows into Golden Bay, is the little village of Collingwood (pop. 200), named after Nelson's Admiral Collingwood. The first settlers arrived here in 1842, and the place enjoyed a boom from 1857 onwards when gold was discovered in the neighbourhood. The village is a good base for interesting walking expeditions in the surrounding area.

### Te Anaroa Caves
8 km south-west of Collingwood are the karstic caves of Te Anaroa. Near the caves are bizarre rock formations.

### Cape Farewell
30 km north of Collingwood is Cape Farewell, the most northerly point on the South Island. From the cape the Farewell Spit, a narrow, desert-like sandbank 30 km long reaches out to the east. It is largely a bird and seal sanctuary and can only be visited on organised coach tours.

### Wharaiki Beach
To the west of the cape are beautiful Wharaiki Beach and **Whanganui Inlet** (Westhaven).

### ★★Heaphy Track
Bainham, 30 km south of Collingwood, is the starting point of the famous Heaphy Track, named after the explorer and surveyor Charles Heaphy. The walk (78 km; 4–5 days) runs through the dense primeval forests of the North-West

Nelson Forest Park and along the west coast, with magnificent views, particularly on the west coast, and ends at Karamea. The track follows an old Maori route to the deposits of greenstone on the coast, later used by gold prospectors. The walk is facilitated by slender suspension bridges spanning gorges overgrown with ferns and huts providing overnight accommodation. Walkers can return on the Heaphy air taxi. Information and vouchers for accommodation in huts are available from the Department of Conservation offices in Takaka and Nelson. All-weather clothing and walking boots are essential. The track is not difficult, though it climbs to 900 m.

### Kaituna Track
The Kaituna Track (ca 3 hours) runs from the Aorere valley (15 km south of Collingwood) to the excavations and spoil heaps of the 19th c. gold-diggers.

### Motueka
25 km south of the national park, on Tasman Bay, is the little port of Motueka (pop. 5000). In its fertile hinterland are large plantations of berry fruits, kiwi fruit, apples, hops and tobacco. Before the arrival of European settlers there was a large Maori population in this area. For many years it was accessible only by boat.

The Te Ahurewa Maori church was built in 1897 on the initiative of Frederick Bennett, who in 1928 became the first Maori bishop.

### ★Kaiteriteri Beach
14 km north of Motueka is the magnificent beach of Kaiteriteri, and 10 km beyond this is the beautiful beach of **Marahau**, at the end of the Coastal Track.

### Upper Moutere
A few kilometres south of Motueka is the fruit-growing area of Upper Moutere, originally settled by German immigrants. The Lutheran church was built in 1905; in the churchyard are gravestones with German inscriptions.

## ★Kahurangi National Park

### Topography
To the west of Motueka extends Kahurangi National Park (4000 sq km; established 1995). The central feature of this park in the wild Tasman Mountains

(up to 1700 m) is the largest and deepest cave system in the southern hemisphere, the sandstone, marble and karstic caves of Kahurangi. There are almost 600 km of trails in the National Park; the most popular are the Heaphy Track (see above) and the Wangapeka Track.

### Riwaka Cave
A favourite excursion from Motueka is to the Riwaka Cave (16 km west). The Riwaka River flows out of the cave.

## Alexandra                          D 12

**Region: Otago**
**Population: 5000**

Alexandra, the largest town in Central Otago, lies on the Clutha River, 200 km north-west of Dunedin and 100 km south-east of Queenstown (see entries).

### History
Alexandria grew up during the gold rush of the 1860s and was originally called Lower Dunstan. It was later renamed in honour of the Danish princess Alexandra, who married the Prince of Wales in 1863.

The alluvial gold in the surrounding area was soon exhausted, but there was a second gold rush in the 1890s when the river beds were dredged out in a search for further deposits. There are now few reminders of the gold-mining days in Alexandra. The construction of reservoirs and irrigation channels has promoted the development of flourishing fruit plantations (stone fruit, particularly apricots). The expanses of green in the valley are in sharp contrast to the bare arid hillsides.

## Sights

### Shaky Bridge
The picturesque Shaky Bridge (now for pedestrians only) was built in 1879.

### Sir William Bodkin Museum
The Sir William Bodkin Museum (Thomson Street) illustrates the methods used for working gold in this area. Old photographs show, for example, the dredging of river beds and the large numbers of Chinese who came here to try their luck.
ⓘ *Summer Mon.–Fri. 2–4pm.*

## Tucker Hill Lookout

From bare Tucker Hill, north-east of Alexandra, there are good views of the little town in its setting of fruit plantations and of the junction of the Clutha River (dredged out in the quest for gold) and the winding Manuherikia River. The peaks of the Remarkables outside Queenstown (see entry) can sometimes be seen in the distance.

## Surroundings

### Old gold-mining settlements (round trip 180 km)

Alexandra is a good base for a tour of gold-mining settlements in Central Otago. The tour begins on Highway 85, which runs north to Omakau (pop. 200), then north-west to Matakanui, now almost a ghost town, at the foot of the Dunstan Range. The route continues to Drybread, the decayed gold-mining town of St Bathans and Hills Creek, and then returns through the Ida valley to the old gold-mining town of Oturehua, now occupied by farmers. The old Golden Progress workings and the Hayes Engineering Works have been partly preserved or restored. Then go by way of Lake Idaburn (curling and skating in winter) to Ophir, where the finding of gold in 1863 attracted thousands of prospectors. The old courthouse and post office here have been preserved. An old suspension bridge then crosses the Manuherikia River to return to Alexandra.

## Clyde

### Region: Otago
### Population: 900

10 km north-west of Alexandra on Highway 8, on the River Clutha, is the little township of Clyde, where gold was found in 1862. The settlement, originally called Dunstan, grew up at the south end of Cromwell Gorge and at one time had a population of 4000 gold miners, with banks and hotels. It has preserved a few buildings from the time of the gold rush.

When the gold was exhausted the water of the river, previously used for gold panning, served for the irrigation of fruit plantations.

### Sights

A prominent feature of the little town is the memorial to the gold miners in the north. The old courthouse (1864) houses the **Clyde Historical Museum**, which vividly illustrates the history of gold mining in this area, including the spectacular gold robbery of 1870, when the gold stored overnight in the supposedly secure local jail disappeared.

🕐 *Tue.–Sun. 2–4pm.*

Other buildings dating from the days of the gold rush are the Athenaeum (1874), a theatre and concert hall, the former town hall (1869), now a hotel, the old Hartley Arms Hotel (1865), Dunstan House (1900), Naylor's Victoria Store (1874), now a restaurant, the old post office, St Michael's Church (1877; Anglican), St Dunstan's Church (1906; RC) and St Mungo's Union Church (1894).

### Clutha Hydroelectric Scheme

In spite of strong objections from environmentalists and the possible earthquake risk the Clutha Hydroelectric Scheme has proceeded in stages since 1977. A massive 59 m high dam was completed in 1992, 1 km north of Clyde, forming a reservoir (Lake Dunstan) 26 km long. It has now filled Cromwell Gorge and submerged the old township of Cromwell (see below). The lake will supply water to a hydroelectric power station (still under construction), and its water is also being used for the irrigation of the local fruit plantations.

## Cromwell

### Region: Otago
### Population: 3000

30 km north-west of Alexandra, at the junction of the Clutha (coming from Lake Wanaka and Lake Hawea) and the Kavarau (coming from Lake Wakatipu), is the new township of Cromwell, built here in substitution for the old one at the north end of Cromwell Gorge, now submerged by the waters of Lake Dunstan.

### Old Cromwell Historic Village

The most important buildings from the old gold-miners' settlement, founded in the 1860s, have been re-erected as Old Cromwell Historic Village in Melmore Terrace. The Cromwell Museum has interesting material on the history of the town.

🕐 *Daily 10am–4pm.*

Other old **gold-mining settlements** round Cromwell, now all but abandoned (ghost towns), are Bendigo and Logantown to the north and Bannockburn and Carricktown to the south.

### ★Kawarau Gorge Mining Centre
8 km west of Cromwell on Highway 6 is the Kawarau Gorge Mining Centre (part of the Otago Goldfields Park), where visitors are introduced to the laborious processes of gold working.
Ⓖ *Presentations daily noon, 3pm.*

### ★Kawarau River
White-water enthusiasts will find plenty of scope on the Kawarau River, whether in kayaks, rubber dinghies or jet boats.

### Naseby
100 km north-east of Alexandra, in the barren Maniototo plain, is Naseby. Once an important gold town, with anything up to 5000 prospectors grubbing for gold in the area from 1863 to the 1930s, it now has a population of about 150.

To supply the gold miners with the water they needed long water channels were constructed, and these are now used for irrigation. Some old buildings still survive to recall the great days of the past, such as the Briton Hotel, a brick building of 1863, St George's Church (1865; Anglican) and the Athenaeum, (1865). The Maniototo Early Settlers Museum is housed in a building of 1878.

There are pleasant walks to the Welcome Inn, on a hill above the little town, and to Naseby Forest (25 sq km), planted with imported conifers (Douglas fir, larch, pine).

### St Bathans
60 km north-east of Alexandra, at the foot of the Dunstan Range, is St Bathans, another gold-miners' town that has lost its one-time importance. Of its once numerous hotels there remains only the Vulcan Hotel (1869). Other old buildings are St Alban's Church (1882; Anglican), St Patrick's Church (1892; RC), and the rather showy post office with the postmaster's house.

### Blue Lake
The Blue Lake occupies a great trench excavated in the search for gold, 800 m long, 50 m across and over 50 m deep. The deep blue colour of the water is clouded only by the inflow of surface water.

### Otago Goldfields Park
The Department of Conservation looks after the widely scattered remains of gold mines and gold-miners' settlements in Otago. Information is available from DoC offices in Alexandra, Queenstown and Dunedin.

## ★Arrowtown                    C 11

**Region: Otago**
**Population: 1000**

20 km north-east of Queenstown (see entry), in the valley of the Arrow River and at the foot of the Crown Range, is the old gold-miners' settlement of Arrowtown. Due to its charming setting it has now developed into an important tourist centre.

Gold was found here in 1862, but only a year later gold mining suffered a severe setback when many prospectors were drowned in a devastating flood.

### Sights
Many old **miners' houses** have been restored in recent years. The old jail in Cardigan Street dates from 1875.

The former Bank of New Zealand building (1875) now houses a branch of the **Lakes District Centennial Museum**, which is devoted to the history of the area round Lake Wakatipu. It has displays on gold mining.
Ⓖ *Daily 9am–5pm.*

On the **Arrow River**, below the town, visitors can hire pans and try their hand at washing for gold.

An unusual feature is the **Chinese quarter** on the west side of the town. In the late 1860s many east Asians came here to work in the gorges of the Arrow and Shotover rivers. They were undemanding and hard-working, and this involved them in disputes with the white prospectors. As a result they were required to live outside the town. Their little stone houses and brick cottages have now been restored, as has the Chinese shop in Bush Creek.

### Macetown
Macetown, another ghost town, lies on the Arrow River 15 km upstream. The town was abandoned because of its remote situation and harsh climate, and

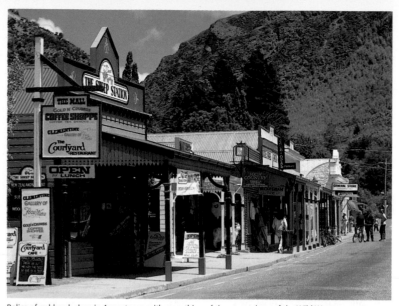

Relics of gold rush days in Arrowtown, with something of the atmosphere of the Wild West

all that now remains is three buildings and a plant for crushing the gold-bearing ore. The old road through the gorge to Macetown, built in 1883, is suitable only for all-terrain vehicles, on horseback or on foot, and there are many fords to cross. It is advisable to enquire about the state of the road before setting out. There is no overnight accommodation in Macetown.

## Arthur's Pass                F 9/10

**Regions: Canterbury and West Coast
Altitude: 921 m above sea level**

**Warning** In winter, when there may be sudden falls of snow, the Arthur's Pass Road may be negotiable only by automobiles with chains, or sometimes not at all. Because of the sharp bends and steep gradients in the Otira Gorge vehicles with trailers, caravans and vehicles over 13 m in length are banned.

**History**
When gold was found on the west coast in 1863 the authorities in Christchurch

were concerned to find some way over the barrier of the Southern Alps into Westland. Most prospectors travelled by boat to Hokitika (see entry) on the west coast and the recovered gold was also shipped from there. But transport overland was safer and more reliable than the voyage on the wild Tasman Sea. There was of course the narrow Harper Pass that had been used by the Maoris to get to the Westland greenstone deposits; but the swarms of prospectors and their heavily laden pack horses soon reduced the track to an impassabile state.

In 1864, therefore, two surveyors, Arthur and George Dobson, set out on horseback through the valleys of the Waimakariri and Bealey rivers. Arthur found the pass that now bears his name, but the steep descent on the west side to the Otira River, and particularly the Otira Gorge, were difficult to negotiate.

In 1865 work began on the construction of a road over the pass. An army of almost 1000 workmen armed with picks and shovels hewed the road out of the rock, and within a year a coach was able to drive on it from Christchurch (see entry) to Hokitika.

Beef cattle, too, were driven over the pass to supply the building workers and gold miners.

In the 1920s a railway line was laid broadly parallel with the road, bypassing the Otira Gorge in a tunnel 8.6 km long.

After the railway line was completed the camp that had accommodated the track layers and tunnellers became an alpine holiday resort, from which beautiful trails lead into the majestic mountains. Here too is the national park visitor centre, with displays on the natural history of this part of the Southern Alps and on the construction of the road and the railway line.

## ★★Arthur's Pass National Park

### Information
Information and maps about trails in the national park can be obtained from the visitor centre in Arthur's Pass village.

### Season
The national park is open throughout the year. The main summer season is in December and January. There is skiing in winter.

### Landscape
The tourist potential of this wild and romantic range was soon realised. The first sightseeing tour was organised in the 19th c., running over the pass to the west coast and continuing south to the Franz Josef and Fox glaciers. In time the view gained ground that the government must take steps to protect the unique vegetation of this area and in 1901 700 sq km of land round the pass were declared a nature reserve. After various extensions to the protected area Arthur's Pass National Park was established in 1929. With an area of almost 1000 sq km, it is New Zealand's fourth-largest national park.

The scenery of the national park shows great variety, since the park takes in the two very different sides of the Southern Alps. The altitude ranges between 245 m on the Tamarakau River and over 2000 m on mounts Rolleston, Murchison and Franklin. Rainfall ranges between an annual 5000 mm on the west side and 1700 mm on the drier east side.

### Walks
Among the finest and best-known walks

The TraNZAlpine Express skirting the Otira Gorge on its way over Arthur's Pass

from Arthur's Pass village are the Devil's Punchbowl Walk (ca 2 hours), the Bridal Veil Nature Walk round the 130 m high Bridal Veil waterfall (ca 2 hours), the Dobson Nature Walk (ca 4 hours) and the Bealey Valley Walk (ca 4 hours).

### Temple Basin ski area
At the higher levels there is an abundance of snow in winter and the Temple Basin skiing area attracts large numbers of skiers.

## Ashburton                        F 10

**Region: Canterbury**
**Population: 16,000**

The town of Ashburton lies on the Ashburton River in the Canterbury Plains, 90 km south-west of Christchurch (see entry). The town and the river are named after Lord Ashburton, a prominent member of the New Zealand Land Company founded by Edward Gibbon Wakefield in London. The wide Canterbury Plains, with the Southern Alps in the distance, are now the granary of New Zealand, reminiscent of the American Midwest, though only 150 years ago, when Bishop Selwyn was travelling about his immense diocese, the plains were arid, treeless and covered with brown tussock grass.

### History
The remains of hunting camps of early Maori nomads have been discovered in this area, and simple rock paintings have been preserved under rock overhangs. The present town grew up by an important ford on a coach route, centred on an inn built here in 1858 for the accommodation of coach drivers. Some 20 years later farmers began to irrigate the arid land; trees were planted and fields brought into cultivation.

## Sights

The Domain Park demonstrates the success of irrigation in making the land fertile: here the steppe vegetation of the 19th c. has given place to grass and trees that afford welcome shade. The town retains a number of 19th c. brick buildings and five churches.

## Surroundings

**Mount Somers**
43 km north-west of Ashburton is Mount Somers, a little town with numerous limestone quarries that supplied stone for building Melbourne in the 19th c..

**Erewhon**
**Mesopotamia**
The two little townships of Erewhon (90 km north-west) and Mesopotamia (100 km north-west) were formerly commercial centres for the huge sheep farms in the area.

**Rakaia Gorge**
50 km north of Ashburton is Rakaia Gorge, a popular destination for excursions, particularly in summer.

**Mount Hutt**
In winter the skiing area on Mount Hutt (50 km north-west) attracts many winter-sports enthusiasts.

## Balclutha                        D 13

**Region: Otago**
**Population: 4000**

**Balclutha**
Balclutha, the commercial centre of a prosperous sheep-farming area, lies 80 km south-west of Dunedin (see entry) on Highway 1, on the lower course of the mighty River Clutha. The river divides into two arms, enclosing the fertile island of Inchclutha. The Gaelic name of Balclutha (town on the River Clutha or Clyde) points to the Scottish origins of the first European settlers here.

**River Clutha**
In the past the River Clutha and many of its tributaries were rich in alluvial gold. Around the turn of the 19th c. almost 200 dredgers gouged out the bed of the river, leaving the huge spoil heaps still visible today.
    In 1878 Otago suffered a hard winter with an abundance of snow, and with the thaw there was severe flooding in the Clutha Valley. As a result the southern arm of the river changed its course and Port Molyneux lost its harbour.

**Clutha Valley Scheme**
The Clutha Valley Scheme, under which a series of dams and associated

View of the Banks Peninsula, where British settlers landed in 1850 and founded the town of Christchurch a few kilometres to the north

hydroelectric power stations will be built in the valley, is aimed at taming the sometimes destructive force of the river. It is feared, however, that this will dramatically change the landscape.

## Banks Peninsula G/H 10

### Region: **Canterbury**

The Banks Peninsula reaches out into the south Pacific south-east of Canterbury (see entry), with Highway 75 as its main artery. The peninsula, with its two deep natural harbours, Lyttleton on the north-west coast and Akaroa on the south-east, consists of two huge extinct volcanic craters. It has a mild climate in which even frost-sensitive kumara (sweet potatoes) grow.

### History
In 1770 Cook named the peninsula, which he took for an island, after the botanist Joseph Banks who was accompanying him. In the early 19th c. seal hunters, whalers and flax and timber dealers established temporary settlements here. In 1835 a Prussian whaler called Georg Hempelmann (1799–1880) settled at Peraki, on the south coast of the peninsula, and established its first whaling station. He claimed to have acquired large tracts of land on the peninsula and was involved in a long and unsuccessful struggle with the government for recognition of his rights. His logbook is displayed in the Canterbury Museum in Christchurch. The European settlements on the peninsula were able to expand unhindered because of a conflict between local Maori groups in the late 1820s, when the practice of exacting *utu* (revenge and retaliation) led to the rival tribes massacring one another. Then Te Rauparaha, conqueror of the North Island, and his warriors fell upon the decimated tribes and almost wiped them out.

In 1838 the French whaler and sea captain Jean Langlois bought land from the few remaining Maoris, and 2 years later, soon after the proclamation of British sovereignty, French immigrants founded the colony of Akaroa (see below).

By 1900 the forests that had previously covered the peninsula had been cleared by felling or burning. Until the building of the road the numerous bays and inlets on the coast of the peninsula could be reached only by boat.

## Sights

### Lyttleton

13 km south of Christchurch (see entry), on a sheltered natural harbour formed by the crater of an extinct volcano, is the port of Lyttleton (pop. 3000). It is named after Lord Lyttleton, a leading member of the Canterbury Association (☞Christchurch, History), which during the 19th c. was the gateway of New Zealand for many thousands of immigrants. The pilgrims of Christchurch landed in 1850 on the north-western shore of Lyttleton Harbour, which is still the city's port. The arrival of the pilgrims is commemorated annually on December 16th by the Bridle Path Walk (8 km) from the harbour over the steep hills to Christchurch. A railway tunnel was driven through the hills in 1867, followed in 1964 by a road tunnel; both provide good connections between Lyttleton and Christchurch.

The best features in the town can be seen by following the ★Lyttleton Historic Walk. Information can be obtained in the excellent Lyttleton Historical Museum on Gladstone Quay, which in addition to its material on local history has sections on oceanography and Antarctic exploration.
◉ *Tue., Thu., Sat., Sun. 2–4pm.*

The Timeball Station (1875) in Reserve Terrace, which signalled the time by lowering the ball, operated until 1935. The building was erected by convict labour.
◉ *Daily from 10am.*

Other notable buildings are Holy Trinity Church (1860; Anglican), St Joseph's Church (1865; RC) and the Presbyterian Church (1864) in Winchester Street.

On the tiny **Ripapa Island** in Lyttleton Harbour there was once a Maori *pa*. In 1885, when there was concern about a possible Russian invasion, a fort was built on the island. For a time the island served as a quarantine station and a prison. Among the prisoners detained here was the 'Sea Devil' Count Felix von Luckner (☞Famous People) after his daring flight from Motuihe Island.

### ★Akaroa

80 km south-east of Christchurch is Akaroa (Maori for long harbour; pop. ca 800). There are a number of old buildings. The Roman Catholic parish church of St Patrick was built in 1864; it was the third church of the mission station established by Bishop Pompallier in 1840. The Maison Langlois-Eteveneaux in Rue Lavaud was built in 1845 by A Langlois and was occupied from 1858 to 1906 by the Eteveneaux family; it is furnished in period style. Associated with it is a small museum with mementos of the brief French episode.
◉ *Museum daily 10.30am–4.30pm.*

The neo-Gothic St Peter's Church (Anglican) in Rue Balguerie was built in 1863. Another fine example of carpentry is the former custom house (1852). On the hill called L'Aube, with a modern lighthouse (1980), is the French settlers' cemetery.

5 km south of Akaroa is a little Maori church (1878).

### Okains Bay

In Okains Bay is the Maori and Colonial Museum, which displays objects from the surrounding area and the Chatham Islands. Items of particular interest are the carved Maori meeting house and the old pioneers' houses.
◉ *Daily 10am–5pm.*

### Walks

There are a number of trails on which the hilly peninsula can be explored, including the Mount Herbert Walk and the Summit Road Scenic Walk. The Banks Peninsula Track is a 4 day walk.

The best known of the trails is the **Bridle Path**, which runs between Lyttleton and Christchurch, the route followed by the first Christchurch settlers.

### Summit Road

From Akaroa you can drive back to Christchurch on the winding Summit Road, which runs round the edge of the old volcanic crater, with fine views. At Hilltop it meets Highway 75.

# Blenheim                          H/J 8

**Region: Nelson-Marlborough**
**Population: 22,000**

The town of Blenheim lies on Highway 1 near the north end of the South Island, on the Wairau plain near the mouth of the Wairau River. The Blenheim area is one of the sunniest in New Zealand, with no fewer than 2600 hours of sunshine in the year. Not surprisingly therefore, this is a great winegrowing area and Blenheim's annual wine festival in February is a major event.

**Name**
The town was originally called Beaver because the first settlers felt like beavers in the mud after the Wairau River overflowed its banks. Then in 1859, when the province of Marlborough was instituted, it was renamed after the Duke of Marlborough's victory over the French at Blenheim in 1704.

**History**
The Wairau affray, the South Island's only serious confrontation between Europeans and Maoris over rights to land, took place in 1843 to the north of Blenheim. Settlers in Nelson who had made what they claimed was a legal purchase of land set out, in spite of warnings, to survey the land. Chiefs Te Rauparaha and Te Rangihaeata then intervened and the conflict escalated. In the affray that ensued some of the settlers were able to make their escape, but others were killed or taken prisoner, including Captain Arthur Wakefield, a brother of Edward Gibbon Wakefield and leader of the Nelson settlers. In retaliation for the death of a female relative of his the chief had all the prisoners killed. The government in Auckland rejected the people of Nelson's demand for severe punishment because the settlers had been in the wrong, and besides the government had neither the troops nor the money for a war against the Maori chiefs. The Maoris, who had withdrawn from the disputed territory, interpreted the governor's leniency as weakness.

In 1855 a severe earthquake caused heavy damage. The level of the plain sank by almost 2 metres and the Opawa River now became navigable as far upstream as Beaver (Blenheim). When Marlborough became a provincial authority in 1859 Blenheim and Picton were rivals for the seat of the provincial government. Blenheim won and remained the provincial capital until such provincial governments were abolished in 1876.

## Sights

The old government buildings in High Street are now occupied by the police. At the corner of High Street and Seymour Street is the cannon in return for which Captain Blenkinsopp claimed to have acquired Te Rauparaha's land in the Wairau area in 1831. In the Brayshaw Museum Park in New Renwick Road are old agricultural implements and a reconstruction of an immigrants' settlement.

## Surroundings

**Wairau Affray Memorial**
At Tuamarina, between Blenheim and Picton on Highway 1, is a monument commemorating the Wairau affray. Those who fell in the battle are buried on the nearby hill.

**Riverlands Cob Cottage**
4 km south of Blenheim on Highway 1 is the Riverlands Cob Cottage (1859), built of cob (a mixture of clay and chopped straw), a reminder of the early European settlement.

**Lake Grassmere**
35 km south on Highway 1 is Lake Grassmere, on which are the only saltpans in New Zealand. Seawater is pumped into the main lake, which has an area of almost 700 ha and is then left to evaporate in small ponds. An average of 50,000 tonnes of sea salt is produced here every year. Gleaming white pyramids of salt are visible everywhere. *Conducted tours by appointment.*

**★Marlborough Wine Trail**
New Zealand's best wines are produced in the Blenheim area and there are regular tours of the wineries. The Marlborough Wine Trail, starting from Blenheim, gives visitors an excellent introduction to New Zealand winemaking, taking in such well-known wineries as Montana, Te Whare Ra, Cellier le Brun and Cloudy Bay.

## Buller River                F/G 8

**Regions: Nelson-Marlborough, West Coast**

### Buller Valley
The Buller River – named after a director of the New Zealand Land Company – is the principal river on the west coast of the South Island. Issuing from Lake Rotoiti, in Nelson Lakes National Park, it flows west through high mountain country, enclosed in steep gorges and flanked by dense forest. After a course of 169 km it flows into the Tasman Sea at Westport. In 1929 and 1968 the area was hit by violent earthquakes that caused massive landslides.

Highway 6 follows the winding course of the river to Howard Junction, with picnic areas at attractive spots. The finest scenery is in Upper Buller Gorge and from Lower Buller Gorge to Sinclair Castle.

### Murchison
130 km south-west of Nelson (see entry), in a bend on the upper course of the Buller River, is the remote little township of Murchison (pop. 700). Above it rears Mount Murchison (1469 m), named after the Scottish geologist Sir Roderick Murchison.

Murchison was founded during the gold rush of the 1860s and thereafter developed into the commercial centre for the remote farms in the interior of the country. In 1929 the area was devastated by a severe earthquake with its epicentre near Murchison and the whole landscape was altered by landslides. Bridges, roads and buildings were destroyed, but due to the sparse population only 17 people lost their lives.

## Canterbury (region)        F–H 9–11

The Canterbury region, bounded on the east by the Pacific and on the west by the Southern Alps, extends for some 100 km from east to west and 300 km from north to south. Within this area are great plains, torrential rivers and New Zealand's mightiest mountains.

### Population
The region has a population of around 440,000, most of them living near the coast. The largest town is Christchurch (see entry). The density of population decreases rapidly towards the interior of the South Island and the mountains. Between 1986 and 1991 the population of the whole region increased by 2.2 per cent.

### Early settlement
In the early days of the Polynesian settlement of New Zealand nomadic Maoris lived on the coast, often hunting moas by lighting fires to limit their movements.

### European settlement
When the first Europeans came to this area the moas had long since died out. The wide plains of Canterbury, grass-covered and treeless, were ideal grazing land. After Te Rauparaha's raids in the 1820s and 1830s, which had decimated the local tribes, the settlers received an almost friendly reception and found the Maoris ready to let them have land. The first settlers established themselves in the early 19th c. on the Banks Peninsula (see entry) and in the Christchurch area.

### Edward Gibbon Wakefield
The main wave of settlers came later. Edward Gibbon Wakefield, the initiator of the New Zealand Land Company, formed to promote the settlement of New Zealand, planned to establish an Anglican settlement and was supported in this by a young Conservative, John R Godley. After the company's earlier foundations at New Plymouth, Wellington, Wanganui and Nelson, which had suffered from a chronic shortage of land, Wakefield hoped that this time his ideal of a 'gentlemen's colony' would be realised. The new settlers – only wealthy men – would buy land on a large scale and establish large farms on the model of English estates. The land would be worked by selected, reliable workers who would have no claim to own land of their own. They were given free passage to New Zealand, 'tween decks, if their honesty was vouched for by an Anglican clergyman. The first ships arrived in 1850 with a consignment of carefully selected craftsmen, workers and tradesmen. From the outset class-consciousness prevailed.

### Wool barons
The well-to-do landowners left the coastal regions to arable farmers, while they themselves acquired vast areas of grazing land on the pattern of the large

sheep runs in the adjoining region of Marlborough to the north and the sheep stations of Australia. Wool was the fastest road to wealth. But Wakefield was once again disappointed. He had envisaged his new colony along English lines – large mixed farms near villages and the village church. But the New Zealand sheep farms were huge, ranging from 150 to 600 sq km in extent, which soon made their owners wealthy wool barons. This was felt to be unjust and undemocratic, and later legislation and tax reforms were introduced enabling small farmers with limited resources to acquire land. Many of the larger farms, overgrazed and ravaged by erosion, were abandoned.

### James McKenzie

James (Jock) McKenzie, a Scottish shepherd and sheep stealer, became New Zealand's first folk hero. With the help of his sheepdog Friday he stole thousands of sheep from the huge Levels Station and drove them into the then unknown highlands of what is now the Mackenzie Country, in the foreland of the Southern Alps.

### Samuel Butler

Closely connected with Canterbury was the English writer Samuel Butler, who lived here for 4 years as owner of the huge farms of Mesopotamia and Erewhon. He then sold his land at a considerable profit and returned to England. In his satirical novel *Erewhon* (1872) he gave literary immortality to the Canterbury region.

### Lake Coleridge

100 km west of Christchurch is Lake Coleridge, a typical elongated glacier-formed lake, surrounded by mountains and open tussock grassland and which is now a Mecca for anglers. It is named after a prominent member of the Canterbury Association (☞Christchurch, History). The first state-owned hydroelectric station came into operation here in 1911. The water that formerly flowed into the Harper River was diverted through underground pipelines into the Rakaia River. Near here are the winter-sports areas of Porter Heights and Mount Olympus.

Sheep in the Canterbury region

# Catlins                    D 13

### Region: Otago

This beautiful but remote and sometimes marshy stretch of upland country, with its many waterfalls and surf coast, lies in south-eastern Otago. It takes its name from a whaler who acquired large tracts of land from the Maoris in around 1840. The government would not recognise the purchase and his descendants were allowed to keep only 92 ha.

### Forests
The great forests on the east coast attracted large numbers of loggers. Sawmills were established and the timber was shipped from Hinahina. The only settlement surviving from the time of the timber boom is Owaka (pop. 400), at the entrance to Catlins Forest Park.

## ★Catlins Forest Park

### Access
The entrance to Catlins Forest Park can be reached from Highway 92 or, coming from the west, via Wyndham. The park office, with a small exhibition on the Catlins area, is in Owaka.

### Virgin forest
Catlins Forest Park, 600 sq km of largely virgin forest, extends along the Catlins River to the sparsely populated coastal area, lashed by heavy surf. There are a number of attractive trails through the forest and along the Catlins River.

On the coast there are numerous inlets and caves. The name Cannibal Bay recalls the bloody deeds of the 1830s, when the notorious Maori leader Te Rauparaha pressed his raids as far as the south of the South Island.

### Penguins and seals
Yellow-eyed penguins breed on the coast, but are very rare elsewhere in New Zealand. Colonies of seals can be seen at some points along the coast.

## Chatham Islands

### Population: 750

The Chatham Islands lie in the south Pacific some 800 km east of Christchurch. There are three main islands: Chatham, Pitt and South-east Island.

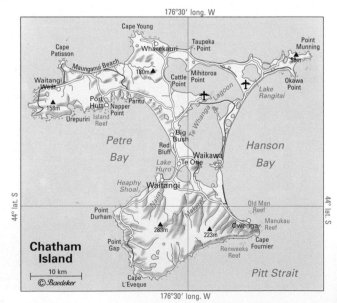

## Getting there

There are scheduled flights to Chatham from Christchurch and Wellington.

## Chatham

The largest of the islands, Chatham, has an area of 900 sq km and a population consisting mainly of fishermen and farmers. Its most striking feature is the large central lagoon (180 sq km), and there are also a number of shallow lakes. The chief place on the island is Waitangi (pop. ca 300).

From Chatham the other islands (mostly bird sanctuaries) can be visited in local fishing boats. There is little in the way of accommodation – a tourist lodge, a modest hotel and a few rooms in private houses. There is no restaurant or baker's shop and only two small general stores.

## History

The first inhabitants of the Chatham Islands, described in the literature as the Moriori, came from Polynesia. According to local tradition the ancestors of the present population came from Hawaiki in two canoes; a third canoe is said to have reached Pitt Island rather later. The Moriori developed in isolation from the inhabitants of the main islands of New Zealand. Their great limitation was the lack of any tall trees whose timber could be used for building houses or canoes, and accordingly their dwellings were very simple. They developed an art of their own in the form of tree carving (cutting figures into the bark of living trees).

Their first contact with white people was in 1791, when Lieutenant Broughton, during an expedition led by George Vancouver, saw land that was not shown on any map. The islands were named after Broughton's ship, the *Chatham*.

After 1800 whalers and seal hunters frequently visited the islands. In the 1820s Maoris who had been driven out of their tribal territory in Taranaki learned of the existence of the Chatham Islands and sought a refuge there. Under pressure from the many Taranaki Maoris who now flocked to the islands, together with the many Europeans who visited them, the numbers of Moriori gradually declined. The last pure-blooded survivor died in 1933.

The New Zealand Land Company bought the Chatham Islands in 1839, and soon afterwards tried to sell them on at a profit to a German colonial syndicate. The proposal was vetoed by the British government, which then incorporated the islands into the colony of New Zealand.

## Te Kooti and the Ringatu sect

The charismatic Maori leader Te Kooti, who had fought on the government side against the Hauhau rebels on the North Island, was suspected of espionage and in 1866, without trial, was interned on Chatham along with 300 Hauhau supporters. While there he founded the Ringatu sect, which used the Old Testament. In 1868 Te Kooti and his followers seized a ship, burned down Waitangi, the chief place on the island, and escaped to the east coast of the North Island, carrying out a brutal massacre at Gisborne. Thereafter Te Kooti and his guerrilla fighters were a thorn in the government's side for many years.

## Crayfish boom

Until the end of the second world war the Chatham Islands remained undeveloped. Between 1968 and 1972 a boom in the crayfish fisheries brought rapid prosperity. Since then fishing has remained the islanders' main source of income.

## Sights

There is a small museum in Waitangi containing Moriori artefacts and documents from the arrival of the Europeans and the Taranaki Maoris. There is also material on the career of Te Kooti.

At some places on the main island, particularly on the west side of the central lagoon and on the east coast, there are rock drawings scratched on the limestone cliffs, almost all depicting seal-like figures.

The tree carvings of the Moriori were always of human figures.

# Christchurch                    G 10

**Region: Canterbury**
**Population: 307,000**

Christchurch, the largest town on the South Island and its economic and cultural centre, lies on the east coast, not far from the Banks Peninsula, in whose natural harbour of Lyttleton the first

settlers landed in the 19th c. The city extends over an almost treeless plain that is bounded on the south-east by the hills, rising to some 400 m, between the city and Lyttleton Harbour. In summer an unpleasant hot, dry wind from the north-west often blows for days at a time.

### Getting there
**Air travel** The city's international airport, which is served by numerous domestic and foreign airlines, is in the suburb of Harewood, north-west of the city centre. There are several connections daily with Wellington and Auckland on the North Island and Dunedin in the south-east of the South Island.

**Rail** Express trains run daily on the Christchurch–Blenheim–Picton, Christchurch–Dunedin–Invercargill and Christchurch–Greymouth (on the west coast; TraNZAlpine Express) lines.

**Boat** Many cruise ships sailing in the south Pacific and cargo vessels carrying some passengers call in at Lyttleton's deep-water harbour.

### Garden City
With its spacious parks, its numerous sports grounds and well-tended gardens – amounting altogether to more than 30 sq km of green space – Christchurch has become known as the Garden City. The city's architecture and atmosphere lead many visitors to declare that it is the most British of New Zealand's towns. Its situation in an extensive plain has allowed its planners to lay it out on a rectangular grid with broad main streets. Only the winding course of the Avon River and the diagonal line of the High Street and Victoria Street disturb the regularity of its plan.

### Name
The city takes its name from Christ Church, Oxford, the college of its founder John Godley.

### History
Every year on December 16th the Canterbury Pilgrims and Settlers Association holds a religious service in the cathedral to commemorate the arrival of the first pilgrims in 1850. On the Sunday nearest the 16th there is a

◄ Christchurch Cathedral

memorial walk from Christchurch through the Port Hills to Lyttleton Harbour, where the first British settlers landed.

The original deal for the purchase of land to build a settlement on had an epilogue many years afterwards, for the land had been bought from Te Rauparaha, a Maori chief from the North Island, and not from the local Ngai Tahu tribes whom he had killed or driven out. It was only in 1920 that the government agreed to pay compensation to the real owners of the land. Since 1973 payments have been made annually towards the cost of health, education and social services for the Ngai Tahu tribes. There were uncertainties about the site of the settlement, for the Otago Association that founded Dunedin was also interested in the plains round the Banks Peninsula. The Canterbury Association grew out of the partnership of Edward Gibbon Wakefield with a young Conservative named John Robert Godley, scion of a family of large landowners. Godfrey was in entire agreement with Wakefield's ideas on colonisation – to sell the land at a high price to capitalists, to enlist reliable Anglican farm workers and tradesmen with a certificate of character from a clergyman, offer them free passage and employ them on large farms on the English model; class distinctions were to be rigidly observed. This was not a democratic community of hungry and landless emigrants like the first settlements of the New Zealand Land Company at Nelson and elsewhere on the North Island, where Wakefield had been unable to realise his idea of a 'gentlemen's colony' (☛Canterbury). Godley arrived in Lyttleton 8 months before the first settlers to prepare for the arrival of his pilgrims. In the early years of the settlement the original conception was realised. Round the town a community of arable farmers developed under the authority of the church, very much on the English model. After the drought years 1850 and 1851 in Australia wealthy sheep farmers from there came to the Christchurch area and established huge sheep runs from which they expected to draw equally huge profits. By 1855 all the available land was taken up. The Canterbury Association, which had brought no fewer than 3500 settlers – mostly Anglicans from England but also some Scottish Presbyterians, Irish

| | | | |
|---|---|---|---|
| 1 | The Victoria Clock Tower | 11 | Library Chambers | 21 | The Press Building |
| 2 | Cranmer Courts | 12 | The Canterbury Club | 22 | State Trinity Centre |
| 3 | Cranmer Centre | 13 | Original Municipal Chambers | 23 | Christchurch Club |
| 4 | Christ's College Dining Hall | 14 | Prov. Government Buildings | 24 | Fishers Building |
| 5 | Canterbury Museum | 15 | Methodist Church | 25 | Shands Emporium |
| 6 | Arts Centre Clock Tower Block | 16 | New Regent Street | 26 | McKenzie and Willis Building |
| 7 | Antigua Street Boatsheds | 17 | New Regent Street | 27 | Former Kaiapoi Woollen Company |
| 8 | Nurses' Memorial Chapel | 18 | Regent Theatre | 28 | Cathedral of the Blessed Sacrament |
| 9 | Pegasus Arms Building | 19 | Former Cheif Post Office | | |
| 10 | St Michael and all Angels | 20 | Former Government Building | | |

Catholics and German Lutherans – to the Christchurch area, was dissolved.

**City**

The Englishness of the original settlement is still evident in the city centre. The settlers planted trees with which they had been familiar at home, mainly oaks and willows, and the architecture of the late 19th c. is very much in the English styles. And the settlers were not slow to form clubs for English games like cricket and tennis.

Visiting the town in its early years, Bishop Selwyn complained that there were not enough churches and schools. In those days the churches, like other buildings, were simple wooden buildings, but in 1855 a start was made on constructing more permanent and more dignified churches. The style preferred for Anglican churches was neo-Gothic: the neoclassical style was felt to be too secular.

### Benjamin Mountfort
The aspect of the city owes a great deal to the architect Benjamin Mountfort, who was responsible for a series of major public buildings, including the Provincial Council Buildings, the Canterbury Museum and the Great Hall of the University (now the Arts Centre).

### Sightseeing
The main sights of Christchurch can be seen in a 3-hour walk. The first stage begins in Cathedral Square and leads past the Regent Theatre and over the Avon Bridge, with the Scott Memorial and the visitor centre. Then along Cambridge Terrace, passing the Bridge of Remembrance, to the Botanic Gardens, with the Arts Centre and the Canterbury Museum.

From the Canterbury Museum the second stage leads past Christ's College to Hagley Park and along Armagh Street to Cranmer Square, with two former schools, the Girls' High School and the Normal School. At the end of Chester Street is the city's oldest stone church, the Methodist Church (1864). At the south end of Durham Street, where it reaches the Avon, are the Provincial Government Buildings. On the far side of the bridge are Victoria Square and the modern Town Hall.

From Victoria Square the third stage continues along Oxford Terrace, skirting the Avon, to Madras Street, and south along this to Latimer Square. From there Worcester Street runs back to Cathedral Square.

### Tramway
There is a nostalgic city tram with which to discover the city centre. It stops near various important sights.

### Entertainment
The Arts Centre houses both ballet and theatre companies (Southern Ballet, Court Theatre, University Theatre). On the university campus in the Ilam district is the Ngaio Marsh Theatre (named after the detective-story writer, a native of Christchurch).

## Sights

### ★Christchurch Cathedral
The city's principal sight is the cathedral, a prominent landmark with its 65 m spire. It was designed by the famous London architect Sir George Gilbert Scott. The foundation stone was laid in 1864, but only a year later the work was halted because of shortage of money and only resumed in 1873. The direction of the work was entrusted to Benjamin Mountfort, who modified Scott's plan by adding turrets, pinnacles and small balconies. The building was completed in 1904, 6 years after Mountfort's death and 40 years after the start of work – though the first services were held in the nave in 1881.

In the interior of this monumental church are a series of pictures illustrating the history of the Anglican church and its bishops in New Zealand. There is also fine stained glass.

The spire has three times suffered damage in earthquakes. Visitors can climb to the viewing balconies halfway up from which there are magnificent views of the city centre.

🅖 *Balconies open Mon.–Fri. 9am–4pm, Sat. 1–4.30pm.*

### Trinity Centre
Behind the cathedral is the State Trinity Centre, originally a church (by Benjamin Mountfort, 1874) and now used for lectures and meetings.

### ★Cathedral Square
The large open square in front of the cathedral is the hub of the city's life and for long the pride of its citizens. There was great indignation when George Bernard Shaw, visiting Christchurch in 1935, admired Petre's neoclassical Roman Catholic cathedral and dismissed the Anglican cathedral as 'too academic'.

### Godley Memorial
In front of the cathedral is a statue of John Robert Godley, founder of Christchurch.

### Post Office
On the south-west side of the square is the old Chief Post Office (by PFM Burrows, 1879; ☛64), a building in Italian Renaissance style.

### Regent Theatre
The Edwardian-style Regent Theatre was

built in 1905 as the Royal Exchange Building. It was converted into a cinema in 1930.

### Press Building

The Press Building, on the north-east side of Cathedral Square, was built (by Collins and Harman, 1909) to house the offices of the *Press*, Christchurch's oldest newspaper (founded 1861). A striking feature of this four-storey building in English late Gothic style is that the windows are different on each of the floors.

### City Mall

To the south of Cathedral Square is City Mall (pedestrian zone), Christchurch's principal shopping street.

### Christchurch Club

In Latimer Square, to the east of the cathedral, is the Christchurch Club (by Benjamin Mountfort, 1861), an imposing wooden building in Italian Renaissance style. This was the meeting place of the wool barons and owners of the great sheep farms. The writer Samuel Butler was also a member, though he complained that his fellow-members could talk of nothing but money and sheep.

### Theatre Royal

The Edwardian-style Theatre Royal in nearby Gloucester Street was built in 1908 to the design of the Luttrell brothers. It has a very handsome auditorium.

### Canterbury Society of Arts Gallery

Further along Gloucester Street is the Canterbury Society of Arts Gallery, which specialises in modern art. There is a showroom with works for sale.
*Mon.–Sat. 10am–4.30pm, Sun. 2–4.30pm.*

### St Michael and All Angels

In Oxford Terrace, to the west of the cathedral, is the church of St Michael and All Angels (by WF Crisp, 1872), the oldest surviving Anglican wooden church. It has a beautiful interior and fine stained glass. The free-standing bell tower (1861) was designed by Benjamin Mountfort.

### ★Provincial Council Buildings

The neo-Gothic Provincial Council Buildings (by Benjamin Mountfort,

1859–65) to the north-east of the cathedral, beyond the little Avon River, are among the finest buildings in the city. There was originally a wooden building centred on a courtyard, a stone extension and tower being added later. The showpiece of the current buildings is the ornate neo-Gothic Council Chamber, with wall mosaics, stained-glass windows, massive and richly decorated barrel vaults and galleries for spectators and the press (completed in 1965). In 1924 an annex was built in Armagh Street.
*Conducted tours by appointment.*

### Visitor information centre

Along the Avon River to the south is the visitor information centre, housed in the former City Council Chambers (1887), a red-brick Queen Anne style building. It stands on the site of the Canterbury Association's Land Office of 1851.

### Women Memorial

Beyond the visitor centre is the Women Memorial, the city's newest bronze memorial, erected in 1993 on the 100th anniversary of the confirmation of women's right to vote.

### Scott Memorial

Opposite the visitor centre is a memorial honouring Robert Falcon Scott, who set out from Christchurch in 1912 on the expedition that took him to the South Pole after Roald Amundsen, and to his death on the return journey. The memorial, erected in 1917, was the work of his widow Kathleen (Lady Kennett), a sculptor.

### ★Boating on the Avon

Visitors can see a different aspect of Christchurch from a punt on the slow River Avon. Punts can be hired at the visitor centre or at the old Antigua Boatsheds in Cambridge Terrace.

### Bridge of Remembrance

Further south is the Bridge of Remembrance, built in 1923 as a memorial to the New Zealanders who fell in the first world war.

### ★Canterbury Museum

On the eastern edge of the Botanic Gardens, in a building of 1870 designed by Benjamin Mountfort, is the Canterbury Museum, which has a fine collection of material on the city's colonial past, as well as magnificent Maori woodcarving and objects carved from greenstone. Displays in the main hall illustrate the history of Antarctic exploration from its beginnings down to the recent past.

The first director of the museum and one of the most important collectors of material was a geologist, Julius von Haast (☞Famous People), who had carried out extensive surveys of the South Island. He used his large collection of moa bones in exchanges with other museums to build up the Canterbury Museum.
◎ *Daily 9am–4.30pm.*

### ★Arts Centre

Near the museum are the neo-Gothic buildings (also designed by Mountfort and built from 1876 onwards) formerly occupied by Canterbury University, which were converted into the Arts Centre in the 1970s, when the University moved west to the Ilam district. The finest features are the Great Hall (1882), the central clock tower (1877) and the main entrance. At the west corner of the main block is the room in which Rutherford (☞Famous People) carried out his early physics experiments. The famous philosopher Karl Popper (1902–94) also taught here (1937–45).

The Arts Centre is home to various dramatic, ballet and musical ensembles, and almost every day there are performances of high quality. Here too there is a great variety of shops, galleries and stalls displaying and selling art and craft objects, as well as cafés and restaurants. It presents a busy and bustling scene, particularly at weekends.

### ★McDougall Art Gallery

Behind the museum is the McDougall Art Gallery, which displays mainly works (paintings, sculpture, ceramics) by older and contemporary New Zealand and British artists.
◎ *Daily 10am–4.30pm.*

### Hagley Park

Beyond the Arts Centre and the Museum is Hagley Park (180 ha). It is planted with trees brought from Europe. Within the park are various sports grounds, including the Harley Cricket Oval, a golf course and a riding track.

The former university building, now the Arts Centre

**Botanic Gardens**
In the centre of the park, enclosed within a loop of the Avon, are the Botanic Gardens.

**Mona Vale**
North-west of Hagley Park, on the banks of the Avon, is the mansion of Mona Vale (1905), set in a 4 ha park planted with mature trees. The mansion is entered from Fenalton Road.
Ⓖ *Daily.*

**Christ's College**
Christ's College, to the north of the Canterbury Museum, was established soon after the foundation of ˜ Christchurch as a boys' secondary school in the tradition of the British grammar school. The earliest buildings date from 1857. The Big School (1863), designed by Superintendent FitzGerald, is the oldest school building still in use in New Zealand. The New Classrooms (1886) were designed by Benjamin Mountfort, the Dining Hall on the street front, the Hare Library with the clock and Jacob's House (1915–25) by Cecil Wood.

**★Town hall**
North-east of the Provincial Council Buildings, in Victoria Square, is the eye-catching modern town hall (1972). This attractive and imposing building was designed by the Christchurch architects Warren and Mahoney. Within the complex are an auditorium seating 2000 and a restaurant.

**Victoria Square**
In Victoria Square are a green-patinated bronze statue of Queen Victoria (1903) and another of Captain Cook (1932).

**Victoria Clock Tower**
North-west of the Town Hall, in Victoria Street, is a clock tower that was originally intended for the Provincial Council Buildings but turned out to be too heavy for their roof. It was moved to its present site on a massive stone plinth in 1930.

**Casino**
Also north-west of the town hall (30 Victoria Street) is New Zealand's first casino, opened just a few years ago.
Ⓖ *Daily 11am–3am.*

**★Cathedral of the Blessed Sacrament**
The Roman Catholic Cathedral of the Blessed Sacrament (Barbados Street, south-east of the city centre) is the finest neo-Renaissance church in New Zealand. The cathedral (1901–05), with a high dome over the crossing, was designed by FW Petre and was much admired by George Bernard Shaw.

**Rugby, Cricket and Sport Museum**
Further to the south-east is Lancaster Park, with the Rugby, Cricket and Sport Museum.
Ⓖ *Daily 10am–4pm.*

**New Regent Street**
New Regent Street was laid out uniformly in Spanish mission style in 1932, after the demolition of the old Coliseum.

## Surroundings: south-east

**Ferrymead Historic Park**
At Mount Pleasant is Ferrymead Historic Park, an open-air museum with a reconstruction of a pioneer settlement, an old tram and a stretch of old railway line on which the first train in New Zealand ran in 1863.
Ⓖ *Daily 10am–4.30pm.*

**★Mount Cavendish**
From the end of Tunnel Road the Mount Cavendish Gondola, a cableway, runs up to the summit of Mount Cavendish, on which there are viewing terraces and a restaurant. There are breathtaking panoramas of the city, the coast and the wide plain extending to the Southern Alps.

**Bridle Path**
The steep Bridle Path followed by the early settlers runs over the hills from Lyttleton Harbour to Christchurch.

**Summit Road**
The beautiful Summit Road runs along the Port Hills, the rim of the crater, with various side paths branching off to viewpoints. The best approach to the Summit Road is from Sumner, in the east, on the Evans Pass Road to Gebbies Pass. The road, with many bends, has a total length of some 70 km. The return route to Christchurch is over Dyer's Pass or via Lyttleton and the road tunnel.

**Red Cliffs**
At Red Cliffs, near Monck's Bay, is a cave

in which Julius von Haast found large numbers of moa bones in 1872.

**Banks Peninsula, Lyttleton**
See Banks Peninsula

## Surroundings: south

**Ngaio Marsh House**
The house (1907) in the Cashmere district once occupied by Ngaio Marsh, the well-known author of detective stories, actress and theatre director, is now a museum.

**Sign of Takahe**
Also in the Cashmere district is the Sign of Takahe. This house, with the aspect of a small castle, was built for Harry Ell, a local politician who was active in the campaign for the preservation of the Port Hills between Christchurch and Lyttleton. Only half-finished when he died in 1934, it was completed by the city in 1949 and is now a restaurant. From the hills there are fine views.

**Sign of Kiwi**
Further south is the Sign of Kiwi, a roadhouse on the Summit Road built on the initiative of Harry Ell.

## Surroundings: west

**Riccarton House (Deans Cottage)**
Some distance west of Hagley Park is Riccarton House (1856), the former residence of the Dean family, in a park that has been left in its natural state. The family was settled here before the arrival of the Canterbury pilgrims. The little cottage that they built in 1843 is open to the public as a museum.

**Air Force Museum**
To the south-west, on the old Wigram airfield (9 km west of the city centre), is the Museum of the Royal New Zealand Air Force, with a number of old military aircraft, aeronautical apparatus and flying equipment. There are also showings of war films.
🕒 *Mon.–Sat. 10am–4pm, Sun. 1–4pm.*

**Yaldhurst Transport Museum**
12 km west of the city centre is the Yaldhurst Transport Museum, with a collection of veteran and vintage cars.
🕒 *Daily 10am–4pm.*

## Surroundings: north-west

**Orana Park Wildlife Reserve**
Near the airport is the Orana Park Wildlife Reserve, Christchurch's zoo, with open-air enclosures reproducing natural conditions and a much-visited nocturnal house for kiwis.

**International Antarctic Centre**
On Orchard Drive, a short walk from the airport building, is the International Antarctic Centre. In the Snow and Ice Experience, an artificial polar landscape with a wind chill machine, visitors can experience the unpleasant climatic conditions to which Antarctic researchers are exposed. The centre illustrates the importance of the Antarctic for the entire globe and has excellent audio-visual shows.
🕒 *Oct.–Mar. daily 9.30am–8pm; Apr.–Sep. daily 9.30am–5.30pm.*

**Tiptree Cottage**
Beyond the airport is Tiptree Cottage (1864), a three-storey building of wood and cob (a mixture of clay and chopped straw) that is open to the public as a museum.

## Surroundings: north

**Te Whatu Manawa Orehua**
This magnificently carved Maori meeting house (1906) stands on the Rehua *marae* (assembly place) in Springfield Road.

## Surroundings: north-east

**Queen Elizabeth II Park**
This large park to the north-east of the city with facilities for various sports was laid out for the 1974 Commonwealth Games. Particular attractions are the giant water slide and a large maze.

## Surroundings: east

**★ Christchurch National Marae (Nga Hau E Wha)**
This new *marae* (assembly place) on Pages Road in the eastern suburb of Aranui is not meant only for Maoris.

Of particular note are the carved entrance gateway and the meeting house, in modern style, with carvings in the tradition of various tribes.

## Dunedin E 12

**Region: Otago**
**Population: 110,000**

Dunedin, the economic and cultural capital of the south, lies in Otago Harbour, a natural harbour reaching far inland, surrounded by hills and mountains. Dun Edin is the Gaelic name for Edinburgh: the name is a reminder that the town was founded by Scottish immigrants, who originally thought of calling it New Edinburgh.

### Getting there
**Air travel** There are several flights daily to and from Christchurch, Queenstown, Wellington and Auckland.

**Sea** Cargo ships with cabins for passengers occasionally call in at Dunedin or the neighbouring port of Chalmers, as do some cruise ships.

**Rail** There are express trains daily between Dunedin and Christchurch and between Dunedin and Invercargill. There are also occasional tourist trains through the Taieri Gorge to Middlemarch.

**Bus** There are regular bus services several times a day between Dunedin and the larger towns on the South Island.

### History
In February 1770 Captain Cook sailed past the Otago Peninsula. He was struck by the long white beaches to the south but did not notice the mouth of Otago Harbour.

Before the arrival of Europeans the Otago Peninsula had a large Maori population, who worked the much sought-after greenstone found on the west coast of the South Island. The tools, weapons and jewellery made from this green jade were also valued on the North Island as objects of exchange. Even before the 19th c. the population had been greatly reduced by inter-family and inter-tribal feuds.

The Maori population was still further reduced by brutal sealers and whalers and by the diseases (influenza, measles) that they brought with them. In 1817 there was bloody fighting between the local Maoris and the crew of a seal-hunting ship, the *Kelly*, in which 70 Maoris were killed and their village, Otakau, burned down. From the name of

Dunedin, capital of the Otago region, lies beside a deep natural harbour

the village came the name Otago that was applied to the natural harbour, the peninsula and finally the whole region.

After the foundation of Nelson Edward Gibbon Wakefield, always looking for new land for immigrants from Europe, won the support of senior Scottish churchmen for the establishment of a new settlement in the south of the South Island, and the Otago Association was formed.

In 1843, in what was known as the Disruption, more than 400 ministers of the Church of Scotland, led by Dr Thomas Chalmers (after whom Port Chalmers, just north of Dunedin, is named), left the established Church and founded the Free Church of Scotland. Two leading members of the Free Church became the founding fathers of Dunedin: William Cargill, a veteran of the Napoleonic wars who became a businessman, and Thomas Burns, a nephew of the poet Robert Burns and a minister of the church.

In 1844, when a delegation from the Otago Association was about to leave London, news came of the Wairau affray, a bloody confrontation between the settlers of Nelson and Te Rauparaha's Maoris, in which Edward Gibbon Wakefield's brother Arthur was killed. After some hesitation Frederick Tuckett was sent out to find a suitable place for the new settlement and he decided on a site in the sheltered natural harbour of Otakau. William Wakefield, who was charged to establish the settlement, persuaded Governor Fitzroy to waive the Crown's exclusive right to acquire land, laid down in the Treaty of Waitangi; the Otago Association was then able to buy land directly from the Maoris, paying only £2400 for 1620 sq km. The first settlers landed in 1848 and established themselves with the support of the local Maoris and an influential whaler named Johnny Jones who had settled nearby.

The finding of gold in Central Otago in 1861 brought a great increase of population: Dunedin was soon larger than Auckland and the wealthiest settlement in New Zealand. Trade and industry flourished in the town.

From 1863 the town's streets were lit by gas. In 1879 a cable tramway system on the model of San Francisco's cable cars began to operate in the hilly Dunedin area. A further upswing in the town's economy began in 1882, when the first refrigerator ship sailed for Britain with a cargo of frozen meat. The first frozen-meat plant in the world was established in Dunedin. Electric trams started to run in 1903.

After the turn of the 19th c., when the gold rush petered out, many young people moved north, where the climate and job prospects were better. This trend has been reversed in recent years and the population is again growing.

### Town

As a result of this stagnation in the economy and population the city centre has been preserved largely unchanged. In the prosperous Dunedin of the 19th c. imposing public buildings were built in stone, at a time when the usual building material in the rest of New Zealand was wood. Easily worked limestone was readily available in the Oamaru quarries.

The town's well-to-do citizens built handsome terraced houses with columns, oriel windows and balconies. There are particularly fine examples in Stuart Street and the High Street.

### Theatres

The former Trinity Methodist Church (1869) at the corner of Moray Place and Stuart Street is the home of the Fortune theatre company. The little Globe Theatre at 104 London Street specialises in avant-garde plays. The fine Regent Theatre, on the Octagon, also offers an excellent repertoire.

### Events

The Otago Agricultural and Pastoral Summer Show (popularly, the A and P Show) at the end of January has a full programme of events. In the middle of February there is the week-long Dunedin Festival (exhibitions, concerts, parades, sporting events). The Scottish Week at the end of March maintains Scottish traditions, with bagpipes, highland dancing and sporting events. Important film festivals are held in April/May and at the end of July.

### Factory visits

Visits to various food and drink factories are very popular – for example to Cadbury Chocolate (Cumberland Street), Speight's Brewery (Rattray Street) or Wilson's Whisky (New Zealand's only whisky distillery). Visits should be booked in advance through the visitor information centre.

## Sights

### Octagon
The central feature of the city is the Octagon, an eight-sided square with a statue of Robert Burns erected in 1887. A market is held in the square on Fridays.

### St Paul's Cathedral
On the west side of the square is the neo-Gothic St Paul's Cathedral (1915; Anglican), built by the London architects Sedding and Wheatley. In the early years of the town, founded as it was by Scottish Presbyterians, there were practically no Anglicans, but as their numbers increased they built their first church in 1862. The wooden bell tower, intended to be only temporary, was built in 1910.

### ★Municipal Chambers
Adjoining the cathedral are the imposing Municipal Chambers (town hall), with a

Renaissance-style facade and a handsome clock tower. It was built in 1880 by the young Melbourne architect RA Lawson.

### Civic Centre
To the south is the Civic Centre, with the public library and the visitor information centre. The library has a collection of books and documents that go back to the town's early days. The archives are often used by genealogists.

### Seventh Day Adventist Church
The oldest Christian church in Dunedin is the former Congregational Church (1864 by David Ross) at the corner of Moray Place and View Street (to the west of the Octagon). It was about to be demolished when it was acquired by the Seventh Day Adventists.

### ★St Joseph's Cathedral
Still further west, in Rattray Street, is St Joseph's Cathedral (1878–86 by FW

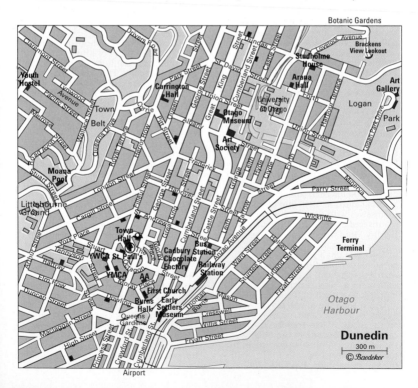

The Law Courts, Dunedin

Petre; RC). The architect seems to have taken as his models the Gothic cathedrals of Amiens and Reims.

Petre, who also designed large churches in Oamaru, Timaru, Invercargill, Wellington and Christchurch, was, along with the Scottish-born RA Lawson, who came to New Zealand by way of Australia, the leading architect working in Dunedin His plan for the cathedral, with a tower over the crossing, proved to be too expensive. There were delays and cutbacks, and the original design was much modified.

### St Dominic's Priory
St Dominic's Priory (1877) is now privately owned.

### Stuart Street
From the Octagon Stuart Street runs south-east. At its lower end are two impressive buildings dating from Dunedin's late-Victorian heyday, the Law Courts and the railway station.

### Law Courts
The Law Courts, designed by the government architect John Campbell,

were built in 1902. Over the main entrance are the royal arms.

Adjoining the Law Courts is the **police station**, a brick building of 1896 that was originally designed as a prison.

### Cadbury chocolate factory
On some days there is a sweet chocolate fragrance over the centre of Dunedin that comes from the Cadbury chocolate factory not far north of the courthouse and railway station.

### ★ Railway station
Diagonally opposite, in Anzac Avenue, the Railway station, a massive fortress-like structure, dominates the scene. In Flemish Renaissance style, it was built in 1904–6 by George Troup. Though mocked for his 'gingerbread' architecture, the architect was knighted for his work. The interior is magnificent, with colonnades, balustrades and mosaic paving.

### ★ Early Settlers' Museum
South of the station is the Early Settlers' Museum, with much material from the town's early days, including many

portraits of the Scottish founding families, and exhibits illustrating the town's technological achievements (street lighting, trams, railway).
ⓖ *Mon.–Fri. 9am–4.30pm, Sat. 10.30am–4.30pm, Sun. 1.30–4.30pm.*

### ★First Church

South-east of the Octagon, on Moray Place and Burlington Street, is the First Church (1868–73 by RA Lawson), a neo-Gothic building with a handsome tower. The foundation stone was laid by Thomas Burns, co-founder of the town.

### ★Princes Street

From the Octagon Princes Street runs south. A street with a fashionable air, it has a number of notable buildings.

### Southern Cross Hotel

To the south-west, at the corner of Princes Street and High Street, is the Southern Cross Hotel, built in 1883 and still retaining its original splendour. Particularly fine are the entrance lobby with its impressive candelabra and the stucco-decorated rooms on the first floor.

### Wain's Hotel

Close by is the sumptuous facade of Wain's Hotel, a luxury hotel opened in 1878. Notable features are the grotesques on the ground-floor windows.

### ANZ Bank

The ANZ Bank occupies a building of 1874 designed by RA Lawson, which retains its neoclassical façade.

### Bank of New Zealand

The Bank of New Zealand (1879–83 by William Armson) is in a richly decorated neo-Renaissance style. The banking hall has a magnificent ceiling.

### ★Otago Museum

1 km north-east of the Octagon, caught between the two carriageways of Highway 1 (Great King Street and Cumberland Street), is the Otago Museum, in a large and handsome building (1876 by David Ross). The museum's rich collections bear witness to the prosperity of Victorian Dunedin and the interest in self-improvement of its citizens, who presented their art treasures to the museum.

There are five main departments: the culture of the Maoris and the Pacific area; the natural history of New Zealand;

archaeology and ancient and classical civilisations; oceanography; and science and technology (with a hands-on science centre for children, Discovery World).

Of particular interest is the large collection of objects made from greenstone, including axe-like weapons and amulets. Many of these items were made by the local Maoris on the Otago Peninsula. There is also a fine carved meeting house of 1872–5 from Whakatane on the Bay of Plenty (North Island).
ⓖ *Mon.–Fri. 10am–5pm, Sat., Sun. 1–5pm.*

### Otago Art Society Museum

Close by, in the handsome old post office of Dunedin North, is the museum of the Otago Art Society.
ⓖ *Daily 2–4.30pm.*

### ★University of Otago

The University of Otago, New Zealand's first university, was founded in 1869. The imposing neo-Gothic buildings (1878 onwards) on the little River Leith, north of the city centre, were designed by Maxwell Bury, who took the University of Glasgow as his model. Particularly impressive features are the handsome clock tower, the main entrance and the staircase. The building in Castle Street is now occupied by the university administration. The first chancellor of the university was Thomas Burns, one of the founding fathers of Dunedin (see above).

Round the old buildings are various later buildings occupied by university faculties, including the Dental School, the only one in New Zealand. Here too are the professors' houses (1879), also designed by Maxwell Bury, built of red brick with contrasting white gable arches.

### Hocken Library

The Hocken Library (Albany Street, Castle Street block) was bequeathed to the city by the bibliophile Dr Thomas M Hocken in 1910 and has since been enlarged. The collection includes printed works, maps, pictures and manuscripts, mainly concerned with New Zealand and the south Pacific.
ⓖ *Mon.–Fri. 9.30am–5pm, Sat. 9am–noon.*

### ★Dunedin Art Gallery

The Dunedin Art Gallery, a few hundred metres east of the university in Logan Park, has a rich collection of early and modern New Zealand and European art. Of particular interest are numerous works by Frances Hodgkins, brought up in Dunedin, who achieved fame in London only late in life. Her father was one of the founders of the art gallery. The work of Colin McCahon is also well represented.

◉ *Mon.–Fri. 10am–4.30pm, Sat., Sun. 2–5pm.*

### ★Bracken's Lookout

From this viewpoint, north-west of the art gallery, there is a good view of the city centre. Thomas Bracken (1843–98) was a poet and politician who wrote the New Zealand national anthem *God defend New Zealand* (☞Introduction, Quotations).

### ★★Botanic Gardens

North-west of Bracken's Lookout are the Botanic Gardens (30 ha), established in 1863. Old trees, both native and European, afford shade, and there is a wide range of New Zealand's flora, well tended and labelled. The gardens are at their most beautiful when the azaleas and rhododendrons are in flower (August to October).

### ★Olveston

To the west of the Otago Museum, in the city's green belt, is the mansion of Olveston (1906), designed by the English architect Ernest George. Its first owner was David E Theomin, a businessman and art collector who came from Olveston, near Bristol, and settled in Dunedin in 1879.

This sumptuous 35-room mansion in late Victorian style gives some impression of the way of life of the prosperous middle class in the early 20th c. The oak staircase and balustrade were made in England. There are numerous paintings illustrating many aspects of life in colonial New Zealand. ◉ *Conducted tours by appointment.*

## Surroundings

### Signal Hill

From Signal Hill (393 m), reached from the Northern Cemetery on Opoho Road and Signal Hill Road, there are magnificent views to the south over Otago Harbour and the city. On the hill is a monument (1940) commemorating the 100th anniversary of the Treaty of Waitangi. It incorporates a piece of rock from Edinburgh Castle, an anniversary gift from Scotland. Bronze figures symbolise the past and the future.

### Mount Cargill

8 km north of Dunedin is Mount Cargill (676 m), from which there are fine views of the city, Otago Harbour and the Otago Peninsula.

### ★Port Chalmers

12 km north of Dunedin, on the north side of Otago Harbour, is the deep-water harbour of Port Chalmers (pop. 3000). The town is named after Dr Thomas Chalmers, one of the founders of the Free Church of Scotland. From here the colonisation of Otago began; the first steamer carrying frozen meat sailed for London; and also from here Scott, Shackleton and Byrd set out on their Antarctic expeditions. In the 1970s, when container shipping became established, Port Chalmers took on a new lease of life. The harbour of Dunedin, which had been developed at great expense, proved unsuitable for this traffic.

The Scott Memorial commemorates Captain Scott, who sailed from here on his last tragic expedition in 1910. Nearby is a monument commemorating the first shipment of frozen meat to London in 1882. The Port Chalmers Flagstaff on the Aurora Terrace Lookout was once a signal station, keeping watch on shipping traffic in Otago Harbour.

Notable churches in the city are the Iona Church (1883), with a 50 m tower, the Anglican church of the Holy Trinity (1874) and the Roman Catholic church of St Mary's Star of the Sea (1874).

The Port Chalmers Museum, in the former post office (1877 by WH Clayton), displays a variety of material on the history of the port and on New Zealand shipping. ◉ *Sat., Sun. 1.30–4.30pm.*

### Glenfalloch Woodland Gardens

10 km east of Dunedin are the Glenfalloch Woodland Gardens, laid out in 1873, with native and exotic trees. The mansion set in the gardens was built of kauri wood 2 years earlier. The gardens are at their most beautiful in spring, when the azaleas, rhododendrons and fuchsias are in bloom.

### Portobello

The **Trust Bank Aquarium** in Portobello

(20 km east of Dunedin) is run by the University of Otago. Here visitors can see examples of almost all New Zealand's marine fauna.

⊙ *Dec.–Feb. daily noon–4.30pm; Mar.–Nov. Sat., Sun. and holidays only.*

## Otakou Maori Site

25 km east of Dunedin, on the former site of a large ancient Maori settlement, a Maori church and meeting house were inaugurated in 1940 on the 100th anniversary of the Treaty of Waitangi. There is a small cemetery containing the graves of three important chiefs.

## ★ Taiaroa Head

Taiaroa Head, the northern tip of the Otago Peninsula, is famed as the nesting-place of royal albatrosses. Nearby are colonies of yellow-eyed penguins, seals and sea lions. There are boat trips from Dunedin to the rugged cliffs of Taiaroa.

## ★ Larnach Castle

50 km from Dunedin, on the Otago Peninsula, is Larnach Castle, also known as the Camp, which was built for a wealthy banker named William Larnach between 1871 and 1887. This

extraordinary building is said to have been modelled on a Scottish castle; its construction was supervised by the well-known architect RA Lawson. The house, which has a ballroom, cost its owner a fortune. William Larnach (1833–98) came to Dunedin in 1867 as manager of the Bank of Otago and had a successful career as a politician. After a series of misfortunes, both financial and personal, he shot himself in the Parliament Building in Wellington. After his death the house suffered many vicissitudes. The surrounding land was broken up into small lots and sold, and the house was bought by the government, with 14 ha of land, and converted into a psychiatric clinic. Later it became a hotel and nightclub. Then in 1940, badly run down, it was sold for a pittance. Only in recent years has its value as a relic of Dunedin's early days been recognised. It has been restored at great expense. From the tower there are fine views.

⊙ *Daily 9am–5pm.*

## Beaches

There are popular beaches in the suburbs of St Kilda and St Clair, to the south of Dunedin on the sandbank linking the

Larnach Castle

Otago Peninsula with the mainland. From St Kilda, where there are many sports clubs, the John Wilson Ocean Drive runs along the edge of the beach.

### ★Taieri Gorge
A half-hour drive north-west of Dunedin is the wild and romantic gorge of the Taieri River. Visitors can jet through the gorge on a jet boat or rattle through it on the Otago Excursion Train.

## ★Fiordland National Park     A–C 11–13

**Region: Southland**
**Area: 12,523 sq km**

The Fiordland National Park, the largest by far of New Zealand's national parks, occupies an immense wilderness of rugged mountain country in the south-west of the South Island, with numerous fjords reaching far inland.

### Information
There is a visitor centre in Te Anau.

### Topography
This is a region of deep fjords in the west, ramified lakes in the east and mountains covered with dense forests of evergreen southern beech. At the higher levels and on the summits grow long beard lichens and various mosses. It is also a region of very high rainfall (up to 6000 mm), which fuels its grandiose waterfalls and locally catastrophic avalanches in winter.

The national park is bounded on the north by the Darran Mountains, which rise to 2700 m at Mount Tutoko. In the east a number of large lakes form a transition to the drier grazing country of Southland. In the west the mountains fall steeply to the Tasman Sea, which is lashed by the roaring forties.

The longest fjords are (from south to north), Preservation Inlet, Dusky Sound, Doubtful Sound, George Sound and Milford Sound (see entry), which is the best known and most accessible of the fjords.

These narrow, deep inlets were originally valleys hewn out by glaciers, which were later drowned by the sea. On the eastern edge of the ridge of mountains that runs down the whole of the South Island the glaciers carved out a series of elongated lakes, of which Lake

Te Anau (see entry) is by far the largest. Others are Lake Manapouri (see entry), Lake Monowai, Lake Hauroko and Lake Poteriteri.

## Trails

### Notes
The grandiose mountain country of the Fiordland National Park appeals particularly to walkers and climbers who like to enjoy the unspoiled beauty of nature. There is plenty of scope in this area for hikes of several days, often very strenuous, exploring lonely mountain forests, lakes and fjords.

Information about trails and accommodation and detailed routes can be obtained from Department of Conservation offices in Te Anau and Tuatapere. Walks must be planned well in advance, since accommodation in mountain huts has to be booked in plenty of time. Except on organised tours, walkers must carry all their gear and food with them. They must be prepared for changeable weather and long spells of rain: rainproof clothing, stout footwear and sandfly and mosquito repellents are essentials.

### ★★Milford Track
The world-famous Milford Track runs from Lake Te Anau to Milford Sound (see entries). At least 4 days must be allowed for this grandiose mountain route. Advance booking of accommodation in huts is essential. Guided walks are available.

### ★Hollyford Track
This route runs along Hollyford Valley, in the north of the national park, follows Lake McKerow and continues to the coast at Martin's Bay. The walk takes at least 4–5 days. Guided walks are available. Accommodation in huts must be booked in advance.

### ★Routeburn Track
Starting from the road to Milford Sound, this track (3-day walk) runs over the Harris Saddle (1279 m) to the north end of Lake Wakatipu at Kinloch. It is often walked as an extension to the Milford Track (see above).

### Kepler Track
The Kepler Track (4 days) runs from Lake Te Anau to Lake Manapouri (see entries).

## Scenic flights

There are scenic flights (in helicopters, seaplanes or light aircraft) from Te Anau and Milford, offering splendid views of mountains, forests and fjords.

## Fiordland cruises

Fiordland Travel offers 6-day cruises in the motor sailing ship *Milford Wanderer*. Visitors can follow in the footsteps of Captain Cook as they sail into the remote fjords in the south of the national park.

FIORDLAND TRAVEL LTD
☎ *(064) 34427509,*
*email info@fiordlandtravel.co.nz,*
*www.fiordlandtravel.co.nz/.*

## Boat trips

There is plenty of scope for rewarding boat trips on Lake Te Anau and Lake Manapouri and in Milford Sound and Doubtful Sound (see entries).

## ★ Dusky Sound

Dusky Sound, New Zealand's longest fjord (44 km), is also one of the most beautiful, with numerous wooded islands and inlets. It was given its name by Captain Cook, who sailed past the fjord on his first voyage, in 1770, as evening was falling. In 1773, on his second voyage, he sailed into the sound and spent over 6 weeks overhauling his ship, the *Resolution*, and taking in supplies. He encountered groups of shy Maoris, who had perhaps withdrawn to this remote area in the face of attacks by more aggressive tribes. George Forster gives a vivid account of the meeting with the Maoris and also of a plague of sandflies. Nowadays the area is almost uninhabited, but the sandflies are still there. The seals that were once common in the fjord were almost wiped out by sealers, but since the ban on seal hunting their numbers have increased.

The fjord can be reached by land only on difficult tracks taking off from the road along Doubtful Sound or, in the south, from Lake Hauroko. The best way of seeing the fjord, with its many islands and inlets, is on a seaplane flight. Cruises in a motor sailing ship, run by Fiordland Travel (see above), start from Deep Cove, in Doubtful Sound. Information from the national park's visitor centre in Te Anau.

## Lake Hauroko

100 km north-west of Invercargill (see entry), in a beautiful setting of steep and densely wooded hills, is Lake Hauroko. Winds and storms blow in from north and south unhindered, sometimes making boating on the lake dangerous. About 6 km east of the lake, on the borders of the national park, is a campsite.

In 1967 a Maori burial site (ca 1700) was discovered in a cave on Mary Island. A steel grille now guards the *tapu* (sacred site).

A number of beautiful trails run round Lake Hauroko, among them the Lookout Bluff Track and the Boundary Track. There is a 4-day walk from the north end of the lake (Hauroko Burn) to Supper Cove on Dusky Sound.

## Doubtful Sound

See Lake Manapouri

## Milford Sound

See entry

## ★★Fox Glacier                    E 10

### Region: West Coast

The Fox Glacier (☞Mount Cook National Park, map) and the Franz Josef Glacier 25 km north reach down from some of the highest peaks of the Southern Alps, in Westland National Park (see entry), to around 300 m above sea level, amid dense forests. They were originally named after Queen Victoria and her consort Prince Albert. But in 1865 the German geologist Julius von Haast renamed the more northerly of the two after the Austrian emperor Franz Josef. And in 1872, when the then prime minister of New Zealand visited the glaciers, the one to the south was given his name.

### View

The glaciers are at their most impressive at sunset. The very high rainfall (up to 7500 mm) produces dense rain forests but also means many rainy days. Stable weather conditions prevail in winter, when the snow-capped peaks that form the backdrop to the glaciers can often be clearly seen. In summer, during the main holiday season, the two holiday resorts at the foot of the glacier are

The Franz Josef Glacier ➤

overcrowded; it is essential, therefore, to book well in advance.

**Visitor centres**
At both glaciers there are good visitor information centres with detailed information about glaciers and rain forests. Both centres run guided walks and excursions and can also arrange accommodation.

**Glaciers**
The 13 km long Fox Glacier and the 10 km long Franz Josef Glacier both make a considerable descent over a relatively short distance. It is because of this relatively rapid descent that they reach so far down. Both glaciers have been growing a few centimetres daily since the 1980s, during the cold and rainy winters.

**Fox Glacier**
A 7 km road and a footpath lead to the mouth of the Fox Glacier. A walk over the glacier is not difficult with suitable footwear. For inexperienced glacier walkers a guided walk (available twice daily) is recommended.

From the Peak Indicator, a viewpoint 9 km further west, there are magnificent views, in clear weather, of the mountain peaks and the creeping glacier. The view is particularly fine at sunrise or sunset.

**Gillespie's Point**
20 km below the village of Fox Glacier, Gillespie's Point reaches out into the wild Tasman Sea. Gold was found here in the 19th c.

## ★★Franz Josef Glacier

Over the last 200 years the relatively steep Franz Josef Glacier has frequently advanced and then withdrawn again. On balance, however, it has retreated markedly. Meltwater from the glacier forms the Waiko River.

A narrow road (6 km) runs along the south side of the Waiko valley to the parking area at the mouth of the glacier. On the way there it is worth taking the side roads going off to Peter's Pool, Sentinel Rock and various lookouts with views of the glacier.

A walk (2 hours there and back) over the wide river bed and rocks polished by the ice leads to a viewpoint at the glacier's mouth. For a walk over the glacier itself it is best to join one of the guided tours, which are available twice a day.

**Alex Knob**
There is a breathtaking view of the glacier from the Alex Knob (1295 m).

**Franz Josef Glacier village**
The village called Franz Josef Glacier is a popular tourist resort. The little church of St James was built in 1931. From its chancel window there was once a good view of the glacier.

**Lake Makourapi**
8 km north of the village on Highway 6 is the idyllic little Lake Makourapi, whose waters mirror the majestic alpine peaks and green expanses of forest. The lake is the haunt of many bird species.

**Okarito**
25 km north of Franz Josef Glacier village is Okarito, a small township founded by gold miners in the 1860s. In good weather there are marvellous views of the Southern Alps from here.

**Okarito Lagoon**
The Okarito Lagoon is a bird sanctuary, established to protect the white heron. This is its only nesting place in New Zealand. There are guided birdwatching walks from November to February.

**Helicopter flights**
A sightseeing flight over the glaciers by helicopter is a memorable experience. Some tours include a landing on one of the peaks, with their deep covering of snow. Popular views for photographers are Lakes Matheson and Gault, in which, in fine weather, the surrounding snow-capped peaks are mirrored (best seen in the early morning).

## Greymouth                                    F 9

**Region: West Coast**
**Population: 11,000**

Greymouth (named after Governor George Grey) is the main commercial centre on the west coast and an important port. Its economy was originally based on gold mining, later on coal and timber, and then also on cattle and dairy farming.

### Flooding

The port, situated at the mouth of the Grey River, is constantly exposed to the threat of flooding, either by the river or by the wild Tasman Sea. Flood protection measures were completed in 1991. Rain is frequent and often goes on for a long time, and a bitterly cold wind known as the Barber blows down the Grey valley. These climatic factors have contributed to the steady decline in population since the end of the 19th c.

### Rail services

There is a rail link between Greymouth and Christchurch on the east coast over Arthur's Pass (see entry). The 5-hour run on the ★TraNZAlpine Express, passing through the Otira Tunnel and the gorges in Arthur's Pass National Park, is a great tourist attraction. The west coast line to Hokitika (see entry) carries only goods.

### History

Greymouth grew up on the site of the Maori settlement of Mawhera. The first European to explore the wilderness on the west coast was Thomas Brunner in 1846. During the Westland gold rush of the 1860s Greymouth was an important supply centre.

### ★Shantytown

13 km south of Greymouth is the reconstructed gold-mining settlement of Shantytown, which attracts crowds of visitors throughout the year. The 1860s are recalled in this open-air museum of old buildings transferred to the site from other parts of the country and furnished in period style. They include a church, Coronation Hall, a general store, stables, a jail, a hotel, a hospital, a printing office and the workshops of various craftsmen. A steam railway line of 1897 runs through the dense forest to an old sawmill. There are old gold-miners' claims at which visitors can try their hand at panning for gold, selling any they find to gold dealers.

### Kumara

The old gold-miners' settlement of Kumara (pop. 300) lies 25 km south of Greymouth on the road that runs through the Otira Gorge to Arthur's Pass. In its heyday it had a population of anything up to 4000. In the nearby

A bar of the gold-rush days in Shantytown

Taramakau River there was large-scale gold prospecting as recently as 1982.

**Woods Creek Track**
11 km east of Shantytown is the Woods Creek Track (ca 1 hour), running through an area that was turned upside down by gold miners in the 1860s.

**Point Elizabeth Walkway**
11 km north of Greymouth, at Raparahoe, is the start of this attractive trail (ca 4 hours each way), which runs along the coast through dense primeval forest with tree ferns and nikau palms. It affords fine views of the coast and the highest peaks of the Southern Alps.

**Brunner**
12 km east of Greymouth on Highway 7 is the Brunner coalfield, with four coal mines that were once of great importance – Dobson, Wallsend, Stillwater and Taylorville. The rich deposits of coal on both sides of the Grey River were discovered by Thomas Brunner while surveying the west coast in 1846–8; mining started in 1864. An accident in the Brunner mine in 1896 cost 67 lives.

An old suspension bridge over the Grey River leads to the Brunner Mine, now closed down and scheduled as New Zealand's first protected industrial monument, ★ Brunner Industrial Site. Industrial heritage trails and displays explain the history of coal mining on the west coast.

**★ Lake Brunner**
32 km south-east of Greymouth, in a setting of great scenic beauty, is Lake Brunner, the largest lake on the west coast, which is ideal for fishing and boating. It was formed in a basin scooped out by a glacier and dammed by terminal moraine.
   The lake is known to the Maoris as Moana Kutuku (lake of the white heron). Herons are still occasionally to be seen on the shores of the lake.

**Lake Hochstetter**
50 km east of Greymouth, on a side road off Highway 7, is Lake Hochstetter. Named after the Austrian geologist Ferdinand von Hochstetter, it was enlarged by the construction of a dam in 1876. Good fishing; picnic spots.

# ★Haast Pass                                    D 11
**Regions: Southland and Otago**

The Haast Pass (named after the German geologist Julius von Haast, first director of Christchurch Museum), the lowest passage through the Southern Alps (564 m), provides a link between the Southland region to the west and the area round Lake Wanaka (see entry) in the Otago region. The road follows an ancient Maori track to the deposits of greenstone on the west coast. The asphalted road was eventually completed in 1965. It runs through grandiose rugged scenery that is often shrouded in cloud. In winter the road is rarely blocked by snow, since in this area the precipitation is mostly rain. There are a number of attractive rest areas.

**History**
The Maori track over the pass was rediscovered by Charles Cameron in 1863 on his way from Dunedin (see entry) to look for gold on the west coast. Mount Cameron (1763 m), on the west side of the pass road, is named after him. Cameron was followed soon afterwards by Julius von Haast.

# ★Hanmer Springs                                 G 9
**Region: Canterbury**
**Population: 1200**

140 km north of Christchurch (see entry), situated in a sheltered hollow at an altitude of 366 m, is the spa and holiday resort of Hanmer Springs, noted for its abundant thermal springs. It is a quiet little place, surrounded by Hanmer Forest, with the hills of the Hanmer Range (skiing in winter) as a backdrop.

**History**
The springs, which had long been used by the Maoris for therapeutic purposes, are said to have been discovered in 1859 by the manager of a farm at Culverton. Soon afterwards the government built a sanatorium, a psychiatric clinic and a soldiers' convalescent home. Since 1971 alcoholics have also been treated here.

**Spa establishment**
The modern spa establishment has water at a temperature of 38°C.
ⓘ Daily 10am–8pm.

### ★Waiau River

For adventurous visitors there are jet-boat trips and white-water rafting on the nearby Waiau River, as well as bungee jumping from the 31 m high bridge over the river.

### ★Hanmer Forest

Hanmer Forest covers an area of 17,000 ha, much of it of natural southern beech. Various exotic species were planted by convict labour in 1902. Nowadays the new plantings are mainly of Californian pine and Douglas fir, timber from which is sold mainly in Christchurch. There are trails of varying length through the forest, and the scenery can also be seen from the 16 km Forest Drive road; permission to drive on it must be obtained from the local visitor centre.

### ★Molesworth Station

In summer all-terrain vehicles can travel from Hanmer Springs to the remote Molesworth Station, the largest in New Zealand. This former sheep farm with some 1800 sq km of grazing land has gradually been acquired by the state. In the past repeated burning of the grass, overgrazing and a plague of rabbits led to severe erosion. Part of the land has now been improved on sound ecological principles and provides grazing for cattle rather than sheep.

## Hokitika                           E/F 9

**Region: West Coast**
**Population: 4000**

The little town of Hokitika lies in a setting of great scenic beauty on the west coast. At the time of the gold rush in the 1860s it had a population of over 10,000, with hotels, theatres, casinos and even an opera house with seating for 1400. Gold is still worked in deep shafts in the Goliath Mine, but the revenue from timber is now much greater than from gold mining.

### ★Greenstone

Fine jewellery is made from greenstone (jade and nephrite) in specialist workshops. The local deposits of greenstone or *pounamu* were known to the Maoris before the arrival of Europeans.

## Sights

In the 19th c. Hokitika was briefly the seat of the provincial government of Westland, and the old Government Building still survives. In front of it is a statue of 'King Dick', as Richard Seddon, the local Member of Parliament for 27 years and prime minister of New Zealand in the 1890s, is known here. At the town's main intersection (Sewell Street and Weld Street) is a clock tower commemorating the New Zealanders who fell in the Boer War and the coronation of King Edward VII. The West Coast Historical Museum has a collection of Maori weapons and jewellery in greenstone, as well as extensive material on the days of the gold rush.

The town's principal landmark is the neo-Romanesque St Mary's Church (RC), built in 1914 in place of an earlier church erected by Irish immigrants in 1865.

## Surroundings

**Lake Kaniere**
20 km south of Hokitika are the idyllic

The Clock tower, Hokitika

Lake Kaniere and the impressive **Dorothy Falls**.

**Hokitika River Gorge**
25 km south is the Hokitika River Gorge, with an old suspension bridge, a popular destination for excursions.

**Ross**
30 km south of Hokitika is the village of Ross (pop. 1000), in an area that in the past yielded great quantities of gold. In 1907 a nugget weighing almost 3 kg was found; it was presented to King George V by the New Zealand government as a coronation gift. After a temporary slowdown, new gold deposits were found in the 1980s, which are now exploited in opencast mines.

The local visitor centre, housed in a restored gold-miner's cottage, has a small museum of relics of gold-mining days. St Patrick's Church (RC) was built by Irish immigrants in 1866.

From Ross the Water Race Walk and the Jones Flat Walk (each 1 hour's walking) lead to the old goldfields.

# Invercargill                    C 13

**Region: Southland**
**Population: 52,000**

Invercargill, New Zealand's southernmost town, lies in an open plain on the banks of the New River estuary. It was laid out from 1856 onwards by the town planner John T Thomson on a geometric plan, with broad streets and open spaces. The town takes its name from William Cargill, one of the Scottish founding fathers of Dunedin; the prefix *inver* refers to its position at the mouth of a river. Many of the streets are named after Scottish rivers.

Originally the New River estuary served as a natural harbour, but its functions as a harbour were later taken over by Bluff, at the southern tip of the South Island. The lush Southland pastures were for many years the town's main source of income. Later a number of large slaughterhouses and meat-freezing plants were established, and a further boost was given to Invercargill's economy by the construction of an aluminium smelter at Bluff (see below).

## Sights

### ★Southland Museum and Art Gallery
The town's principal sight is the Southland Museum and Art Gallery. It has fine natural history collections from the Southland region (including petrified wood from nearby Curio Bay) and relics of the wild days of the whalers, but its particular treasures are its examples of Maori arts and crafts. The art gallery is housed in a striking pyramidal building at the entrance to Queen's Park.

### Tuatara House
The Tuatara House provides near-natural conditions for specimens of this lizard-like reptile that dates back to the time of the dinosaurs and is now very rare.

### Queen's Park
Queen's Park, (80 ha) with various sports grounds, a duckpond, a game park and a children's playground, is entered from Queen's Drive.
◎ *Winter Gardens open daily.*

### Town centre
The town hall, a symmetrical building built in 1906 by ER Wilson, reflects the prosperity of the town in those days. The Kelvin Chambers (1864) recall Southland's short-lived independent provincial government; the region broke away from Otago in 1861 but was reincorporated in it in 1870. Lennel House (102 Albert Street), a mansion set in a beautiful garden, was built in 1880 by John T Thomson; it is still in private ownership.

The town's principal **churches**, all built in brick, are close together: St John's (1887; Anglican), the neo-Byzantine First Church (1915; Presbyterian) and St Mary's (1894–1905 by FW Petre; RC). St Mary's has a beautiful interior in white Oamaru limestone.

## Surroundings

### ★Anderson Park and Art Gallery
7 km north of the town centre is Anderson Park (24 ha), with a mansion that belonged to Robert Anderson, a local entrepreneur who presented the whole property to the town. It now houses a large art collection which includes some fine Maori portraits, early views of Bluff and some good examples of New Zealand modern art. Also in the

Nugget Point, at the southern tip of New Zealand

park is a magnificently carved Maori meeting house.
🕐 *Tue.–Thu., Sat., Sun. 2–4.30pm.*

### Oreti Beach
10 km west of Invercargill is the beautiful sandy Oreti Beach.

### Bluff
30 km south of Invercargill, at the southern tip of the South Island, is the port of Bluff (pop. 2500). It lies on a promontory reaching out into the Foveaux Strait under the Old Man Bluff (265 m), from which there are wide views. The port's main trade is in frozen lamb and it also has a small fishing fleet. The oysters and crayfish of the Foveaux Strait are much valued. The town's maritime museum is devoted to the history of the town and the oyster fisheries.

There is a ferry service between Bluff and Halfmoon Bay on Stewart Island.

On Tiwai Point, on the north-east side of Bluff Harbour, is New Zealand's only ★**aluminium smelter**, a joint New Zealand-Japanese enterprise. Since the discovery of large deposits of bauxite at Weipa on the Cape York peninsula in Australia (Queensland), aluminium oxide has been shipped from there to Tiwai Point and smelted in Bluff, the huge quantities of electricity required being provided by the hydroelectric station on Lake Manapouri. The smelter employs some 1200 workers. The aluminium is mainly exported to Japan.
🕐 *Conducted tours (no under-12s) by appointment Mon.–Fri. 10am.*

### Stewart Island
Stewart Island (see entry), across the Foveaux Strait from Invercargill, can be visited either by air or by ferry (ca 2½ hours from Bluff) to Halfmoon Bay.

### ★Southern Scenic Route
An attractive alternative to the inland route to Balclutha and Dunedin on Highway 1 is the Southern Scenic Route coast road running through Catlins Forest Park (☛Catlins). Via Fortrose, Waipapa Point (lighthouse) and Otara you reach the delightful ★**Curio Bay**, whose main attraction is a fossilised kauri forest and frequent sightings of Hector's dolphins in the bay. A short distance further on is the magical

Waikawa Bay. Continuing to Balclutha, do not miss detours to Cathedral Caves, Purakaunui Falls, Jack's Blowhole or Nugget Point.

# Kaikoura                           H 9

**Region: Nelson-Marlborough**
**Population: 2200**

The little town of Kaikoura lies on the north-east coast of the South Island at the foot of the Seaward Kaikoura Range (2600 m), just north of the rocky Kaikoura Peninsula, which is famed for its seal colony.

The Maori name Kaikoura (eating crayfish) is a reference to the rich crayfish fishing grounds that were much prized by the Maoris. In the 19th c. whaling also made a major contribution to the economy of the town. There are still a few relics of the old whaling stations in the form of whalebones (e.g. in the Garden of Memories).

## Sights

### Fyffe House
Fyffe House (Avoca Street) was built around 1860 for a whaler named George Fyffe. It is now a historic monument.

### Maori meeting house
Near the hospital is the Takahara Marae (assembly place), which has been given a new lease of life by the construction of a modern Maori meeting house. From the little Maori cemetery there is a good view of the mountains across the bay. The old Maori *pa* was taken in 1828 by Te Rauparaha, the warlike chief from the North Island. From here it is a short distance to the Kaikoura Lookout.

## Surroundings

### Maori Leap Cave
3 km south of Kaikoura is the Maori Leap Cave, a karstic sea cave hollowed out by the surf with fine stalactite formations and in which large numbers of bird and seal skeletons were found.
ⓖ *Guided tours by arrangement through the local visitor centre.*

### ★Wildlife
On the rocks at the end of Kaikoura Island is a colony of several hundred seals with some yellow-eyed penguins. They do not appear to have any fear of humans. A trip on a boat will yield sightings, from an appropriate distance, of not just seals but also of black and Hector's dolphins, sperm whales, and albatrosses with wingspans of over 3 m.
☎ *Information (0800) 655121, email res@whalewatch.co.nz, www.whalewatch.co.nz.*

# Karamea                          G 8

**Region: West Coast**
**Population: 500**

Karamea, near the north-western tip of the South Island, is the end point of the Heaphy Track (☛Abel Tasman National Park). It has a dry, sunny climate. In 1874 incomers from Nelson settled in the fertile surrounding area. Until the building of a road from Westport in 1915 Karamea could be reached only by sea or via the Heaphy Track. A severe earthquake in 1929 destroyed the harbour at the mouth of the river.

### Wanga Peka Track
South-east of Karamea is the start of the Wanga Peka Track, which runs through the North-west Nelson Forest Park.

### ★Fenian Range
North of Karamea is the Fenian Range, in which is a system of karstic caves. In the Opara Valley are a number of natural bridges formed by the collapse of caves. The Honeycomb Caves, in which the remains of extinct bird species were found, can be entered only with permission from the Department of Conservation.

# ★★Lake Manapouri              B 12

**Region: Southland (Fiordland National Park)**

Lake Manapouri, perhaps New Zealand's most beautiful lake, lies 30 km west of Te Anau. With an area of 142 sq km, it has no less than three dozen islands and islets. The lake is surrounded by high hills; only on the east, where the Waiau River flows out of the lake to link it with

Lake Te Anau, is the landscape more open. The surface of the lake is 178 m above sea level; at its deepest point (443 m) the bed of the lake is well below sea level.

In the 1960s plans to raise the level of the lake by 12 m under a proposed hydroelectric scheme to supply power to the aluminium smelter at Bluff aroused fierce controversy and in 1972 led to the fall of the government. Thereafter a compromise was reached under which the water level of the lake remained unchanged. The hydroelectric station was installed in a cavern deep under the lake – a technological achievement that draws thousands of visitors every year. (The power plant can be seen only on an organised excursion, see below).

## ★★Manapouri power plant

In order to carry out the project it was necessary to construct a landing stage for ships carrying equipment and supplies at Deep Cove in Doubtful Sound (see below). These were then carried in trucks up a steep works road and over the Wilmot Pass (671 m) to the construction site. Nowadays the landing stage and the road are used mainly for tourist traffic.

## ★★Doubtful Sound

**Organised whole-day excursion**
One of the very few fjords in Fiordland National Park easily accessible for tourists is Doubtful Sound. It can only be reached, however, on an organised excursion. Excursions are run throughout the year by Fiordland Travel (☛Fiordland National Park).

The first stage of the excursion, which starts from Manapouri town, is by boat over **Lake Manapouri** (see above).

The next stage is by bus to the **power plant** (see above). A steep spiral tunnel leads up to the underground power plant, where seven giant turbines are installed in a huge cavern 200 m below the surface of the lake.

After a conducted tour of the power plant the bus continues over Wilmot Pass (670 m) to **Deep Cove**, at the east end of **Doubtful Sound**, a fjord running 20 km inland between steep rock walls, with many branches and inlets. It was given its name in 1770 by Captain Cook, who did not venture in through the narrow entrance to the fjord, being doubtful whether he would find a harbour there and be able to get out again. After a cruise on a catamaran to the mouth of the fjord on the Tasman Sea, the bus returns to the power plant; then by boat across Lake Manapouri to Manapouri town, with the possibility of continuing by bus to Te Anau.

## ★Lake Ohau              D 11

**Region: Canterbury**

Lake Ohau, in a beautiful setting 30 km west of Twizel, forms the boundary between the Canterbury and Otago regions. This glacier-formed lake has an area of 60 sq km. In good weather the snow-capped peaks of the Southern Alps are mirrored in its waters. It is linked

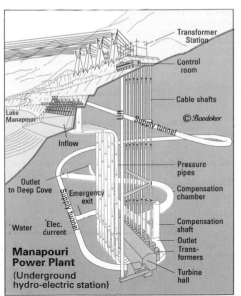

Transformer Station

Control room

Cable shafts

Lake Manapouri

Lift

Supply tunnel

© Baedeker

Inflow

Outlet to Deep Cove

Supply tunnel

Emergency exit

Water

Elec. current

Pressure pipes

Compensation chamber

Compensation shaft

Outlet Transformers

Turbine hall

**Manapouri Power Plant**
(Underground hydro-electric station)

Idyll in Doubtful Sound

by canal with Lake Pukaki and Lake Tekapo – all three lakes being integrated into the hydroelectric scheme on the upper course of the Waitaki River.

Lake Ohau is a popular holiday resort in summer, attracting many fishing and boating enthusiasts and campers.

**Mount Sutton**
Visitors also come here in winter to ski on Mount Sutton, high above the lake.

## Lake Pukaki                    E 10/11

### Region: Canterbury

13 km north of Twizel is Lake Pukaki, the second largest glacier lake in Canterbury region (81 sq km). The mighty Tasman River, fed by meltwater from great glaciers, flows into the north end of the lake, which lies 500 m above sea level. The lake's high content of rock flour (finely ground particles of rock held in the glacial meltwater) gives its water a milky turquoise colour.

**Waitaki River hydroelectric scheme**
With the construction of the Pukaki

Dam and Pukaki Canal in the late 1970s, the lake was incorporated in the hydroelectric scheme on the upper course of the Waitaki River. The dam at the south end of Lake Pukaki, along the top of which Highway 8 runs, was built to control the water level of the lake. The hydroelectric station is near the east side of the lake at the mouth of the Tekapo Canal. Lake Pukaki is also linked with Lake Ohau by a canal.

### ★ Mount Cook National Park route
The asphalted road to Mount Cook National Park (Highway 80) branches off Highway 8 south-west of Lake Pukaki and runs along the western shore of the lake. In good weather there is a magnificent view of the majestic mountain peaks to the west.

## ★Lake Tekapo                    E 10

### Region: Canterbury

Lake Tekapo, the largest of the three glacier lakes in Canterbury's Mackenzie Country (88 sq km), lies 50 km north-east of Twizel in a magnificent setting under the peaks of the Southern Alps, its milky turquoise waters surrounded by slopes covered with tussock grass.

**Tekapo power plant**
At the south end of the lake, near the village of Tekapo, is a dam built in 1954, which regulates the level of the lake. It is normally between 704 m and 710 m above sea level. The first hydroelectric station, Tekapo A, was built in 1951. The second, Tekapo B, was built in 1977 and supplied with water by a 25 km long canal (1977) from Lake Pukaki (see entry) to Lake Tekapo.

**Tekapo (village)**
The village of Tekapo (pop. 400) at the south end of Lake Tekapo is famed for the Church of the Good Shepherd, built in 1935 for the shepherds on the huge sheep farms of the Mackenzie Country Through the chancel window there is a view of Lake Tekapo and the snow-capped summits of the Southern Alps. Beside the church is a bronze figure of a sheepdog carved by a sheep-farmer's wife.

**★ Sightseeing flights**
Sightseeing flights are operated from Tekapo, taking visitors over the largest glaciers and the highest peaks in the Southern Alps.

**Irishman Creek**
16 km south of Tekapo on Highway 8 is the Irishman Creek farm, where William Hamilton (☛Famous People), inventor of the jet boat, once lived. He is commemorated by a small museum.

**Burke Pass**
Above Lake Tekapo to the south-east is Burke Pass (671 m), which carries the road (Highway 8) from the Mackenzie Country to Fairlie. It is named after Michael John Burke, who surveyed the area in 1855. His interest in the area was aroused during the trial of the sheep stealer James Mackenzie (☛Mackenzie Country), when he heard of the great plains in this highland region where the stolen sheep had been hidden.

The Church of the Good Shepherd on the shores of Lake Tekapo

## ★★Lake Te Anau     B 11/12

**Region: Southland (Fiordland National Park)**

Lake Te Anau, the largest lake on the South Island (344 sq km), lies in the north-east of Fiordland National Park. With three arms branching off (South, Middle and North fiords), it reaches deep into the mountain country of the national park with its dense rain forests. The shores of the lake vary considerably in character; the east side is flat, with less rain, and is almost treeless.

### Name
The name of the lake probably derives from the Maori name for the cave system, Te Ana Au (cave of the rushing waters; see below). The caves are difficult of access and though known to the Maoris since early times were forgotten for many years.

### Hydroelectric scheme
The surface of Lake Te Anau is around 200 m above sea level, but the bottom of the lake, which is 417 m deep, reaches well below sea level.

Lake Te Anau is linked with Lake Manapouri (see entry) and is thus an important element in the Manapouri hydroelectric scheme.

### Te Anau (town)
At the south-east end of the lake is the tourist resort of Te Anau (pop. 3000), which has increased enormously in size in recent years. It offers a wide range of accommodation for visitors and is a good base for excursions in Fiordland National Park and the Southern Alps.

### Murchison Range
In 1948 a few specimens of the takahe, a flightless bird which was thought to be extinct, were rediscovered in the remote Murchison Range, on the west side of Lake Te Anau. They can also be seen in the wildlife park at Te Anau.

### ★★Te Ana Au Caves
In the same area and at about the same time (1948) the unique glow-worm caves were rediscovered after much searching. The Te Ana Au Caves, which are accessible only from the lake, are, in geological terms, very young and have little in the way of stalactitic formations. To a visitor entering the caves through the low entrance passage after the half-

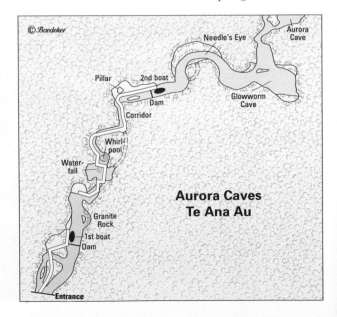

hour crossing of the lake, however, they are still extraordinarily impressive. The boat travels into the cave as far as an underground waterfall, from which visitors are taken in another boat to the marvellous Glow-worm Cave. Glow-worms, the larvae of insects that can live only in conditions of fairly high humidity, produce long sticky threads like a spider's web to which other small insects are attracted by the faint light generated by the glow-worms during the digestive process. It is dark and quiet in the Glow-worm Cave, with the glow-worms twinkling like stars. The trip to the caves starts and finishes at the Te Anau landing stage; the caves can only be reached by boat.

### ★★Milford Road
From Te Anau there is a fascinating drive through the mountains of Fiordland National Park to Milford Sound (see entry). The Milford Road runs along the east side of the lake and through the Homer Tunnel to reach the world-famous fjord.

### ★Mirror Lakes
The route passes the enchanting Milford Lakes in which are mirrored the mountain peaks.

### ★★Milford Track
For keen walkers with a day or two to spare there is the strenuous Milford Track, which runs through scenery of breathtaking beauty. The starting point is at Glade House, in the valley of the Clinton River, at the northern tip of Lake Te Anau.

### ★Excursion to Lake Manapouri and Doubtful Sound
Another attractive excursion, taking a whole day, is to Lake Manapouri (see entry) and the underground hydroelectric station on its western arm; then over the Wilmot Pass and down the steep road to Deep Cove, on Doubtful Sound. From there visitors can cruise in a catamaran to the mouth of the sound on the Tasman Sea. This trip is possible only as an organised tour.

### ★Sightseeing flights
From Te Anau a sightseeing flight in a helicopter or seaplane offers an easy way to view the grand mountain scenery of Fiordland National Park and the South Island's world-famed fjords.

## ★★Lake Wanaka   C/D 11

**Region: Otago**

70 km north-west of Queenstown (see entry) is the quietly beautiful Lake Wanaka, set in a magnificent landscape of gentle mountains. It is 45 km long, with an area of 193 sq km. The Clutha River, the mightiest on the South Island, flows out of the south-east corner of the lake.

### Getting there
From Queenstown (see entry) there are two routes to Lake Wanaka, the shorter being ★Cardrona Road (SR 89) which requires some driving expertise. It branches off Highway 6 at Arrow Junction and after traversing the pass follows the Cardrona River where the beautiful surroundings are reward for the strenuous drive.

The easier alternative is the 50 km Highway 6 via Cromwell which passes through the broad Clutha River valley on its way to Wanaka village.

### ★★Mountain panorama
From Lake Wanaka, in good weather, there are magnificent panoramas, with the peaks in Mount Aspiring National Park (see entry) visible in the distance. The country round the lake is particularly beautiful in autumn, when the many deciduous trees brought here from Europe take on their russet colouring. The finest view of the lake is from Glendhu Bay, 14 km west of Wanaka village.

### History
In early times there were Maoris living round the lake and exchanging greenstone (jade), which they found in the rivers on the west coast. But around 1836 raids by tribes from the north almost depopulated the area. When settlers looking for new grazing grounds came here – Dr Chalmers in 1853, John T Thomson in 1857 and John McLean in 1858, who established the first large sheep farms – the land was almost uninhabited.

### Gold
Gold was found on the Cardrona River in the 19th c. and within a short time the beds of the Cardrona and the Clutha, almost as far up as Lake Wanaka,

Lake Wanaka against a majestic backdrop of mountains

had been thoroughly dug over by prospectors.

### Wanaka (village)
At the south-east end of the lake is the little township of Wanaka (pop. 2000), the largest settlement for many kilometres round. It was known as Pembroke until 1940.

### Skiing areas
There are good skiing areas at Cardrona (south-west of Wanaka) and on the Treble Cone (west of Lake Wanaka).

### Lake Hawea
15 km north of Wanaka village is Lake Hawea, the smallest of the three alpine lakes in the Otago region (30 km, area 140 sq km). Highway 6 runs along the west side of the lake on its way to the Haast Pass. The village of Lake Havea, at the south end of the lake, occupies the site of a Maori village that was attacked and destroyed in 1836.

The damming of the lake under the Clutha River hydroelectric scheme in 1958 raised the water level by around 20 m. The water stored in the lake serves as a reserve supply in winter, when the catchment area of the Clutha River is blocked by ice.

The lake, which offers good trout and salmon fishing, is 410 m deep, so that its bed is 64 m below sea level.

## Lawrence                                D 12

**Region: Otago**
**Population: 600**

90 km south-west of Dunedin (see entry) is the little settlement of Lawrence, founded in 1862 and named after General Sir Henry Lawrence, a hero of the Indian Mutiny (1857–8). It became the first gold-mining town in Otago after a Tasmanian prospector named Thomas Gabriel found rich deposits of alluvial gold nearby, in Gabriel's Gully, and announced his find in a newspaper. Within a short time the little settlement grew to a population of well over 10,000 – twice the size of Dunedin. Gold ceased to be worked in the area in the late 1930s and Lawrence has now become the commercial centre of a wide farming area.

## Sights

Lawrence retains a number of Victorian buildings dating from heyday, including the courthouse and the post office. Anthem House was for many years the home of John J Woods, a local government official who composed the music of *God defend New Zealand*, the country's national anthem. There is an local museum in Ross Place.

### ★Golden Gully

Near the village is the Golden Gully (Gabriel's Gully), where the first gold in the region was discovered. Adjoining it is the Weatherston goldfield, with the ruins of a brewery.

### Waitahuna

11 km south-east of Lawrence is the little village of Waitahuna, which in the 19th c. was also a flourishing gold-miners' town .

## ★Lewis Pass                    G 9

### Region: Canterbury

### Pass road

100 km west of Hanmer Springs (see entry) Highway 7 goes over the Lewis Pass (907 m). The mountain pass road, which links the Canterbury region with the north-west coast of the South Island, was completed in 1937. This route was well known to the Maori tribes of the region, who used it on their way to the greenstone deposits in the rivers on the west coast. Cannibal Gorge, near the summit of the pass, recalls the days when the Maori caravans making for the west coast took slaves with them as carriers; then on the way back, it is said, the slaves were killed and eaten.

### Walks from summit

A number of short trails start from the summit of the pass (e.g. Tarn Nature Walk, Lewis Pass Lookout Walk). The St James Track (70 km) over the Ada Pass and Anne Saddle takes 5 days.

### Hurunui Hotel

One place of interest on the road, which runs through beautiful scenery, is the Hurunui Hotel (1869, restored).

### Maruia Springs

Further on is the little spa of Maruia Springs, with hot springs.

### ★Lake Sumner Forest Park

At Springs Junction, 20 km west of the pass, a road goes off on the south to the beautiful Lake Sumner Forest Park. There are attractive trails in the dense forest of southern beeches, round Lake Sumner, the Robinson River and Lake Christabel.

## Mackenzie Country          D/E 10/11

### Region: Canterbury

The Mackenzie Country is a highland region of some 5000 sq km below the mountains of the Southern Alps, within which are the three large glacier lakes Tekapo, Pukaki and Ohau. It can be reached from the east either by the Burke Pass (Highway 8) or by the little-known Mackenzie Pass (unmade track), to the south of the Burke Pass. This bare plateau covered with tussock grass, cold and snowbound in winter, was settled mainly by Scottish sheep farmers with experience of hill farming.

### Name

The region takes its name from a Scottish shepherd and sheep stealer, James (Jock) McKenzie, who is said to have stolen whole flocks of sheep in 1855 and driven his booty over a pass that he had discovered into the unexplored highland region. He was assisted in his thefts by a marvellously skilled sheepdog named Friday. McKenzie was finally arrested – an event commemorated by a memorial stone on the Mackenzie Pass – and imprisoned in Lyttleton jail. He and his dog soon became legendary figures throughout the country, the subject of numerous stories.

### Farming

Sheep farming, once practised on a large scale here, is now in decline. Some sheep farms have been turned into game farms surrounded by high wire fences.

### Upper Waikati Power Development Scheme

In recent decades the Mackenzie Country has been much changed by the huge hydroelectric projects of the Upper Waikati Power Development Scheme. The large glacier lakes have been dammed, land on their shores has been drowned by rises in water level and new artificial lakes such as Lake Benmore have been created.

### Twizel

The centre of all this activity is Twizel (pop. 1800), the largest place in this sparsely populated region.

### Tourism

The Mackenzie Country has been opened up for tourism by the asphalted Highway 8. Large numbers of visitors now come here, attracted mainly by the glacier lakes but increasingly by the recently established skiing areas; many others pass through the region on their way to Mount Cook National Park.

### Fairlie

On Highway 8, an hour drive north-west of Timaru, is the little township of Fairlie (Canterbury region; pop. 800), the commercial and administrative centre of the Mackenzie Country. Until 1968 it was the terminus of a railway line from Timaru. The Transport Museum of the Mackenzie Carnival Society displays old carnival floats, coaches and agricultural equipment; the old railway station is incorporated in the museum. Nearby is an old smithy, grandly named the Mabel Binney Cottage Museum.

### Two Thumb Ranges

Near Fairlie are the Two Thumb Ranges. Mount Dobson (25 km in the Tekapo direction) and Fox Peak (40 km north of Fairlie by way of Clayton) are popular winter-sports areas.

### ★Lindis Pass

Lindis Pass (970 m) links the alpine landscapes of the Mackenzie Country with the bare arid hills of central Otago. The old Maori track through the hills was rediscovered by John T Thomson while surveying this region in 1857 and was soon travelled by large numbers of gold prospectors. In the valley of the Lindis River a number of old farmsteads dating from the time of the early settlers still survive; particularly notable is Morven Hills farm.

## ★★Marlborough Sounds Maritime Park      H/J 7/8

### Region: Nelson-Marlborough

The Marlborough Sounds, at the north-east corner of the South Island, are one of the most popular holiday areas in New Zealand – a beautiful landscape of drowned river valleys and intricate waterways, islands, beaches and wooded hills. This much indented coast with its many islets and inlets offers endless scope for boating enthusiasts, anglers and campers. On land, too, this is a quiet and peaceful area, for the roads running along the drowned valleys are narrow, winding, steep and usually not asphalted. Nowhere else in New Zealand is there as much sunshine: over 2000 hours per year.

### Name

The Marlborough Sounds are named after John Churchill, the Duke of Marlborough, a war hero like those other military heroes who have given their names to places in New Zealand – Nelson and Wellington.

### Maori mythology

Maori tradition has it that the legendary figures Kupe and Ngahue, while fishing in Hawaiki, found a giant octopus eating their prey and pursued it across the Pacific. Kupe almost caught it in a cave on the Wairarapa coast of the North Island (near present-day Castlepoint), but it got away and was finally caught and killed in the labyrinthine waters of the Marlborough Sounds.

### History

Captain Cook (☛Famous People), like many after him, liked this sunny region of water and hills. On his first visit in January 1770 he climbed a hill on Arapawa Island and, seeing the open sea to the east, realised – as Abel Tasman had done before him – that the North and South Islands of New Zealand were separate. Cook took possession of the South Island in the name of King George III and named Charlotte Sound after his queen. On his second voyage Cook put in at Ship Cove several times.

Later explorers like the French navigator Dumont d'Urville were taken by the beauty and the mild climate of the region. D'Urville discovered that the large island to the north that now bears his name was indeed an island and not part of the mainland.

From 1827 onwards whalers began to settle in the Sounds, including John Blenkinsopp, whose dubious land deal with Chief Te Rauparaha led to the Wairau affray, the only serious clash between Maoris and *pakehas* (whites) on the South Island.

The Marlborough Sounds: a paradise for nature lovers and sailing enthusiasts

Some years later the first sheep farmers arrived. Huge sheep farms were established inland from the Marlborough Sounds and these steadily expanded. By 1870 there were more than a million sheep in the region.

In the 20th c. sheep farming in the area declined but the favourable local climate allowed a switch to fruit growing and wine production.

The Marlborough Sounds made headline news in 1986 when a Soviet cruise ship, the *Mikhail Lermontov*, sank in Port Gore.

**Havelock**
At the north-east corner of the South Island, 40 km north-west of Blenheim (see entry), is the little township of Havelock (pop. 500), in a beautiful setting in the Marlborough Sounds. The settlement, named after General Sir Henry Havelock, who distinguished himself in the Indian Mutiny, was established on the site of an old Maori village to supply the needs of gold miners working at Wakamarina, 10 km west. The inhabitants now live mainly by fish farming (mostly shellfish) in the

inlets of the Marlborough Sounds.

Havelock's main claim to fame is that the atomic physicist Ernest Rutherford and the missile scientist William Pickering went to school here. The old schoolhouse is now a youth hostel. In the former Methodist church is a memorial room commemorating Rutherford and Pickering.

**Pelorus Bridge**
At Pelorus Bridge, 20 km further west, on the river, is a scenic reserve with a number of attractive trails. From Pelorus Bridge a road runs into the romantic Maungatapu Valley, through which the old road from Blenheim to Nelson (see entry) pursues a winding course.

**★★ Endeavour Track**
Endeavour Track follows the footsteps of Captain Cook from Camp Bay over the Kenepuru Saddle to Ship Cove. The walk takes about 10 hours; on the way there are a modest inn and a number of possible campsites.

**★ Nydia Track**
The attractive Nydia Track starts from

Mahau Sound, goes over the Kaiuma Saddle into Nydia Bay and continues to Tennyson Inlet. It too is a 10-hour walk; camping facilities in Nydia Bay.

**Boat trips**
A variety of boat trips in the Marlborough Sounds, either regular services or charters, are on offer from Picton and Havelock. A trip in a sailing boat has a particular appeal. At some places dinghies, luxurious yachts and large catamarans can be hired. Information is available from the Marlborough Sounds Maritime Park office in Auckland Street, Picton.

## ★★Milford Sound                  B 11

**Region: Southland (Fiordland National Park)**

**Getting there**
**Car or bus** From Te Anau (☞Lake Te Anau) on Highway 94 to Milford (120 km).
**Air travel** From Queenstown (see entry) and Te Anau.

**Information**
Fiordland National Park headquarters, Te Anau.

On the south-west coast of the South Island is one of New Zealand's scenic jewels, Milford Sound. Its characteristic landscape is familiar from many photographs: in the foreground lush vegetation, beyond this the still blue waters of the fjord and as a backdrop the massive pyramid of Mitre Peak.

Among the first Europeans to see this magnificent landscape was Captain Stokes, who put into the sound in the survey ship HMS *Acheron* in 1851. He anchored near the Bowen Falls and named the mountain towering above the bay (1692 m) Mitre Peak, from its resemblance to a bishop's mitre.

Milford Sound extends inland for 15 km from its narrow mouth on the Tasman Sea and the high hills that enclose it rise steeply. Rainfall is high at an annual 6000 mm.

**History**
Before the arrival of Europeans the Maoris came here in the search for

◄ Mountain and meadow in the Milford Sound

greenstone. Then in the early 19th c. sealers found their way into the area. Among them was a Welshman called John Grano, who named the sound after Milford Haven in south Wales. The fjord became more widely known after Captain Stokes's visit. Then in 1878 a Scotsman named John Sutherland, a former soldier and seaman, came here to live a hermit's life. He discovered the Sutherland Falls (580 m high), some distance inland, which can be seen only from the Milford Track. Quintin McKinnon, another Scot, surveyed the land route to Milford Sound and discovered the Mackinnon Pass. Later, when increasing numbers of people began to come here, John Sutherland built an inn on Milford Sound which in 1923 was acquired by the state.

**★★Milford Road**
The beautiful mountain road (120 km) from Te Anau (☞Lake Te Anau) through the Eglinton Valley and the Homer Tunnel (named after the surveyor Henry Homer) has made Milford Sound an easily accessible and very popular tourist attraction. (Note that in winter the road can be temporarily blocked by avalanches.)

**★Boat trips**
A variety of boat trips are on offer from Milford. The *Milford Wanderer* sails on cruises lasting several days to the many fjords along the coast (including Doubtful Sound). The finest views of the landscape are to be had from the water.

**★★Milford Track**
The Milford Track, New Zealand's best-known trail, is 54 km long and can be walked in 4–5 days. It begins at Glade House, near the north end of Lake Te Anau (see entry), and at first follows the Clinton River. It then continues through rain forest and an alpine landscape, going over the Mackinnon Pass, passing the wild and romantic Sutherland Falls and finally running down into the valley of the Arthur River.

The track, which is usable from November to March, may be walked only in one direction, from Glade House to Milford Sound; walking in the opposite direction is not allowed. Walkers going on their own must put their names down at the Fiordland National Park office. Guided walks can be booked through travel agencies. The return from Milford

# Milford Sound

5 km

© Baedeker

Musket Bay

Yates Point

Mt. Barton
573m

Brig Rock

John O'Groats River

Ongaruanuku
1690m

Halfway Peak
1937m

Stripe Point

Te Hau
1701m

Lake Never Never

Mt. Parariki
2140m

Pembroke Wilderness Area

Paranui Peak
2194m

St. Anne Point

Mt. Pembroke
2000m

Anita Bay

The Elephant
1518m

Bowen Col

Mt. Grave
2232m

Mt. Tutoko
2746m

Dale Point

Transit Beach

Harrison River

The Lion
1302m

Mills Peak
1831m

Mackenzie Falls

Lake Ronald

Transit River

Milford Sound

Harrison Cove

Cascade Peak
1221m

Bowen River

Maire Peak
1692m

Sinbad Gully

Tutoko River

Llawrenny Peaks
1932m

Mt. Phillips
1469m

Bowen Falls

Milford Sound

Milford Hotel

Terror Peak
1786m

Devils Armchair
1634m

Lake Moeron

Arthur River

Sheerdown Peak
1871m

Steep Hill
1640m

Milford Track

Lake Ada

Odyssey Peak
1832m

Sheerdown Range

Mt. Isolation
1634m

Grave Talbot Pass

Lady of the Snows
1832m

Mt. Edgar
1689m

Diamond Creek

Lake Brown

Mt. Ada
1991m

Access Peak
1878m

Moraine River

Mt. Macpherson
1935m

Homer Tunnel

*Lake Te Anau, Lake Manapouri, Doubtful Sound*

Sound to Te Anau, after the usual boat trip, is by bus. In view of the high probability of rain suitable protective clothing should be taken. Insect repellent is also essential equipment, for the tiny black sandflies are a perpetual plague. The Maori tradition is that the goddess of death created sandflies in order to sour people's enjoyment of the perfect beauty of the landscape.

## ★ Bowen Falls

It is a short walk from Milford to the Bowen Falls (160 m high), which plunge down from a hanging valley. They are named after a former governor.

## ★ Sutherland Falls

The Sutherland Falls can be viewed only by walking the Milford Track. They are too far away to be seen on a day trip.

Mount Aspiring, which soars to over 3000 m

## ★★Mount Aspiring National Park  U/D 10/11

**Regions: Otago and West Coast**
**Area: 3555 sq km**

### Information
Mount Aspiring National Park headquarters and visitor centre, Wanaka; ranger stations at Glenorchy on Lake Wakatipu and Makarora on the Haast Pass road (Highway 6).

New Zealand's second-largest national park, a region of alpine landscape bordering on Fiordland National Park (see entry) to the south, centres on 'New Zealand's Matterhorn', the 3027 m Mount Aspiring. The mountain was given its name by the surveyor John T Thomson, who saw it from a distance in 1857. It was first climbed in 1909. Round this massive rock pyramid other peaks, form a mountain rampart when seen from a distance. Lake Wanaka and Lake Wakatipu are fed by rivers flowing down from the Mount Aspiring massif. The national park displays almost the complete range of glacial features,

including glacier lakes, ground, lateral and terminal moraines, *roches moutonnées*, hanging valleys and glacial striations. The main access route is the Haast Pass road (Highway 6), an impressive mountain road that runs along the east side of Lake Wanaka and bounds the National Park on the north.

### View of Mount Aspiring
The road from Wanaka through the Matukituki Valley runs close to Mount Aspiring. It can often be first seen from Glendhu Bay, south-west of Wanaka.

## Walks on Mount Aspiring

### ★★Routeburn Track
This magnificent mountain track begins in Fiordland National Park (see entry), on the road to Milford Sound (see entry) and continues through Mount Aspiring National Park to the north end of Lake Wakatipu (☛Queenstown). The walk takes 4 days. There are guided walks along the track and on sections of it.

### Rees-Dart Track
This 4-day walk – almost a round trip –

begins at Paradise, near the north end of Lake Wakatipu, and ends at the Invincible Mine in the valley of the Rees River.

### Wilkin Valley Track
This track follows the course of the Wilkin River and then runs close to the eastern boundary of the national park to the junction of the Wilkin with the Makarora River, to the south of the Makarora ranger station (Highway 6).

## ★★Mount Cook National Park                           D/E 10

**Region: Canterbury**
**Area: 699 sq km**

### Getting there
Mount Cook National Park, which marches on the west with Westland National Park (containing the Fox and Franz Josef glaciers), is readily accessible in spite of the relatively high altitude at which it lies.

From Twizel and Lake Pukaki (see entry) an asphalted road (Highway 80)

runs through magnificent mountain scenery to the little township of Mount Cook.

From Christchurch and Queenstown (see entries) there are flights by light aircraft to the Mount Cook airstrip.

### Information
The Mount Cook National Park headquarters and visitor centre, Mount Cook, offers full information on the geology, flora, fauna and ecology of this mountain region. Here too can be obtained information about the condition of tracks, rock climbing and glacier routes and skiing facilities.

### Skiing
The high-altitude skiing areas on Mount Cook offer skiing almost all year round. There are no ski lifts, but light aircraft and helicopters take skiers up to the ski fields.

### Topography
Mount Cook National Park takes in the heart of the Southern Alps and their highest peaks (☛240). Round the highest of all, Mount Cook (3753 m) and Mount Tasman (3496 m), cluster 15

Mount Cook – king of the Southern Alps

other peaks over 3000 m and some 200 others over 2500 m. Through the national park extends the Tasman Glacier, the largest in the Southern Alps, 29 km long and up to 3 km wide. Like most of the world's glaciers, it is steadily retreating.

In December 1991 Mount Cook lost 11 m in height when a massive avalanche of snow, ice and rock detritus plunged off the summit.

## Wildlife

The game introduced into the park in the early 20th c., mostly from Europe, have multiplied to such an extent as to become a real plague. Large numbers of animals have had to be culled, captured or kept in game farms.

## History

Probably Abel Tasman and Captain Cook (☛Famous People) did not see the mountains named after them when they sailed along the west coast of the South Island, since the country's highest peaks were likely shrouded in clouds, as they so often are today. The highest peak was named after Cook by Captain Stokes, who made a careful survey of the coasts of New Zealand in HMS *Acheron* in 1851. Mount Tasman was given its name 11 years later by the German geologist Julius von Haast. Mount Cook was first climbed on Christmas Day in 1894.

## Mount Cook (village)

The little tourist resort of Mount Cook (alt. 762 m; pop. 600) lies at the foot of Mount Sefton, with a grandiose mountain backdrop. It has a luxury hotel complex, the Hermitage, a number of chalets and, 2 km away at White Horse Flat, a large campsite. There is another big campsite at the tourist village of Glentanner Park, 20 km south.

## ★★ Copland Track

Copland Track, the finest but most strenuous mountain trail in Mount Cook National Park, runs right across the park and into Westland National Park (see entry). It goes over the Copland Pass (2149 m) and climbs into the fields of névé on the majestic summits. This walk (at least 4 days) is for thoroughly experienced walkers and climbers only and should only be done with a local guide.

There are many other waymarked trails of varying length in Mount Cook

National Park, for example the Bowen Track, the Governor's Bush Walk, the Kea Point Walk, the Hooker Valley Walk, the Red Tarns Track and the Wakefield Track; all of them offer breathtaking views. Detailed descriptions of the routes can be obtained in the visitor centre in Mount Cook village.

## ★★ Sightseeing flights

Scenic flights from Mount Cook village offer tremendous bird's eye views of the summits and glaciers of Mount Cook National Park and Westland National Park. A flight in a helicopter is an unforgettable experience as it often gets in closer to the peaks than a light plane.

# ★Nelson                                H 8

**Region: Nelson-Marlborough**
**Population: 48,000**

The port town of Nelson lies on the south-east side of Tasman Bay, in an area famed for its mild climate. In its fertile hinterland various fruits (particularly apples and pears) for export are grown, as well as grapes, hops and tobacco. In the surrounding hills there is lucrative forestry, the timber from which is processed in the Nelson area and shipped from the port. The population of the area is increasing markedly, growing within a decade by over 5 per cent.

## Nelson town

The town's harbour, Nelson Haven, is sheltered by a long breakwater. The town itself has many old wooden houses, both mansions and cottages. Modern amenities include seafront promenades and many parks and gardens.

**Artists' colony** In recent years Nelson's beautiful situation has attracted many artists and craftsmen. South of the town on the road to Richmond is the Craft Habitat, an arts and crafts centre.

## History

Abel Tasman was the first European to anchor in the bay, which now bears his name, in 1642. He did not land because the Maoris had attacked his ship's boat. Before any European settlement Maori tribes from the North Island frequently crossed to the Nelson area, attracted by the rich fishing grounds and the

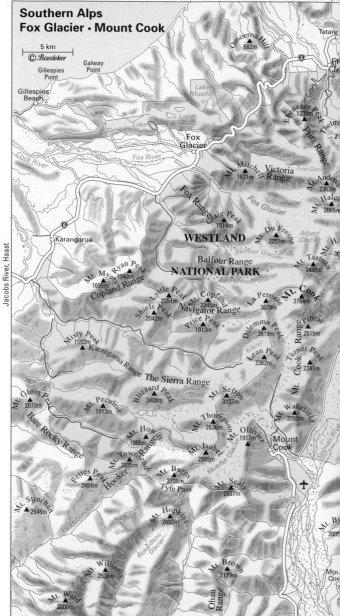

**Southern Alps**
**Fox Glacier · Mount Cook**

5 km
© *Baedeker*

Whataroa, Hokitika, Greyn

Tatare

Omoeroa Hill
682m

Gillespies
Point

Galway
Point

Gillespies
Beach

Lake
Mueller

Lake
Gault

Lake
Matheson

Cook River

Fox River

Fox
Glacier

Ebenezer Peak
1333m

Thelm

Fritz Range

Mt. Mitchel
1631m

Victoria
Range

Fritz Glacier

Mt. Ander
2362m

Mt. Halc
2665n

Fox Range

Craig Peak
1914m

Fox Glacier

Mt. Du Fresne
2251m

Albert
Glacier

WESTLAND

Balfour Glacier

Balfour Range

Mt. Tasman
3498m

Mt. H

NATIONAL PARK

La Perouse Glacier

Mt. Myo

Ryan Peak
1943m

Karangarua

Copland Range

Little Peak
2251m

Mt. Copland
2345m

La Perouse
3079m

Mt. Cook
3764m

1699m

Shiels Peak
2042m

Navigator Range

Price Peak
1913m

Dilemma Peak
2619m

Cook Range

Pibrac
2515m

Misty Peak
1593m

Copland River

Karangarua Range

Lean Peak
2362m

Turner Peak
2341m

The Sierra Range

Douglas
Neve

Mt. Strachan
2545m

Mt. Gloin Peak
2073m

Bare Rocky Range

Mt. Peculiar
1913m

Blizzard Peak
2408m

Douglas Glacier

Mt. Sefton
3157m

Mt. Wakefield
2050m

Karangarua River

Mt. How
1966m

Mt. Townsend
2035m

Mt. Thompson
2636m

Mt. Ollivier
1917m

Mount
Cook

Tasman Rive

Fettes Peak
2454m

Hooker River

Mt. Isabel
2545m

Mueller Glacier

Mt. Burns
2738m

Fyfe Pass

Mt. Sealy
2637m

Landsborough

Arthur
Glacier

Mt. Hopkins
2682m

Mt. B
203

Richardson Glacier

Mt. Williams
2536m

Mt. Brown
2179m

Mou
Coo

Ohau
Range

Mt. Ward
2200m

Jacobs River, Haast

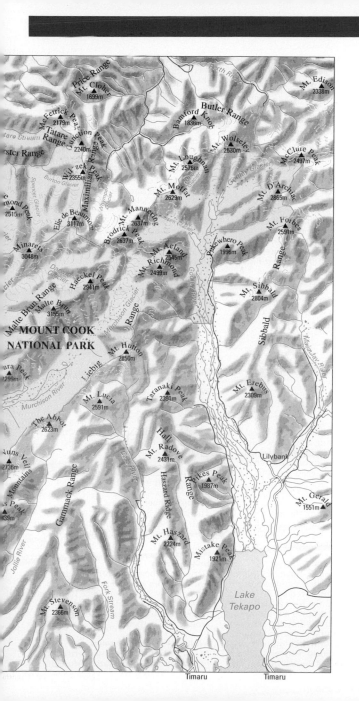

Price Range
Mt. Clober
1699m

Mt. Edison
2338m

Butler Range
Bamford Knob
1836m

McFetrick Peak
2179m
Tatare Range
Junction Peak
2240m

Mt. Wolseley
2530m

Mc Clure Peak
2497m

Tatare Stream
ster Range

Mt. Loughnan
2576m

Burton Glacier

Wil zek Peak
2355m

Mt. Moffat
2629m

Mt. D'Archiac
2865m

Maximilian Peak

Gunby Glacier

Elie de Beaumont
3117m

Mt. Mannering
2637m

Mt. Forbes
2591m

mond Peak
2515m

Spencer Glacier

Brodrick Peak
2637m

Patuwhero Peak
1996m

Minarets
3048m

Mt. Aeland
2545m

Mt. Richmond
2499m

Godley River

Glacier

Haeckel Peak
2941m

Malte Brun Range

Mt. Sibbald
2804m

Malte Brun
3155m

Murchison Glacier

Range

Sibbald Range

MOUNT COOK
NATIONAL PARK

Mt. Hutton
2850m

Makaulay River

ara Peak
2299m

Murchison River

Liebig

Taranaki Peak
2301m

Mt. Erebus
2309m

The Abbot
2623m

Mt. Lucia
2591m

Gammack Range

Cass River

Hall

Lilybank

Nuns Veil
2736m

Mt. Radove
2431m

Pikes Peak
1987m

Range

s Peak
439m

Mountains

Haszard Ridge

Mt. Gerald
1551m

Jollie River

Mt. Haszard
2224m

Mistake Peak
1921m

Fork Stream

Lake
Tekapo

Mt. Stevenson
2366m

Timaru            Timaru

greenstone deposits. In the late 1820s Te Rauparaha and his allies several times attacked the villages and fortified settlements in Tasman Bay; when William Wakefield came here in 1839 in search of new land he found only a few Maoris living in the Nelson area. The first settlers arrived in 1842, and the population soon grew to over 2000. A year later they were joined by large parties of German immigrants. Many of them settled in a valley at the south end of Tasman Bay and established a thriving farming community. In 1858 Nelson, which then had a population of just under 3000, became the first settlement in New Zealand to be granted the status of a borough. It was then enjoying something of a boom, due mainly to the discovery of gold to the north-west and east of the town. In 1862 the first horse-drawn railway was established to transport copper from the Dun Mountains, 20 km away, to the port. The great physicist Ernest Rutherford (☛Famous People) was born in Nelson in 1871, and later became Lord Rutherford of Nelson.

### Name
The town was named after the great naval hero. It main thoroughfare is Trafalgar Street.

## Sights

### City tour
A brochure describing a 30 km scenic drive round the town can be obtained from the visitor and information centre at the corner of Trafalgar Street and Halifax Street.

### Flea market
Every Saturday morning there is a flea market at the Montgomery car park (reached by way of Trafalgar Street, Hardy Street and Bridge Street).

### Christ Church Cathedral
Prominently situated in Trafalgar Square, Christ Church Cathedral stands on the site of a Maori *pa* destroyed by Te Rauparaha. In 1842 the New Zealand Land Company established a settlement here. After the Wairau affray the settlers, fearful of attack, fortified the settlement, calling it Fort Arthur in honour of their leader Arthur Wakefield, who was killed in the affray. The first church on this site was built in 1850. Work on the cathedral was begun in 1925, and after various changes to the plan, partly to make the building earthquake-proof, it was finally completed in 1967.

### Trafalgar Street
The town's busy main artery is Trafalgar Street, lined with many shops. A notable building in the street is Melrose House, an Italian-style mansion (ca 1875) that is now used by the municipality for ceremonial occasions. At the south end of the street is another handsome mansion, Fairfield House (1883).

### Milton Street
In Milton Street are two grand houses, Fellworth House and Grove House, built for wealthy local businessmen in the late 19th c.

### Botanical Hill
Botanical Hill (150 m), covered with gardens, is regarded as the geographical centre of New Zealand. From the top of the hill there is a fine view of the town.

### ★ Suter Art Gallery
The Suter Art Gallery, between Bridge Street and Hardy Street, was founded by Bishop Suter in 1889. It has an excellent collection of paintings, with works by Woollaston, Gully, Lindauer, Van der Velden, Hodgkins and Richmond.
ⓖ *Daily 10.30am–4.30pm.*

Close by, in Nile Street, is an exhibition of works by **New Zealand artists**
ⓖ *Daily 10am–5pm.*

Near here are a number of **cottages** built in the 1860s for military personnel.

### Bishop's School
The Bishop's School in Nile Street was built in 1844 on the initiative of Bishop Selwyn. It is furnished in period style and is open to the public as a museum.

### Nelson Haven
Nelson's harbour is a scene of busy activity. From here every conceivable type of New Zealand produce is shipped, particularly fruit, wine, timber and timber products. There are cruises around the harbour.

### ★ Nelson Provincial Museum
In Isel Park, in the south-western district of Stoke, is Nelson Provincial Museum,

which is devoted to the history of the town and the region. In addition to an excellent collection of Maori objects it has material on the Wairau affray, the only serious clash between Maoris and whites on the South Island.

@ *Tue.–Fri. 10am–4pm, Sat., Sun. 2–5pm.*

### Isel House
This 19th c. mansion beside the museum is furnished in period style.
@ *Oct.–Easter Sat., Sun.*

### Broadgreen House
Broadgreen House, in Nayland Road, is another 19th c. mansion with beautifully decorated windows, gable and porch.
@ *Summer, usually in the afternoon.*

## Surroundings

### ★Founders Park
2 km north of the town centre (Atwahai Drive) is Founders Park, an open-air museum in which various buildings of the Victorian period (some of them reconstructions) are displayed. Of particular note are a windmill and an exhibition on the history of Nelson Haven.
@ *Daily 9am–6pm.*

### ★Princess Drive
From Princess Drive, the road to the Davis Lookout, there are a series of fine views.

### Beaches
At the end of Rocks Road is **Tahunanui Beach**, the most popular of the town's beaches, with a campsite and leisure facilities. Also popular is the beach on Rabbit Island (25 km).

### ★Cable Bay
### Croisilles Harbour
The lovely landscape is ample reward for the difficult drive from Nelson northwards to Cable Bay, with its fine beach, and on via Rai Valley to the idyllic Croisilles Harbour. The more adventurous may drive on to Admiralty Bay and the strongpoint at French Pass.

### ★Mount Richmond Forest Park
The densely wooded and beautiful Mount Richmond Forest Park extends to the south and east of Nelson, over the hills of the Richmond Range and down into the valley of the Wairau River. A popular trail is the Wakamarina–

Onamalutu Track, which follows in the footsteps of the gold prospectors. The walk, which begins 20 km south of Canvastown, takes 2 days.

### ★North-west Nelson Forest Park
The North-west Nelson Forest Park covers 3760 sq km of densely wooded mountain country extending from Tasman Bay (Motueka Valley) over the Tasman Mountains to the west coast (Karamea Bay). A number of trails run through this primeval landscape with its expanses of lush vegetation. The best known are the Heaphy Track (☛Abel Tasman National Park) and the Wangapeka Track (4-day walk).

## ★Nelson Lakes National Park    G 8/9

**Region: Nelson-Marlborough**
**Area: 960 sq km**

Nelson Lakes National Park lies 120 km south of Nelson (see entry) and 100 km south-west of Blenheim (see entry). The gateway to the park is the township of St Arnaud on Highway 63.

### Information
Nelson Lakes National Park headquarters and visitor centre, St Arnaud; ranger station on Lake Rotoroa

### Topography
The national park covers a wide expanse of wild mountain country traversed by the highly visible Alpine Fault. This fault accounts for the difference in height between the hills to the north-east, which rise to over 2000 m, and those to the north-west, which are around 1000 m high. The national park is bounded on the east by the high St Arnaud Range. The highest peaks are snow-capped until well into summer. At a number of points in the park, particularly on the shores of lakes, there are expanses of dense beech and rain forest.

### Lakes
Two long narrow lakes, Lake Rotoiti (alt. 610 m) and Lake Rotoroa, which lies around 100 m lower, occupy valleys gouged out by glaciers and dammed by terminal moraine. A minor road leads to Lake Rotoiti, which attracts water-sports

enthusiasts and others seeking a relaxing holiday. Lake Rotoroa is difficult to get to and therefore quieter; it attracts mainly anglers.

### History
This rugged mountain country was first explored from Nelson. The first European to reach Lake Rotoiti, in 1842, was a young surveyor called John S Cotterell, who was killed in the Wairau affray in June the following year. Lake Rotoroa was discovered in 1846 by William Fox, later prime minister of New Zealand, the surveyor Thomas Brunner and a Maori named Kehu. Soon afterwards Brunner and Kehu set out on a strenuous journey of exploration, lasting nearly 2 years, in the north-west of the South Island. In 1859 the geologist Julius von Haast was commissioned by the provincial government to survey the mountain country and in the course of his travels gave names to some of the mountains and rivers within the national park.

### Walks
There are a number of trails of varying length in the national park. There are longer walks in the Travers, Sabine and D'Urville valleys.

Descriptions of the various routes can be obtained in the visitor centre in St Arnaud and the ranger station on Lake Rotoroa.

### Winter sports
There are skiing areas on Mount Robert (south-west of Lake Rotoiti) and at Rainbow (25 km south of St Arnaud).

## Oamaru                                      E 12

### Region: Otago
### Population: 14,000

Oamaru, 120 km north of Dunedin on Cape Wanbrow, is the commercial centre of northern Otago. The town rose to great prosperity in the 19th c. The climate is warm and dry. Inland from the town are extensive market gardens; beyond these, further inland, is a region of intensive sheep farming.

### Oamaru limestone
The white Oamaru limestone worked in many quarries in the surrounding area was used in the construction of many public buildings in New Zealand and even in Australia. The stone is easy to work when freshly quarried but hardens when exposed to dry air.

## Sights

### Historic Walk
The town's principal sights can be seen on a signposted Historic Walk, which starts from the Boer War memorial in Thames Street. The most notable monuments are the Court House (1883 by Forrester and Lemon), the simple Old Post Office (1864), the imposing New Post Office (1884) with its noticeable clock towers, and the Athenaeum (1882), which houses a small regional museum.
ⓘ *Museum Mon.–Fri. 1–4.30pm.*

### Forrester Art Gallery
Opposite the post offices are two imposing banks designed by RA Lawson, the National Bank (1871) and the Bank of New South Wales (1883), which is now occupied by the Forrester Art Gallery.
ⓘ *Mon.–Fri. 10am–4.30pm, Sun. 1–4.30pm.*

### Churches
Notable churches are St Luke's (1865; Anglican), at the corner of Itchen Street and Thames Street, St Paul's (1876; Presbyterian), in Coquet Street, and St Patrick's Basilica (1893; RC), in Usk Street.

## Surroundings

### ★Penguins
On the coast at Oamaru there are some delightful, relatively small penguins that can be observed close up. The yellow-eyed penguins are more shy. These birds, associated more with the Antarctic than with New Zealand, are driven in by the waves and waddle along the beach or up the cliffs.

### ★Totara Estate
8 km south of Oamaru on Highway 1 is the Totara Estate, where frozen meat was first produced in this area. Visitors can see the old slaughterhouses and production plant. The trim farmhouse (1868) stands in the shade of tall trees. On the nearby hill is a monument to Thomas Brydone, who established frozen-meat production in this area.

### ★Clark's Mill

4 km further south is Clark's Mill (1865), the only surviving watermill in the Oamaru area, now preserved as an industrial monument.

### ★★Moeraki Boulders

35 km south of Oamaru, scattered about on the beach, are the Moeraki Boulders – massive spherical rocks up to 3 m in diameter and weighing several tonnes. In Maori tradition they are calabashes and food baskets thrown ashore from the ancestral canoe long ago and since turned to stone.

The scientific explanation is that the boulders were formed on the seabed millions of years ago by the deposit of chemical concretions on hard cores. When the seabed was thrust upwards they were washed out of the softer rock by the surf and left on the beach. Some of them are still embedded in the rock. The net patterns on the surface of the boulders were produced by the extrusion of yellow calcites.

Although the boulders are strictly protected as natural monuments, the smaller ones, regrettably, are steadily eroding.

### Moeraki

The pretty fishing village of Moeraki nearby has a mainly Maori population. In the past there was a whaling station here.

## Otago                    C–E 11–13

The Otago region, which is bounded on the north by the wide Waitaki River and on the south by Catlins Forest Park, takes in a green and often mist-shrouded coast, in which the chief towns are Balclutha in the south, Dunedin in the centre and Oamaru in the north (see entries). The interior of the region is sparsely populated; here the climate is of continental, with hot, dry summers and very cold winters.

### Topography

Central Otago consists of a plateau broken up by the folding movements in the Southern Alps, falling sharply to the west but with a gentler gradient to the east. The Clutha, one of New Zealand's wildest and most abundant rivers, has carved out deep gorges in its westward course from the alpine lakes Wanaka and

The Moeraki Boulders

An arid landscape in Otago

Hawea. During the ice ages the landscape was reshaped. The hills, worn smooth by the ice, have rounded contours and are covered with tussock grass. The long fjord-like lakes were formed by glaciers and closed off by moraines.

In the west the Otago region reaches into the Southern Alps. Its highest peaks are Mount Aspiring (3027 m), Mount Earnslaw (1816 m) and the Remarkables, near Queenstown, which rise to almost 2500 m.

### Name

The region takes it name from the former Maori settlement of Otakau on the Otago Peninsula, north-east of Dunedin. The name of the village was applied to the peninsula and later to the whole region.

### History

Archaeological evidence shows that the region was originally inhabited by moa hunters, who moved north after the moas died out. In this southern latitude it was too cold to grow kumara (sweet potatoes), and the small groups that remained in the region moved to the coastal areas, where they lived on fern roots, fish and seals.

When Captain Cook passed this way he saw no Maoris on the Otago coast. In the early 19th c. sealers and whalers, mostly coming from Sydney, established themselves in the bays. Following the murderous raids by Te Rauparaha and his allies the local Maoris were ready to sell land to the settlers, only to be decimated by the diseases the Europeans brought with them.

**Gold rush** In the early 1860s the first gold was found at Lawrence in Central Otago, and thereafter prospectors flocked into the interior. In 1860 the population of the whole area was almost 12,000; 11 years later it had risen to 70,000.

The prospectors were deterred neither by the heat of summer nor the snowstorms of winter, and gold-miners' camps sprang up like mushrooms all over the place – at Lawrence, but also at Clyde, Cromwell, Arrowtown, Macetown, Queenstown, Naseby, Ophir and St Bathans. These tented towns had large numbers of bars and hotels, casinos, saloons and music halls. When the alluvial goldfields were exhausted the gold had to be won by mining for gold-bearing seams of quartz and dredging the beds of the rivers.

**After the gold rush** Some of the gold-miners' settlements managed to live on as market and commercial centres for the surrounding farming country. Irrigation converted barren valleys into flourishing fruit-growing and market-gardening areas. The export of frozen meat, as well as the sale of wool, brought increased prosperity. But as a result of erosion and a plague of rabbits many of the large sheep runs became uneconomic and were broken up by the government into smaller units that could be more intensively worked.

### Hydroelectric potential

In the course of time the economic potential of the great masses of water flowing down from the mountains was realised, and great dams were built to store water for hydroelectric power, irrigation and to provide protection against flooding. In parallel with this development new roads were built. As a result the landscape of central Otago has been transformed.

The Pancake Rocks in Paparoa National Park

### Tourism

The infrastructure provided primarily for the hydroelectric schemes also opened up the region for modern – car-borne – tourism. Some of the old gold-mining settlements, like Queenstown, which had subsided into rural slumber, were given a fresh lease of life, and Otago now attracts large numbers of visitors – walkers, climbers, winter-sports enthusiasts and ordinary tourists.

## ★Paparoa National Park      F 9

**Region: West Coast**
**Area: 306 sq km**

The Paparoa National Park lies on the west coast of the South Island, roughly half way between Greymouth and Westport (see entries).

### Information

Paparoa National Park visitor centre, in Punakaiki, has an exhibition about the flora and fauna of the park, with a display explaining the origin of the Pancake Rocks. Advice about walking in the park can also be obtained here.

## ★★Pancake Rocks

The principal feature of interest in the small national park, only established in 1987, is the Pancake Rocks, a curious limestone formation in which the strata look like piles of pancakes. In the rocks are blowholes, through which, when there is a heavy surf, water spurts high into the air.

The warm marine current that passes this way and the shelter afforded by the rocks produce a microclimate in which a rich subtropical vegetation (including many nikau palms) flourishes.

The best way to see the Pancake Rocks is to follow a ★footpath alongside the sea, which starts at Dolomite Point. On the way there are safe platforms looking straight down into the seething blowholes. There are also beautiful views inland, as far as the Southern Alps in good weather.

### Walks

There are a number of short trails leading to interesting places on the wild coast – the Punakaiki Cavern Track, the Truman Track to Perpendicular Point, and the Te Miko Track. There are also a number of longer walks into the hills and the valley of the Pororari River, notably the Punakaiki–Pororari Loop Track and the Upper Pororari Track.

### ★Inland Pack Track (Razorback Road)

A very strenuous but worthwhile trail is the Inland Pack Track, following a route used in the 1870s, which runs through the hills between the valley of the Punakaiki River to the south and the Fox River to the north. This tough walk takes at least 3 days. (Note that there are no bridges over the rivers and streams.)

## Picton                                    H/J 8

### Region: Nelson-Marlborough
### Population: 3300

Picton, where the ferries sailing between the South and the North Island (Wellington) put in, lies at the north-eastern tip of the South Island, at the head of one branch of picturesque Queen Charlotte Sound, 30 km north of Blenheim (see entry).

This little port, where Katherine Mansfield (☞Famous People) often stayed, is hemmed in by steep hills. In spite of the busy ferry traffic it has retained its original character. As the many yachts in its marina indicate, it is a popular holiday resort.

### History

Picton was founded in 1848 on the site of an abandoned Maori fortified settlement. The name commemorates one of Wellington's generals, who was killed in the Battle of Waterloo. For many years Picton was in fierce competition with the neighbouring town of Blenheim (see entry) to be the seat of the provincial government of Marlborough province. As early as 1862 there were calls in the press for a steamer service to link the railway systems on the North and South Islands. More than 30 years later, in 1898, Prime Minister Richard Seddon proposed the establishment of a train-ferry service, and the proposal was soon put into effect. In 1962 the ferry *Aramoana*, which carries both rolling stock and motor vehicles, was brought into service.

### Sights

The Smith Memorial Museum on London Quay commemorates the whaling tradition in this area since the mid-19th c. Whaling ceased only in the 1960s.

On the way to Waikawa Bay (north-east of the town) is the Victoria Domain Lookout, from which there are fine views of the town and Queen Charlotte Sound.

### Karaka Point

8 km away, to the north of Waikawa Bay, is the Karaka Point Reserve, in which are the remains of a Maori *pa*.

### ★Queen Charlotte Sound

North of Picton is Queen Charlotte Sound, a beautiful arm of the sea with many picturesque inlets. The best way to see the marvellous coastal scenery is by boat – the finest places are Mistletoe Bay, the Bay of Many Coves, Endeavour Inlet, Resolution Bay and Ship Cove. The Queen Charlotte Walkway, a beautiful trail offering no great difficulties, runs from Anakiwa to Ship Cove. There is also a road, Queen Charlotte Drive, through this picturebook landscape. From Picton there are organised boat excursions and fishing trips that take visitors, among other places, to Ship Cove, where Captain Cook called in several times, Queen Charlotte Sound and further out

Lively Picton Harbour

into the Marlborough Sounds (see entry). For divers there is a trip to the wreck of the Soviet cruise ship *Mikhail Lermontov*, which sank in Port Gore in 1986.

### ★ Robin Hood Bay

It is well worth an excursion from Picton to the picturesque Robin Hood Bay in the east; the steep sections of road require a confident driver.

### Cook Strait

At its narrowest point Cook Strait, the storm-swept channel between the North and South Islands of New Zealand, is only 23 km wide. The ferry crossing takes nearly 3½ hours. The first hour (from Picton) is spent sailing through the beautiful Marlborough Sounds; then follows an hour and a half in the open sea, and finally three-quarters of an hour in Wellington's huge natural harbour.

## Queenstown      C 11/12

**Region: Otago**
**Population: 4000**

This old gold-miners' settlement on the east side of Lake Wakatipu is unchallenged as the leading tourist centre on the South Island. It is well supplied with hotels and other accommodations and offers a varied programme of entertainment and leisure activities throughout the year. For the more energetic tourist there is a choice of activities, including bungee jumping, jet-boat trips, white-water rafting, paragliding and rock climbing.

### Getting there

**Road** From the west coast and Invercargill (see entry) on Highway 6, from Dunedin (see entry) on Highway 8. There are buses to and from all the major centres on the South Island.

**Air travel** There is an airstrip, used by scheduled services and charter flights, at Frankton, 6 km north-east of Queenstown.

### Information

Clocktower Information Centre, at the corner of Shotover Street and Camp Street.

### History

The Queenstown area was first explored

in 1857 and 1859, and soon afterwards a sheep farmer named William Rees staked out huge areas of grazing land. It was not long, however, before he had to leave his farm, the Camp, when a prospector called William Fox found gold in the Arrow River. Rees's farm rapidly developed into a gold-miners' settlement. The considerable quantities of gold found in the Shotover River and its tributaries Skipper's Canyon and Stoney Creek attracted large numbers of prospectors and adventurers. After the gold rush petered out and most of the prospectors left, Queenstown fell into a kind of twilight sleep, from which it awoke only when the great tourist potential of the area (mountain walks and climbs, white-water rafting, winter sports) was recognised.

### ★Town centre

The town centre is charmingly situated beside a promontory that reaches far out into Lake Wakatipu, now beautifully laid out as Queenstown Gardens. The best starting point for a tour of the sights is the Old Stone Library (1877), which is built on to the courthouse. From here the route runs under magnificent old trees into Camp Street. St Peter's Church (1932; Anglican) looks much older than it really is. Church Street leads down to the shores of the lake. Passing the Lake Lodge of St Ophir (1873), you come to the place where William Rees established his sheep farm, the Camp, in the early 19th c.

Continue to Queenstown Gardens (see above). On the way back, at the end of the Mall (pedestrian zone), you come to Eichardt's Tavern, which has been on this site since 1871. On the pier at the end of the Mall is Underwater World, where trout and eels are visible in the clear waters of the lake; they are fed here, but otherwise live freely in the lake. Beside the pier are marks showing the level to which the lake rose in the floods of 1878 and 1983.

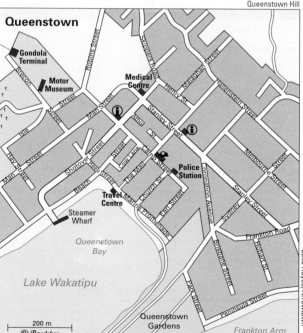

At Steamer Wharf is moored the old-time steamer *Earnslaw*. Then along the Esplanade on the seafront to St Omer Park, from which there are views of the lake and the town centre.

In the north-west of the town, near the lower station of the Skyline Gondola, is the Motor Museum (collection of vintage and veteran cars).
ⓖ *Daily 9am–5.30pm.*

### ★Bob's Peak
From Brecon Street an cableway, the **Skyline Gondola**, runs up to the summit of Bob's Peak (446 m; ☞252), from which there is an overwhelming view. Immediately below is Queenstown; beyond this is Lake Wakatipu; and beyond this again, forming a striking backdrop, are the peaks of the Remarkables.

### ★SS Earnslaw cruises
Cruises on the SS *Earnslaw*, which first went into service in 1912, are very popular. Some of the cruises include visits to sheep farms that are accessible only by boat. (The ship is taken out of service in June for its annual overhaul.)

### ★Skipper's Canyon
A trip through the 20 km long Skipper's Canyon in a specially equipped bus is an exciting experience. Drivers who do the trip in a hired car are not covered by insurance.

The return trip can be by jet boat for part of the way.

### ★Shotover River
The Shotover River is a challenge to the adventurous visitor, with trips by jet boat in which the steersman has to battle against strong currents, and white-water rafting in kayaks or rubber dinghies. There are organised rafting trips lasting several days, with overnight accommodation in tents.

### ★Kawarau River
There are jet-boat and rafting trips on the Kawarau River as well. The supreme experience for the daring, however, is a **bungee jump** from the Kawarau Bridge (☞254, Baedeker Special).

### Winter sports
Queenstown is the most popular winter-sports centre in New Zealand, the season lasting from June to September or October. Coronet Peak (1650 m), 15 km

north of the town, has excellent facilities (including ski lifts) for skiers, as have the skiing areas high up in the Remarkable Mountains. They are reached by way of Highway 6 (signposted to Kingston) and the Tollgate (10 km east of Queenstown), from which it is a 14 km climb to the ski fields. There is a shuttle bus service. Queenstown's Winter Festival is held annually in July.

### Pony trekking
There is plenty of scope for pony trekking in the hills round Queenstown, and for rides to some of the large sheep farms or abandoned goldfields in the area.

### Adventure sports
Other activities for the adventurous are tandem parachute jumps, paragliding and ballooning. A trip in a balloon is a marvellous way of seeing the beautiful country round Queenstown.

### Scenic flights
There are sightseeing flights from the Queenstown airstrip to the Southern Alps, Fiordland National Park and Milford Sound.

### Steam train
An steam train, the *Kingston Flyer*, runs between Kingston, at the south-east end of Lake Wakatipu, and the little township of Fairlight.

## Walks

### Information
Information about walks in the Queenstown area can be obtained from the Department of Conservation's visitor centre at the corner of Ballarat Street and Stanley Street.

### Short walks
There are many attractive walks in the beautiful highland country round Lake Wakatipu, for example to One Mile Creek, Queenstown Hill, Sunshine Bay, the Frankton Arm, Lake Sylvan, Ben Lomond or the Big Hill.

### ★★Routeburn Track
This route runs from the Dart Valley over the Harris Saddle and down to the Te Anau–Milford Road, through the grand mountains of Fiordland. The track is closed in winter. The walk, which takes

3–4 days, can be combined with the Milford Track (☛Fiordland National Park).

### Greenstone–Caples Track
This walk, a circuit which takes about four days, runs through the valleys of the Greenstone and Caples Rivers, which both flow into Lake Wakatipu. The best starting-point is Elfin Bay, on the west side of Lake Wakatipu.

### Rees–Dart Track
This walk (4 days) runs through the valleys of the Rees and Dart rivers, going over the Mount Cunningham Saddle (1447 m). The best starting points are Paradise, at the north end of Lake Wakatipu, or the Invincible Mine.

### ★Remarkables
There are a number of tracks, of varying grades of difficulty, through the beautiful mountain landscape of the Remarkables, which rise to 2300 m.

### ★Lake Wakatipu
This Z-shape lake, hemmed in by high hills, has an area of 293 sq km. It is some 80 km long, barely 5 km across at its widest point, and up to 378 m deep.

According to a Maori legend the lake came into being when a sleeping giant was burned to death. His heart still beats, however, at the bottom of the lake, causing variations in the level of the lake, which can rise or fall by several centimetres within 5 minutes.

The first Europeans reached Lake Wakatipu in 1853, and some years later the whole lake was surveyed. The Otago gold rush of the 1860s brought thousands of prospectors into the area. In those days there were 30 or 40 passenger ships, including four steamers, plying on the lake. One old steamer, the *Earnshaw* (1912), is now one of the lake's tourist attractions (see above).

## Reefton                                F 9

### Region: West Coast
### Population: 1200

Reefton lies in the valley of the Inangahua River, 80 km north-east of Greymouth and about the same distance

◀ Queentown and Lake Wakatipu, seen from Bob's Peak

south-east of Westport (see entries). Once a flourishing gold-mining town, it is now merely a supply centre for farmers, forestry workers and workers in the local coal industry. Its former importance as a gold-mining centre is reflected in its name (reef town); it was also known as Quartzopolis.

### History
Large quantities of gold were found in the area in 1866, and the gold-bearing seams of quartz were mined from 1870 until well into the 20th c. In those days Reefton had its own stock exchange. Shares in the local gold mines rose to unprecedented heights and then collapsed. After the gold mines closed coal mining was intensified, but this too is now in decline.

### Sights
Notable buildings that bear witness to the town's gold-mining heyday are the Church of the Sacred Heart (1878), St Stephen's Church (1878), the courthouse (1872) and the School of Mines (1886), which has a rich collection of minerals.

2 km east of Reefton is Black's Point Museum, which vividly illustrates the history of gold mining in the area.
◉ *Aug.–May Tue.–Sun. 1–4pm.*

At Crushington, 2 km further east, are two monster machines, the Wealth of Nations and the Globe Battery, in which the gold-bearing quartz was crushed.

### ★Victoria Forest Park
North and east of Reefton extends Victoria Forest Park (2090 sq km), in which are a number of old gold and coal mines (warning: the old and often overgrown shafts can be dangerous). Also within the park, 40 km south of Reefton, is the ghost town of Waiuta, where gold was worked until 1951. Information about walks in the gold- and coal-mining area can be obtained from the Department of Conservation office in Reefton (Crampton Road).

## Southland                        A–D 12/13

The Southland region, an area of rolling uplands and former swampy lowlands traversed by rivers, occupies the southern tip of the South Island.

### Topography
The Fiordland area in the south-west is

# *Baedeker* SPECIAL

# The High Jump

What makes people – some young, some not so young – jump from a great height into the void with only an elastic rope to save them from destruction? Is it that they have no sense of fear, is it the thrill, or is it 'the quickest way to a new self-awareness', as some have claimed? No one knows for sure. But there is no doubt that the extraordinary sport of bungee jumping, invented in New Zealand and introduced to Europe some years ago by a New Zealander who jumped from the Eiffel Tower, has caught on in a big way.

The origin of bungee jumping has been traced by ethnographers to the island of Vanuatu in the New Hebrides – not so far from New Zealand. Until recently adolescent boys on Vanuatu used to throw themselves from a high bamboo tower with only lianas to save them. A boy who summoned up the courage to jump had taken an important step towards becoming a man. Bungee jumping was thus seen as an essential element in the rites of passage to manhood.

Others believe that it was Tarzan and Jane who invented bungee jumping. Cinema-goers may recall how they moved about the forest by swinging on lianas.

Modern bungee jumping originated in New Zealand – or rather the Queenstown area to be more precise. Round Queenstown there are a number of gorges into which it is possible to jump with reasonable safety. In the mid-1980s, however, a New Zealander went one stage further. Attached to a high-tech rope made of strands of rubber, he jumped from the old bridge over the Kawarau River into the gorge 43 m below. Since then there has been a steady stream of intrepid jumpers from the bridge, as well as those who go only to watch, seeking to get, one way or the other, a big shot of adrenalin.

The elastic rope tied to the jumper's ankle brakes their fall relatively gently and safely. Then the rope springs back and pulls them up, then lets them down again. After bobbing up and down several times like a yo-yo, the jumper finally comes to rest and dangles helplessly at the end of the rope until they are picked up by a rubber dinghy.

There are now a variety of facilities for bungee jumping throughout New Zealand. Some practitioners jump from a platform on the jib of a crane, others from the roof of a sports stadium.

In Queenstown the hot spots for bungee jumpers are the Kawarau Bridge and, more recently, the 70 m high Skipper's Bridge. The supreme challenge, however, is a jump from the 102 m high Pipeline on the upper Shotover River.

A bungee jump costs between NZ$80 and $180, depending on the degree of difficulty and the arrangements for picking up the jumper after the jump.

The dernier cri among the adventure sports practised in New Zealand is 'parapenting', a combination of parachute jumping and hang-gliding. Instruction in this sport can be obtained in the Queenstown area on Crown Terrace and in the skiing area on the Remarkables. Experienced parapenters seek out areas in the mountains of Central Otago with good thermals.

A flock of Romney sheep in Southland

one of the most inaccessible and least populated parts of New Zealand. Here the deep valleys gouged out by glaciers were filled with water when the sea level rose and became fjords. On the east side of the mountains the valleys were dammed by terminal moraines and became long narrow lakes, such as Lake Te Anau (the largest lake on the South Island), Lake Manapouri, Lake Monowai and Lake Hauroko.

### History

Long before the arrival of Europeans this area was occupied by moa hunters and Maoris, who caught fish and hunted waterfowl and rats. These early inhabitants were driven out or decimated by Maori tribes from the north with a more advanced culture. The shy Maoris whom Cook encountered in Dusky Sound on his second voyage in 1773 had probably been driven out of their original territory by these invading tribes.

The first sealers came here from Sydney in 1792 and established temporary settlements in Dusky Sound and elsewhere. From the 1830s whalers established permanent settlements like Jacob's River (now Riverton, west of Invercargill) and Bluff.

In 1854 the colonial government acquired large territories in Southland, expropriating property from many of the large landowners. Scottish settlers then moved in from Dunedin and founded Invercargill, laying it out on a regular plan. The forests were cleared and the swamps drained, producing rich grazing land for Romney sheep and dairy cows.

To improve employment in this sparsely populated region an aluminium smelter was built some 20 years ago at Bluff, using power supplied by the controversial Manapouri hydroelectric station in Fiordland. In spite of massive economic incentives and the increasing development of tourism in the beautiful Fiordland region the population has in recent years been declining.

### Gore

Gore (pop. 11,000), Southland's second-largest town, lies at an important road intersection north-east of Invercargill (see entry) in an area of fertile pastureland, with some arable farming (grain) and horticulture. The former landscape of swamp and tussock grass was brought into cultivation by the early settlers.

Gore is known beyond the bounds of New Zealand for its ★★**Country Music Festival**, held annually in June.

The South Island's **sheep-shearing championship** is held annually in Gore.

### Mandeville
At Mandeville, 30 km north-west of Gore, is a homestead of pioneering days, now protected as a national monument.

## ★Stewart Island     B/C 13/14

**Region: Southland**
**Population: 700**

Stewart Island lies 30 km off the south coast of the South Island, separated from it by the Foveaux Strait. Triangular with many inlets, it has an area of 1700 sq km and a total coastline of over 1600 km.

### Getting there
A small ferry takes 2 hours to make the crossing from Bluff to Halfmoon Bay, the only place of any size on the island. During the main holiday season (December and January) there is a daily service. There are also day trips in light aircraft from Invercargill (see entry).

### Accommodation
The island's only commercial and tourist centre is the village of Halfmoon Bay (Oban). Here too are the only accommodations (a hotel, a lodge, a motel, an inn and a camping park with caravans for hire), which in the main holiday season are rapidly booked up. Advance reservation is essential.

### Topography
The island has a much indented coastline and is surrounded by a host of small islands. It is hilly and densely wooded, its principal peaks being Mount Anglem (980 m) in the north and mounts Rakeahua (676 m) and Allen (749 m) in the centre.

A marine current off the west coast warms the island and the fairly high hills provide shelter from the prevailing stormy winds. In consequence the climate is surprisingly mild for this latitude (47°S). In addition to peace and

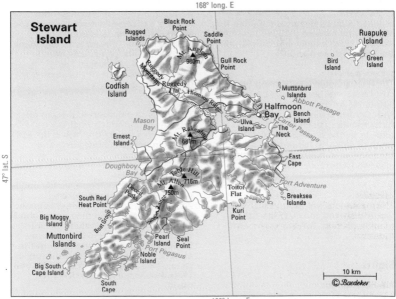

quiet and its almost intact natural flora and fauna, the island's attractions include sunsets of great beauty.

### Wildlife
The densely wooded island is a retreat for numerous endangered species (including kiwis) and large areas are already subject to conservation orders. A **national park** is being planned.

### History
Stewart Island, which in ancient times was very sparsely populated, was discovered by Captain Cook in 1770 – though he took the island for part of the mainland of New Zealand.

The Foveaux Strait was named after the deputy governor of Norfolk Island. One of the earliest European visitors to the island was William Stewart, first officer of the sealing ship *Pegasus*, who landed in 1803 with a party of sealers and gave the island its name. His ship is commemorated by Port Pegasus, an inlet on the south-east coast. The sealers were followed by whalers, as happened everywhere when the seals had been almost exterminated by overhunting. The whaling season was in winter; in summer the whalers grew potatoes and kept sheep and cattle.

In 1864 the colonial government acquired most of Stewart Island from the Maoris, who retained the right to catch waterfowl (particularly muttonbirds) on the little offshore islands.

### Johann Wohlers
The German missionary Johann Wohlers (1811-85) spent his last days on Stewart Island. He arrived on Nelson in 1843 with German settlers, but soon moved further south in order to establish a mission station on Ruapuke Island, south of Bluff. His harmonium is kept in the museum in Halfmoon Bay. Wohlers grave and a memorial are situated on Ringaringa Beach.

### Economy
The main sources of income are fishing (particularly cod and crayfish), fish farming (salmon, Foveaux oysters) and tourism.

## Sights

### Rakiura Museum
The Rakiura Museum, on the beach at Halfmoon Bay (Oban), illustrates the island's flora and fauna and the history of seal hunting and whaling.

### Acker House
Acker House, at the south end of Halfmoon Bay, was built of stone, clay and shells by an American whaler called Lewis Acker, who lost his land to the government.

### Walks and boat trips
There is plenty of good walking on Stewart Island, with mountain huts for overnight accommodation. In summer there are guided walks.

There are attractive boat trips to Port Adventure Bay on the east coast and to the beaches in Paterson Inlet.

## Timaru                                    F 11

**Region: Canterbury**
**Population: 28,000**

The port of Timaru, the second-largest town in Canterbury region, lies on the east coast, on the southern edge of the great Canterbury Plain, halfway between Christchurch and Dunedin (see entries). Along the coast extend the Tertiary basalts known as Timaru bluestone, forming a sheltered natural harbour. The Maori place name Te Maru means 'sheltered place'. Timaru is an important port for exports (particularly frozen meat) and the commercial and administrative centre of an extensive hinterland.

### History
There was an old Maori settlement on this site, within which whalers established a base in the 18th c. In 1859 British immigrants landed here and founded a town.

### Sport personalities
Timaru has produced some world-famous sportsmen, among them Robert Fitzsimmons, a world boxing champion in the late 19th c., and the runner John E Lovelock who won a gold medal for the 1500 metres at the 1936 Olympics in Berlin. Timaru also produced one of the most famous racehorses in the history of racing, Phar Lap, which in the 1920s and 1930s won major races all over the world.

# Sights

### ★Caroline Bay

The place to go to in Timaru is Caroline Bay, with its parks and entertainment and leisure facilities. It is particularly lively and busy in summer. At Christmas it is the venue of the Timaru Christmas Carnival, a great annual occasion.

### Maori Park

At the north end of Caroline Bay is Maori Park, in which is an eye-catching wooden lighthouse (1877).

### ★South Canterbury Museum

In a modern octagonal building in Perth Street is the South Canterbury Museum. It offers a survey of the history and natural history of the Timaru area, as well as material on the early flights by the aviation pioneer Richard Pearse in 1903. Opposite the museum is an obelisk commemorating the victims of two shipwrecks in 1882.

ⓖ *Tue.–Fri., Sun. 1.30–4.30pm.*

### St Mary's Church

Beside the museum is St Mary's Church (1886; Anglican), built in the local bluestone in Early English style.

### Basilica of the Sacred Heart

In Craigie Avenue is the Basilica of the Sacred Heart (1911 by FW Petre; RC), with twin towers and a copper dome.

### Aigantighe Art Gallery

The Aigantighe Art Gallery, housed in an elegant building of 1905 in Wai-iti Road, has a fine collection that includes works by New Zealand artists. Attached to the gallery is a sculpture garden.

ⓖ *Tue.–Fri. 11am–4.30pm, Sat., Sun. 2–4pm.*

### Washdyke

To the north of the town is the Washdyke industrial zone. The name refers to an old installation that once existed in this area, in which sheep were washed before shearing. Visitors can see round a brewery, textile factories and milling works (by appointment through the visitor centre in George Street).

# Surroundings

### City Walkway

The popular City Walkway runs through Centennial Park and continues along the coast.

### Walks

On the Opihi River (10 km north), on the north bank of the Pareora River (13 km south-west) and on Otaio Beach (20 km south) there are attractive paths running through beautiful scenery.

### Cave

35 km west of Timaru on Highway 8 is the hamlet of Cave (pop. 130), which grew up round an outpost of the huge Levels sheep station that once belonged to the Rhodes brothers. It was from this farm that the notorious Scottish sheep stealer James McKenzie allegedly stole sheep and then drove them into the unexplored highland country.

On a hill 2 km from Cave is St David's Memorial Church (Presbyterian), which commemorates the pioneers of the Mackenzie highlands. This beautiful little neo-Romanesque church with a battlemented tower is built of natural ice-smoothed stone.

ⓖ *Daily.*

### ★Maori rock paintings

In a wide area round Timaru, in caves and rock overhangs, are rock paintings by Maoris or their predecessors from a very early period. The finest are at Dog Rock, 1 km east of Cave, and Craigmore, 30 km south-west. Information is available from from the visitor centre in George Street, Timaru.

# Geraldine

### Region: Canterbury
### Population: 2000

The little agricultural market town of Geraldine lies 35 km north of Timaru, between the plain and the highlands. Early settlers planted European species of trees here.

### Surroundings

In Pleasant Valley, 17 km west of Geraldine, is St Anne's Church (1862; Anglican), the oldest church in South Canterbury.

16 km north-west of Geraldine is Orari Gorge Farm, established in the mid-19th c. The farm buildings, including a cottage of 1859, are protected as national monuments

(restored by the Historic Places Trust). The farm is still occupied and there is only restricted public access.

Two local beauty spots are the Waihi Gorge (13 km north-west) and the Te Moana Gorge (19 km west).

### ★Peel Forest Park

23 km north of Geraldine is Peel Forest Park, 600 ha of largely unspoiled woodland with romantic waterfalls and attractive picnic areas.

Nearby are the old buildings of Mount Peel Station, a sheep farm established in the 1860s.

### Mesopotamia

The track ends at Mesopotamia (70 km north-west of Geraldine), which, like the neighbouring **Erewhon** Station, belonged to the English writer Samuel Butler. (Erewhon can be reached only on a roundabout route by way of Mount Somers).

## Waikouaiti                    E 12

**Region: Otago**
**Population: 1000**

An hour drive north of Dunedin (see entry) on Highway 1 is Waikouaiti, the oldest European settlement in Otago.

### History

In the 1830s a whaler named Johnny Jones (1809–69), a sharp businessman, settled here and established a chain of whaling stations all the way down the west coast as far as the Foveaux Strait. When the whaling industry declined he switched to farming and property dealing. He organised the settlement of immigrants, and as a supplier of foodstuffs he was virtually indispensable to the newly founded town of Dunedin in its formative years. In Waikouaiti itself he showed himself a generous benefactor and patron.

### Sights

Two handsome wooden buildings dating from the pioneer days are the Presbyterian Church (1863) and St John's Church (1858; Anglican). St Anne's Church (RC) was built in 1871. The old farmstead of Matanaka at the north end of the bay also dates from this period.

The Early Settlers Museum, housed in a former bank dating from the turn of the 19th c., contains mementos of the early settlement.

### ★Beach

Waikouaiti's safe bathing beach attracts many day visitors. The dunes were consolidated around the turn of the 19th c. by sowing grass and later by planting pines.

## Waimate                      F 11

**Region: Canterbury**
**Population: 3000**

50 km south of Timaru (see entry) is Waimate, the commercial centre of a large agricultural area. On land that in the 19th c. was covered with totara forests grain is now grown, as well as flower bulbs and berry fruits.

### History

The first settlers in this area in the 19th c. were loggers and sawmill workers engaged in clearing the ancient totara forests. In 1854 the Studholme brothers came here from Christchurch looking for new grazing land. With the agreement of the old Maori chief Huruhuru they established a huge sheep farm, the Te Waimate Station, which also reared cattle and horses. The horses bred here found markets as far afield as Australia.

## Sights

### ★Studholme Farm

The first farmhouse, the Cuddy, was built by the Studholme brothers in 1854 of wood from a single totara tree. A sheep-shearing shed and a wool shed were built at the same time. The buildings, still in private ownership, are protected as national monuments.

### St Augustine's Church

St Augustine's Church (Anglican) was built in 1872 of rough-sawn wood, with a striking little tower over the crossing. The interior bears witness to the prominent position of the Studholme family in the local community.

### Historical Museum

This museum of local history is housed in the old courthouse (1879).
ⓘ *Mon.–Fri. 1–5pm, Sun. 2–4pm.*

### Seddon Square

In Seddon Square, the well looked-after village square, there are monuments to Michael Studholme, the Maori chief Huruhuru and Dr Margaret Cruickshank, New Zealand's first woman doctor, who cared for the town's people until 1916.

### Mount John

From the summit of Mount John (446 m), in the nearby Hunter's Hills, you can get some idea of the vastness of the Canterbury Plains.

## Waitaki River      E/F 11

### Regions: Otago and Canterbury

The broad Waitaki River is fed by the snowfields and glaciers of the Southern Alps, and its principal tributaries come from the alpine lakes Tekapo, Pukaki and Ohau (see entries). With these and numerous other tributaries it has a catchment area of almost 12,000 sq km. It forms the boundary between the Canterbury and Otago regions.

### Hydroelectric power

Two gigantic hydroelectric schemes have transformed both the course of the river and the landscape. On the upper course of the river, near Twizel, there is the Upper Waitaki Power Development Scheme, and on its middle course are the Benmore, Aviemore and Waitaki hydroelectric stations, each supplied by an artificial lake created by damming the river. Much of the river's course is now a chain of lakes. The water stored in the lakes is also used for agricultural and horticultural irrigation in the arid plains on the lower course of the river.

There are fish ladders at the dams for the benefit of trout and salmon anglers – and of the fish

### ★Maori rock paintings

At Takiroa, near Duntroon (on the south bank of the river), are very fine rock paintings by nomadic Maori tribes. They are easily accessible from Highway 83.

### Twizel

A few kilometres south of Lake Pukaki, on the Twizel River in the Mackenzie highlands, is Twizel (pop. 1800), originally a camp for construction workers on the Upper Waitaki Power Development Scheme. Under this

project the water level of lakes Tekapo, Pukaki and Ohau was raised by the construction of dams, the lakes were linked by canals and lower down, in the middle Waitaki Valley, other dams were built, creating artificial lakes like Lake Benmore. In the course of these developments, which were highly controversial, a holiday and leisure complex, the Mackenzie Hydro Lakes, was established round Twizel. This offers excellent facilities for fishing, boating and cruising on the lakes. In recent years a number of skiing centres have also been developed.

## West Coast      B–F 8–11

The West Coast or **Westland** region extends for more than 500 km along the west coast of the South Island, from Jackson Bay and the Haast River in the south to Karamea in the north. It is a narrow coastal belt of dense rain forest backed inland by high mountains that is nowhere more than 50 km wide. The region has a population of only 35,000, which has been steadily declining for many years.

The principal towns in the region are Greymouth, Westport and Hokitika (see entries). It has many relics of the pioneer days of loggers and gold miners – although the infrastructure has been much improved since then by the building of roads.

### Discovery

Abel Tasman and Captain Cook sailed along this inhospitable coast, and the hinterland was later explored by Thomas Brunner and Julius von Haast, who discovered the region's extensive coalfields.

### History

Before the 19th c. the Maoris on the west coast greatly prized the hard *pounamu* (greenstone, nephrite, jade) found here, from which they made weapons and jewellery. In the mid-19th c., when Brunner and von Haast travelled through the dense rain forests, iron had long replaced greenstone for making weapons. But in 1864 two Maoris were still looking for greenstone when they found gold in the Greymouth area. When news got round boatloads of prospectors began arriving in Hokitika, and many found their way through the Southern Alps over little-known passes to the rainy west coast with its promise of wealth. Within a year there were no fewer than 40,000 prospectors in Westland, digging up swamps, impenetrable forests and river beds in the quest of gold. The newly established settlement of Hokitika grew within a short time into a town of 10,000 inhabitants, New Zealand's most important port after Auckland. By the end of the 1870s the goldfields were largely exhausted and only a few gold miners were left, laboriously scratching at gold-bearing veins of quartz at Reefton and in the interior.

Something of the atmosphere of the West Coast in the 19th c. can be felt in the reconstructed gold-miners' settlement of Shantytown to the south of Greymouth.

### Coal

After the end of the gold rush the economy of the region increasingly depended on timber and coal. Coal mining began to flourish, particularly to the north of Westport and on the Grey River. In spite of the large deposits still available, however, mining has declined sharply in recent years – many abandoned mines are already overgrown by the rain forest.

### ★★Lowland rain forest

The high rainfall on the west coast has produced a type of rain forest that is unique in the world. This lowland rain forest has a variety of species rarely found anywhere else. Recent proposals to exploit its economic potential by extensive felling have met fierce resistance from conservationists all over the world.

### Agriculture

Fishing and pastoral farming have become major contributors to the economy of the region. Fishing and fish farming (particularly salmon and trout) are widely practised, and large cattle and sheep farms have been established in many places. A recent development is game farming, with large enclosures containing game whose meat brings the highest prices in export markets (e.g. roe deer and fallow deer).

Primeval landscape in the west of the South Island

The Fox Glacier in Westland National Park

### Tourism

The isolation of the southern West Coast was ended by the opening of the road over the Haast Pass in 1965, which gave a great boost to tourism on the west coast. It now became possible to make a circuit of the whole South Island. The imposing Fox and Franz Josef glaciers (see entry) are major attractions. The Westland National Park (see entry) was opened in 1960 and much extended in 1982.

## ★★Westland National Park D/E 10

**Region: West Coast**
**Area: 1176 sq km**

### Information

Westland National Park headquarters and visitor centre, Franz Josef village; information bureau in Fox Glacier village.

### Te Wahipounamu Nature Reserve

Westland National Park and Mount Cook National Park together form the large Te Wahipounamu Nature Reserve, which because of its unique expanse of rain forest it is also a UNESCO World Heritage Site.

### Topography

Westland National Park, established in 1960 and considerably enlarged in 1982, extends from the west coast at Gillespie's Point and Okarito (white heron reserve) to Mount Tasman (3498 m), one of the highest peaks in the Southern Alps. The national park's main attractions are the Fox and Franz Josef glaciers (see entry), which flow down from the permanent ice caps of the 3000 m peaks of the Southern Alps to an altitude of 300 m above sea level, where evergreen rain forest and tall tree ferns flourish.

### Climate

Directly on the coast it is relatively warm and less wet, with an annual rainfall of around 2500 mm. In the western foothills of the Southern Alps rainfall is around 5000 mm, and in the alpine and summit regions it is over 7600 mm. In Westland National Park you must expect to encounter violent and long spells of rain and snow – without which there would of course be no snowfields, glaciers or rain forests.

### Highway 6

The main road through the national park is Highway 6, which gives access to all the major natural attractions and many lesser ones.

### Walks

There are a number of waymarked trails in the national park. Before setting out on a walk it is essential to enquire about the condition of the trail at the visitor centre in Franz Josef or the Fox Glacier tourist village, which also supply detailed descriptions of the routes.

## Westport                                        F 8

### Region: West Coast
### Population: 4500

The little port of Westport, the second-largest place in the West Coast region, lies on the north side of the estuary of the Buller River. In spite of its isolated location it is an important commercial centre for the northern part of the west coast, serving a large area.

Its economic resources are the abundant supplies of timber in the surrounding area, the huge coalfields in the hinterland of the Paparoa Range and the limestone quarries on Cape Foulwind, which have promoted the development of a large cement industry.

### History

Westport grew out of a 19th c. gold-miners' camp, but it survived after the end of the gold rush due to the large deposits of coal in the area. This 'black gold' is shipped abroad from Westport and transported to Christchurch by rail.

### Sights

The town centre is laid out on a regular plan. The **Coaltown Museum**, housed in an old brewery in Queen Street, displays the history of coal mining.
ⓖ *Daily 8.30am–4.30pm.*

Two other features of interest are the venerable **St John's Church** (Anglican) and the imposing **Bank of New South Wales**.

## Surroundings

### Beaches

Two popular beaches are Carter's Beach (5 km from the town in the direction of Cape Foulwind; surfing) and North Beach (suitable for families).

### ★Cape Foulwind

20 km west of Westport is Cape Foulwind, with a handsome lighthouse. The cape was given its name by Captain Cook in 1770, who had to battle with contrary winds here.

### ★Tauranga Bay

Tauranga Bay, with its friendly seal colony, attracts many day visitors.

### Walks

There are attractive trails round Cape Foulwind and in the old gold- and coal-mining areas. Information, particularly on the Britannia Track and the Denniston Walkway, is available from from the visitor information centre, 1 Brougham Street, Westport.

### ★Coal mining

Coal was, and to some extent still is, mined north of Westport at Waimangaroa (16 km), Denniston (25 km), Granity (29 km), Stockton (35 km) and Ngakawau (32 km). In the past transportation of the coal, mined high up on steep hills, was difficult. At Denniston the coal was brought down by funicular railway.

### Mitchell's Gully Goldmine

A gold mine established in 1866 by the great-grandfather of the present owner stands on the road from Westport to Punakaiki. It is still worked with equipment from the 19th c.

**COOK ISLANDS**
After the exertions of sightseeing, or to escape the stress of modern life, where better to relax than the idyllic beaches of the Cook Islands.

# Cook Islands

The Cook Islands epitomise the dream of an idyllic island in the south Pacific. Scattered like pearls in the vast ocean, they lie between longitude 156° and 170°W and between latitude 8° and 23°S, some 3500 km north-east of New Zealand. Their charms – unspoiled natural beauty and palm-shaded beaches – have not been ruined by mass tourism.

## ★★Topography

The Cook Islands consist of a northern group of seven and a southern group of eight islands, lying 1000 km apart. Their national territory extends over a total area of 2,201,490 sq km, but their land area is no more than 240 sq km. Lagoons within the islands cover 566 sq km. The total area of the islands with their lagoons is thus only 0.04 per cent of the national territory.

The islands in the northern group (total area 28 sq km) are Penrhyn, Rakahanga, Manihiki, Pukapuka, Suwarrow, Palmerston and Nassau. The southern group consists of Rarotonga (the chief island in the archipelago), Mangaia, Atiu, Mauke and Mitiaro, Aitutaki, Manuae and Takutea (total area 212 sq km). The most visited of the islands, and the best equipped to cater for visitors, are Rarotonga and Aitutaki. On the other islands there are only modest hotels and accommodation in private houses; but it is a marvellous experience to pay a flying visit to one or other of these almost entirely unspoiled islands. A 40- or 50-minute flight from Rarotonga will take you deep into the past.

## Getting there

Air New Zealand flies twice weekly from London via Los Angeles to Rarotonga. It is also possible to combine a visit to New Zealand with a trip to the Cook Islands. Air New Zealand flies from Auckland to the islands, and reasonably priced package deals are available. Cook Islandair and Air Rarotonga fly regular services to almost all the islands in the northern and the southern groups.

On arrival in the islands visitors are required to produce a return ticket and evidence that they have booked hotel accommodation.

## Geology

Like most of the Pacific islands the Cook Islands are either purely volcanic or coral atolls on a basalt base. Five types of island can be distinguished: the high volcanic island of Rarotonga; the raised coral islands of Mangaia, Mauke, Atiu and Mitiaro, with a volcanic core and a surrounding plain of coralline limestone; Aitutaki, consisting of a central volcanic island and a surrounding barrier reef; the atolls of Manuae, Palmerston, Penrhyn, Manihiki, Rakahanga, Pukapuka and Suwarrow; Takutea and Nassau, islands of sand on a coralline limestone base.

Mangaia, Atiu, Mauke and Mitiaro are islands of a type that is very rare in the Pacific. In a term borrowed from the Maori language, they are described as *makatea* islands: islands that consist of a central volcanic hill surrounded by a broad, gently sloping plain of coralline limestone. They originated soon after the ending of volcanic activity, when the volcanic islands were gradually sinking into the sea. As they sank their fringing coral reefs rose. Later, forces from the earth's interior thrust the extinct volcanoes with their fringing reefs up again, and these were then levelled off by the surf and later by weathering. The *makatea* was born.

Both in origin and in age the atolls in the northern group share common characteristics. With the exception of Penrhyn, which lies on top of its own volcano, all of them came into being at about the same time on the highest points of a massive submarine volcanic ridge.

The islands in the southern group, however, do not have had a common origin. It is established that the string of islands from Aitutaki to Mauke follow the WNW–ESE line of a series of submarine volcanoes. This points to a common origin in plate-tectonic activity, with a hot spot in the earth's upper mantle over which the Pacific plate is moving north-west. The disposition of the islands is comparable with other island chains in the Pacific, for example Hawaii. Mangaia and Rarotonga are out on their own and completely isolated. They are the oldest and the youngest of the Cook Islands, all of which came into

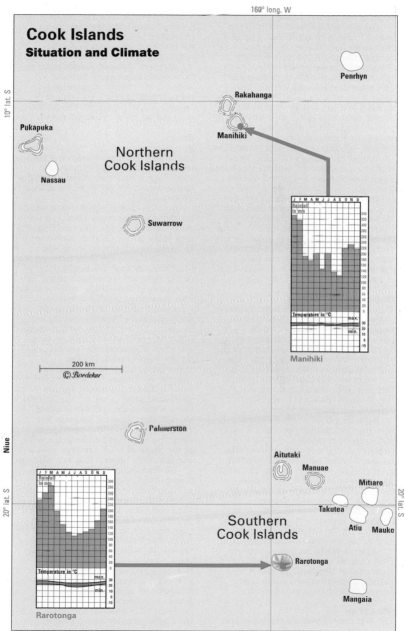

# Cook Islands
## Situation and Climate

160° long. W

10° lat. S

Penrhyn

Rakahanga

Pukapuka

Manihiki

Nassau

### Northern Cook Islands

Suwarrow

J F M A M J J A S O N D
Rainfall in mm
340
320
300
280
260
240
220
200
180
160
140
120
100
80
60
40
20
0
Temperature in °C
max.
30
20
min.
10
0
-10

**Manihiki**

200 km
© Baedeker

Palmerston

Niue

Aitutaki

Manuae

Mitiaro

Takutea

20° lat. S

Atiu

Mauke

J F M A M J J A S O N D
Rainfall in mm
300
280
260
240
220
200
180
160
140
120
100
80
60
40
20
0
Temperature in °C
max.
30
20
min.
10
0
-10

### Southern Cook Islands

Rarotonga

**Rarotonga**

Mangaia

160° long. W

being in the Tertiary period.

The geological development of the islands began with the building up and emergence from the sea of the first volcanic islands in the early Tertiary (Palaeocene), some 65–60 million years ago. In the Eocene, 60–38 million years ago, some of them sank into the sea again. The reef corals then began to grow upwards and the first atolls and reef islands came into being. The building up of Rarotonga occurred only towards the end of the Tertiary (Pliocene), between 2.8 and 2.3 million years ago. It ended at the turn of the Tertiary (Pleistocene), with the last eruptions, which evidence suggests took place less than 2 million years ago.

During the ice ages, when even the tropics were markedly cooler than they are today, the growth of the reefs continued. Depending on the level of the sea (100–120 m) and the movements of the islands resulting from tectonic activity, almost all the islands have marine terraces and cliff and beach lines at varying heights.

**Climate**

The Cook Islands lie within the sphere of influence of the marine climate of the tropics, which is characterised by slight annual variations in temperature, high air humidity and rainfall throughout the year. Between December and April the northern group of islands falls within the inner tropical convergence zone. In this area whirlwinds can occur, hitting the northern islands in particular between December and March.

High temperatures (☞269) combined with high air humidity produce a sultry and sometimes extremely oppressive climate on all the islands. The months January to April are particularly trying: even at night the air is not much cooler. December to March are the rainiest months (annual average ca 2200 mm). Overcast days with rain, however, are rare even during these months. Prolonged periods of bad weather occur only during the (relatively rare) passage of tropical disturbances and storms.

Water temperature ranges between 24°C (August to September) and 27°C (February) in the southern group of islands; in the northern group it is around 28°C throughout the year.

**When to go**

The best time of year for European and American visitors to go to the southern group of islands is from May to December, when fewer rainy days and the cooling trade winds make the sultriness of the air perfectly tolerable. In the northern group of islands there are no seasonal differences. In these latitudes the climate is oppressive throughout the year – visitors not accustomed to the tropics should limit their stay to no more than 2 weeks.

**History**

When the Cook Islands were discovered and settled by Polynesians is not known with certainty, though excavated arcaeological material indicates that the islands have been occupied for at least 1100 years.

Nor is it known where the original inhabitants came from. There is much evidence that the Maoris came from the area of the Society Islands and were followed by tribes from Tonga and Samoa. The great distances between the islands meant that there were only occasional contacts between them, so that many of the islands underwent their own distinctive cultural development.

A survivor from the early period is the Maori god of fertility and the sea, Tangaroa. Figures of the god are found frequently across the islands, in parks and even in apartments, but noticeably on the 1-dollar coin. The first missionaries (see below) started to destroy the Tangaroa figures, but local belief in the god persisted. Figures continued to be carved on the islands, albeit without the symbolic phallus, though more recently Tangaroa has appeared in his original naked form. Souvenirs of the god are popular today, in the shape of small carvings, jewellery and key rings, often acting as a talisman.

Western contacts with the islands began with Portuguese and Spanish navigators, who sighted, and landed on, some of the northern atolls between 1595 and 1606. The first more detailed description of the archipelago was by Captain Cook, who reached Manuae on September 23rd 1773 during his second voyage. He named the southern group the Hervey Islands, after Augustus Hervey, a lord of the Admiralty. After him came others, mostly seafarers or missionaries: among them were the *Bounty* mutineers.

From 1823 onwards the influence of the English missionaries on Rarotonga

The Maori god Tangaroa

adoption of British law that followed strengthened the bonds between Britain and the islands. Soon practical and geographical considerations pointed to the advisability of putting the islands under the protection of New Zealand; on June 11th 1901 they were annexed by New Zealand and given their present name of Cook Islands.

These eventful years were followed by a long period of peace and stability, until in the early 1960s, under pressure from the United Nations who suspected New Zealand of colonial ambitions in the south Pacific, government was gradually transferred to the Rarotonga Parliament, and in 1965 the Cook Islands became independent. Since then they have remained in close association with New Zealand, which retains responsibility only for defence and foreign policy.

### Society

The islands have a population of some 19,000 (78 inhabitants per sq km). The overwhelming majority are Maoris of Polynesian descent. More than 31,000 'Cook Maoris' live and work in New Zealand. Rarotonga, with almost 11,000 inhabitants, is by far the most densely populated island, followed by Aitutaki (pop. 2400) and Mangaia (pop. 1100). Three of the islands are uninhabited. The national languages are English and Maori. Some 70 per cent of the population are Protestants, around 10 per cent Catholics.

### Economy

The economic base of most Pacific island states is agriculture. Their smallness and remoteness are usually obstacles to economic development, the scope for which is dependent on the size of the island and its natural conditions. The economic production of most island states is directed in varying degrees to meeting the needs of the domestic market.

The Cook Islands themselves are constrained by the size of the individual islands and to a large extent also by the poor fertility of the soil. This is particularly the case with the islands in the northern group and with Takutea and Manuae in the southern group, where the coralline limestone has only a thin soil. In these islands the only economic resource is the undemanding and salt-tolerant coconut palm. The volcanic islands are more favoured by

gradually spread to all the islands in the group. They brought the Christian message, which put an end to tribal wars and the tradition of human sacrifices, but they also brought diseases that in the next few years would carry off half the native population. Since the widely scattered islands were never united under a single ruler, the British mission centre on Rarotonga, with its schools and Takamoa College (founded in 1837), became the unifying factor in the islands. For many years the islanders' fears about possible European claims on their territory were groundless: at first neither Britain nor France showed any territorial interest in the remote islands west of Tahiti. This situation changed with the French intervention in Tahiti and the first Maori rebellions in New Zealand. It was the chiefs of Rarotonga who, fearful of French intentions, first sought British protection in 1844. A formal application followed in 1865, but it was another 23 years until a British protectorate over Rarotonga was proclaimed in 1888. In subsequent years this was extended to all the islands.

The establishment of a parliament on the British model in Rarotonga and the

nature, with soils that in many places are highly fertile. These islands, inheriting the colonial plantation economy (a monoculture), grow tropical fruits and tuberous plants. On Rarotonga, Atiu and Mauke the main crops are pawpaws, bananas and, on a smaller scale, coffee, while Mangaia specialises in pineapples and Aitutaki in bananas.

The islands export tropical fruits (mainly pawpaws, bananas, pineapples and copra), as well as processed products such as orange juice and tinned pineapples. The production of cultured black pearls also makes a contribution to the economy. Fishing and fish processing play only a subordinate role. A canning plant, two small clothing factories and a number of craft workshops provide some industrial employment. The largest employer, however, is the government, which has over 900 employees. The opening of Rarotonga's international airport in 1974 gave a boost to tourism, which has become increasingly important to the islands' economy. Some 30 per cent of the working population are now employed in the tourism, compared with 20 per cent in industry. Only 6 per cent of the population work in agriculture, which accounts for 17 per cent of the gross domestic product (1990). Even with the increasing revenue from tourism – the annual number of visitors, mainly from New Zealand and Australia, is now over 40,000 – the

prospects for further economic development are limited. And this is in spite of the fact that the islands' political and economic relationship with the former protecting power, New Zealand, brings great economic and financial advantages, which have given the people of the Cook Islands a relatively high standard of living. The islanders' unrestricted access to the New Zealand labour market, however, has a downside. Continuing emigration, particularly of skilled workers, has had negative effects on the social structure and on the national sense of identity, which have created a feeling of national disorientation and hopelessness among those who remain.

## Southern Cook Islands

### ★Rarotonga

With an area of 67.2 sq km, Rarotonga is the largest of the Cook Islands, with almost 60 per cent of the total population of the archipelago. Its bizarre landscape and lush tropical vegetation make it, in the opinion of many visitors, one of the most beautiful of the Polynesian islands. The chief place, Avarua, is the administrative, economic and cultural centre of the Cook Islands.

Rarotonga is the visible tip of a volcanic cone that reaches down to 4500 m below sea level. The hilly

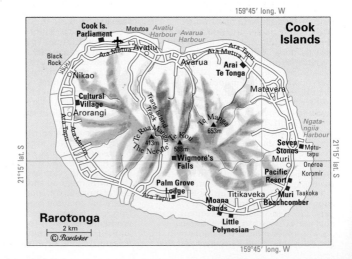

interior consists of a number of much weathered overlapping volcanoes. Due to rapid weathering in the moist tropical climate the slopes of the hills have been deeply indented by rivers. Round the rugged interior is a coastal plain about 1 km wide, covered with fertile alluvial sands and dunes in which grow various ornamental and useful plants, coconut palms, pawpaws, bananas, coffee. Between the belt of dunes and the volcanic hills is a swampy depression that, as on other islands, is used for growing taro.

The island is fringed by a reef that encloses a narrow lagoon, linked with the open sea by a number of gaps in the reef. Only on the south and south-east is the reef further from the coast, separated from it by the Muri Lagoon, with three sand islands and an island formed of a volcanic rock known to the inhabitants as *taakoka*.

Rarotonga can be explored on the regular buses, in a hired car or on a moped or bicycle. All the places on the island can be reached on a 30 km asphalted ring road, and most of the hotels and other accommodations are on this road within sight of the sea. A second road, negotiable almost all the way, serves the agricultural areas at the foot of the hills, and from this route minor roads and a number of tracks lead into the interior. A good way of getting to know the island is to join a guided walk. The cross-island walk from the north coast up to the pinnacle rock Te Rua Manga (413 m) and then via Wigmore's Falls to the south coast takes about 4 hours. Only those with a good head for heights should attempt the ascent of Te Kon (588 m), from which there are breathtaking views. Another possible excursion is to the Marae Trai-te-tonga, the most sacred cult site on the island, with ancient Polynesian stone buildings.

## Mangaia

Mangaia (51.08 sq km; up to 169 m), the most southerly and the second-largest island in the archipelago, is in the shape of an irregular circle. The lower slopes of the central volcanic ridge are deeply indented by rivers. Round the central core are numerous irregularly shaped swampy depressions up to 366 m across, bounded at the lower end by limestone cliffs up to 60 m high, sometimes dropping almost vertically. The cliffs are

part of the 1.2–1.6 km wide plain of coralline limestone (*makatea*), much affected by karstic action, which surrounds the island's volcanic core. The water flowing down from the hills seeps away into dolines and extensive cave systems, to re-emerge on the shore or in karstic springs near the coast.

The island is well provided with roads and tracks. Its fertile volcanic soil yields good yields of pineapples, coffee and other tropical produce for export.

## Atiu

Atiu (27 sq km; up to 72 m), almost square in shape, lies north-east of Rarotonga. The third largest of the Cook Islands, it consists of a much weathered central volcanic massif in the form of a shallow dome, the slopes of which are slashed by radial gorges. Round the foot are swampy depressions (taro land) completely surrounding the island's volcanic core. These in turn are succeeded by a 1 km wide raised platform of coralline limestone (*makatea*), which falls down to the sea, at some points edged by cliffs 6–9 m high. The surface of the *makatea* is much affected by karstic action, with underground cave systems. Surface water drains down to the coast through dolines and caves. The island is surrounded at a distance of 45–90 m by a surf-lashed reef some 90 m wide, with gaps at intervals that allow small ships to reach the landing stages.

From Taunganui Landing a road cuts through the interior of the island, with narrow roads or tracks leading to individual houses or to the taro swamps. Another road runs along the north and west coasts to the Tarapaku and Vai Piaka Landing. Almost all the inhabitants live in the five small villages on the volcanic plateau, in which are the island's shops and administrative buildings, as well as a small coffee-roasting plant. There are a number of trails through the island's tropical jungle and pineapple plantations. Characteristic features of Atiu are the large limestone caves, which can be explored with the help of guides. There are many sandy beaches but the coral reefs near the coast tend to make bathing unappealing.

## Mitiaro

The island of Mitiaro (22.25 sq km), north-east of Rarotonga, is in the form of an irregular oval. Like Atiu and Mauke, it has a raised reef surrounding the volcanic core and is enclosed by a continuous fringing reef. But unlike these islands, it consists not of a single volcano but of four low volcanic hills no more than 12 m high surrounded by a belt of swampy land.

The only settlement on the island is at Omutu Landing, with all the houses clustered round the post office, radio station, health centre and copra drying building. From here gravel roads, each 2 km long, run along the coast; the way over the swamps into the interior is on stone causeways. Two features of interest are a doline, 8 m deep, and a stalactitic cave containing a lake of cold milky water that smells strongly of sulphur.

There are almost no sandy beaches, but visitors can cool off in a number of pools on the fringing reef.

### Mauke

Mauke (18.4 sq km) is the most easterly of the Cook Islands. The interior of the island is occupied by a much weathered basalt plateau with fertile soils, rising to a height of 30 m, which is surrounded by a plain of coralline limestone up to 1.6 km wide. In between the two there are occasional swampy depressions that are used for growing taro. The island is enclosed by a narrow fringing reef with a surf platform on the inner side. Six gaps in the reef allow small boats to reach the landing stages.

There are two villages on Mauke, one near Taunganui Landing, with the post office, school and administrative offices, the other on the central plateau, with the church and a number of shops. The villages are linked by a good road and another road runs round the island. There are a number of large limestone caves. Like Atiu, Mauke has beautiful beaches, but here too the nearby reef with its broad surf platform restricts bathing.

### ★Aitutaki

Aitutaki (18.02 sq km) – which is almost an atoll – is a popular holiday island, particularly for day or longer excursions from Rarotonga. It consists of a main island of deeply weathered basalt (area 16.8 sq km), which is surrounded by a wide lagoon. Its highest hill is Maungapu (124 m). The lagoon, which at many points is shallow, is surrounded by a triangular barrier reef marking the outline of the volcano that rises from a depth of 4000 m below sea level. On the eastern reef are 12 small coral islands (*motus*) with a total area of 2.2 sq km. The only sand island is on the south-western reef. Two little basalt islets, Rapota and Moturakau, lie off the reef in the south-west of the lagoon. All 15 *motus* are fringed with coconut palms. The coastal areas of the main island also have coconut and pandanus palms. The scanty vegetation of the higher islands reflects the fact that they have less rainfall than Rarotonga.

On the west side of the island there is a gap in the reef that allows boats and motor lighters access to the little harbour of the chief place on the island, Arutanga, in which are the island's post office, administrative offices, hospital and shops. There are other small settlements in the north and east of the island, easily reached on good roads. Most of the accommodations for visitors are on the west side of the island, in sight of the lagoon. Aitutaki's main source of income apart from tourism is its banana plantations.

### Manuae

The atoll is formed by two horseshoe-shape islands, Manuae and Auoto (or Te-Au-O-Tu), separated from one another by a lagoon. The two islands, which have a total area of only 6 sq km, consist of coral sand. The islands and the lagoon are surrounded by a continuous coral reef.

Of the two islands only Manuae – an island of coconut plantations – has a permanent, if fluctuating, population. In addition to houses and administrative offices the little settlement has a health centre and a number of copra-drying plants. Extra seasonal workers come from the neighbouring islands. Outside the lagoon there is an anchorage for seagoing ships while a gap in the reef allows smaller vessels through. The other island, Auoto, can be reached only by boat over the lagoon. Within the lagoon and in the scrub near the shore white and blue herons and some other seabirds make their home. The turtles that are numerous here bring up their young in the lagoon. Visitors can reach Manuae only by boat at irregular intervals.

### Takutea

Takutea is an oval sand island (area 2.2 sq km) surrounded by a coral reef. It is planted with coconut palms, which, since Takutea is uninhabited, are looked after from Atiu.

## Northern Cook Islands

The atolls in the northern group consist of narrow elongated reef islands (*motus*), reaching a maximum height of 3–6 m above sea level, set round a central lagoon. Some of the *motus* were once larger, as old beach defences and cliff lines show, but have been partly destroyed by tidal waves resulting from hurricanes (as, for example, in 1942). On the seaward side the beaches have been raised by the shingle and boulders thrown up by the surf and by beach defences; on the lagoon side they fall away gently. The concave coastline of many atolls is the result of displacements of the reef and submarine faults. The gaps in the atoll are mostly narrow and very shallow. There are anchorages for larger vessels within the lagoon only on Penrhyn and Suwarrow. The islands receive necessary supplies from Rarotonga in small vessels that call several times a year and on their return voyage carry the islands' produce, mainly coconuts and copra.

The larger buildings on the islands (churches, administrative offices, schools) are built of coralline limestone, which offers protection against the storm tides that can sweep over these low islands. Other buildings are mainly of wood and roofed with corrugated iron or palm leaves. The Polynesians still prefer the traditional method of construction, adapted to the climate, using pandanus wood and leaves. Rainwater is collected in large cisterns to meet local needs. Apart from rats and mice there are no wild animals on the islands. Pigs and poultry are kept for domestic consumption. Large numbers of seabirds nest on most of the islands, particularly on Suwarrow. Outside the reefs there are good fishing grounds.

### Penrhyn
Penrhyn is the largest atoll in the Cook Islands, with an area of 9.8 sq km. There are three passages through the reef, which has two *motus* of some size on the south-west side and numerous smaller ones to the north, east and south. Near the western passage through the reef is Omoka village, the chief place on the islands, with public buildings and

administrative offices. Tautua village, the second-largest settlement, lies 14 km from Omoka on the opposite side of the lagoon.

### Manihiki
Manihiki (5.3 sq km) is one of the most beautiful atolls in the Cook Islands. It resembles Aitutaki in its triangular conformation. The lagoon is surrounded by a continuous reef, with no navigable passages through it. The two *motus*, which are among the longest in the group, rise no higher than 5 m above sea level. The water between individual *motus* is rarely more than 1 m deep. The chief place on the island is Tauhunu village, which has the necessary public buildings and a shed for storing coconut products. There is a smaller village, which can be reached only by boat over the lagoon, at the northern tip of the atoll. Visitors can see round the pearl farm in the lagoon.

### Rakahanga
Rakahanga (4.04 sq km) is square in form. There are only shallow passages through the surrounding reef. The long and relatively broad reef islands have been broken up into smaller *motus* only near the gaps in the reef. There are broad sandy beaches on the north-eastern shore of the atoll; elsewhere the beaches are of shingle, sometimes very coarse. The only village with shops is to the south-west.

### Palmerston
Palmerston (2 sq km) is an irregularly shaped atoll with 35 *motus*. The shallow lagoon is surrounded by a continuous reef with no passages of any depth. Only one of the *motus* is permanently inhabited. Many buildings in the neat little village were built with timber from shipwrecks. In addition to public buildings such as the church and the radio station there are rainwater tanks for collecting the community's water supply. The lagoon is shallow and suitable only for small outboard motorboats and canoes.

### Pukapuka
Pukapuka (1.2 sq km), also known as Danger Island, is a triangular atoll consisting of three *motus* and a sandbank. Motu Kotawa and Motu Ko are uninhabited but are under cultivation. On Motu Pukapuka are three

small villages (Roto, Yato and Ngake) of low houses and huts. Roto is the main centre, with the post office, church, administrative offices and shops. Here too are substantial houses built of wood and coralline limestone. The only vehicles on the island are bicycles. The shallow lagoon is suitable only for motorboats or outrigger boats.

25 km south-east of Pukapuka is Tima Reef, a small flat coral island only 450 m across. It is believed to be a fragment of the Pukapuka atoll, which was formerly much larger.

### Nassau

The oval sand island of Nassau (1.2 sq km) is covered by chains of dunes up to 9 m high and surrounded by a broad reef platform ranging in width between 90 and 130 m, which makes landing on the island extremely dangerous. The island has large coconut plantations, and in the swampy depressions between the dunes taro is grown. There are a number of springs of fresh water. The land on Nassau is worked from the neighbouring island of Pukapuka.

### Suwarrow

This atoll has the form of an irregular circle. Its small size (0.4 sq km) and few *motus* are the result of the destruction caused by violent whirlwinds within the last hundred years. The atoll was uninhabited until the mid-1960s, when an Englishman named T Neal settled here and lived as a hermit for more than 10 years. The population has now risen to 10.

# Practical
# Information
# A to Z

# Practical Information

## Air Travel

### International airports

**Auckland**
Auckland International Airport
24 km south of city centre
Half-hourly shuttle bus service between
airport and downtown terminal (journey
time 45 minutes); taxis.

**Christchurch**
Christchurch International Airport
11 km north-west of city, at Harewood
Shuttle bus service to and from airport;
taxis. Information from:
AIR NEW ZEALAND
☎ *(03) 3795200*

**Wellington**
Wellington International Airport
9 km south-east, near Lyall Bay
To and from airport: shuttle bus service;
taxis. Information from:
AIR NEW ZEALAND
☎ *(04) 4952910*

**Cook Islands (Rarotonga)**
Rarotonga International Airport
Information from:
AIR NEW ZEALAND
☎ *26302*

Note: passengers flying with Air New
Zealand have the option of a stopover in
Rarotonga. Air New Zealand flies Los
Angeles–Honolulu–Rarotonga–Auckland.

### Domestic airports

In addition to New Zealand's three
international airports a number of
important airports serve as regional hubs
for domestic flights: on the North Island
Rotorua, Hamilton and Palmerston
North; on the South Island Nelson,
Queenstown and Dunedin.
    Other New Zealand airports are: on
the North Island Kaitaia, Kerikeri,
Whangarei, Tauranga, Whakatane,
Gisborne, New Plymouth, Wanganui,
Napier/Hastings and Paraparaumu; on
the South Island Takaka, Motueka,
Blenheim, Westport, Hokitika, Mount

Cook, Timaru, Wanaka, Milford Sound,
Te Anau and Invercargill.

**Cook Islands**
**Niue**
Rarotonga, the principal island in the
Cook Islands group, is included in Air
New Zealand's network of services. From
Rarotonga Polynesian Airlines fly to the
other islands in the archipelago and to
Niue, using smaller aircraft.

### Airlines

**New Zealand airlines**
The leading New Zealand airline is **Air
New Zealand**, which flies both
international and domestic services. Its
international services include one-stop
flights to and from London Heathrow
via Los Angeles. It occupies a dominant
position in domestic services, flying to
and from 31 domestic airports as well as
the Cook Islands.

**Ansett New Zealand** flies to a number of
airports in New Zealand, Australia and
other neighbouring countries.

The **Mount Cook Airline** flies to major New
Zealand airports, particularly tourist
centres, and also to many smaller places.
It also does air tours and charter flights.
    A number of smaller regional airlines
mainly provide connecting services with
the major airlines and also do charter
flights.

**Information and reservations**
AIR NEW ZEALAND
Head Office, Private Bag 92007,
Auckland
☎ *(09) 3573000, fax (09) 3362649, email
info@airnz.co.nz, www.airnz.co.nz*
United Kingdom
☎ *(020) 87412299*
United States
☎ *(800) 9267255 (freephone reservation)*
Canada
☎ *(800) 6635494 (freephone reservation)*
ANSETT NEW ZEALAND
Head Office: PO Box 4168, Auckland
☎ *(09) 5268300, fax (09) 5268400, email
international@ansett.co.nz,
www.ansett.co.uk*

MOUNT COOK AIRLINE
Head Office, PO Box 4644, Christchurch
☎ *(0800) 800737 (freephone reservation)*

### Polynesian Airlines
Polynesian Airlines serve the Cook
Islands and the island of Niue, and also
provide connections with major New
Zealand and foreign airlines.

### Foreign airlines
The main foreign airlines flying to
Auckland, Wellington or Christchurch
(☞Arriving) are Air Pacific, British
Airways, Cathay Pacific, Garuda
Indonesia, Malaysia Airlines, Qantas,
Royal Tongan Airlines, Singapore
Airlines, Thai International and United
Airlines.
   British Airways have one-stop flights
from London to Auckland, with fast
airside transfer at Los Angeles.
Information from:
BRITISH AIRWAYS
New Zealand head office, 191 Queen
Street, Auckland
☎ *(09) 3568690*

### Air passes and discounts
The three New Zealand airlines offer
various special rates for visitors. The
Explore New Zealand Air Pass, which is
valid on all domestic flights on Air New
Zealand, Mount Cook Airline, Eagle Air
and Air Nelson, consists of 3–8 flight
coupons offering a considerable
reduction on standard fares. The pass
must be bought before leaving home
along with a ticket to New Zealand.
   The Mount Cook Airline has the Kiwi
Air Pass, which covers an unlimited
number of flights on its whole network,
though each route may be flown only
once.
   Ansett New Zealand has a variety of
special rates, including the Discover New
Zealand Tariff, which gives a reduction
of 20 per cent.

### Departure tax
A departure tax (airport tax; at present
NZ$25) is payable by all passengers
leaving airports in New Zealand (and the
Cook Islands) for foreign destinations.

### Private flying
Light aircraft can be hired by visitors
holding a pilot's licence and an English
radio-telephony certificate after a check
on their competence. For information
enquire locally.

## Arriving

The majority of visitors to New Zealand
go by air. Some cruise ships call in at
New Zealand ports, but there are no
longer regular passenger services by sea
from either Europe or North America.
   From the United States the most
frequent services are from Los Angeles;
there are also some flights from San
Francisco and other American airports.
From Europe there is a choice of routes –
either westward via the United States
(Los Angeles and Honolulu) or eastward
via Hong Kong, Singapore or other
intermediate points. The most
convenient route from Britain, flown by
British Airways and Air New Zealand, is
from London Heathrow via Los Angeles
to Auckland.

### International airports
New Zealand's leading international
airport is Auckland (☞Air Travel). Some
airlines also fly to Wellington (North
Island) or Christchurch (South Island).

### Stopovers
A flight to New Zealand from Europe or
North America is long and tiring. Most
airlines allow one or more stopovers on
the way. Stopovers on the western route
from Europe are possible, for example, at
Los Angeles, Honolulu, Tahiti, Fiji,
Western Samoa, Tonga and the Cook
Islands, and on the eastern route at
Singapore, Bangkok, Denpasar
(Indonesia), Kuala Lumpur (Malaysia),
Hong Kong, Seoul (South Korea) and
Tokyo.
   Since a flight from Europe to New
Zealand involves travelling halfway
round the world, it is possible, with a
round-the-world ticket offered by Air
New Zealand and other airlines, to make
a complete circuit of the globe by taking
the eastward route on the outward
journey and the westward route when
flying home, or vice versa.

### Foreign airlines
The principal foreign airlines flying to
Auckland, Wellington or Christchurch
are:
Air Pacific (Los Angeles–Fiji–Auckland/
   Christchurch)
British Airways (London–Los Angeles–
   Auckland)
Cathay Pacific (Frankfurt/Zurich–Hong
   Kong–Auckland)
Garuda Indonesia (Berlin/Frankfurt/

# Air Services

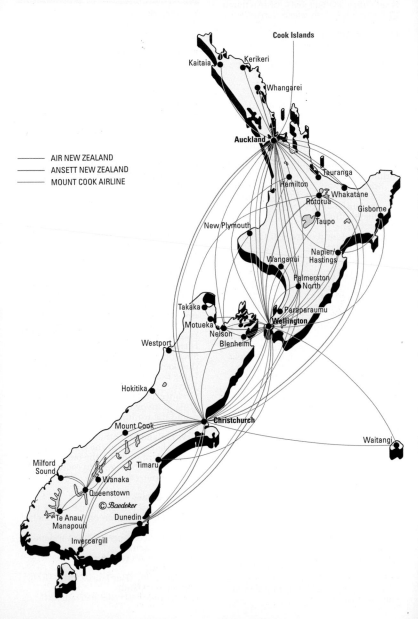

Munich/Zurich–Denpasar–Auckland)
Malaysia Airlines (Frankfurt/Munich/
Zurich–Kuala Lumpur–Auckland)
Qantas (Frankfurt/Zurich–Hong
Kong/Bangkok/Singapore/Bali–Sydney–
Auckland/Christchurch)
Royal Tongan Airlines (Los Angeles–
Honolulu–Tongatapu–Auckland–
Sydney)
Singapore Airlines (Frankfurt/Berlin/
Zurich–Singapore–Auckland/
Christchurch)
Thai International (Frankfurt/Zurich–
Bangkok–Sydney–Auckland)

### Jet lag
To combat jet lag it is advisable to avoid
high-protein food on the flight and
drink plenty of liquid (but not too much
alcohol). To get into the new daily
rhythm it is best, on arrival in New
Zealand, not to go to bed until the
evening, after an easily digestible meal.

### Baggage
Before leaving home it is advisable to
check on the free baggage allowance.
Some airlines have a fairly low limit.

### Airport transfer
For transfers between the airport and
your hotel there are service buses, taxis
and shuttle buses (usually large taxis)
with a fixed and very reasonable charge.

### Return flight
You should confirm your return flight at
least 72 hours in advance, otherwise the
booking is cancelled. It is advisable to
check in 2 hours before departure, since
some airlines tend to overbook.

## Beaches

### Secluded beaches
Seafronts lined with high-rise hotels,
massed ranks of beach umbrellas and
sunbathers are rare – so far – in New
Zealand. Most beaches are secluded and
uncrowded, and usually enclosed by lush
vegetation. There are still many little
bays and inlets where you will scarcely
see another human being all day.

### Sandy beaches
New Zealand's sandy beaches show a
wide spectrum of colour – black volcanic
sand on the west coast, white calcareous
sand in subtropical Northland, pinkish-
red sand on the Coromandel Peninsula,

golden sand at the northern tip of the
South Island.

### Popular beaches
It is almost impossible to list all of New
Zealand's bathing beaches. The following
places are where bathing is a particular
delight:

**North Island** Bay of Islands, Bay of Plenty,
Hawke's Bay near Napier, Hot Water
Beach and Hahei on the Coromandel
Peninsula, Ninety Mile Beach at the
northern tip of the North Island, Orewa
Beach near Auckland.

**South Island** Banks Peninsula, beaches at
the northern tip of the island in the Abel
Tasman National Park, round Nelson and
in the Marlborough Sounds, at the
Moeraki Boulders, round Dunedin
(particularly Tunnel Beach), Papatowai
and Purakanui Bay in the Catlins, on
Stewart Island and round Christchurch
(particularly Sumner Beach and Taylor's
Mistake).

### Season
The bathing season is from the end of
October to the beginning of March. On
beaches in the north and east of the
North Island water temperatures reach
20°C or more. On the most popular
beaches in the South Island, for example
in Golden Bay, Tasman Bay and the
Marlborough Sounds and round
Christchurch, water temperatures are
usually around 18°–20°C.

### Nude bathing
Nude bathing is, in general, frowned on
in New Zealand. Even topless bathing or
sunbathing is not generally acceptable.

### Dangers
Some of the most popular beaches have
lifeguards but in many places bathers are
left on their own. Great caution is
required on long beaches exposed to the
open sea, since there are sometimes
dangerous currents.
    Sandflies, which can give very painful
bites, can be troublesome, particularly in
the late afternoon and evening.

## Camping

New Zealand is an ideal country for
tourists who like to get about on their
own with a tent or caravan. The roads

are good and there is little traffic. There are well over 500 official campsites, but also plenty of scope for camping without using the official sites. Wild camping is permitted provided that permission is asked from the owner of the land and the regulations about the disposal of waste are observed.

Information about current regulations can be obtained from offices of Tourism New Zealand or from car rental firms (☛Car Rental) that hire camper vans (RVs).

### Campsites

There is no lack of campsites in New Zealand. Even quite small places have sites for tents and caravans, ranging from sites with basic facilities to motor camps provided with every amenity. The sites – usually well situated – are clean and tidy and well equipped with facilities (communal kitchens, refrigerators, washing machines, driers). Motor camps have power sockets for camper vans and arrangements for the disposal of waste. There may also be accommodation for people travelling without either a tent or camper van, ranging from a modest cabin to a comfortable (and relatively expensive) holiday apartment.

### DoC campsites

The 200 or so Department of Conservation (DoC) campsites have usually only the most basic facilities but compensate for this by the beauty of their settings. They are also fairly cheap.

### Charges

Since most campsites are run by local authorities the charges are relatively low. On the best sites the charge for two people with a camper van is at present around $30 per night. Average rates per person per night are around $10 (tent), $10–20 (camper van), $15–50 (cabin) and $40–100 (holiday apartment).

### Lists of sites

The Camp and Cabin Association and the New Zealand Automobile Association publish complete lists of all campsites in New Zealand, updated annually. The Department of Conservation also produces an annual list of its sites.

CAMP AND CABIN ASSOCIATION OF NEW ZEALAND

4A Kanawa Street, Waikanae

DEPARTMENT OF CONSERVATION

PO Box 10–420, Wellington (site list also obtainable through Tourism New Zealand offices; ☛Information).
☎ www.nzcamping.co.nz,
www.nzcamping@clear.net.nz

### Camping in the wild

Tents may be pitched and camper vans parked anywhere in New Zealand except where there is a 'No camping' sign. No more than 7 days may be spent in the same place. As a matter of politeness the farmer or owner of the land should be asked for permission, and the site must be left clean and tidy.

### Spirit stoves

Methylated spirits may be used in spirit stoves but not white spirit.

## Car Rental

### Car rental firms

International car-rental firms such as Avis, Hertz and Budget operate in New Zealand and have offices at the international airports and elsewhere. They offer advantageous deals, which can be booked before leaving home. There are also many local rental firms, among the largest of which are Maui and NZ Rent-a-Car. A list of recommended car rental firms can be obtained from Tourism New Zealand offices (☛Information).

### Booking

The minimum age for renting a vehicle is 21. A valid driving licence must be produced (United Kingdom, United States, Canadian and Australian licences, among many others, are accepted in New Zealand).

It is cheaper to book through one of the international car-rental firms before leaving home, and it is advisable, particularly during the main holiday season, to book well in advance.

Rental charges vary according to the time of year, the type of vehicle and the period of hire. Currently the minimum charge per week (including unlimited mileage, tax and insurance) is of the order of NZ$400. There is also the additional cost of GST (goods and sales tax) as well as any supplementary insurance required. (It is advisable to take out insurance against the breakage of glass, which is usually not covered and is liable to occur on New Zealand's many gravel roads).

### Deposit

When hiring a car or camper van a deposit of around NZ$500 is required; this can be met by production of a credit card.

### One-way rental

There is no difficulty, moreso with the larger rental firms, in arranging one-way hire without additional charge, for example between Auckland and Christchurch. The vehicle can be returned to the firm's depot at Wellington (North Island) or Picton (South Island) and a new one picked up on the other side.

### Insurance

Before signing the rental agreement you should check which roads may be used: on some roads there is no insurance cover.

### Fly/drive

Travel operators and airlines offer attractive fly/drive packages that include flights, hire of car or camper van and accommodation, if required, in hotels or motels. Visitors are then free to choose their own route.

### Rental vehicles

Many types of vehicle are available for hire, from small cars to limousines (with or without driver) and all-terrain vehicles.

### Camper vans (RVs)

A camper van is an ideal vehicle for a touring holiday in New Zealand. You are relatively independent and can spend the night almost wherever you like, either in open country or on one of the numerous campsites. The Maui, Newmans and Mount Cook rental firms offer a wide choice of camper vans (from NZ$150 upwards per day) and rather larger motor homes. The condition of these vehicles, however, sometimes leaves much to be desired: poor insulation, defective heating, inadequate water containers, no waste-water tank, no mosquito screens on the windows to provide protection against the bloodthirsty sandflies are not uncommon defects. And the hard suspension gives anyone travelling in the living compartment an uncomfortable ride.

### Motorcycles

Motorcycles are also available for hire and are much in demand during the New Zealand summer. A helmet can be hired at an extra charge of NZ$20.

### Buying a car

For a stay of more than 2 months it may be worthwhile to buy rather than hire a car or motorcycle. You may find attractive offers in the car fair held in Auckland (Newmarket district) every Saturday morning. Before buying it is essential to check that the car has a new WoF (warrant of fitness). Selling the car at the end of your stay can be a time-consuming business. Some second-hand car dealers, however, are prepared to agree on a price at which they will buy the car back.

## Children

Apart from the long flight, a holiday in New Zealand has a great deal to offer families with children, in particular plenty of open space where children can play without danger from traffic or wild animals. Even small places have children's playgrounds, and in restaurants there are children's menus and high chairs as a matter of course.

Children are particularly at home on the beaches of the Coromandel Peninsula, the Hauraki Gulf, Great Barrier Island, the Marlborough Sounds and the northern tip of the South Island.

## Attractions for children

Royal Albatross Colony
Taiaroa Head, Otago Peninsula
Here albatrosses can be watched nesting, sitting on their eggs and flying.
Admission charge.
☎ *(03) 4780499, fax (03) 4780575*
◉ *Dec.–Aug.*

Kelly Tarlton's Antarctic Encounter and Underwater World
23 Tamaki drive, Auckland
Admission charge.
☎ *(09) 5280603, fax (09) 5285175, www.new-zealand.com/kellytarltons*
◉ *Daily 9am–9pm.*

Paradise Valley
Paradise Valley Road, Rotorua
A park with animals from many parts of the world. Visitors are allowed into the lion cubs' enclosure when they are being fed. Children should be carefully

watched so that they don't get into any danger. Admission free, but a voluntary contribution is asked for.
☎ *(07) 3489667, fax (07) 3493359*
🕐 *Daily 9am–7pm.*

PENGUIN PLACE
Dunedin
Yellow-eyed penguins and seals can be seen in their natural surroundings. Previous notice required to tourist information office, Dunedin; admission free.

## Conversions

To convert metric to imperial multiply by the imperial factor; e.g. 100 km equals 62 mi. (100 × **0.62**).

**Linear measure**

| | |
|---|---|
| 1 m | **3.28** ft |
| | **1.09** yds |
| 1 km (1000 m) | **0.62** mi. |

**Square measure**

| | |
|---|---|
| 1 sq m | **1.2** sq yds |
| | **10.76** sq ft |
| 1 ha | **2.47** acres |
| 1 sq km (100 ha) | **0.39** sq mi. |

**Capacity**

| | |
|---|---|
| 1 litre (1000 ml) | **1.76** pints |
| | **2.11** US pints |
| 1 kg (1000 grams) | **2.21** pounds |
| 1 tonne (1000 kg) | **0.98** ton |

**Temperature**

| °C | °F | °C | °F |
|---|---|---|---|
| –5 | 23 | 20 | 68 |
| 0 | 32 | 25 | 77 |
| 5 | 41 | 30 | 86 |
| 10 | 50 | 35 | 95 |
| 15 | 59 | 40 | 104 |

## Crime

New Zealand's crime rate is, surprisingly, relatively high. Tourists have so far been little troubled, but it is advisable for visitors, particularly those travelling by car or camper van, to take sensible precautions. Break-ins to cars have considerably increased in recent years. In hotels, motels and other holiday accommodation the safes should be used for keeping valuable documents and other items. Jewellery is best left at home.

## Currency

New Zealand's unit of currency is the New Zealand dollar (NZ$1 = 100 cents). There are notes for 5, 10, 20, 50 and 100 dollars and coins in denominations of 1, 2, 5, 10, 20 and 50 cents and 1 and 2 dollars.

### Banks
Banks are open Mon.–Fri. 9.30am–4.30pm. There are bank branches at airports and almost every large shopping centre.

### Currency regulations
There are no restrictions on the import or export of either New Zealand or foreign currency in the form of banknotes, coins, traveller's cheques or other means of payment.

### Changing money
There are exchange offices as airports and seaports. It is better to change most of your money in New Zealand rather than at home, since you will get a better exchange rate in New Zealand, but some money should be changed before leaving home in order to avoid the long queues at the airport.
    Any surplus New Zealand money left at the end of your stay should be changed in plenty of time, particularly if your departure is at night. You are unlikely to get a good rate for New Zealand money outside New Zealand.

### Credit cards
Credit cards – particularly American Express, Diners Club, MasterCard (Eurocard) and Visa – are a common form of payment in New Zealand. A credit card is also useful when you are hiring a car, since it can be used in place of a deposit.

### Traveller's cheques
Traveller's cheques denominated in New Zealand dollars can be cashed in banks, hotels, restaurants and many shops. Some banks and large hotels also accept traveller's cheques denominated in British sterling or American dollars.

### Cash
Cash in any currency can be exchanged in New Zealand.

### Currency for a long stay
If you are spending some time in New

Zealand it is worth while opening a giro account with the Bank of New Zealand. You can then draw cash at any branch of the bank in New Zealand, and in the meantime your money can earn interest.

### Loss of money
If you lose traveller's cheques or a credit card you should inform the police and the appropriate bank as soon as possible. If you are left without money your embassy or consulate will help (☛Embassies and Consulates).

### Prices
Prices in New Zealand are comparable with those in Europe, though imported goods are more expensive. Two people with average standards of expenditure will spend perhaps NZ$250 to $350 per day for food, car hire and accommodation in a motel.

### Goods and services tax
Goods and services tax (GST) is payable on all goods and services; the current rate is 12½ per cent.

## Customs Regulations

In addition to personal effects, visitors over the age of 17 are allowed the following concessions, free of duty and tax: 200 cigarettes or 50 cigars or 250 grams of tobacco, or a mixture of all three not weighing more than 250 grams; 4.5 litres of wine and 1.125 litres of spirits or liqueur; and gifts up to a total combined value of NZ$700.

To prevent the importation of animal and plant diseases (from which New Zealand is relatively free) it is unlawful to bring most untreated or unprocessed animal and plant materials into New Zealand, even packaging materials made of natural products.

New Zealand's customs controls are thorough and there are heavy penalties for evasion of duty.

To prevent the spread of epidemics and disease the cabins of aircraft are disinfected before the passengers leave, as is their luggage. Shoes and other items of equipment may be imported only if they are clean.

### Information
Full information about New Zealand's customs and entry regulations is obtainable from Tourism New Zealand offices or:
MINISTRY OF AGRICULTURE AND FISHERIES
PO Box 10–814, Wellington
🌐 www.customs.govt.nz

### Duty-free shopping
Visitors to New Zealand may purchase duty-free goods, which are not liable to local taxes, from airport duty-free shops on arrival and departure. Duty-free shops in downtown Auckland, Wellington and Christchurch will deliver purchases to airport departure lounges.

## Cycling

A cycling tour of New Zealand is an special experience. From north to south of each of the two main islands it is a 2-week trip at an average of 70 km a day. The best time of the year for cycle touring, now becoming increasingly popular, is between October and April, when numbers of cycling enthusiasts, including many from overseas, take to the roads.

Visitors contemplating a cycle tour in New Zealand should be fit and in good training, for the roads are often winding, sometimes narrow and not infrequently very hilly. They must also be prepared to contend with almost permanent wind and showers, which, though usually brief, can be very heavy. The main roads are mostly asphalted but minor roads – for example New Zealand's highest road, from Arrow Junction to Wanaka, east of Queenstown – are often merely gravel tracks. Cities and busy main roads are best avoided, both because of the traffic fumes and because bus and lorry drivers tend to overtake cyclists by very narrow margins. The best plan is load your bicycle on to some form of public transport and head for quieter roads.

### Helmets
It has been compulsory since 1994 for cyclists to wear helmets.

### Bicycle rental
Bicycles can be rented in almost every New Zealand town, costing between NZ$15 and NZ$25 per day. Service facilities and spare parts are readily available in larger towns.

### Bringing your own bicycle
Your bicycle should be a sturdy machine with good gears.

In addition to a good bicycle you should have proper equipment: watertight cycle bags, rainproof clothing, headgear, a light tent for emergencies, and a sun cream with a high protection factor.

If you are attached to your own machine you can bring it with you. Most airlines carry bicycles free or at a very reasonable charge.

**Organised cycle tours**

Some specialised travel operators offer cycle tours lasting one or more weeks, with an accompanying vehicle to carry luggage. Information from:

PEDALTOURS
PO Box 37–575, Parnell, Auckland
☎ *(09) 3020968, fax (09) 3020967*
VENTURETREKS
PO Box 37–610, 164 Parnell Road, Parnell, Auckland
☎ *(09) 3799855, fax (09) 3770320*

See Crime; Health (sunburn, sandflies, parasites)

# Diving

New Zealand's 10,000 km coastline offers endless opportunities for scuba divers and snorkellers. The best diving grounds on the North Island are the Poor Knights Islands (a particularly colourful underwater world, visibility up to 70 m) and the Bay of Islands (also good visibility) and on the South Island are Fiordland and Stewart Island (huge forests of seaweed and paua shells). The waters of the Cook Islands, with their numerous reefs of coralline limestone and atolls, are a Mecca for scuba divers. The reefs formed by the calcareous deposits left by tiny marine creatures and the lagoons they enclose are a biotope inhabited by vividly coloured marine life.

Hazards to watch out for, however, are dangerous and poisonous denizens of the sea like moray eels and sea snakes.

Exploring wrecks is also a popular activity. Round the islands approximately 50 ships lie on the seabed, including the Greenpeace ship *Rainbow Warrior* and the Russian cruise ship *Mikhail Lermontov*, which sank in the Marlborough Sounds in 1986.

**Protection of nature**

Some areas round the coasts are now statutorily protected, and scuba diving and snorkelling in these areas is strictly controlled. The hunting and killing of marine animals is prohibited in some areas. Certain biotopes that are particularly endangered may not be entered, or may be entered only with special permission.

**Scuba diving**

In New Zealand and in the Cook Islands there are well-equipped diving centres that are of particular help to visitors who have come by air. If you have brought your own equipment you may need an adaptor for air cylinders of a different type. When hiring scuba equipment you will usually be asked for a certificate of competence.

**Rainbow Warrior**

The wreck of the Greenpeace ship *Rainbow Warrior*, which was sunk in Auckland harbour by French secret agents in 1985, was towed to the Bay of Islands and sunk in Matauri Bay at a depth of 26 m. The wreck is now overgrown with marine flora and provides a home for a variety of sea creatures. There are organised diving trips from Paihia (day trips, with two dives). Information from:

PAIHIA DIVE HIRE AND CHARTER LTD
PO Box 210, Bay of Islands
☎ *(09) 4027551*

**Goat Island Marine Reserve**

This marine reserve at Leigh, north of Auckland, is a happy hunting ground for scuba divers and snorkellers. At quite a shallow depth and with excellent visibility a great variety of underwater life (particularly fish) can be observed at close quarters.

**Information**

NEW ZEALAND UNDERWATER ASSOCIATION
PO Box 875, Auckland
☎ *(09) 6233252, fax (09) 6323523, email nz@nzunderwater.org.nz, www.nzunderwater.org.nz*

# Electricity

Electricity is supplied throughout New Zealand at 230/240 volts, 50 hertz, though most hotels and motels have 110 volt sockets for electric razors. For all other apparatus an adaptor will be required, since power sockets take only

Australian-type plugs with three flat prongs.

# Embassies and Consulates

## New Zealand diplomatic and consular offices

### United Kingdom
High Commission, New Zealand House, Haymarket, London SW1Y 4TQ
☎ *(020) 79308422, fax (020) 78394580*

### United States
Embassy, 37 Observatory Circle NW, Washington DC 20008
☎ *(202) 3284848, fax (202) 6675227, email nz@nzemb.org*
Consulates in Chicago, Houston, Los Angeles, New York, Salt Lake City, San Diego, San Francisco and Seattle

### Canada
High Commission, Suite 727, Metropolitan House, 99 Bank Street, Ottawa, Ontario K1P 6G3
☎ *(613) 2385991, fax (613) 2385707, email nzhcott@istar.ca*
Consulate in Vancouver

### Australia
High Commission, Commonwealth Avenue, Canberra ACT 2600
☎ *(6) 2704211, fax (6) 2733194, email nzhccba@dynamite.com.au*
Consulates in Brisbane, Melbourne and Sydney

## Diplomatic and consular offices in New Zealand

### United Kingdom
High Commission, 44 Hill Street, Thorndon
Wellington
☎ *(04) 4726049, fax (04) 4711974 (consular), www.brithighcom.org.nz*
Consulates in Auckland and Christchurch

### United States
Embassy, 29 Fitzherbert Terrace, Thorndon, Wellington
☎ *(04) 4722068, fax (04) 4723537*
Consulates in Auckland and Christchurch

### Canada
High Commission, 61 Molesworth Street, Wellington
☎ *(04) 4739577, fax (04) 4712082, email wlgtn@dfait-maeci.gc.ca*
Consulate in Auckland

### Australia
High Commission, 72–78 Hobson Street, Thorndon, Wellington
☎ *(04) 4736411, fax (04) 4987103 (consular)*
Consulate in Auckland

# Emergencies

☎ *111*
In the larger towns dial 111 for police, fire or ambulance services.

Other emergency numbers can be found at the beginning of the local telephone directory. In country areas the emergency numbers are shown on the telephone keypad.

# Events

### A and P shows
Visitors will enjoy a visit to one of the A and P shows (agricultural and pastoral shows) – more than a hundred all told – that are held at many places in New Zealand throughout the year. In the early days of settlement these shows were important occasions for farmers in the surrounding area, enabling them to learn about the latest farming methods and equipment. Some of them have taken on the aspect of a popular festival. There are often special events such as sheepdog trials and sheep-shearing competitions.

### Information
Events are listed in the *What to See and Do Guide*, available from Tourism New Zealand offices.

# Calendar of events

### January
**Auckland** Annual Yachting Regatta (end Jan./beginning Feb.). The regatta celebrates the anniversary of the foundation of the town on January 29th 1840: the sporting event of the year, in which over 1000 boats take part.
Kiwi Dragon Boat Festival

Cup Day
**Christchurch and Napier** Summertime
Festival
**Glenorchy** Horse racing and rodeo
(beginning of January; north of Lake
Wakatipu)
**Kataia** Far North Rodeo and A and P
Show
**Levin** Horowhenua A and P Show on
Lake Horowhenua (January 24th/25th;
between Wellington and Palmerston
North)
**Te Anau** Fiordland Summer Festival
**Waipu** (Northland) Highland Games and
New Zealand Championship Heavy
Field Events (New Year's Day)
**Wellington** National tennis
championships

**February**
**Bay of Islands** Waitangi Day (New Zealand
Day; February 6th) commemorating
the signing of the Treaty of Waitangi in
1840
New Zealand National Deep Sea
Fishing Competition
**Brancott Estate** (between Nelson and
Blenheim) Marlborough Wine and
Food Festival (beginning of February)
**Napier** Art Deco Weekend: jazz and art
festival
**Speight's Coast to Coast Triathlon** (mid-
February) from Kumara Beach on the
west coast to Sumner Beach, near
Christchurch, on the east coast: a
running, cycling and kayaking race of
over 200 km.

**March**
**Auckland** Round the Bays Run: one of the
largest mass runs in the world, with
70,000 runners
**Hastings** Highland Games (Easter)
**Hokitika** Wild Food Festival: food and
drink of the early settlers
**Masterton** Golden Shears sheep-shearing
competition (beginning of March)
**Ngaruawahia** Maori Canoe Regatta at
(between Hamilton and Auckland).
**Taupo** Ironman Triathlon: the second
oldest competition of this type in the
world (first Sat. in March)
**Wellington** International Festival of the
Arts (in even-numbered years): classical
and modern music, ballet, poetry
readings, arts and crafts

**April**
**Arrowtown** Autumn Festival (mid-April)
**Dargaville** Kumara Festival
**Taihape** Gumboot Day

**May**
**Lake Rotorua** Fletcher Challenge
Marathon (beginning of May)
**Te Puke** (kiwi capital of the world) Kiwi
Festival (mid-May)

**June**
**Christchurch** DB Draught Marathon
**Hamilton** National Agricultural Field Days
(mid-June): New Zealand's most
important agricultural show
**Wellington** Film Festival

**July**
**Queenstown** Winter Festival (mid-July)

**August**
**Invercargill** Solo Highland Piping
Championship
**Nelson** Festival of Fashion and Art
**Wellington** Boat Show

**September**
**Alexandra** Spring Festival
New Zealand Luge Championships, at
changing venues
**Rotorua** International Trout-Fishing
Competition (mid-September)
**Wanaka** Snow Festival at .

**October**
AMP New Zealand Open Golf
Championship (October/November)
**Auckland** International Marathon (end
October)
**Greymouth** (on west coast of South
Island) Whitebait Festival
**New Plymouth** Taranaki Rhododendron
Festival (end October/beginning
November)
**Palmerston** North International Orchid
Show
**Queenstown** Freshup Alpine Ironman
Triathlon

**November**
**Christchurch** Canterbury Show (first week
in November): 3-day agricultural show
with horse racing
**Otago** Goldfields Heritage Celebrations
(mid-November)
**Rotorua** International Trout-Fishing
Tournament

**December**
**Auckland** International Air New
Zealand/Shell Golf Open
Pre-Christmas parades by children in the
larger towns

## Ferries

### Wellington–Picton
Ferries ply between Wellington on the North Island and Picton on the South Island; in winter there are at least two crossings daily, in summer up to four. They have comfortable seats on deck and cabins, a restaurant and bar, cinemas, rooms with video games and a children's playroom.

The crossing of the Cook Strait, one of the windiest and most turbulent waterways in the world, takes about 3½ hours. The fare (one-way) is NZ$35 for an adult and for a vehicle, depending on length, from NZ$110. You must arrive at the ferry terminal an hour before departure. Between November and March and on public holidays it is essential to make an advance booking.

### Bluff–Stewart Island
There is a regular ferry service between Bluff, at the southern tip of the South Island, and Halfmoon Bay (Oban) on Stewart Island. On this service too booking is essential in the main holiday season.

### Information and booking
INTERISLANDER
Railway Station, Bunny Street, Wellington
☎ *(04) 4983303, freephone (0800) 802802, fax (04) 4983090, email bookings@tranzrail.co.nz, www.theinterislander.co.nz*

### Boat charter
In all coastal towns boats can be chartered for deep-sea angling expeditions or sailing trips.

In many of the larger ports there are passenger ferries that will take visitors, for example, to Fiordland or some of the sub-Antarctic island groups.

## Cruises

Many of New Zealand's coastal towns, particularly Auckland, Wellington, Christchurch and Dunedin, as well as the Cook Islands (e.g. Atiu, Takutea, Aitutaki, Rarotonga, Palmerston) are ports of call for cruise ships operating in the Pacific, and New Zealand ports are frequently staging posts in cruises in the South Seas. There are also short cruises from the Australian ports of Sydney and Cairns to New Zealand and/or the Cook Islands.

## Food and Drink

### Cuisine
Breakfast in New Zealand is the traditional British breakfast, consisting of eggs and bacon, sausages, or fish with hash browns (fried potatoes). Typically British, too, is the national dish of many New Zealanders – roast lamb with mint sauce and greens. For many years these were the main specialities of New Zealand cuisine. Not surprisingly, therefore, New Zealand cooking, until well into the 1980s, was looked down on by gourmets as a mere variant of the unimaginative cuisine of the home country. Things are now very different. For some time now New Zealand chefs have been going to Europe for training and immigrants from many countries have brought in their national culinary skills and recipes. New Zealand now has a number of gastronomic high spots, and not only foreign speciality restaurants; and there is now a distinctive New Zealand cuisine that gourmets and restaurant critics can appreciate. The basis for it is the wide range of high-quality foodstuffs produced in New Zealand.

## Food

### Lamb
Among the specialities of New Zealand cuisine are various lamb dishes. (How could it be otherwise, with 70 million sheep?) Unlike Europeans, New Zealanders prefer a rather older lamb (a yearling or hogget), which is equally tender but with a rather stronger taste. Visitors should seek out a restaurant that has won the Lamb Award and will offer a wide range of lamb dishes. Particular favourites are lamb chops, lamb's kidneys and lamb's liver, as well as sushi-style lamb balls.

### Beef and pork
Beef and pork feature on the menu in the form of tender and succulent steaks.

### Poultry
New Zealanders are particularly fond of

chicken served in a range of variations. It is a favourite lunch dish.

### Game

Game, particularly venison, is becoming increasingly popular, but it lacks the typical gamey taste, since it comes from roe deer and red deer that have been reared on game farms and are almost tame. Some restaurants also serve wild boar, rabbit and wild duck.

### Fish and seafood

Several dozen species of fish, many of them completely unknown in Europe (for example hapuka, tarakihi and snapper), feature on the New Zealand menu, as do various crustaceans – lobsters, crayfish, shellfish and oysters – and dory. Two particular delicacies are whitebait and toheroa, a rare species of shellfish.

Fish and seafood are usually served fresh, since no part of New Zealand is more than 130 km from the sea. Oysters are usually not 'fresh', being sold without their shells.

New Zealand has the largest trout in the world, but the sale of trout is prohibited by law, so that if you want to eat a trout you must either catch it yourself or go to a restaurant.

### Fruit and vegetables

Due to its good climate and good soil New Zealand produces an enormous range of fruit and vegetables. Succulent accompaniments to the main dish are tamarillos (tree tomatoes), which are little known in Europe, and the kumara, the world's softest and juiciest sweet potato. New Zealanders are health fanatics and many of them have only fruit and vegetables for lunch. Apples, pears, nashis (a cross between apple and pear), strawberries and all kinds of citrus fruits are only a few of the varieties of fruit that are exported worldwide. And of course there is the kiwi fruit, developed in New Zealand from the humble Chinese gooseberry, which is now known all over the world.

### Desserts

A sweet that has become a kind of national dish is the pavlova (named in honour of the Russian ballerina Anna Pavlova, who was a popular star in New Zealand in the 1920s). This consists of a meringue base topped with whipped cream and fruit (particularly kiwi fruit).

Another passion of New Zealanders is ice cream, of which they are said to be the largest consumers in the world.

### Fast food

A sudden pang of hunger can be eased in one of the countless branches of American hamburger and pizza chains. There are also numerous Chinese takeaways and fish and chip shops (the fish usually being hoki). Also very popular are meat pies, served up piping hot from the microwave.

### Hangi

A special gastronomic experience is a meal cooked in a *hangi*, a Maori open-air earth oven. Various kinds of meat (pork, beef, poultry), fish and vegetables (particularly sweet potatoes) are wrapped up in large leaves and laid on a red-hot lava stone in a hole in the ground. The food is then covered with damp cloths and the hole is filled up with earth. After cooking for 1–2 hours the dish is served on the leaves.

Some hotels, particularly in the Rotorua area, offer *hangi* meals, often combined with a Maori show. *Hangi* meals are also put on by various organisations as fund-raisers.

It should be added that a *hangi* meal does not agree with everyone.

### Cheese

Cheese lovers will find plenty to interest them in New Zealand. In recent years creameries and cheese factories have steadily increased the range of New Zealand cheeses, creating new sorts such as Aihette and Kapiti.

### Bread

New Zealand's bread is not its strongest point. Most of it is flabby and lacking in nutrition; it is best suitable for toasting. But here too there are signs of improvement due to increased health consciousness. Well-made bread incorporating unmilled grains is now available, and health stores sell nourishing and satisfying loaves. In the larger towns there are French bakeries selling French white bread (baguettes) and croissants.

## Soft drinks

### Water

Still or slightly carbonated table and

mineral waters are widely available, though tap-water is pure and drinkable.

### Tea
As is to be expected in a country with so many people of British descent, tea is one of New Zealand's most popular drinks.

### Coffee
Coffee does not play a great part in New Zealand life and much of it is instant coffee. There are increasing numbers of cafès, however, offering authentic espresso or cappuccino (though with a dash of cinnamon rather than cocoa on the frothed-up milk).

### Fruit juices
Surely no country in the world has so many different kinds of fruit as New Zealand. Unsurprisingly, therefore, it has a great range of high quality fruit juices, such as apple, pear, cherry, kiwi fruit.

## Alcohol

### Sale of alcohol
Alcoholic drinks can be obtained only in licensed restaurants and hotels and in special shops known as 'bottle stores'. Bottle stores are open Mon.–Sat. until 10pm. Bars are normally open Mon. Sat. 11am–10pm; no alcohol may be supplied on Sunday.

### BYO
Restaurants showing the sign BYO (bring your own) have no licence to serve alcohol, but guests may bring their own wine or beer. There may be a small charge for corkage.

### Beer
New Zealand has one of the highest rates of consumption of beer per head in the world. It is drunk cold, full to the brim, with no head. Almost every pub serves both lager and ale. The best known New Zealand brands are Steinlager, Lion Brown, Lion Red, Rheineck, Speight's and Dominion Brown.

### Wine
See entry

### Restaurants
See entry

## Health

### Inoculations
Inoculations are not required for visitors from Europe, North America and many other countries unless they have travelled by way of a problem area identified by the World Health Organisation.

### Sandflies
New Zealand has no poisonous snakes or other dangerous animals, but it is plagued by sandflies. They seem to have troubled Captain Cook, who mentions them in his account of his voyages. A Maori legend relates that sandflies were created by the goddess Hine Nui Te Po when she saw Fiordland for the first time, fearing that without them people would want to stay for ever in that beautiful region. In areas with high air humidity, along the banks of rivers and on beaches, there can be up to 10 species of these tiny (2 mm long) midges, whose bite is painful and gives rise to an annoying itch. An effective repellent is Dimp; but it should be borne in mind that while it does no harm to the skin it does dissolve plastic. The best plan is to cover up as much as possible, with long trousers and long sleeves.

### Wasps
Recently wasps have also become a problem, particularly in the riparian forests in the north and centre of the South Island. Visitors should carry suitable sprays, creams or antihistamines for treating wasp stings.

### Parasites
Since 1990 numerous rivers and lakes including those of the national parks have become infested with the parasite *Giardia lamblia*, which is spread in human and animal excreta. The parasite finds its way from the mouth into the intestinal tract and soon gives rise to severe diarrhoea. This clears up quickly with suitable drugs. Water from rivers or lakes should always be boiled or chemically purified before drinking. In still waters and springs dangerous micro-organisms may be encountered that enter the body through the ear or nose and may cause meningitis, so it is essential never to submerge one's head.

## Medical care

Medical services in New Zealand are well up to European and North American standards. Even in country areas every place of any size will have a doctor and/or a pharmacist. All hospitals have an accident and emergency service. The larger hotels and motels usually have a doctor on call to deal with emergencies.

### Insurance

Medical care in New Zealand can be expensive (see below), and visitors are strongly advised to take out short-term health insurance for the period of their visit. Cover should include transport home by air if required. Sample charges for medical care:

General practitioner, surgery consultation, ca NZ$50–80
General practitioner, domiciliary visit, ca NZ$50–100
Specialist, consultation, from NZ$80
Dentist, from NZ$60
Hospital stay, per day (public hospital, including doctors' fees), ca NZ$700
Private nursing home, per day (accommodation only), ca NZ$350

### Drugs

Visitors bringing in a quantity of drugs are advised to have a doctor's certificate to avoid possible problems with the New Zealand customs.

### Emergencies

☎ 111

### Accident Information Service

☎ (09) 5290488
This service is available 24 hours a day to provide advice on which doctor to consult; it will arrange house calls.

## Chemists

Chemists are open during normal business hours. Emergency service outside these hours is provided on a rota system, details of which are published in the local press.

## Ozone layer

In recent decades increasing levels of carbon dioxide and fluorocarbons, among many other substances, have risen into the upper atmosphere (the stratosphere, between 11 km and 50 km above the earth) and caused the protective layer of ozone at that height to become steadily thinner. The destruction of the ozone layer is particularly dramatic above the southern hemisphere. Over the South Pole there is now a hole in the ozone layer, the size of which varies with the seasons. From time to time patches of thinner ozone layer extend over New Zealand, where they can remain for a considerable time.

### Sunbathing

The ozone layer normally shields the earth against the short-wave ultraviolet radiation, which is harmful to many organisms. When the ozone layer becomes thinner these ultraviolet rays are able to filter through. The result is an increase in the ultraviolet B rays that are dangerous for the human skin. In this situation visitors who spend hours tanning themselves in the sun are exposing themselves to the probability of sunburn, premature ageing of the skin and a much increased risk of skin cancer.

### Warning system

The New Zealand meteorological service is actively concerned with the problem of the ozone layer. It publishes regular forecasts of the condition of the layer and of cloud cover that may block the ultraviolet B rays. An ultraviolet index has been created that acts as a measure of the intensity of radiation and thus of the danger of sunburn and the risk of skin cancer.

A low index figure means that ultraviolet radiation is low and no particular protective measures are required. At the first warning level, indicating moderate radiation, long periods of sunbathing should be avoided and the skin (particularly of small children) should be protected against the sun. At the second level, indicating high radiation, sunbathing should be avoided altogether and protection against the sun by suitable clothing, sunglasses and sun cream is essential. At the third level, indicating extremely high radiation, sunbathing is dangerous and outdoor activities should be undertaken only with complete protection against the sun for all parts of the body, including the face, the back of the neck, arms and legs.

### Ultraviolet forecasts

The radiation forecasts and warnings of

the New Zealand meteorological service
are broadcast daily on New Zealand radio
and are available by telephone (☎ *0900
999* plus area code). People of different
skin types can then judge how long they
can stay in the sun without risk of
sunburn.

**Advice for sunbathers**
Your skin should be gradually
accustomed to sunlight. Around midday,
when radiation is particularly strong,
you should keep in the shade. The use
of sun creams with a high protection
factor is strongly recommended, and
sunglasses with maximum ultraviolet
protection should be worn. When out
in the sun you should avoid the use of
perfume and decorative cosmetics,
which make the skin more sensitive to
light. When using certain drugs
sunbathing is inadvisable: you should
seek medical advice on this point if
necessary.

## Drinking water

Tap water is safe anywhere in New
Zealand, but bottled table and mineral
waters are available all over the country.

**Warning**
Water from springs, rivers, streams and
lakes should always be boiled before
drinking. In recent years parasites have
been a danger in many parts of the
country (see above).

## Quarantine

Due to the country's remoteness many
kinds of organisms and diseases are
unknown in New Zealand. Accordingly,
the authorities maintain strict control on
the importation of plants and animals.
On arrival in New Zealand visitors must
complete a declaration listing any food
or articles of plant or animal origin they
have brought with them. Even dirty
shoes, clothing and bicycles are regarded
with extreme suspicion. Offending items
may be removed for cleaning,
quarantined or even refused admission.

## Hotels

**Hotel chains**
Luxury hotels belonging to the big

international chains – e.g. Hyatt, Regent,
Sheraton – are found only in large cities
and tourist centres, for example in
Auckland, Rotorua and Christchurch. All
of them are in the highest price
categories.

There are hotels in the upper and
middle price ranges, motels and motor
inns in all the main tourist areas and
beauty spots. Most of them are up to
international standards of comfort and
amenity. Among them are the hotels in
various chains such as Parkroyal and
Travelodge run by the Southern Pacific
Hotel Corporation. The state-run Tourist
Hotel Corporation (THC) hotels are
found in areas of outstanding natural
beauty, for example in some of the
national parks. Many hotels belong to
international chains, making it possible
to arrange bookings or purchase hotel
vouchers before leaving home.

**Small hotels and pubs**
In many provincial towns you will find
small and reasonably priced hotels.
Many pubs also have a few rooms to let,
usually rather noisy. More than three
dozen such establishments have formed
the Pub Beds group.

**Motels**
Visitors who like to cater for themselves
will find what they want in motels,
which are equipped with cooking
facilities, crockery and cutlery, television
and other amenities.

**Lodges**
A lodge in New Zealand offers luxurious
accommodation in a setting of largely
unspoiled natural beauty, combined with
various sport activities, good cooking
and exemplary service – all this, of
course, with a price to match. The cost
of full board ranges between NZ$250 and
NZ$1000 per day.

**Bed and breakfast**
The fastest-growing sector of the hotel
industry is bed and breakfast, a type of
accommodation following the British
model. There are now large numbers of
homes throughout New Zealand offering
bed and breakfast accommodation,
which have joined up to form the
Federation of Bed and Breakfast Hotels.
In many of these houses, with standards
of comfort and amenity ranging between
modest and luxurious, guests are treated
as members of the family.

### ★Heritage Inns of New Zealand
Bed and breakfast accommodation of a special kind is provided in restored houses of the colonial period. More than two dozen such houses have formed an association, the Heritage Inns of New Zealand. A night in one of these houses, some of which are of great elegance, costs between NZ$50 and NZ$200. It is essential to book in advance.

### Qualmark
Tourism New Zealand and the New Zealand Automobile Association have developed the Qualmark classification system. It applies in the first place to the various types of tourist accommodation such as hotels, motels and campsites, which are awarded from one to five stars. It is planned to extend the system to other service providers to tourists, including buses and taxis.

### Tariffs
The price of a double room in modest hotels and motels ranges between NZ$50 and NZ$130 a night; in hotels with high standards of comfort and amenity prices range up to NZ$250 a night; and in luxury hotels and some lodges a charge of several hundred dollars is not unusual.

### Price categories
In the following list hotels are classified in three categories of price (for a double room):

A over $160
B $75–160
C below $75

# North Island hotels (selection)

### Auckland
**ASCOT PARNELL (A)**
36 St Stephen's Avenue
☎ *(09) 3099012, fax (09) 3093729, email ascotparnell@compuserve.com, www.ascotparnell.com*
9 r. Comfortable accommodation in a historic building situated in a side street. The centre of Parnell Village is within easy reach. Smoking is not permitted.

**AUCKLAND CENTRAL BACKPACKERS (C)**
9 Fort Street
☎ *(09) 3584877, fax (09) 3584872, email backpackers@acb.co.nz, www.acb.co.nz*
144 r. (300 beds). Centrally located, this

is Auckland's biggest information exchange for backpackers. Restaurant with harbour view. The rooms are adequate but the place is sometimes noisy.

**BAVARIA GUEST HOUSE (B)**
83 Valley Road, Mount Eden
☎ *(09) 6389641, fax (09) 6389665, email bavaria@xtra.co.nz, www.mysite.extra.co.nz/~bavarian*
11 r. As the name suggests, this comfortable bed and breakfast hotel is German-run.

**BERLIN LODGE (C)**
5A Oaklands Road, Mount Eden
☎ *(09) 6386545*
14 r. Under German-Swiss management.

**★HYATT REGENCY AUCKLAND (A)**
Corner of Princes Street and Waterloo Quadrant
☎ *(09) 3551234, fax (09) 3032932, email auckland@hyatt.co.nz*
275 r. A luxury hotel with an excellent restaurant on the top floor.

**★REGENT (A)**
Albert Street
☎ *(09) 3098888, fax (09) 3796445*
332 r. and suites. Centrally situated. Large and elegantly furnished rooms; best rooms on harbour side. Heated pool on roof.

**THE GREAT PONSONBY BED AND BREAKFAST (B)**
30 Ponsonby Terrace, Ponsonby
☎ *(09) 3765989, fax (09) 3765527, email great.ponsonby@xtra.co.nz, www.ponsonbybnb.co.nz*
11 r. and studios. Attractive accommodation in a prettily restored late 19th c. house.

### Bay of Islands
**★KIMBERLEY LODGE (A)**
Pitt Street, Russell
☎ *(09) 4037090, fax (07) 4037239, www.lodges.co.nz*
5 r. and suites. The most luxurious hotel on the Bay of Islands; magnificent views of Russell and Kororareka Bay.

### Katikati
**★FAINTAIL LODGE (A)**
Rea Road; 4 km south of Katikati (north of Tauranga)
☎ *(07) 5491581, fax (07) 5491417*
12 suites. A well cared for country house, famed for its cuisine.

## Mangatawhiri Valley
### Hôtel du Vin (A)
Mangatawhiri Valley; 60 km south of Auckland
☎ *(09) 2336314, fax (09) 2336215*
46 r. A five-star hotel in a beautiful setting of forests and vineyards. An excellent place for sport activities or merely for relaxation. The restaurant is one of the best in New Zealand.

## Mangonui
### Old Oak Inn (C)
66 Waterfront Drive
☎ *(09) 4060665*
8 r. A small and very comfortable hotel in a handsome historic building. Round the corner is the bus stop of the overland coaches.

## Masterton
### Victoria House (C)
15 Victoria Street
☎ *(06) 3770186, fax (06) 3770186*
6 r. A bed and breakfast hotel near the town centre, in a lovingly restored building built pre-1886.

## Napier
### Edgewater Motor Lodge (B)
359 Marine Parade, Beachfront
☎ *(06) 8351148, fax (06) 8356600*
20 units. A centrally located motel with facilities for guests with disabilities. Well furnished rooms, some of which have a magnificent sea view.

### Pinehaven Travel Hotel (C)
259 Marine Parade
☎ *(06) 8355575, fax (06) 8355575, email pinehaven@napier.co.nz*
6 r. A bed and breakfast hotel with a fine view of the sea. Just round the corner are the railway station and bus station.

## Ngaruawahia
### Brooklands Country Estate (A)
Waingaro, RD 1
☎ *(07) 8254756, fax (07) 8254873*
8 r. A small luxury hotel in the beautiful Waikato region, an hour drive from Auckland. The main building dates from the turn of the 19th c. Golf course.

## Paihia
### Austria Motel (B)
36 Selwyn Road
☎ *(09) 4027480, fax (09) 4027480, email austriamotel@xtra.co.nz*
7 units. Clean and attractive rooms. A short walk from the shops and the seafront.

### Waitangi Resort Hotel (B)
Waitangi National Trust Grounds
☎ *(09) 4027411, fax (09) 4028000*
138 r. The largest hotel north of Auckland; much patronised by coach parties. Some of the rooms are more comfortable and more tastefully appointed than others.

## Pauanui
### Puka Park Resort (A)
Pauanui Beach
☎ *(07) 8648088. fax (07) 8648112, email pukapark@pukapark.co.nz, www.pukapark.co.nz*
50 chalets. This luxury hotel on the Coromandel Peninsula is one of the finest in New Zealand. The chalets are scattered about in the bush – not a single tree had to be felled to make room for them. Service is good, and the restaurant in the main building has an excellent reputation. Nearby is a beautiful beach.

## Rotorua
### Cedar Motor Lodge (B)
312 Fenton Street
☎ *(07) 3490300, fax (07) 3462855*
16 units. This well-appointed motel is particularly suitable for families with children. Each apartment has its own courtyard, 15 apartments with spa.

### ★Sheraton Rotorua (A)
Fenton Street
☎ *(07) 3495200, fax. (07) 3495201*
130 r. and 8 suites. The best rooms are on the top two floors, with magnificent views. The hotel is famed for its *hangi* meals.

## Russell
### Okiato Lodge (A)
James Clendon Place, Okiato Point
☎ *(09) 4037948, fax (09) 4037515*
4 suites. A few minutes' drive from Russell. The suites are furnished in modern/rustic style. Facilities for all types of water sports in the bay.

### Te Maiki Villas (A)
Flagstaff Road
☎ *(09) 4037046, fax (09) 4037106, email te.maiki@xtra.co.nz*
9 villas. Comfortably furnished rooms with fine views of the bay below Flagstaff Hill.

**Taupo**
★HUKA LODGE (A)
Huka Falls Road
☎ (07) 3785791, fax (07) 3780427
17 suites. This stylish lodge sets the standard for all other sport lodges in New Zealand. Radio, television and telephone are banned from all suites.

**Thames**
BRIAN BORU HOTEL (B)
200 Richmond Street
☎ (07) 8686523, fax (07) 8689760
23 r. and 8 apartments. This little hotel occupies a venerable 19th c. building. The owners run tours to little-known spots on the Coromandel Peninsula, and on alternate weeks organise Murder Mystery Weekends.

**Wanaka**
WANAKA HOLIDAY PARK (C)
212 Brownston Street
☎ (03) 4437883, fax (03) 4437883
33 units (flats, cabins, lodge). A few minutes' drive from the town. Open throughout the year. The cabins are well equipped and some have a high standard of amenity. It is less than an hour drive to the Treble Cone skiing area.

**Wellington**
MUSEUM HOTEL DE WHEELS (B)
90 Cable Street; opposite Te Papa National Museum
☎ (04) 3852809, fax (04) 8028909, email reservations@museum-hotel.co.nz, www.museum-hotel.co.nz
36 r. This hotel is in a busy commercial street and is much favoured by business people. As a result it is possible to get reduced rates at weekends.

★PARKROYAL WELLINGTON (A)
Corner of Featherston Street and Grey Street
☎ (04) 4722722, fax (04) 4724724
232 r. and 7 suites. The hotel was opened in 1990. Many people who have stayed here say that it is the best hotel in New Zealand, a reputation due mainly to its excellent service. When booking ask for a room with a sea view.

★PLAZA INTERNATIONAL (A)
148–176 Wakefield Street
☎ (04) 4733900, fax (04) 4733929, email ressies@plazainternational.co.nz, www.plazainternational.co.nz
192 r. An elegant and luxurious hotel.

**TINAKORI LODGE (B)**
182 Tinakori Road, Thorndon
☎ (04) 4733478, fax (04) 4725554
10 r. This bed and breakfast hotel is situated in a quiet street in a historic quarter of the town. The rooms are plain but well appointed.

# South Island hotels (selection)

**Arrowtown**
See Queenstown

**Arthur's Pass**
THE CHALET (B)
Main Road (PO Box 5), Arthur's Pass, Canterbury
☎ (03) 3189236, (03) 3189200, email thechalet@arthurspass.co.nz, www.arthurspass.co.nz
11 r. This bed and breakfast hotel is in the style of a Swiss chalet.

**Christchurch**
ANTRIM GLEN MOTOR INN (B)
22 Riccarton Road
☎ (03) 3480909, fax (03) 3489876
34 r. Pleasant, well-appointed rooms.

KINGSGATE CHRISTCHURCH HOTEL (A)
766 Colombo Street
☎ (03) 3795880, fax (03) 3654806
90 r. A centrally located and well-run hotel. Shopping mall and parks within easy reach.

PACIFIC PARK HOTEL (B)
263 Bealey Avenue; 2km north of the city centre
☎ (03) 3798660, fax (03) 3669973, email helpdesk@pacificpark.co.nz
66 r. The rooms are neat and attractive.

PARKROYAL CHRISTCHURCH (A)
Corner of Durham Street and Kilmore Street
C(03) 3657799, fax (03) 3650082, email reservations@christchurch.parkroyal.co.uk
297 r. Ask for a room with a view of Victoria Square and the river. There are four restaurants.

**Clyde**
OLIVER'S LODGE
34 Sunderland Street
☎ (03) 4492860, fax (03) 4492862
12 r. This comfortable lodge, which will appeal especially to nature lovers, is set in a particularly beautiful part of Central Otago, with excellent facilities for

fishing, riding, shooting, boating and, in winter, skiing.

## Dunedin
### CARGILLS HOTEL (B)
678 George Street
☎ *(03) 4777983, fax (03) 4778098, email cargills@es.co.nz, www.cargills.co.nz*
50 r. Near the city centre. Tastefully appointed rooms.

### SOUTHERN CROSS HOTEL (A)
Corner of Princes Street and High Street
☎ *(03) 4770752, fax (03) 4775776, email cross@es.co.nz*
134 r. Externally this hotel has a nostalgic air of the past, but the interior is modern and equipped with every amenity. Casino.

## Greymouth
### GOLDEN COAST BED AND BREAKFAST (C)
10 Smith Street
☎ *(03) 7687839, fax (03) 7687869*
4 r. This family guesthouse, set in a beautiful garden, is only a short walk from the town centre.

## Invercargill
### ASCOT PARK MOTOR HOTEL (B)
Corner of Tay Street and Racecourse Road
☎ *(03) 2176195, fax (03) 2177002, email ascot@ilt.co.nz*
68 r., 24 motel units. The best hotel in the town, beside a beautiful park.

## Lake Brunner
### LAKE BRUNNER LODGE (A)
Mitchell's Road, Kumara, Westland
☎ *(03) 7380163, fax (03) 7380163*
9 suites. A comfortable lodge on the south side of Lake Brunner, just under an hour drive from Hokitika. It offers a range of outdoor activities, particularly trout fishing.

## Lake Moeraki
### LAKE MOERAKI WILDERNESS LODGE (B)
Hokitika, to the north of Haast
☎ *(03) 7500881, fax (03) 7500882*
20 r. This lodge does not offer the luxury of other hotels in the same price category, but the beauty of its unspoiled natural surroundings fully makes up for this. Guests can fish for trout and observe the rare dwarf penguins.

## Mount Cook village
### ★HERMITAGE AORAKI MOUNT COOK ALPINE VILLAGE (A)
☎ *(03) 4351809, fax (03) 4351879*
104 r. This mountain hotel complex is one of the best of its kind in New Zealand.

### MOUNT COOK TRAVELODGE (B)
☎ *(03) 6271809, fax (03) 4351879*
55 r. This lodge is suitable for mountain walkers and climbers who do not require a high degree of luxury. It has magnificent views of some of the highest peaks in the Southern Alps.

## Nelson
### BEACHSIDE VILLAS (B)
71 Golf Road
☎ *(03) 5485041, fax (03) 5485078, email beachside@clear.net.nz*
6 apartments. Comfortable, tasteful accommodation and a plentiful breakfast including home-baked bread.

### CAMBRIA HOUSE (B)
7 Cambria Street, Nelson
☎ *(03) 5484681, fax (03) 5466649*
5 r. A bed and breakfast hotel in a house dating from 1860. It offers very comfortable accommodation and a peaceful location.

### HECATE HOUSE (C)
181 Nile Street East, Nelson
☎ *(03) 5466890, fax (03) 5466895*
6 r. Small and reserved for women, just a few steps east of the town centre.

## Oamaru
### TOKARAHI HOMESTEAD (A)
47 Dip Hill Road, Tokarahi
☎ *(03) 4312500, fax (03) 4312551, email tokarahi@xtra.co.nz, www.homestead.co.nz*
A pretty 19th c. mansion, about a 30-minute drive north-west of Oamaru in the Kakanui Mountains. Comfortable bed and breakfast accommodation and attentive service. A delicious dinner can be ordered.

## Picton
### ADMIRAL'S LODGE BED AND BREAKFAST HOTEL(B)
22 Waikawa Road
☎ *(03) 5736590, fax (03) 5738318, email admiralb&b@xtra.co.nz, www.nzbnbhotels.com*
10 r. This comfortable bed and breakfast establishment is near the beach and is a short walk from restaurants and shops.

## Queenstown
### LITTLE PARADISE LODGE (C)
Glenorchy Road; 28 km north-west of

Queenstown
☎ *(03) 4426196, fax (03) 4421145*
20 suites. The pleasant lodge lies right by
the lake and is a good base for all kinds
of outdoor activity.

### MILLBROOK RESORT AND COUNTRY CLUB (A)
Malaghan Road, Arrowtown; 20 km from
Queenstown
☎ *(03) 4417000, fax (03) 4417007*
20 suites. A luxurious hotel complex,
designed in rustic style, with a popular
golf course.

### ★NUGGET POINT RESORT (A)
Arthur's Point Road
☎ *(03) 4427273, fax (03) 4427308*
35 r. Situated high above the Shotover
River, this is perhaps the best hotel in
the Queenstown area. In winter there is
skiing on nearby Coronet Peak.

### Te Anau
### TE ANAU HOLIDAY PARK (C)
1 Te Anau/Manapouri Road
☎ *(03) 2497457, fax (03) 2497536, email
teanau@xtra.co.uk*
Located beside Lake Te Anau, this motor
camp has well-kept and reasonably
priced cabins and tourist apartments.

### Waiau
### ★SHERWOOD LODGE (A)
919 Sherwood Road, Waiau
☎ *(03) 3156078, fax (03) 3156424*
This classic luxury accommodation for
hunters and anglers is in the Canterbury
Highlands.

## Stewart Island hotels (selection)

### Halfmoon Bay
### RAKIURA HOTEL (C)
Horseshoe Bay Road; 2 km from town
☎ *(03) 2191096*
5 r. A simple motel in a quiet location.
The rooms can accommodate up to six
people.

### STEWART ISLAND LODGE (A)
Nichol Road
☎ *(03) 2191085, fax (03) 2191085*
4 r. The most luxurious hotel on Stewart
Island, with superb views of the bay and
the surrounding mountains. The island
is a paradise for birdwatchers; this is the
only place where the brown kiwi can still
be seen in its natural surroundings. The
hotel is famed for its cuisine (fish a
speciality).

## Cook Islands/Niue hotels (selection)

### Rarotonga
### EDGEWATER RESORT (A)
7 km from Avarua
☎ *25475, fax 25475, email
stay@edgewater.co.uk*
182 r. Situated on the north-west coast of
Rarotonga, this is the largest and liveliest
hotel in the Cook Islands. It has its own
swimming pool and several tennis
courts, and guests can use snorkelling
equipment free of charge. Bicycles,
mopeds and cars can be hired.

### ★MANUIA BEACH BOUTIQUE HOTEL (A)
Near Arorangi, on the west coast
☎ *22461, fax 22464, email
rooms@manuia.co.uk*
20 bungalows. A luxurious hotel on an
idyllic beach, with marvellous sunsets. It
has an excellent restaurant and a bar; the
service is excellent. Golf, tennis, squash,
sailing, snorkelling; swimming pool.

### MURI BEACHCOMBER (A)
Muri Beach
☎ *21022, fax 21323, email
muri@beachcomber.co.uk*
16 bungalows. This small holiday
complex, with its own swimming pool,
lies in a tropical garden on picturesque
Muri Lagoon (east side of Rarotonga).
Sailing boats, surfboards, snorkelling
equipment and bicycles can be hired
nearby.

### ★PACIFIC RESORT AND VILLAS (A)
Muri Beach
☎ *5320427, fax 5320427, email
thomas@pacificresort.co.uk,
www.pacificresort.com*
53 apartments (some of them in
bungalows). One of the finest hotels in
the Cook Islands, on the east side of
Rarotonga. The bungalows are situated
in a tropical park. There are two
restaurants and a bar on the beach.
Sailing, windsurfing, snorkelling, scuba
diving, tennis and squash.

### RAROTONGAN BEACH RESORT (A)
☎ *25800, fax 25799, email
info@raratongan.co.nz*
151 r. This was the first large hotel on
Rarotonga and is still the island's
favourite rendezvous; it is particularly
good for families. Its Polynesian nights,
with a generous buffet supper and music

and dancing, attract large numbers of people. It has its own floodlit tennis courts and a large swimming pool. Canoeing, windsurfing, sailing, snorkelling, scuba diving.

### Aitutaki
**AITUTAKI PEARL BEACH RESORT (A)**
☎ 31201, fax 31202, email akitua@aitutaki.net.ck
25 apartments. This Polynesian-style hotel, a private island resort, lies on the dazzlingly white sandy shores of the Aitutaki Lagoon. It offers ample scope for water-sports enthusiasts – sailing (HobieCats), snorkelling, scuba diving, deep-sea angling.

### Niue
**NIUE HOTEL (B)**
3 km south of Alofi
☎ 4092
30 r. The hotel has an excellent restaurant and two bars. It is famed for its Polynesian dance shows, mainly during the holiday season. Tennis and golf nearby. There are organised snorkelling and diving trips and walks (fairly strenuous) round the island.

## Private accommodations

### Farmstay
The best way to see something of rural life in New Zealand is to take a farm holiday. Many farmhouses have rooms or holiday apartments for let. On some farms there are opportunities for riding.

### Homestay
Visitors can experience everyday life in New Zealand by taking a room in a private house (private home, city home). Many house owners are glad to meet visitors from abroad and make very good hosts. Dinner, bed and breakfast in a private house cost between NZ$60 and $200. Advance booking is essential.

### Information
Many local tourist offices will arrange short farmstays and homestays. Addresses are given in a brochure, *Where to Stay*, obtainable from Tourism New Zealand offices. Accommodation can also be arranged by the following agencies:
RURAL TOURS NZ LTD FARMSTAYS
92 Victoria Street, PO Box 228, Cambridge

☎ (07) 8278055, fax (07) 8277154, email stay@ruraltours.co.nz
FARMHOUSE AND COUNTRY HOME HOLIDAYS
Auckland
☎ (09) 4108280, fax (09) 4108380

### Other accommodations
See Camping; Youth Hostels

## Information

### Tourism New Zealand

Tourism New Zealand produces a range of information about New Zealand's tourist attractions and facilities. The main offices are:

### New Zealand
TOURISM NEW ZEALAND
Level 7, 89 The Terrace, Wellington
☎ (04) 9175400, fax (04) 9153817, www.nztb.govt.nz

### United Kingdom
New Zealand House, Haymarket, London SW1Y 4TQ
☎ (020) 79301662, fax (020) 78398929, www.purenz.com

### United States
1111 North Dearborn Street, Suite 2705, Chicago IL 60610
☎ (312) 4401345, fax (312) 4403808
501 Santa Monica Boulevard, Suite 300, Santa Monica, Los Angeles CA 90401
☎ (310) 3957480, fax (310) 3955453
Suite 1904, 780 Third Avenue, New York NY 10017–2024
☎ (212) 8328482, fax (212) 8327602

### Canada
888 Dunsmuir Street, Suite 1200, Vancouver BC V6C 3K4
☎ (604) 6842117, fax (604) 6841265

## North Island tourist offices

Tourist offices, or VIN (Visitor Information Network) centres, throughout New Zealand are marked by a green 'i'.

### Auckland
Auckland Airport
International Terminal, Arrivals Lounge
☎ (09) 2568535,
email intlauc@aucklandnz.com

Auckland Airport
Air New Zealand Domestic
☎ *(09) 2568480,*
*email domavc@aucklandnz.com*

NZ Visitor Centre
Corner of Quay Street and Hobson Street
☎ *(09) 9792333,*
*email nzuc@aucklandnz.com*

Auckland Travel and Information Centre
287 Queen Street
☎ *(09) 9792333,*
*email reservations@aucklandnz.com*

North Shore City
49 Hurstmere Road, Takapuna
☎ *(09) 4868670,*
*email visitorinfo@nthshore.govt.nz*

**Bay of Islands**
Pahia Wharf, Marsden Road, Paihia
☎ *(09) 4027345,*
*email visitorinfo@fndc.govt.nz*

**Coromandel**
355 Kapanga Road
☎ *(07) 8668598, email coroinfo@ihug.co.nz*

**Dargaville**
Normandy Street
☎ *(09) 4398360,*
*email info@kauricoast.co.nz*

**Foxton**
Main Street
☎ *(06) 3638940*

**Gisborne**
209 Grey Street
☎ *(06) 8686139,*
*email info@gisbornenz.com*

**Hamilton**
Corner of Ward Street and Anglesea
Street
☎ *(07) 8393580,*
*email hamiltoninfo@wave.co.nz*

**Hastings**
Russell Street North
☎ *(06) 8735526,*
*email vic@hastingstourism.co.nz*

**Hawera**
55 High Street
☎ *(06) 2788599,*
*email visitorinfo@stdc.govt.nz*

**Kaitaia**
Jaycee Park, South Road

☎ *(09) 4080879,*
*email fndckta@xtra.co.nz*

**Katikati**
34 Main Road
☎ *(07) 5491658*

**Masterton**
5 Dixon Street
☎ *(06) 3787373*

**Matamata**
45 Broadway
☎ *(07) 8887260, email matvin1@xtra.co.nz*

**Mount Maunganui**
Salisbury Avenue
☎ *(07) 5755099,*
*email trgvin@tauranga.govt.nz*

**Napier**
100 Marine Parade
☎ *(06) 8341911,*
*email info@napiervic.co.nz*

**New Plymouth**
Liardet Street and Leach Street
☎ *(06) 7596080,*
*email info@newplymouth.govt.nz*

**Ohakune**
54 Clyde Street
☎ *(06) 3858427,*
*email ruapehu.vic@xtra.co.nz*

**Opotiki**
Corner of St John Street and Elliott
Street
☎ *(07) 3158484,*
*email infocentre@odc.govt.nz*

**Otorohanga**
57 Maniapoto Street
☎ *(07) 8738951, otovin@xtra.co.nz*

**Palmerston North**
52 The Square
☎ *(06) 3546593,*
*email manawatu.visitor-info@xtra.co.nz*

**Rotorua**
1167 Fenton Street
☎ *(07) 3485179, email gdela@rdc.govt.nz*

**Stratford**
Broadway South
☎ *(06) 7656708,*
*email stratford@info.stratford.govt.nz*

**Taumarunui**
Railway Station, Hakiaha Street

☎ *(07) 8957494,*
*email info@ruahudc.govt.nz*

**Taupo**
30 Tongariro Street
☎ *(07) 3760027,*
*email taupovc@laketauponz.com*

**Tauranga**
95 Willow Street
☎ *(07) 5788103,*
*email trgvin@tauranga.govt.nz*

**Te Aroha**
102 Whitaker Street
☎ *(07) 8848052,*
*email infotearoha@xtra.co.nz*

**Te Kuiti**
Rora Street
☎ *(07) 8788077,*
*email tkinfo@voyager.co.nz*

**Thames**
206 Pollen Street
☎ *(07) 8687284, email thames@ihug.co.nz*

**Tokoroa**
State Highway 1, Tokoroa
☎ *(07) 8868872,*
*email tokoroa.info@xtra.co.nz*

**Turangi**
Ngawaka Place
☎ *(07) 3868999,*
*email turangi@laketauponz.com*

**Waitomo Caves**
Main Street, Waitomo Caves
☎ *(07) 8787640,*
*email waitomomuseum@xtra.co.nz*

**Waiuku**
2 Queen Street
☎ *(09) 2358924,*
*email waiukvin@ihug.co.nz*

**Wanganui**
101 Guyton Street
☎ *(06) 3490508,*
*email info@wanganui.govt.nz*

**Wellington**
101 Wakefield Street, Civic Square
☎ *(04) 8024860,*
*email bookings@wellingtonnz.com*

**Whakatane**
Boon Street
☎ *(07) 3086058,*
*email whakataneinfo@xtra.co.nz*

**Whangarei**
Tarewa Park, 92 Otaika Road
☎ *(09) 4381079,*
*email whangarei@clear.net.nz*

**Whitianga**
66 Albert Street
☎ *(07) 8665555,*
*email whitvin@ihug.co.nz*

**Woodville**
42 Vogel Street
☎ *(06) 3761023, email info@tararua.com*

## South Island tourist offices

**Alexandra**
22 Centennial Avenue
☎ *(03) 4489515, email info@tco.org.nz*

**Arthur's Pass**
Main Road
☎ *(03) 3189211,*
*email mlimpus@doc.govt.nz*

**Ashburton**
East Street and Burnett Street
☎ *(03) 3081064,*
*email infocentre@ashburton.co.nz*

**Balclutha**
4 Clyde Street
☎ *(03) 4180388,*
*email clutha.vin@cluthadc.govt.nz*

**Blenheim**
2 High Street
☎ *(03) 5789904,*
*email blm_info@clear.net.nz*

**Christchurch**
Christchurch and Canterbury Visitor
Centre, Old Chief Post Office, Cathedral
Square, Christchurch
☎ *(03) 3799629,*
*email info@christchurchnz.net*

Christchurch Airport
Domestic Terminal
☎ *(03) 3537774/5*

**Cromwell**
47 The Mall
☎ *(03) 4450212,*
*email cromwellvin@extra.co.nz*

**Dunedin**
48 The Octagon
☎ *(03) 4713300,*
*email visitor.centre@dcc.govt.nz*

**Franz Josef**
Main Road
☎ *(03) 7520796, email vctemp@doc.govt.nz*

**Gore**
Hokonui Drive and Norfolk Street
☎ *(03) 2089908, email goreinfo@esi.co.nz*

**Greymouth**
Mackay Street and Herbert Street
☎ *(03) 7685101,*
*email vingm@minidata.co.nz*

**Haast**
Main Road and Jackson Bay Road
☎*(03) 7500809, email haastfc@doc.govt.nz*

**Hanmer Springs**
42 Amuri Avenue West
☎ *(03) 3157128, email info@hurunui.com*

**Hokitika**
The Carnegie Building
☎ *(03) 7556166, email hkkvin@xtra.co.nz*

**Invercargill**
Queens Park, 108 Gala Street
☎ *(03) 2149133, email*
*tourismandtravel.invercargill@thenet.net.nz*

**Kaikoura**
Westend
☎ *(03) 3195641,*
*email info@kaikoura.co.nz*

**Methven**
93 Main Street
☎ *(03) 3028955,*
*email methven@clear.net.nz*

**Motueka**
Wallace Street
☎ *(03) 5286543, email mzpvin@xtra.co.nz*

**Mount Cook**
Bowen Drive
☎ *(03) 4351186,*
*email mtcookvc@doc.govt.nz*

**Nelson**
Trafalgar Street and Halifax Street
☎ *(03) 5482304,*
*email vin@latitudenelson.co.nz*

**Picton**
The Foreshore
☎ *(03) 5737477,*
*email pictonvin@xtra.co.nz*

**Punakaiki**
Main Road

☎ *(03) 7311895,*
*email punakaikivc@doc.govt.nz*

**Queenstown**
Clocktower Building, corner of Shotover
Street and Camp Street
☎ *(03) 4424100, email qvc@xtra.co.nz*

**Stewart Island**
Main Road, Halfmoon Bay
☎ *(03) 2191218, email*
*stewartislandfc@doc.govt.nz*

**Takaka**
Willow Street
☎ *(03) 5259136*

**Te Anau**
Lakefront Drive
☎ *(03) 2498900,*
*email vin@fiordlandtravel.co.nz*

**Timaru**
Lower George Street
☎ *(03) 6886163,*
*email info@timaru.co.nz*

**Twizel**
Wairepo Road
☎ *(03) 4350801*

**Wanaka**
Ardmore Street
☎ *(03) 4431233,*
*email info@lakewanaka.co.nz*

**Westport**
1 Brougham Street
☎ *(03) 7896658,*
*email westport.info@xtra.co.nz*

# Maori Affairs

**Information**
TE PUNI KOKIRI (MINISTRY OF MAORI
DEVELOPMENT)
143 Lambton Quay, PO Box 3943,
Wellington
☎ *(04) 9226000, fax, (04) 9226299,*
*email tpkinfo@tpk.govt.nz, www.tpk.govt.nz*

**Maori villages**
Riki Rangi Maori Centre, Christchurch
Maori Arts and Crafts Centre, Rotorua/
  Whakarewarewa
Maori Village, Rotorua/Ohinemutu
Rewa Village, Kerikeri (Bay of Islands)
Maori Marae, Waitangi (Bay of Islands)
Turangawaewae Marae, Ngaruawahia
  (near Hamilton)

### Maori art
War Memorial Museum, Auckland
Waikato Museum, Hamilton
Museum of New Zealand Te Papa
Tongarewa, Wellington

# Media

### Radio
The two state-run stations, Radio New
Zealand and National Radio, broadcast
programmes on medium wave and VHF
throughout New Zealand. Away from the
larger towns listeners can sometimes
receive only a few medium-wave
transmissions. There are also a number
of private radio stations that broadcast
news for tourists.

### Tourist Information FM
Tourist Information FM broadcasts round
the clock. In addition to programmes on
the history and culture of New Zealand it
carries advertisements by hotels,
restaurants and other items of interest to
tourists.

### Television
Television services are provided mainly
by Television New Zealand Ltd, with two
channels. The programmes consist
largely of American soap operas and
films, though there are also some
programmes with New Zealand themes.
A privately run channel, TV3, came
on air in 1989. In the two tourist centres
of Rotorua and Queenstown there are
local television stations with non-stop
programmes on the sights of the region.

# Motoring

### Rule of the road
As in the United Kingdom, traffic goes
on the left, with overtaking on the right.
Nevertheless, traffic coming from the
right has priority.
Particular care is required when
turning off into a road on the right.

### Road network
There are multi-lane motorways only
round the cities of Auckland, Wellington
and Christchurch. Main roads (State
Highways, numbered in single figures)
and country roads (Highways, numbered
in double figures) are asphalted and well
signposted, though in some areas there
are many bends.

Some roads are not asphalted, and on
such roads, because of the dust and the
loose chips that are thrown up, drivers
should drive carefully.

### Narrow bridges
Drivers will frequently encounter narrow
bridges that can carry only one line of
traffic and must be crossed alternately in
each direction. In some areas,
particularly on the South Island, the
density of traffic is so low that it would
not be worthwhile building two-lane
bridges over rivers and valleys.
It can also happen that a bridge
carries both the road and the railway. In
such a case a give-way sign will indicate
that traffic coming in the other direction
has priority. The railway, however,
always has priority.

### Traffic density
Motoring is a pleasure in New Zealand,
for outside the larger towns there is
relatively little traffic. In New Zealand
eyes a rush hour is when there is a queue
of three cars at traffic lights.

### Driving style
Most New Zealand drivers drive carefully
and defensively. However, watch out for
the car in front of you pulling up sharply
or turning off without indicating. The
real danger on New Zealand roads,
however, comes from the animals that
can suddenly stray on to the road.

### Sheep
In country areas sheep always have
priority. Woe betide the motorist who
injures a sheep by inconsiderate driving!

### Speed limits
Outside built-up areas: 100 kph
Built-up areas: 50 kmph
Within 100 m of a level crossing: 30 kph
When overtaking a stopping school bus:
  20 kph

### Traffic signs
Traffic signs are in line with
international standards. Distances are
given in kilometres (km) and speeds in
kilometres per hour (kph).

### Seat belts
Seat belts must be worn. There are heavy
fines for not wearing one.

### Alcohol
The blood alcohol limits are 30 mg

# Distances in kilometres

SOUTH ISLAND

Nelson    Picton

Greymouth

Franz Josef

Mount Cook

Christchurch

Lake Pukaki

Milford Sound

Timaru

Queenstown

Cromwell

Te Anau

© Baedeker

Dunedin

Invercargill

**Journey times in hours and minutes**

alcohol per 100 ml blood for drivers aged under 20; 80 mg alcohol per 100 ml blood for drivers aged 20 or over.

### Police
Police vehicles in action switch on a flashing red light and sound their siren. To stop a driver they sit on their tail with light flashing and siren sounding.

### Parking ban
No-parking areas in towns are marked by road signs and yellow lines. Drivers parking in these areas are liable to heavy fines and may have to pay a recovery charge if their car is towed away.

### Driving licence
See Travel Documents.

### Fuel
Much the same brands of petrol and

diesel fuel as in Europe are available in New Zealand, and at similar price levels.

### Filling stations
In well-populated areas and on main trunk roads there are plenty of filling stations, but there may be problems in remoter areas. In country areas, too, many filling stations close from Saturday noon to Monday 6am. It is advisable, therefore, to fill up regularly.

## Automobile Association

The New Zealand Automobile Association (AA) has offices in all major towns. Members of the United Kingdom Automobile Association and other motoring organisations are entitled to the services of the AA free of charge, and on presentation of their membership

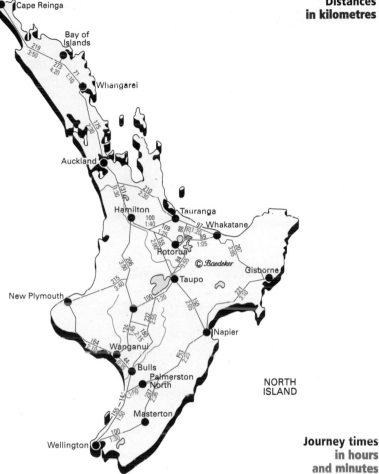

**Distances
in kilometres**

Cape Reinga

Bay of
Islands

219
3:50

273
4:20

71
1:10

Whangarei

175
2:30

Auckland

210
2:30

131
1:30

Hamilton

100
1:40

Tauranga

109
1:25

97
1:20

Whakatane

88
1:05

89

Rotorua

84

206
3:30

215
3:40

100
1:20

Taupo

207
3:05

Gisborne

221
3:0

New Plymouth

232
2:55

164
2:10

124
1:45

180
2:15

Wanganui

130
2:0

Napier

44

Bulls

63
2:20

Palmerston
North

**NORTH
ISLAND**

155
1:50

140

Masterton

100
1:30

Wellington

© *Baedeker*

**Journey times
in hours
and minutes**

card can obtain certain AA publications
free of charge and others at reduced
prices. In addition to road maps the AA
publishes brochures on camping,
accommodations and outdoor pursuits.

**Breakdown**
☎ *Freephone (0800) 500222*

**North Island**
NEW ZEALAND AUTOMOBILE ASSOCIATION
*www.nzaa.co.nz*
*www.aaguides.co.nz*

99 Albert Street, Auckland
☎ *(09) 3774660, fax (09) 3094564*
342–352 Lambton Quay, Wellington
☎ *(04) 470999*

**South Island**
210 Hereford Street, Christchurch
☎ *(03) 3791280*

**Maps**

The map of New Zealand supplied with

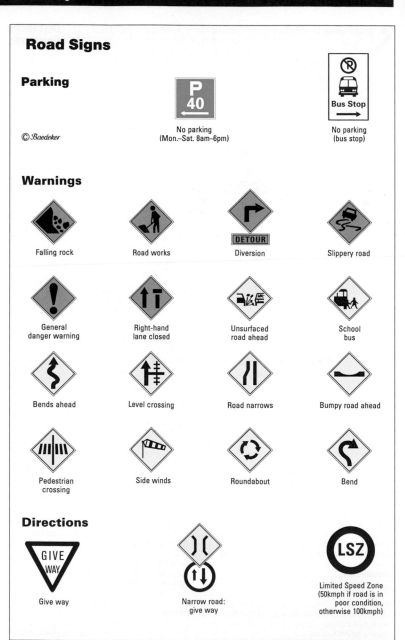

# Road Signs

## Parking

© *Baedeker*

No parking
(Mon.–Sat. 8am–6pm)

No parking
(bus stop)

## Warnings

Falling rock

Road works

Diversion

Slippery road

General
danger warning

Right-hand
lane closed

Unsurfaced
road ahead

School
bus

Bends ahead

Level crossing

Road narrows

Bumpy road ahead

Pedestrian
crossing

Side winds

Roundabout

Bend

## Directions

Give way

Narrow road:
give way

Limited Speed Zone
(50kmph if road is in
poor condition,
otherwise 100kmph)

this guide can usefully be supplemented by maps on a larger scale for particular areas. Up-to-date maps can be obtained in New Zealand at filling stations, in bookshops and from the New Zealand Automobile Association.

The following is a selection of the maps available.

### 1:1,000,000

Department of Survey and Land Information; 2 sheets, with contours, roads, national parks and index of places.

### 1:500,000

Department of Survey and Land Information *Coast to Coast*; 4 sheets, with contours, shading and roads.

### 1:250,000

Department of Survey and Land Information; 18 sheets, with roads, shading and index of places.

### Special maps

A variety of maps for special purposes can be obtained in New Zealand (walking, cycling and climbing maps, geological maps).

## Museums

In most towns and in many smaller places there are museums – some of them with very large collections – devoted to the history and natural environment of New Zealand and the Pacific region.

The country's most important museums are the Auckland Museum, the National Museum in Wellington, the Canterbury Museum in Christchurch and the Otago Museum in Dunedin.

The principal museums are mentioned in the Sights from A to Z section of this guide. Opening hours and admission charges should be checked with the local tourist office. Many museums are closed on Monday or some other day of the week. In some cases admission charges are quite high; some museums have concession rates for children, students and senior citizens.

### Art galleries

With the increasing interest in the arts since the second world war, there are now more than 20 public art galleries in New Zealand.

## National Parks

New Zealand's 13 national parks (four on the North Island and nine on the South Island), with a total area of more than 23,000 sq km, occupy around 10 per cent of the country's land area. In addition there are three maritime parks on the coast and 19 forest parks. Thus just under a fifth of New Zealand's total area is protected in this way. All the national parks and nature reserves are open to the public. The Department of Conservation (DoC) is responsible for the maintenance of these reserves.

The forest parks offer scope for pleasant short walks and are much frequented by town dwellers. For longer hikes, sometimes lasting several days, there are the national parks, which are traversed by a network of trails and have huts provided by the Department of Conservation for overnight accommodation. The trails maintained by the DoC are carefully planned to allow walkers to choose which way to go and which sights to see en route.

During the main holiday season the national parks attract large numbers of hikers, and some parks find it necessary to limit the numbers admitted. Some of the national parks are open throughout the year, others are closed in winter. Before setting out on a walk, therefore, you should check with the local DoC office that the trail will be open.

### Information

DEPARTMENT OF CONSERVATION
59 Boulcott Street, PO Box 10–420, Wellington
☎ *(04) 4710726, fax (04) 4711088, www.doc.govt.nz*
Liverpool Street/Karangahape Road, Private Bag 68–908, Newton, Auckland
☎ *(09) 3079279, fax (09) 3772919*

### Conduct in national parks

All plants and animals are protected.

Toilet waste must be buried well away from water points and paths. Other rubbish must be taken with you and properly disposed of.

Rivers, streams and lakes must be kept clean. Do not wash in them with soap or shampoo.

Take great care in lighting fires.

Do not leave the waymarked trails.

Be particularly careful in your behaviour in Maori settlements and respect their sacred places.

## National parks

### North Island

**Urewera National Park** (opened 1954, area 2126.72 sq km). The largest continuous area of primeval forest on the North Island, with lonely Lake Waikaremoana; innumerable small Maori settlements; unsurfaced roads.

**Tongariro National Park** (opened 1887, area 786.51 sq km). New Zealand's oldest National Park, in a mountainous region marked by volcanic activity, with several Maori cult sites. A UNESCO World Heritage Site.

**Egmont National Park** (opened 1900, area 335.34 sq km). Named after the extinct volcano of Taranaki (Mount Egmont, 2518 m), one of New Zealand's most photographed mountains. Popular skiing area.

**Whanganui National Park** (opened 1968, area 742.31 sq km). Named after the Whanganui River, which follows a winding course through a picturesque valley and is navigable by boat or canoe.

### South Island

**Abel Tasman National Park** (opened 1942, area 225.3 sq km). The smallest national park but one of the most beautiful. Idyllic coastal scenery.

**Kahurangi National Park** (opened 1995, area 4000 sq km). At the north-western tip of the South Island. Striking geological formations, caves, lowland forest; many endemic plants and animals.

**Nelson Lakes National Park** (opened 1956, area 961.21 sq km). Beautiful lakes with facilities for water sports and fishing.

**Paparoa National Park** (opened 1987, area 303.27 sq km). Its particular attractions are the Pancake Rocks and the blowholes that shoot up jets of water when the tide is high.

**Arthur's Pass National Park** (opened 1929, area 992.7 sq km). Valleys, gorges, cliffs, rock walls, mountains, dense forests, waterfalls and keas.

**Te Wahipounamu**, an area (UNESCO World Heritage Site) taking in the Westland, Fiordland and Mount Cook national parks.

**Westland National Park** (opened 1960, area 1175.47 sq km). Glaciers (Franz Josef, Fox, Tasman) and subtropical rain forest. Trout fishing.

**Mount Cook National Park** (opened 1953, area 700.13 sq km), with New Zealand's highest peak (3754 m). Alpine flora. Glacier walks, climbing, nature walks.

**Mount Aspiring National Park** (opened 1964, area 3555.18 sq km). Named after Mount Aspiring (3035 m). Alpine landscape. Climbing and hill walking.

**Fiordland National Park** (opened 1952, area 12,000 sq km). New Zealand's largest national park, with imposing mountains, lakes, fjords and almost impenetrable forests. The last retreat of two almost extinct species of flightless birds, the takahe and the kakapo.

## Maritime parks

### North Island

**Bay of Islands** At the subtropical north-eastern tip of the North Island, with quiet inlets and lonely islands. Water sports. Of historical interest as the place where the Maoris first landed in New Zealand and the Treaty of Waitangi was signed in 1840.

**Hauraki Gulf**, to the east of Auckland. Some 50 islands. Rare species of animals and plants.

### South Island

**Marlborough Sounds**, at the northern tip of the South Island. Rias (drowned valley systems).

## Nightlife

## Casinos

Gaming houses on the Las Vegas model are a recent development in New Zealand, and there are now casinos in Auckland and Christchurch, open only to adults aged 20 or over. In contrast to Las Vegas, a reasonable standard of dress is required (no jeans).

## National Parks and Walking Trails

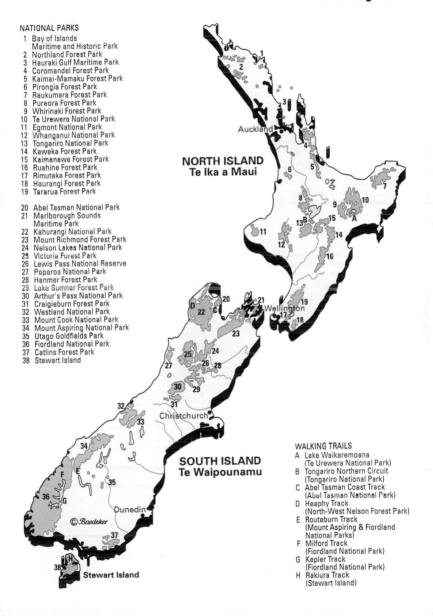

NATIONAL PARKS

1  Bay of Islands
   Maritime and Historic Park
2  Northland Forest Park
3  Hauraki Gulf Maritime Park
4  Coromandel Forest Park
5  Kaimai-Mamaku Forest Park
6  Pirongia Forest Park
7  Raukumara Forest Park
8  Pureora Forest Park
9  Whirinaki Forest Park
10 Te Urewera National Park
11 Egmont National Park
12 Whanganui National Park
13 Tongariro National Park
14 Kaweka Forest Park
15 Kaimanawa Forest Park
16 Ruahine Forest Park
17 Rimutaka Forest Park
18 Haurangi Forest Park
19 Tararua Forest Park

20 Abel Tasman National Park
21 Marlborough Sounds
   Maritime Park
22 Kahurangi National Park
23 Mount Richmond Forest Park
24 Nelson Lakes National Park
25 Victoria Forest Park
26 Lewis Pass National Reserve
27 Paparoa National Park
28 Hanmer Forest Park
29 Lake Sumner Forest Park
30 Arthur's Pass National Park
31 Craigieburn Forest Park
32 Westland National Park
33 Mount Cook National Park
34 Mount Aspiring National Park
35 Utago Goldfields Park
36 Fiordland National Park
37 Catlins Forest Park
38 Stewart Island

Auckland

**NORTH ISLAND**
**Te Ika a Maui**

Wellington

**SOUTH ISLAND**
**Te Waipounamu**

Christchurch

Dunedin

© Baedeker

**Stewart Island**

WALKING TRAILS

A  Lake Waikaremoana
   (Te Urewera National Park)
B  Tongariro Northern Circuit
   (Tongariro National Park)
C  Abel Tasman Coast Track
   (Abel Tasman National Park)
D  Heaphy Track
   (North-West Nelson Forest Park)
E  Routeburn Track
   (Mount Aspiring & Fiordland
   National Parks)
F  Milford Track
   (Fiordland National Park)
G  Kepler Track
   (Fiordland National Park)
H  Rakiura Track
   (Stewart Island)

**Auckland**
Harrah's Sky City Casino
A casino designed by contemporary
artists, with a large gaming hall, a
theatre seating 700 people, several
restaurants and various other gambling
and sports facilities.

**Christchurch**
Christchurch Casino
30 Victoria Street
◉ *Thu. 11am–Mon. 3am (non-stop)*
☎ *(03) 3659999*

## Opening Hours

**Banks**
See Currency

**Bottle stores**
Mon.–Sat. 9am–6pm, often to 10pm.
    Alcoholic drinks can be bought only
in licensed bottle stores.

**Dairies (corner shops)**
Daily 7am–10pm.
    Dairies in New Zealand are the
equivalent of the corner shop or store. In
cities and tourist centres some of them
stay open until midnight.

**Post offices**
Mon.–Thu. 8.30am–5pm, Fri.
8.30am–8pm.

**Public offices**
Mon.–Fri. 9am–5pm.
    Some travel agencies and airline
offices have longer opening hours.

**Shops**
Mon.–Thu. 9am–5.30pm, to 9pm Fri. (or
another weekday for late-night
shopping).
    In the larger towns shops are also
open Sat. 9.30am–2pm (sometimes to
4.30pm); some also open Sun.
9am–4.30pm.

## Outdoor Life

New Zealand is a Promised Land for all
those – particularly young people – who
enjoy an adventurous outdoor holiday.
Its great tracts of largely unspoiled and
sparsely populated natural landscape
offers endless scope for all kinds of
outdoor activities – trekking and
camping, fishing, shooting, riding,
flying, climbing, walking, mountain
biking, motorcycle scrambling,
swimming, scuba diving and snorkelling,
golf and cricket, skiing and heli-skiing,
sailing, white-water canoeing, jet
boating, bungee jumping, survival
training and many more. Those looking
for risk, those who want to see what
they are made of, will find what they
want in New Zealand.
    But such pursuits have not been
without cost to the natural environment,
as those concerned for the protection of
nature had long feared. Thoughtless
holidaymakers have left scars on the
landscape with their all-terrain vehicles
and mountain bikes. The national park
authorities are attempting to control the
problem by admission charges and strict
regulations, but the problem is still
there. All users of the countryside,
therefore, are reminded of their
responsibility to the environment.

## Photography

**Films**
Films of all kinds can be bought in
chemists, photographic shops and
supermarkets. They tend to be dearer
than in Europe and North America, so
you should take a sufficient supply of
films from home.

**Processing**
Films are developed in many specialist
shops within a day. Prints, slides and
enlargements are also produced very
rapidly.

**Protection**
Cameras and lenses should be protected
from the heavy rain that can occur in
New Zealand by keeping them in a stout
plastic bag (e.g. a cool bag). Some camera
bags are not completely rainproof.

**Photographing people**
Before photographing people you should
ask their permission. This is particularly
important in the case of Maoris.

## Post

Normally postal services are provided by
post offices, but in some country areas
the post office may be combined with a
shop.
    In addition to the usual postal

services post offices are also responsible for telecommunications (telephone, fax, internet).

### Opening hours
See Opening Hours

### Postage
An airmail letter (up to 20 grams; with 'fast post' sticker) to Europe costs NZ$1.80. It takes 7–12 days for the letter to reach its destination.

An airmail postcard (up to 10 grams) or aerogram to Europe costs NZ$1.

Mail sent by sea takes at least 8 weeks to reach Europe.

Poste restante mail is kept by the post office for a month and then returned to the sender by sea. Visitors can also arrange in New Zealand for mail to be forwarded to their next address. Hotels will keep mail for delivery on arrival.

### Postboxes
In New Zealand there are separate postboxes for ordinary mail (red) and airmail or 'fast post' (blue).

### Postcards
New Zealand post offices also sell attractive postcards.

## Public Holidays

### Statutory holidays

#### National holidays
New Year's Day (January 1st)
Waitangi Day or New Zealand Day (February 6th): commemorating the foundation of New Zealand
Good Friday (March/April)
Easter Monday (March/April)
Anzac Day (April 25th): commemorating the New Zealand and Australian troops who fell at Gallipoli in 1915
Queen's Birthday (first Monday in June)
Labour Day (fourth Monday in October)
Christmas Day (December 25th)
Boxing Day (December 26th)

#### Regional holidays
Each province has its own anniversary day:
Wellington: January 22nd
Auckland: January 29th
Northland: January 29th
Nelson: February 1st
Otago: March 23rd

Southland: March 23rd
Taranaki: March 31st
Hawke's Bay: November 1st
Marlborough: November 1st
Canterbury: November 9th
Westland: December 1st

#### Long weekends
Since New Zealanders like a long weekend, public holidays are usually moved to the Monday before or after the actual date.

#### School holidays
The long school holidays, and thus the main holiday season, are from mid-December to the end of January. There are shorter holidays in the second and third weeks of May and a week in July. The winter holidays begin at the end of August and end in mid-September.

## Public Transport

Public transport is reasonably adequate only in and around the larger towns. For longer distances air services (☛Air Travel) are used. There are large numbers of flights between the cities of Auckland, Wellington and Christchurch. Rail travel is comfortable, but there is usually only one train a day between towns. Seats must therefore be booked in advance. Coaches are the most popular from of public transport.

## Coach services

The most important public transport in New Zealand is the coach. A dense network of coach services links all the major cities and towns and the main tourist centres. Most services, however, operate only on weekdays; on Sundays there are very few coaches and in some areas none at all. It is essential to book in plenty of time, particularly during the main tourist season (December to March).

#### Coach companies
The largest private coach companies in New Zealand are Newmans on the North Island and Mount Cook Landline on the South Island. In addition there are the state-owned inter-city coachlines and a number of smaller companies such as the Kiwi Experience and Magic Bus Company.

### New Zealand Travelpass

Visitors to New Zealand can obtain various kinds of travel pass that allow unlimited coach travel within a given area and are very good value for money.

The New Zealand Travelpass covers travel on trains, ferries and coaches run by InterCity and Newmans Coachlines.

The 2-in-One Travelpass includes coach and ferry and the 3-in-One coach, ferry and rail travel. The 4-in-One Travelpass includes one flight with Air New Zealand between the North and South Islands or within either of them.

Travelpasses can be bought only outside New Zealand or on arrival in New Zealand. The current price is NZ$720 for 22 days' travel over 8 weeks. Children under 4 can travel free; children between 4 and 15 pay NZ$500. Information from: ☏ *www.travelpass.co.nz*

### Kiwi Coach Pass

Another good bargain is Mount Cook Landline's Kiwi Coach Pass, which also covers travel on all InterCity and Newmans routes, as well as those of Great Sights Gray Line, Northliner and Kiwi Experience. Also included is one flight with Air Nelson over the Cook Strait from Wellington to Nelson or Blenheim. Holders of this pass also enjoy a reduction of up to 20 per cent on sightseeing flights with the Mount Cook Airline and boat trips with Fuller's Cruises.

The Kiwi Coach Pass at present costs around NZ$400 for 11 days and NZ$800 for 45 days. It is obtainable outside New Zealand, but can also be bought in New Zealand on production of the visitor's passport and air ticket.

### Newmans Coach Pass

The Newmans Coach Pass is also accepted by the Northliner, Mount Cook Landline and Kiwi Experience companies. A One Island Pass covers either the North or the South Island; a Two Island Pass covers both. The difference in price is between NZ$40 and NZ$50, depending on the number of days.

### Backpacker's Pass

Other coach companies offer a variety of inducements for backpackers, like Kiwi Experience's Backpacker's Pass.

### Information

INTERCITY COACHLINES

395 Manukau Road, PO Box 26–601, Epsom, Auckland
☏ *(09) 9136100, fax (09) 9136121, email info@coachnet.co.nz, www.intercitycoach.co.nz*

MOUNT COOK LINE
PO Box 4644, Christchurch
☏ *(03) 3482099, fax (03) 3438159*

NEWMANS COACHLINES
395 Manukau Road, PO Box 26–601, Epsom, Auckland
☏ *(09) 9136200, fax (09) 9136121, email info@coachnet.co.nz, www.newmanscoach.co.nz*

KIWI EXPERIENCE
Heard Park, 170 Parnell Road, Parnell, Auckland
☏ *(09) 3669830, fax (09) 3661374, www.kiwiexperience.com*

## Railways

Rail travel in New Zealand is a comfortable means of getting about the country, though only on the main lines. The branch lines – more and more of which are being closed down – are not well known for their comfort.

New Zealand has a total rail network of 4300 km. The track is narrow-gauge. Trains usually take longer than overland coaches to cover the same distance. Passengers travel in comfortable coaches with panoramic windows, and there are modern and well-equipped restaurant cars. Many of the lines run through magnificent scenery, and provide a running commentary on points of particular interest.

The following are the principal trains run by Tranz Scenic:

### Overlander (day train)

Auckland–Wellington (685 km)
Journey time: 10 hours 10 minutes

### Northerner (night train)

Auckland–Wellington (685 km)
Journey time: 10 hours 40 minutes

### Kaimai Express

Auckland–Tauranga
Jourhey time: 3 hours 18 minutes

### Geyserland Express

Auckland–Rotorua
Journey time: 4 hours 9 minutes

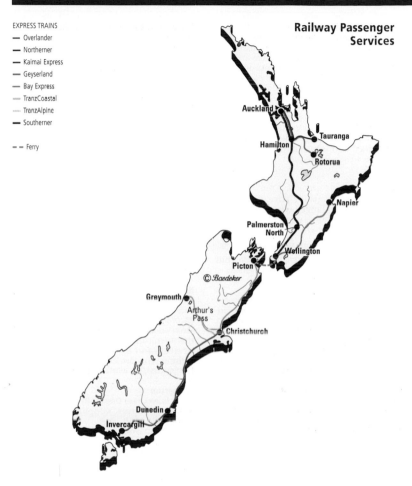

EXPRESS TRAINS
— Overlander
— Northerner
— Kaimai Express
— Geyserland
— Bay Express
--- TranzCoastal
···· TranzAlpine
— Southerner

– – Ferry

**Railway Passenger Services**

Auckland
Tauranga
Hamilton
Rotorua
Napier
Palmerston North
Wellington
Picton
© Baedeker
Greymouth
Arthur's Pass
Christchurch
Dunedin
Invercargill

**Bay Express**
Wellington–Napier (334 km)
Journey time: 5 hours 30 minutes

**Southerner (day train)**
Christchurch–Invercargill (594 km)
Journey time: 9 hours 40 minutes

**TranzCoastal**
Christchurch–Picton (350 km);
connection to Picton–Wellington ferry
Journey time: 5 hours 20 minutes

**TranzAlpine**
Christchurch–Greymouth

Journey time: 9 hours 30 minutes

**Information and booking**
Tranz Rail, Railway Station, Wellington
☎ (04) 4983303, fax (04) 4983090, email
*passengerservices@tranzrail.co.nz,*
*www.tranzrailtravel.co.nz*

## Restaurants

In all the larger towns and in holiday
resorts there is a wide range of
restaurants, and in addition there are
numerous pubs, bistros, cafes, American-

style fast-food establishments and takeaways offering meals at very moderate prices. Due to the influx of immigrants in recent years there are now numerous speciality restaurants offering a variety of national cuisines, particularly Chinese, Indian, Italian and even Mexican.

In New Zealand it is usual to book a table in advance by telephone. On entering a restaurant guests should wait to be taken to a table. They may be reminded of this by a notice at the entrance with the request 'Wait to be seated'.

### Prices
In good restaurants the price of the main dish is likely to range between NZ$20 and NZ$50. In some establishments it can be much higher.

### The bill
In most restaurants there is only one bill per table. It is then up to the guests to decide who should pay.

### Dining
As a rule New Zealanders eat out only in the evening and they tend to eat early. Many restaurants serve meals only until 9.30pm.

Many restaurants do not serve à la carte dishes on Saturdays but only a smorgasbord (buffet).

### Alcohol
See Food and Drink

## Restaurants on the North Island (selection)

### Auckland
**★ANTOINE'S**
333 Parnell Road
☎ (09) 3798756
Auckland's best and most expensive restaurant, which has long been a Mecca for gourmets.

**CIN CIN ON QUAY**
Ferry Building, 99 Quay Street
☎ (09) 3076966
Freshly caught fish and pizzas cooked in a charcoal oven are specialities. The wine list offers a choice of over 100 wines, mostly from New Zealand. From the restaurant there is a fine view of the harbour. Some guests may be disturbed by the music, which is often very loud.

**HARBOURSIDE SEAFOOD BAR AND GRILL**
Ferry Building (first floor), 99 Quay Street
☎ (09) 3070486,
www.harboursiderestaurant.co.nz
On warm evenings guests can enjoy lobster (a speciality of the restaurant) and also a magnificent view of Waitemata Harbour and Hauraki Gulf. Unusually for a fish restaurant, it also has excellent game and lamb dishes.

**★THE FRENCH CAFÉ**
210 Symonds Street
☎ (09) 3771911
An elegant restaurant whose chefs have won many awards. Its specialities are lamb, game and salmon. Opening off the street is its associated Brasserie, with excellent food at lower prices.

**LEFT BANK RESTAURANT**
34 Marlborough Place
☎ (07) 8393350
A very popular restaurant, famed for its cooking.

### Hastings
**VIDAL WINERY BRASSERIE**
913 St Aubyn Street
☎ (06) 8768105
Situated amid vineyards to the south of the town, this restaurant is renowned for its steaks and above all for its wine. In summer you can eat on the terrace in the garden, in winter round an open fire.

### Masterton
**SWEET INSPIRATIONS DESSERT RESTAURANT**
434 Queen Street, Kuripuni
☎ (06) 3782641
Even those who don't care for sweet things can enjoy a meal here. The menu offers a wide range, particularly soups and poultry and fish dishes.

### Napier
**BAYSWATER BISTRO**
8 Harding Road, Ahuiri
☎ (06) 8358517
The cuisine is creative, with new menus every few weeks. The restaurant offers an excellent selection of New Zealand wines. Prices are moderate. On fine days there is a beautiful view from the terrace over Hawke's Bay.

**BEACHES RESTAURANT**
War Memorial Building, Marine Parade
☎ (06) 8358180
Excellent fish dishes. Magnificent view over Hawke's Bay.

**Ju Ju's**
80B Emerson Street
☎ *(06) 8353976*
Those who like Thai cuisine – now increasingly popular – will find what they want here.

**New Plymouth**
THE DEVON SEAFOOD SMORGÅSBORD
390 Devon Street East
☎ *(06) 7599099*
The restaurant's fish and meat dishes and vegetarian food appeal to many guests, but its speciality is Swedish-style smorgasbord, a cold and hot buffet with a variety of meat and fish, egg dishes, vegetables, salads and cheese.

**Paihia**
ESMAE'S
41 Williams Road
☎ *(09) 4028400*
Typical New Zealand cuisine (lamb, fish, game, pork, poultry). Vegetarian dishes are also on the menu.

**Pauanui**
★PUKA PARK RESORT
Pauanui Beach
☎ *(07) 8648088, reservations (0800) 785272, www.pukapark.co.nz*
The restaurant of this exclusive lodge (☛Hotels) is noted for its fine cuisine. Booking essential.

RELF KEITH AND MARGARET
El Dorado Ldr, Pauanui Beach, Coromandel Peninsula
☎ *(07) 8647015*
The best restaurant on the Coromandel Peninsula, where gourmets can spoil themselves. A quick snack can be had at the bar.

**Rotorua**
★POPPY'S VILLA RESTAURANT
4 Marguerita Street
☎ *(07) 3471700*
This elegant restaurant, in an Edwardian villa, is famed for its exquisite cuisine.

RENDEZVOUS RESTAURANT
1282 Hinemoa Street
☎ *(07) 3489273*
A friendly restaurant, famed for its fish dishes and grills, occupying a building of the colonial period in the commercial district of Rotorua.

YOU AND ME
31 Pukuatua Street

☎ *(07) 3476178*
This restaurant offers interesting combinations of New Zealand and French cuisine.

**Russell**
★GABLES RESTAUARANT
The Strand
☎ *(09) 4037618*
One of the best restaurants on the Bay of Islands, offering excellent New Zealand cuisine (fish, seafood, lamb, game).

**Stratford**
MOUNTAIN HOUSE MOTOR LODGE
Mount Egmont, Taranaki
☎ *(06) 7656100,*
*www.mountainhouse.co.nz*
This restaurant, located in the Egmont National Park, offers the best of New Zealand cuisine.

**Taupo**
TRUFFLES RESTAURANT
116 Lake Terrace
☎ *(07) 3787856*
Mainly New Zealand dishes (lamb, game, poultry), Marvellous view of Lake Taupo and the mountains.

**Thames**
OLD THAMES RESTAURANT
705 Pollen Street
☎ *(07) 8687207*
Specialities are fish and lamb dishes.

**Wellington**
BRASSERIE FLIP
RSA Building, 103 Ghuznee Street
☎ *(04) 3859493*
A French-style restaurant offering international dishes and excellent New Zealand wines. Booking essential in the evening.

PETIT LION
8 Courtney Place
☎ *(04) 3849402*
Everything here is top class: the food, the service – and the prices.

★PIERRE'S
342 Tinakori Road, Thorndon
☎ *(04) 4726238*
The chef's preference for Mediterranean cuisine is unmistakable.

★THE GRAIN OF SALT
232 Oriental Parade (first floor)
☎ *(04) 3848642*
This restaurant, from which there is a

view of the town and the harbour, is not cheap, but the chef has won awards for his New Zealand-cum-French cuisine.

### Tinakori Bistro
328 Tinakori Road, Thorndon
☎ (04) 4990567
New Zealand dishes presented with French refinement. In good weather you can eat out of doors.

## Restaurants on the South Island (selection)

### Blenheim
#### Rocco's Restaurant
5 Dodson Street
☎ (03) 5786940
The best Italian restaurant within a wide area. In winter guests are warmed by an open fire.

### Christchurch
#### Mykonos
112A Lichfield Street
☎ (03) 3797452
The excellent Greek cuisine here attracts a large clientele. Booking essential.

#### Pegasus Arms
14 Oxford Terrace
☎ (03) 3660600
Dining in the oldest house in Christchurch.

#### Pedro's Restaurant
143 Worcester Street
☎ (03) 3797668
Excellent New Zealand cuisine and Spanish specialities.

#### ★ Scarborough Fare
corner of Scarborough Road and Sumner Esplanade
☎ (03) 3266987
Rated one of the best restaurants in the country.

#### Sign of the Takahe
Dyers Pass Road, Cashmere Hills
☎ (03) 3324052
The restaurant, housed in a castellated building in the Cashmere Hills, has marvellous views of the Southern Alps and the city. Its specialities are game and lobster. Booking essential. Male guests must wear jacket and tie.

### Clyde
#### Oliver's Restaurant and Lodge

34 Sunderland Street
☎ (03) 4492860
This restaurant, in a house dating from 1863, is famed for its cuisine and for its fine wines from Central Otago.

### Dunedin
#### Palm's Café
64 High Street
☎ (03) 4761604
A good restaurant for people who prefer not to eat meat.

### Fairlie
#### Rimuwhare Motel and Restaurant
53 Mount Cook Road
☎ (03) 6858058, reservations (0800) 723723
An excellent restaurant, with a view of the Queen's Gardens.

### Hokitika
#### ★ Chez Pierre
Sewell Street
☎ (03) 7626856
One of the best restaurants on the west coast. French cuisine.

### Invercargill
#### Aino's Steakhouse and Restaurant
Waikiwi Shopping Centre
☎ (03) 2159568
The oldest restaurant in Invercargill. Its specialities are steaks and fresh fish.

#### ★ Donovan
220 Bainfield Road, Waikiwi
☎ (03) 2158156
Housed in a late 19th c. building on the outskirts of the town. The chefs have won a number of awards.

### Nelson
#### Chez Eelco Coffee House
296 Trafalgar Street
☎ (03) 5487595
The oldest street cafe in New Zealand, offering a choice of imaginative snacks. Patronised by locals and younger visitors.

### Picton
#### Marlborough Terranean
31 High Street
☎ (03) 5737122
New Zealand cuisine with a French touch, appealing both to local people and to visitors.

### Queenstown
#### Cow Restaurant

Cow Lane
☎ *(03) 4428588*
Famed locally for its pizzas and pasta dishes. You will usually have to wait until a table is free.

**QUALITY HOTEL AND RESORT, QUEENSTOWN TERRACES**
88 Frankton Road
☎ *(03) 4427950*
Specialities are game and lamb, but the restaurant's fish and seafood are also excellent. Fine views of Lake Wakatipu and the Remarkable Mountains.

**ROARING MEG'S**
57 Shotover Street
☎ *(03) 4429676*
A pleasant restaurant in a late 18th c. gold-miner's house, one of the oldest buildings in the town.

**Te Anau**
**BLUESTONE RESTAURANT**
Kingsgate Hotel, 20 Lakefront Drive
☎ *(03) 2497421*
Specialities are crayfish, lamb, game – that is, typical New Zealand dishes. From the restaurant there is a fine view of the snow-capped peaks of the Southern Alps.

**Wanaka**
**CAPRICCIO RESTAURANT**
123 Ardmore Street
☎ *(03) 4438579*
Italian and New Zealand specialities. Fine views of Lake Wanaka and the mountains.

## Restaurants on Stewart Island (selection)

**ANNIE HANSEN'S DINING ROOM**
South Sea Hotel, Elgin Terrace
☎ *(03) 2191120*
Good New Zealand cooking; prices are high. Dinner served 6pm–8pm.

**STEWART ISLAND LODGE**
Nichol Road, Halfmoon Bay
☎ *(03) 2191085*
A gourmet restaurant famed for its fish dishes.

## Restaurants on Cook Islands and Niue (selection)

**Rarotonga**
★**FLAME TREE**
Muri Beach

This is the best and most expensive restaurant on the island, located on the idyllic Muri Lagoon. Fish dishes and Asian specialities. Open evenings only.

**SAILS**
Muri Beach
A well-run restaurant in the Muri Lagoon Sailing Club. Outstanding fish dishes.

**TRADER JACK'S**
Avarua
This quayside restaurant, with the atmosphere of a cosy pub, serves Polynesian dishes (particularly fish and seafood) at reasonable prices.

**Aitutaki**
**RAPAE HOTEL RESTAURANT**
Near Arutanga
Every Friday evening there is an Island Night, with a tasty Polynesian buffet.

**Niue**
**NIUE HOTEL RESTAURANT**
South of Alofi
This restaurant, recently restored after storm damage, offers both Polynesian and international specialities.

**SAILS**
Coral Garden Motel (4 km from Alofi)
You can eat well in this little restaurant, which also has a bar.

## Shopping

**Markets**
The largest markets in New Zealand are the Victoria Market in Auckland, the Wakefield Market in Wellington and the Art Centre Market in Christchurch. Some markets are open daily, but the busiest times are at the weekend.

**Shopping malls**
The principal shopping malls in Auckland are Queen Street, Karangahape Road and the Downtown complex at the harbour; in Wellington Willis Street and Customhouse Quay; and in Christchurch the shops round Cathedral Square. In Queenstown souvenir shops are everywhere.

## Souvenirs

The most popular – and the best – souvenirs of New Zealand are articles made from natural materials such as wool, leather, wood and jade.

### Sheepskins and wool products
With more than 60 million sheep, New Zealand is one of the world's largest producers of wool. Wool products are on offer in every conceivable form and colour, from hand-knitted pullovers, scarves and blankets to carpets and rugs. New Zealanders themselves are fond of the 'swanny', a check-patterned woollen jacket that provides protection against rain as well as cold. If you go in for knitting or weaving you will be able to stock up with wool. Particularly popular in New Zealand is wool from Perendale sheep, which is good for knitting and dyeing.

### Furs
Furs are a popular buy, particularly Persian lamb and fur from the opossum, which has become a regular plague in New Zealand.

### Leather
Popular items are jackets, coats, waistcoats, boots and shoes, handbags and gloves of leather or lambskin. Articles made of polished lambskin are particularly light and soft. There are bargains to be had, too, in leather articles made from game animals (particularly roe deer).

### Woodcarving
Typical souvenirs from New Zealand are examples of Maori woodcarving, which can be both beautiful and decorative. The best places to look for them are the Maori Arts and Crafts Centre in Rotorua and in some places in the East Cape area. Work by trained Maori woodcarvers, however, is difficult to find. The export of works of art of the classic Maori culture – i.e. of antiques – is prohibited.

**Warning** The numerous wooden articles with the Maori look offered to tourists are industrially produced reproductions of traditional themes.

### Jewellery
Greenstone or *pounamu* (the New Zealand form of jade) is used in the making of jewellery, particularly on the west coast of the South Island (Hokitika). The Maoris formerly used greenstone in the manufacture of weapons and tools. Many items of greenstone jewellery such as the *hei-tiki*, a kind of necklace, are still made in traditional Maori style. Jewellery is also made from other semi-precious stones like agate and amethyst. In the old gold-mining areas tourists are offered nuggets of gold and pieces of gold jewellery in the form of small earrings.

### Paua shells
A very popular souvenir is an ashtray made from the shimmering blue-green shell of the paua, a type of abalone. The shells are also used to make jewellery. If you are very lucky you may find an undamaged paua shell on a lonely beach.

### Pottery and glass
New Zealand pottery is much sought after by foreign visitors, and New Zealand glass is also beginning to make a name for itself. Fine examples of pottery and glass are found in the increasingly numerous craft shops.

### Foodstuffs
Natural products such as honey, jam, smoked meat and kiwi-fruit wine also make good souvenirs.

### Wine
New Zealand wines are excellent. In the United Kingdom it is the full-tasting dry whites (Chardonnay, Sauvignon Blanc, Riesling) that are most highly regarded.

### Sports articles
Some items of sporting equipment can be bought in New Zealand at lower prices than in Europe or North America.

### Books
New Zealand claims to read more books and periodicals per head of population than any other country in the world. There are, therefore, plenty of bookshops in which visitors can buy – among much else – guide books and illustrated books on New Zealand.

### Postage stamps
Post offices in the larger towns have special counters for philatelists.

### Garage sales, demolition yards
Second-hand objects can be bought cheaply in privately run garage sales (boot sales) and in 'demolition yards', a type of flea market usually run by professional dealers.

**Goods and services tax**
See Currency

## Social Customs

### Dress
New Zealanders prefer light casual
clothing. Ties are obligatory only in
some top restaurants, and evening dress
is rarely worn.

In late spring, summer and autumn
(October to May) summer clothing can
be worn, with something warm for the
evening. In the winter months and early
spring (June to September) warm
clothing is required.

Essential items of clothing, at any
time of year, are windproof and
rainproof clothing, a hat or cap,
sunglasses and sun cream, a pullover and
stout footwear.

### Hongi
The Maoris traditionally do not greet
one another by shaking hands or kissing
but by rubbing noses with one another:
a form of greeting known in the Maori
language as *hongi*.

## Sport

New Zealanders are great sports
enthusiasts. At every opportunity,
particularly at weekends, they get away
from their work to follow their sporting
interests, whether as active participants
or as spectators. All the elements are
called into play – land (walking, tennis,
rugby), water (fishing, swimming,
surfing) and air (gliding, parachute
jumping).

## Participatory and spectator sports

### Basketball
Excitement centres on the National
League matches during the winter and
the stadia are packed.

### Netball
Netball is the most popular women's
sport in New Zealand. The netball
championships in May and June attract
large numbers of spectators.

### Bowls
The British and New Zealand form of
bowls is rather sedater than its French
and Italian equivalents, boules and
boccia. It is played on an immaculate
bowling green and the players are
dressed in white.

### Cricket
Cricket has a large and enthusiastic
following in New Zealand. Important
matches attract large and sometimes
unruly crowds in the same way as rugby
matches. International teams visit New
Zealand during February and March.

### Football
Since New Zealand first played in the
World Cup in 1982 football has become
increasingly popular. Matches are
played throughout New Zealand on
Sundays.

### Hockey
Hockey has long been popular in New
Zealand, and it was given a great boost
when the New Zealand team won a gold
medal in the Montreal Olympics in
1976.

### Marathon
All types of light athletics are popular in
New Zealand. Championships are held at
many places in summer and early
autumn.

There is particular interest in long-
distance running. New Zealand runners
won gold medals in the marathon at the
Olympic Games in Rome (1960) and
Montreal (1976). Tens of thousands of
competitors take part in the Round the
Bays Run that takes place annually in
March in the Auckland area.

### Horse riding and racing
In few parts of the world are there so
many horses per head of population as
in New Zealand, and riding is, not
surprisingly, a very popular sport. On
many farms visitors can hire a horse, and
pony trekking is an attraction offered by
many farms and lodges, for example in
the Urewera National Park, where
visitors can explore the ancestral lands of
the Maoris on horseback.

Flat races and steeplechases draw
large numbers of spectators. Every town
of any size has its own racecourse, and
there are something like 450 race
meetings (usually on Sundays and
Wednesdays) every year.

The two big events of the year are the
Auckland Cup (during the Christmas

holidays) and the Great Northern meeting at the beginning of June.

### Rugby
Rugby is by far the most popular spectator sport in New Zealand, and at weekends between April and September tens of thousands of fans flock to rugby grounds throughout the country to support their team. The All Blacks, New Zealand's national team, have a formidable international reputation and are famed for their performance, before a match, of the intimidating Maori war chant, the *haka*. Enthusiasm, of course, rises to fever pitch at international matches, usually played in Auckland's Eden Park, which can accommodate 47,000 spectators.

### Shooting
New Zealand offers a variety of game for shooting enthusiasts, including red deer, chamois, ducks, geese and other small game. There are no close seasons and no limits on bags. Visitors are not allowed to bring in their own guns, but professional guides, whose help should always be sought, supply guns and ammunition.

Further information can be obtained from Tourism New Zealand (☛Information).

### Tennis
New Zealand towns are well supplied with tennis courts (some of them grass courts), and most hotels in the top price category have their own courts.
Information from:
NEW ZEALAND TENNIS INC.
PO Box 11–541, Wellington
☎ *(04) 4731115, fax (04) 4712152, email info@tennis.org.nz, www.tennis.org.nz*

### Bungee jumping
The challenging sport of bungee jumping originated in New Zealand but has now spread all over the world (☛254, Baedeker Special).

## Fishing

Angling is a very popular recreation in New Zealand, whose coastal waters, rivers and lakes are well stocked with fish. Fishing in the sea is free, but fishing in inland waters is permitted only with a licence obtainable from fishing tackle and sports shops.

### Freshwater fishing
The main fishing season on inland waters is from October to March. The species preferred by anglers are trout and salmon.

### Surfcasting, deep-sea angling
Surfcasting and deep-sea angling are also very popular. A world-famous big-game angling area is off the north-east coast of the North Island. The season is from January to May.

### Information
NEW ZEALAND PROFESSIONAL FISHING GUIDES ASSOCIATION
PO Box 16, Motu, Gisborne
☎ *(06) 8635822, fax (06) 8635844, www.flyfishing.net.nz/nzpfga.htm*

## Flying

### Light aircraft
Conditions for flying are particularly good in the Queenstown area. There are a number of airfields where aircraft can be hired by holders of the appropriate pilot's licence. Some pilots also like to take passengers.

### Parapenting
Parapenting is a cross between hang-gliding and parachuting that is initially easier to learn than either. There are courses of instruction at Queenstown, with the Crown Terrace (620 m) as jumping-off point. In the skiing area on the Remarkables parapenters take off and land on skis.

### Hang-gliding and paragliding
There are a number of areas in New Zealand that offer excellent conditions for hang-gliding and paragliding. Among the best places are Coronet Peak and the mountains on Lake Wanaka.

### Gliding
New Zealand is also a good place for gliding enthusiasts, as was demonstrated by the world championships of 1995.

## Golf

Golf is a popular sport in New Zealand, not an elite recreation as it is in some countries. There are around 410 golf courses in New Zealand and many of them are set in beautiful surroundings.

Among the most attractive are the courses at Waitangi and Titirangi (near Auckland), Wairakei (near Taupo), Queenstown (one of the most beautiful courses in the world) and Rotorua (Arikikapakapa, the only golf course in the world where pools of boiling mud are among the hazards).

Foreign visitors are welcome in most clubs, though on certain days or at certain times the course may be reserved for club members. There are few countries in the world where golf can be played at less expense, on courses that are almost always relatively empty, than in New Zealand.

### Green fees

Green fees for visitors are usually between NZ$25 and NZ$50 and over NZ$50 for the most exclusive courses. Clubs and trolleys can be hired and professionals are available for coaching.

### Season

The main golfing season is from October to May.

### Information

NEW ZEALAND GOLF ASSOCIATION
PO Box 11–842, Wellington
☎ (04) 3854330, fax (040) 3854331,
email nzga@xtra.co.nz, www.nzga.co.nz

## Water sports

As is to be expected in an island state, New Zealanders are strongly drawn to the water. Round the coasts are bathing beaches of enchanting beauty; off the North Island and round the Cook Islands are happy hunting grounds for scuba divers and snorkellers; and in many parts of the country there are superb sailing waters. And it is not only salt water that appeals to New Zealanders and foreign visitors: the wild rivers of the interior are travelled by hosts of tourists in jet boats, canoes and rubber dinghies, and the lakes offer endless scope for boating and water sports of all kinds.

### Rowing

New Zealand is one of the great rowing nations of the world. In recent years its oarsmen have won world championships and gold and silver Olympic medals. The national rowing championships are held annually in February.

### Sailing

Sailing is a very popular sport in New Zealand. Sometimes in the Hauraki Gulf it seems as if every single inhabitant is in a boat on the water. New Zealand yachtsmen have been successful in all the world's great sailing races, such as the America's Cup (won in 1995).

Among the finest sailing waters in the world are the Hauraki Gulf and the Bay of Islands on the North Island and the Marlborough Sounds at the north-eastern tip of the South Island.

Boats can be hired with or without a skipper and crew, and in many regattas – for example in the classic race from Auckland to Nouméa in New Caledonia – it is possible to join the crew of one of the competing boats or get a place on an escort boat. Information from:
NEW ZEALAND YACHTING FEDERATION
PO Box 33–789, Takapuna, Auckland
☎ (09) 4889325, fax (09) 4889326,
email mail@yachtingnz.org.nz,
www.yachtingnz.org.nz

## Other water sports

### Jet boats

The commercial development and operation of jet boats originated in New Zealand, and a high-speed trip on a jet boat through beautiful river scenery and narrow gorges or in a Hamilton jet (named after the inventor; ☛Famous People) over a great expanse of shallow water is one of the special holiday experiences of New Zealand. Passengers in a jet boat need no particular qualities of fitness or training – only strong nerves as the boat jets at hair-raising speed towards rocks and cliff faces. Life jackets are provided.

Jet-boat trips as a tourist attraction began in Queenstown, where passengers were taken on a breathtaking journey through the Shotover Canyon. Trips are now on offer on other rivers as well, for example on the South Island the Waimakariri at Christchurch, the Buller and the Makarora, on the North Island the Rangitikei, at the east end of the Bay of Plenty, and the Whanganui.

### White-river rafting

White-river or white-water rafting is one of the special attractions of an adventure holiday in New Zealand. It can be practised on both the North and South Islands. The rivers suitable for the sport are not long but they are certainly wild. Several dozen specialist travel operators in New Zealand offer rafting holidays in varying grades of difficulty, and some offer guided kayak and canoe trips. Participants must be at least 13 years old; equipment and accommodation are part of the package.

**Rafting areas** The best rafting rivers on the North Island are the Wairoa, the Rangitikei and the Mohaka. On the South Island there are the Buller, the Shotover, the Kawarau, the upper course of the Rangitata (all in the Queenstown area) and the 64 km Landsborough River, which has the steepest gradient of any New Zealand river and flows through country of great scenic beauty. The best months for rafting are October and April/May, when the climate is most pleasant, but it is perfectly possible to enjoy rafting at other times of year, provided that the rivers have a sufficient flow of water. Information from:
NEW ZEALAND PROFESSIONAL RIVER RAFTING ASSOCIATION
PO Box 77, Tauranga
GO WEST RAFTING
PO Box 99, Buller River
☎ (03) 5239315
PUNAKAIKI CANOE HIRE
PO Box 2, Punakaiki
☎ (03) 7311870, fax (03) 7311870

**Black-river rafting**
Black-river rafting is the name given to rafting on underground rivers, for example on the Ruakuri, one of the underground rivers in the Waitomo Caves (North Island). To reach the river it is necessary to abseil down into these deep caves with their fossils and their glow-worms.

**Kayaking**
A trip by canoe or kayak on the rivers, lakes and the quieter coastal waters of New Zealand is a delightful way of enjoying the country's beautiful scenery. Particularly good areas are the Abel Tasman National Park at the northern tip of the South Island; on the east coast off Great Barrier Island; and in the Marlborough Sounds. A variety of organised trips are available. You can also go on your own, but it is safer and more interesting to have a knowledgeable local guide. The necessary equipment is provided by local travel operators. Information from:

ABEL TASMAN KAYAKS
Marahau Beach, Motueka
☎ (03) 5278022, fax (03) 5278032,
email wp@kayaktours.co.nz,
www.kayaktours.co.nz
OCEAN AND RIVER ADVENTURE COMPANY
Main Road, Marahau Beach, Motueka
☎ (03) 5278266, fax (03) 5278006,
email abeltasman@seakayaking.co.nz,
www.seakayaking.co.nz

**Surfing and windsurfing**
Surfing and windsurfing are popular sports, particularly in the warmer part of the year, at many points on the New Zealand coast. At the main centres there are instructors to teach newcomers to the sport, and surfboards and surfing suits can be hired from many sports shops. New Zealand's surfing beaches offer plenty of scope for both beginners and experts. Winds are often strong, for example on the north coast of the North Island or on the Tasman Sea, where the waves are sometimes several metres high.

A good place for beginners is Takapuna Beach, near Auckland, with a light east wind. Windsurfing is also possible on some inland waters, for example on Lake Taupo in the centre of the North Island. Information from:
SURFING NEW ZEALAND
PO Box 13289, Johnsonville, Wellington
☎ (04) 4790468, fax (04) 4790467, email surfingnz@xtra.co.nz

**Other sports**
See Cycling; Diving; Walking; Winter Sports

# Taxis

There are plenty of taxis at airports and in towns and tourist centres. They can be picked up at a taxi rank or called by telephone (24-hour service). They are expensive and in addition the driver expects a suitable tip. More reasonably priced are the communal taxis and minibuses (shuttle buses) that ply, for example, between airports and their town terminals.

# Telephone

**Public telephones**
Modern public telephones are operated either by coins (payphones) or telephone cards (cardphones). Subscriber trunk

dialling (STD) is available in all new telephone kiosks.

**Card-operated telephones**
Increasing numbers of public telephones are now card-operated. Telephone cards (NZ$5, NZ$10 and NZ$20) can be bought in post offices, Telecom sales points, hotels, motels and motor camps, and also in all dairies (corner shops).

**Private and hotel telephones**
Trunk and international calls can be made from all private telephones and from the telephones installed in most hotel and motel rooms.

**Charges**
Local calls from a public telephone cost 50 cents. An STD call to Europe costs at present around $4 a minute during the day and $3 a minute 10pm–8am.

**Freephone information**
For freephone directory enquiries dial 018 for New Zealand and 0172 for other countries.

**International dialling codes**
From New Zealand to the United Kingdom: 0044
From New Zealand to the United States or Canada: 001
From the United Kingdom to New Zealand: 0064
From the United States or Canada to New Zealand: 01164

# Time

New Zealand lies near the International Dateline and is thus one of the first places in the world to see the new day. It is 12 hours ahead of Greenwich Mean Time.

In summer New Zealand has Daylight Saving, when the clocks are put forward an hour. Daylight Saving begins on the first Sunday in October and ends on the last Sunday of the following March.

# Tipping

In principle tips are given in New Zealand only in appreciation of extra-special service, consideration or kindness at the discretion of the visitor, particularly in restaurants, for waiter service in bars or for room service.

Service charges are not added to hotel or restaurant bills. Nevertheless the practice of tipping is creeping in, particularly in the larger towns and tourist centres. If you have been well served in a restaurant you may feel like leaving a tip of perhaps 5–10 per cent of the bill. Taxi-drivers and porters will usually expect a suitable tip.

# Travel Documents

**Entry**
All visitors to New Zealand must have a passport. British citizens do not need a visa, and on arrival in New Zealand will be issued with a permit for a stay of up to 6 months. United States and Canadian citizens do not require a visa, and on arrival in New Zealand will be issued with a permit for a 3-month stay. Australian citizens do not need a visa and can stay as long as they like.

On arrival in New Zealand visitors will be asked to produce their passport, a ticket for return or onward travel, the arrival card giving their personal details that they will have filled in on the plane and, more rarely, evidence that they have sufficient means, in the form of cash, traveller's cheques or credit cards, for the duration of their stay (with a guide figure for sufficiency of means of NZ$1000 a month).

If you decide that you want to stay longer than your entry permit allows you must apply to the Immigration Office for a visa. But if you know from the start that you are likely to stay longer it is advisable – and cheaper – to get the visa before leaving home.

**Driving licence**
British, American, Canadian and Australian driving licences are accepted in New Zealand. To hire a car in New Zealand you must produce your driving licence and must be at least 21.

**Other documents**
It is advisable to carry your inoculation record, your AA (or other motoring organisation) membership card and details of your insurance cover.

It is a good idea to carry photocopies of important documents, since if you lose the originals this makes it easier to get them replaced. If you lose your passport you must inform the police and your local embassy or consulate.

## Visitors with Disabilites

Many New Zealand hotels, restaurants, tourist sights and even the railways have facilities for people with disabilities; Air New Zealand has special seats and wheelchairs. However, there can be problems with buses. In some national parks, for example in the Paparoa and Tongariro national parks, there are special paths for wheelchair users. Wheelchairs can be hired free of charge at certain points in the town of Rotorua, for instance at the Mike Hale, John Cubbon and David Meek pharmacies.

### Information

DISABLED PERSONS ADVICE BUREAU
Disabled Resources Trust, 60 Woburn Road, Lower Hutt
☎ *(04) 5693091, (04) 5693707*
DISABILITIES INFORMATION SERVICE
26 North Street, Timaru
☎ *(03) 6885515, freephone (0800) 500896, email mmaddren@aoraki.ccs.org.nz*
ENABLE NEW ZEALAND
467 Selwyn Street, Christchurch
☎ *(03) 9620011, freephone (0800) 170606*

# Walking

Some 30 per cent of the area of New Zealand is now protected by nature and landscape reserves of one kind or another. Nor surprisingly, therefore, walking and climbing – trekking, tramping, bushwalking, backpacking – are among the New Zealanders' most popular leisure activities.

### Walks and tracks

There is plenty of scope everywhere in New Zealand, even in the outskirts of the cities, for short walks taking no more than a day. Some of these are waymarked with the letter 'W'. Longer routes are often described as tracks.

### ★★Milford Track, ★★Routeburn Track

The two finest routes in New Zealand – some would say the finest in the world – run through the magnificent scenery of Fiordland National Park on the South Island. They are the Milford Track (over 50 km long) and the Routeburn Track (40 km). A fit walker can do each of them in 4 days, with overnight accommodation in simple huts.

### Other tracks

There are numerous other tracks (for example the Hollyford Valley Walk) that are maintained by wardens or the Department of Conservation rangers.

### Notification, guides

Many walks can be done at any time of year, but others, particularly walks in mountain country, should not be attempted in winter. On many tracks walkers are required to let the local Department of Conservation (DoC) office know that they propose to do the walk. Some walks should be done only with a guide who knows the country.

### Huts

Most walks do not call for the very highest standard of fitness, since there are more than 1000 huts only a 4–5 hour walk apart. These huts do not, of course, offer any great luxury but they do provide a place to sleep, water, toilets and sometimes cooking facilities. Since they tend to be overcrowded during the main holiday season, it is a sensible precaution to take along a small, light tent. The charge for a night in a hut ranges between NZ$5 and NZ$20; more than 350 of them are free.

### Guided walks

Many agencies run guided walks, normally for quite small parties. Accommodation is usually in comfortable huts (with hot showers), and the participants need take only a light pack and weatherproof clothing. Everything else (e.g. sleeping bags) is provided by the organisers.

### Season

The best time for walking is the months of February and March, after the main holiday season. There are fewer walkers on the tracks then and there is less difficulty in getting accommodation in huts. Moreover the weather tends to be more settled and it is not so hot.

### Equipment

Essential items of equipment for walkers are stout footwear, a not-too-heavy rucksack, a light sleeping bag and perhaps a light tent, cooking utensils, provisions, rainwear, a warm pullover, a hat or cap, protection against the sun and against sandflies, and good maps. Maps and brochures can be obtained from DoC offices.

### Rules of conduct

Before setting out on a long walk (i.e. one lasting several days) you should inform the local Department of Conservation office, sign the register in each hut and inform the DoC office when you have completed the walk. There are risks about walking on your own. It is highly dangerous to cross rivers when they are in spate. Never wash your hands in a river. Excreta should not be disposed of in rivers or streams but should be buried well away from the path. Leave no litter: take your litter with you and dispose of it in a suitable place. In dry weather be very careful about lighting fires.

## Climbing

Most people know that Sir Edmund Hillary (☞Famous People) is a New Zealander. He trained for his ascent of Everest on Mount Cook, the country's highest peak. New Zealand's climbers are world class, as are its climbing schools. And not surprisingly, for climbers can find in the Southern Alps mountains that put the highest demands on their skill and endurance. Favourite climbing areas in the Southern Alps are Mount Cook, Mount Tasman and the mountains in Mount Aspiring National Park; and on the North Island there are Taranaki (Mount Egmont) and Mount Ruapehu. In all these areas visitors can join climbing trips led by experienced guides. Information from:
DEPARTMENT OF CONSERVATION
PO Box 10–420, Wellington (☞National Parks for addresses)

## When to Go

### Climate

Broadly speaking, the North Island lies in the subtropical climatic zone, the South Island in the temperate zone, with sub-Arctic conditions in the mountains (☞Introduction, Climate).

### Reversed seasons

New Zealand's seasons are the reverse of those of the northern hemisphere. Spring lasts from September to November, summer from December to February, autumn from March to May and winter from June to August.

### Weather

The North Island, lying nearer the equator, has a subtropical climate, while on the South Island the climate is temperate, comparable with the climate of northern Europe but rather warmer. There is no marked rainy season, though there is rather more rain in winter. Showers of rain do not usually last long, though they can be very heavy. Temperature variations are relatively small, with a range of around 10°C. Winter temperatures seldom fall below freezing point. Snow usually falls only on land above 1000 m. Winds are predominantly westerly.

### Weather forecasts

Telephone forecasts: dial 0900 999 plus area code
Weather bulletins: every hour on New Zealand Radio

## Wildlife

With its great expanses of almost intact natural landscape New Zealand offers wide scope for the observation of wildlife. Sunbathing seals, yellow-eyed penguins and albatrosses will become as familiar to the nature lover as the playful mountain parrots (keas; ☞Introduction, Flora and Fauna) and nocturnally active kiwis (☞22, Baedeker Special). Various travel firms and local tourist organisations offer specially organised trips for the observation of wildlife.

### Royal albatrosses

On the Otago Peninsula, near Dunedin, you can, if you are very lucky, see the royal albatross, whose nesting places are normally near Antarctica. These albatrosses, with a wingspan of up to 3 m, are among the largest birds in the world.

### Muttonbirds

Muttonbirds nest mainly on Stewart Island and the small neighbouring islands. From time immemorial the young birds have been prized by the Maoris for their down. Tens of thousands of them are caught every year.

### Gannets

Gannets nest on the east coast of the North Island. Excellent divers, they are easily recognised by their pointed wings, their powerful beaks and their heads with black-rimmed eyes.

### Seals
Seals can be observed on the remote west coast of the South Island. They also find their way up Milford Sound.

### Whales and dolphins
Whales are no longer hunted off the coasts of New Zealand with harpoons, as they were until 1964, but with cameras and camcorders. On the Kaikoura coast, some 130 km south of Blenheim on the east side of the South Island, they can – with luck – be seen close up from a rubber dinghy with an experienced guide. In the course of their travels over the oceans of the world they regularly appear in the coastal waters off the north-east of the South Island, where they find abundant food. Under the Mammals Protection Act of 1978 they are now protected within the 200-mile fishing zone round New Zealand. From April to June sperm whales can be seen, in summer killer whales, in June and July the 'singing' humpbacked whales.

The season for dolphins is from October to May. At some points they are particularly friendly, and many a tourist has had the experience of swimming with a dolphin. Occasionally Hector's dolphins, a species so far found only in New Zealand waters, can be seen.

### Penguins
Near the town of Oamaru on the South Island it is possible to see a colony of very cute blue penguins that float in with the waves to waddle along the shore. Further away up the beach are the slightly larger yellow-eyed penguins.

# Wine

As recently as 1975 a German visitor and wine lover, when asked what he thought of New Zealand wines, replied 'You can't call *that* wine!'. Much has changed since then and New Zealand wines now enjoy a very different reputation. They can expect to win medals in international competitions and wine critics agree that the best New Zealand wines can challenge the great wines of the world.

The first vines were brought to New Zealand by immigrants in 1819, but until the early 1980s New Zealanders – traditionally beer drinkers – showed no interest in wine. Until then mixtures of grapes were used to produce sickly sweet wines of port and sherry style and and mediocre table wines sold in 3-litre plastic packs. In order to moderate the acidity of such mass-produced wines they were, quite legally, diluted with tap-water. Practically none of this wine could be marketed abroad. Then a kind of wine euphoria set in. The slogan now was 'quality, not quantity'. New Zealand winegrowers brought in new types of grape and the necessary knowledge from France, Germany and California; and many European winemakers, mainly from Austria and Germany, emigrated to New Zealand, bringing their experience and skills with them.

With its good soil and excellent climate, New Zealand offers ideal conditions for winegrowing. Its temperate summers and mild winters make it a cool-climate wine country. To some extent conditions for winegrowing in New Zealand are comparable with conditions on the Rhine and Moselle, in Burgundy and Bordeaux. Its winegrowing areas have expanded rapidly: whereas in the mid-1980s New Zealand had around 4000 ha of vineyards it now has some 6100 ha. The main winegrowing areas are north of Auckland (around 4 per cent of the total area under vines), on the east side of the North Island (Gisborne and Hawke's Bay, each 25 per cent) and round Blenheim on the South Island (33 per cent). The remaining tenth consists of wine estates in the Bay of Plenty, Northland and the Wairarapa area on the North Island and round Canterbury and Nelson and in Central Otago on the South Island, the most southerly winegrowing area in the world. The Blenheim area alone produces around 15,000 tonnes of grapes a year.

The wineries have no difficulty in selling their products on the domestic market: New Zealanders have acquired a taste for wine. Annual consumption per head in New Zealand is now around 21 litres per head, and in certain social circles it has become obligatory to know about wine, or at least to be able to talk about it.

### Buyer's guide
There is now extensive literature about New Zealand wines. The front-runner among works of reference, picture books and periodicals devoted to wine is the

*Buyer's Guide to New Zealand Wines* by Michael Cooper, a New Zealander who also knows about the winegrowing areas of France, Germany, California and Australia. His book covers the whole subject from the first vines planted in New Zealand to the wineries of the present day. Wine lovers take it with them on holiday.

### Sale of wine

Until a few years ago the sale of wine was strictly regulated, but controls are now much relaxed. Since 1990 wine can be bought not only direct from a wine dealer or in a bottle store, as previously, but also in ordinary food shops. The pricing of wine has also adjusted to international standards, and for a bottle of top New Zealand wine you may have to pay anything up to NZ$50.

### White wines

The grapes most used in making white wine are Chardonnay, Müller-Thurgau, Sauvignon Blanc and Riesling. Formerly the most used variety was Müller-Thurgau, but this has recently been overtaken by Chardonnay, which now accounts for 21 per cent of the total area under vines, particularly in the Marlborough, Hawke's Bay and Gisborne areas. Chardonnay is used in the making of a great variety of wines – young, fruity, heavy, dry and so on. Since it is almost invariably dry it has been called the red-wine drinker's white wine. In the spring of 1993 the leading British wine magazine *Decanter* set up an enquiry to find out where the best Sauvignon Blanc was grown, and after 130 wines had been tested the winner was adjudged to be New Zealand, more specifically the Marlborough area.

Fourth place among the most grown types of grape is taken by Riesling, which is grown mainly on the South Island, particularly in the Marlborough, Nelson, Canterbury and Central Otago areas. New Zealand Riesling is more like the lighter German version than the drier Alsatian and Australian ones.

Other types of white wine are Breidecker, Chenin Blanc, Ehrenfelser (a cross between Riesling and Sylvaner), Gewürztraminer (which is declining because of its poor resistance to bad weather), Morio-Muskat, Osteiner, Pinot Blanc, Pinot Gris, Scheurebe (very rare in New Zealand) and Sémillon, which is added to Sauvignon in the proportion of

15 per cent to redu

New Zealand al
wines, including s
méthode champen

### Red wines

First place among
Cabernet Sauvigno
commonest of grap
New Zealand wines
Zealand from Bord
grown mainly in th
In second place is
grown mainly in th
the south end of th
Merlot, the princip
Bordeaux region, is
with Cabernet Sauv
soft, fruity taste. M
Zealand's Merlot is
Bay region. Other
Cabernet Franc (ov
North Island) – a g
small quantities to
Zealand red wines
Pinotage, Refosco a
Shiraz).

### Wineries

Almost all wineries
who are given con
tastings.

## Winter Sports

### Season

The best months f
months with the b
snow – are July, Au
when the snowlin
1000 m. Skiing eq
in ski resorts, whic
ski tows and skiing
the winter months
available, covering
skiing instruction
Information about
obtained from Tou
(☛Information). T
areas are all above
offer plenty of spa

### Heli-skiing

An increasingly po
heli-skiing, in whi
to the skiing area
aircraft fitted with
heli-skiing are ava
and in other areas
can now be reache

:e its high acidity.
:o produces sparkling
ne made by the
:ise.

:d wines is taken by
:a, the fourth
:e types among all
. First brought to New
:aux in the 1890s, it is
:e Hawke's Bay area.
:inot Noir, which is
:e Wairarapa area, at
:e North Island.
:al grape of the
: frequently mixed
:ignon to give it a
:ore than half New
: grown in the Hawke's
:rapes used are
:er 75 per cent on the
:ape that is added in
: many top New
:- Durif (very rare),
:nd Syrah (Australian

: welcome visitors,
:lucted tours and wine

:r skiing – that is, the
:st prospects of good
:gust and September,
: comes down to
:ipment can be hired
:n also have chairlifts,
:, instructors. During
: package holidays are
: accommodation,
:nd lift passes.
: skiing areas can be
:ism New Zealand
:ne New Zealand skiing
:the treeline and thus
:e.

:pular form of skiing is
:h skiers are taken up
:n helicopters or light
: skids. Facilities for
:lable on Mount Hutt
: More than 400 pistes
:d in this way. The

# Source of Illustrations

## Imprint

97 illustrations, 37 maps and plans, 1 large fold-out map

Editorial work German edition: Baedeker-Redaktion (Rainer Eisenschmid, Helmut Linde)
Cartography: Christop Gallus, Hohberg; Haupka-Verlag, Bad Soden (large fold-out map)
General direction: Rainer Eisenschmid, Baedeker Ostfildern

Editorial work English edition: g-and-w PUBLISHING, Kate Parker
English translation: James Hogarth, Carole Porter
Design English edition: The Company of Designers, Basingstoke, Hampshire, UK

2nd English edition 2001

© Baedeker Ostfildern
Original German edition 2000

© Automobile Association Developments Limited 2001
English language edition worldwide

Published by AA Publishing (a trading name of Automobile Association Developments
Limited, whose registered office is Norfolk House, Priestley Road, Basingstoke,
Hampshire RG24 9NY; registered number 1878835).

Distributed in the United States and Canada by:
Fodor's Travel Publications, Inc.
201 East 50th Street
New York, NY 10022

A CIP catalogue record of this book is available from the British Library.

Licensed user: Mairs Geographischer Verlag, Ostfildern

Typeset by Fakenham Photosetting Ltd, Fakenham, Norfolk, UK
Printed in Italy by G Canale & C SpA, Turin

ISBN 0 7495 2966 0

Only a selection of hotels and restaurants can be given; no reflection is implied
therefore on establishments not included.
   In a time of rapid change it is difficult to ensure that all the information given is
entirely accurate and up to date, and the possibility of error cannot be eliminated.
   Although the publishers can accept no responsibility for inaccuracies and
omissions, they are constantly endeavouring to improve the quality of their guides
and are therefore always grateful for criticisms, corrections and suggestions for
improvement.